The Cambridge Companion to Won

This Companion explores women's work in music since 1900 across a broad range of musical genres and professions, including the classical tradition, popular music, and music technology. The crucial contributions of women to music education and the music industries feature alongside their activity as composers and performers. The book considers the gendered nature of the musical profession in areas including access to training, gendered criticism, sexualisation, and notions of 'gender appropriate' roles or instruments. It covers a wide range of women musicians, such as Marin Alsop, Grace Williams, Billie Holiday, Joni Mitchell, and Adele. Each thematic section concludes with a contribution from a practitioner in her own words, reflecting upon the impact of gender on her own career. Chapters include suggestions for further reading on each of the topics covered, providing an invaluable resource for students of feminist musicology, women in music, and music and gender.

LAURA HAMER is Staff Tutor and Lecturer in Music at The Open University. She is the author of *Female Composers, Performers, Conductors: Musiciennes of Interwar France, 1919–1939* (2018) and co-editor, with Helen Julia Minors, of *The Routledge Companion to Women and Musical Leadership: The Nineteenth Century and Beyond* (forthcoming).

Cambridge Companions to Music

Topics

The Cambridge Companion to Ballet
Edited by Marion Kant

The Cambridge Companion to Blues and Gospel Music
Edited by Allan Moore

The Cambridge Companion to Choral Music
Edited by André de Quadros

The Cambridge Companion to the Concerto
Edited by Simon P. Keefe

The Cambridge Companion to Conducting
Edited by José Antonio Bowen

The Cambridge Companion to the Drum Kit
Edited by Matt Brennan, Joseph Michael Pignato and Daniel Akira Stadnicki

The Cambridge Companion to Eighteenth-Century Opera
Edited by Anthony R. DelDonna and Pierpaolo Polzonetti

The Cambridge Companion to Electronic Music
Edited by Nick Collins and Julio D'Escriván

The Cambridge Companion to the 'Eroica' Symphony
Edited by Nancy November

The Cambridge Companion to Film Music
Edited by Mervyn Cooke and Fiona Ford

The Cambridge Companion to French Music
Edited by Simon Trezise

The Cambridge Companion to Grand Opera
Edited by David Charlton

The Cambridge Companion to Hip-Hop
Edited by Justin A. Williams

The Cambridge Companion to Jazz
Edited by Mervyn Cooke and David Horn

The Cambridge Companion to Jewish Music
Edited by Joshua S. Walden

The Cambridge Companion to the Lied
Edited by James Parsons

The Cambridge Companion to Medieval Music
Edited by Mark Everist

The Cambridge Companion to Music in Digital Culture
Edited by Nicholas Cook, Monique Ingalls and David Trippett

The Cambridge Companion to the Musical, third edition
Edited by William Everett and Paul Laird

Composers

The Cambridge Companion to Women in Music since 1900

Edited by

LAURA HAMER

The Open University, Milton Keynes

CAMBRIDGE
UNIVERSITY PRESS

CAMBRIDGE
UNIVERSITY PRESS

University Printing House, Cambridge CB2 8BS, United Kingdom

One Liberty Plaza, 20th Floor, New York, NY 10006, USA

477 Williamstown Road, Port Melbourne, VIC 3207, Australia

314–321, 3rd Floor, Plot 3, Splendor Forum, Jasola District Centre, New Delhi – 110025, India

79 Anson Road, #06–04/06, Singapore 079906

Cambridge University Press is part of the University of Cambridge.

It furthers the University's mission by disseminating knowledge in the pursuit of education, learning, and research at the highest international levels of excellence.

www.cambridge.org
Information on this title: www.cambridge.org/9781108470285
DOI: 10.1017/9781108556491

© Cambridge University Press 2021

This publication is in copyright. Subject to statutory exception and to the provisions of relevant collective licensing agreements, no reproduction of any part may take place without the written permission of Cambridge University Press.

First published 2021

A catalogue record for this publication is available from the British Library.

Library of Congress Cataloging-in-Publication Data
Names: Hamer, Laura, author.
Title: The Cambridge companion to women in music since 1900 / edited by Laura Hamer.
Description: New York: Cambridge University Press, 2021. | Series: Cambridge companions to music | Includes bibliographical references and index.
Identifiers: LCCN 2020056954 (print) | LCCN 2020056955 (ebook) | ISBN 9781108470285 (hardback) | ISBN 9781108556491 (ebook)
Subjects: LCSH: Women musicians. | Women composers. | Women in the music trade. | Music by women composers – 20th century – History and criticism. | Music by women composers – 21st century – History and criticism.
Classification: LCC ML82 .C36 2021 (print) | LCC ML82 (ebook) | DDC 780.82/0904–dc23
LC record available at https://lccn.loc.gov/2020056954
LC ebook record available at https://lccn.loc.gov/2020056955

ISBN 978-1-108-47028-5 Hardback
ISBN 978-1-108-45578-7 Paperback

Cambridge University Press has no responsibility for the persistence or accuracy of URLs for external or third-party internet websites referred to in this publication and does not guarantee that any content on such websites is, or will remain, accurate or appropriate.

For all our students

Contents

Afterword: Challenges and Opportunities: Ways Forward
for Women Working in Music

Figures

Boxes

Notes on Contributors

VICTORIA ARMSTRONG is a Lecturer at the University of Surrey. Her research revolves around gender and inclusion. She is the author of *Technology and the Gendering of Music Education*, and her second monograph, *Women's Musical Lives*, uses digital ethnography to explore the gendered dimensions of labour in cultural work. She serves on the editorial board of *Music Education Research*.

MANUELLA BLACKBURN is Lecturer at Keele University in Music Technology (since 2019) and previously worked at Liverpool Hope University between 2010 and 2019. Her practice-based research covers the exploration of short sound-file use within compositional activity along with methodologies for handling larger quantities of these materials. Manuella has written on topics such as sampling, cultural sound borrowing, intercultural creativity, and music education.

LEAH BRANSTETTER, PhD, is a music historian and educator. She runs womeninrockproject.org, a web project preserving the stories of women in early rock and roll. She has also contributed to education initiatives for the Rock & Roll Hall of Fame and Steven Van Zandt's Rock and Roll Forever Foundation.

MICHAEL BROCKEN was one of the first Popular Music Studies PhDs at the Institute of Popular Music (University of Liverpool). While Senior Lecturer at Liverpool Hope University he devised and taught the world's first master's degree concerning the Beatles. He currently presents *Folkscene* on BBC Radio Merseyside and lectures at Wirral 3Ls.

FLANNERY CUNNINGHAM is a composer and musicologist who investigates the voice, compositional processes, and live electronics aimed at amplifying the musicality of human performers. She is a winner of the National Sawdust's Hildegard Competition and her work has been performed at festivals including Aspen, June in Buffalo, and Copland House's CULTIVATE.

CLARE K. DUFFIN is Lecturer in Commercial Music at the University of the West of Scotland and has a portfolio career that sees her practice span over a wide range of musical operations, including her role as an artist manager; as a drummer with Suspire; and in various community music practice positions.

SOPHIE FULLER'S main research interest is in ensuring that women composers' voices are given the hearing they deserve. She is the author of *The Pandora Guide to Women Composers* (1994) and numerous articles and chapters on women's engagement with music and music making. Sophie currently works at Trinity Laban Conservatoire of Music and Dance (London).

LAURA HAMER is Staff Tutor and Lecturer in Music at the Open University. Her research interests lie in women in music. She is the author of *Female Composers, Performers, Conductors: Musiciennes of Interwar France, 1919–1939* (Routledge, 2018) and co-editor, with Helen Julia Minors, of *The Routledge Companion to Women and Musical Leadership: The Nineteenth Century and Beyond* (Routledge, forthcoming).

ELIZABETH HOFFMAN is a New-York-City-based composer. She works in acoustic and computer-driven media. Compositional interests include a focus on timbre and spatialisation as means of creating signification and immersive sound worlds.

ELAINE KELLY is Senior Lecturer in Music at the University of Edinburgh. Her work focuses on music and politics during the Cold War, with a particular emphasis on the GDR. She is currently a Leverhulme Major Research Fellow and is researching musical relations between the GDR and the postcolonial world.

TAMMY L. KERNODLE is Professor of Musicology at Miami University in Ohio. Her scholarship, which focuses primarily on African American music (popular and classical) appears in a number of anthologies and journals. She is the author of *Soul on Soul: The Life and Music of Mary Lou Williams* (Second Edition; University of Illinois Press, 2020).

VIRGINIA KETTLE is a singer-songwriter born in Manchester, UK. She performs both solo and with award-winning folk rock band Merry Hell. Since childhood, Virginia has been influenced by all styles of popular music. Her songs create snapshots of humanity, using equal measures of beautiful imagery and kitchen-sink irony.

ASTRID KVALBEIN is a researcher at the Norwegian Academy of Music, specialising in Nordic music history, particularly twentieth-century processes of modernisation, gender issues, and contemporary music. Her PhD was on the composer Pauline Hall (1890–1969), and she has written for *A Cultural History of the Avant-Garde in the Nordic Countries* (Brill, forthcoming).

ROBERT LEGG's research uses critical social theory and narrative methods to interrogate aspects of schooling. He has written extensively on social justice in music education. In addition to his regular involvement in music theatre, he is active as a choral conductor and as a composer of music for young voices.

KRISTIN J. LIEB is an Associate Professor at Emerson College. Her interdisciplinary research, about the production and consumption of popular music, sits at the intersection of media studies, production studies, and gender and sexuality studies. Her writing often investigates how popular music stars are created, branded, popularised, credited, and received.

RHIANNON MATHIAS is Lecturer and Music Fellow at Bangor University, and is the author of *Lutyens, Maconchy, Williams and Twentieth-Century British Music* (Ashgate, 2012). She is Editor of the *Routledge International Handbook on Women's Work in Music* (forthcoming), and Editor-in-Chief of Cambridge University Press's Elements: Women in Music series.

LOUIS NIEBUR is Associate Professor at the University of Nevada, Reno, and received his PhD from UCLA. His research examines post-war music bridging high and low culture through media technology. *Special Sound: The Creation and Legacy of the BBC Radiophonic Workshop* was published in 2010 by Oxford University Press.

FRANCESCA PLACANICA (PhD, University of Southampton, 2013) currently lectures and directs the Performance Programme at Maynooth University (Republic of Ireland). She is co-editor of *Cathy Berberian: Pioneer of Contemporary Vocality* (Ashgate, 2014). She is the recipient of a Marie Curie Individual Fellowship at the University of Huddersfield, due to start in September 2021.

STEPH POWER is a composer, writer, and critic. Recent commissions include music for Uproar and the Vale of Glamorgan and Fishguard International Festivals. Amongst other publications, she writes for *BBC Music Magazine* and *The Stage*. A contributor to *The Music of Simon Holt* (Boydell, 2017), she chairs Tŷ Cerdd, Music Centre Wales.

MARGARET SCHEDEL has an interdisciplinary career blending classical training, audio research, and innovative education, which transcends the boundaries of disparate fields to produce work at the nexus of computation and the arts. She has a diverse output, ranging from books to sculptures, and is internationally recognised for the creation and performance of ferociously interactive media.

JACQUELINE WARWICK is Professor of Musicology at Dalhousie University, Canada. She is the author of *Girl Groups, Girl Culture: Popular Music and Identity in the 1960s* (Routledge, 2007) and co-editor, with Allison Adrian, of *Voicing Girlhood in Popular Music: Performance, Authority, Authenticity* (Routledge, 2016). She is currently preparing *Musical Prodigies and the Performance of Childhood* for Oxford University Press.

KATHERINE WILLIAMS is Lecturer in Music and Performance Pathway Leader at the University of Plymouth. She has published on the singer-songwriter and on songwriting more widely; gender and music; music and geography; jazz; improvisation; and Duke Ellington. She is currently editor of the *Jazz Research Journal*.

Preface

The situation of women in music has evolved significantly since 1900. At the start of the twentieth century, female musicians faced considerable gender-specific barriers. Prior to the First World War, much of women's musical work was confined to the private sphere; strict social conventions still dictated which instruments were deemed appropriate for women (piano, harp, guitar, the higher strings, and voice) and which were not (woodwind, brass, and percussion); and the work of female composers was largely confined to smaller-scale genres. The situation improved undeniably over the course of the twentieth and twenty-first centuries. Access to education and training increased; the full range of genres within which to write music became available to female composers, as the full range of instruments did to performers; and women's music was performed, published, broadcast, and recorded with increased frequency. In the period since 1900, women musicians have achieved many significant firsts, although a number of these have come shockingly recently. In 1913, Lili Boulanger became the first woman to win a Premier Grand Prix de Rome in composition, and in 1930 Ruth Crawford Seeger became the first woman composer to be awarded a Guggenheim Fellowship. Despite these early victories, however, it was not until 1983 that Ellen Taafe Zwilich became the first woman to win the Pulitzer Prize for Music, and 1990 that Joan Tower became the first woman to win the Grawemeyer Music Award. More shockingly still, Marin Alsop could claim a first for women in 2013, when she became the first woman to conduct the Last Night of the BBC's Proms, and Rebecca Saunders could claim one as late as 2019 when she became the first woman composer to win the Ernst von Siemens Music Prize. Alongside these developments in the world of classical music, popular music has developed rapidly since 1900, and women's voices have been present across a vast range of genres, although there too they have faced significant gender-based barriers and obstacles. In recent years there has been both a growing awareness of the gendered nature of the music industries, and some steps taken towards enabling positive change; as seen, for instance, in the PRS Foundation's Keychange initiative to encourage 'festivals and music organisations to achieve a 50:50 gender balance by 2022'.[1]

That such enterprises are necessary highlights the fact that – despite undeniable improvements in some areas – the music industries remain highly gendered, and significant gender-based constraints for women still exist. In particular, women musicians are still regularly subjected to gendered criticism, which often undermines their artistry by focusing upon their appearance and is sometimes highly sexualised. The career choices of women musicians are often dictated by their family circumstances. Much musical work takes place outside of family-friendly hours, childcare remains extremely expensive, and the gender pay gap persists. Some musical fields – including, but not limited to, conducting, music technology, parts of the music industries (company executives, managers, promoters, and producers amongst other roles spring readily to mind), and certain popular music genres (such as hip-hop and heavy metal) – remain extremely male dominated. And gender, of course, is only one factor – amongst which, race, ethnicity, class, sexuality, age, disability, faith, and others are also of great significance – in exclusion, from music and more widely. That we are now more consciously aware of the gendered nature of the music industries stems in part from the development, over recent decades, of the branch of musical scholarship which seeks to address the work of women musicians. Intended as both celebration and critique of women's musical work since 1900, this book fits within this wider academic trend which seeks to create a more gender-balanced music studies.

Notwithstanding the work of such early pioneers as Sophie Drinker, women in music studies – sometimes referred to as feminist musicology or included more broadly within music and gender studies – developed through the critical work of such as scholars as Eva Rieger, Nancy B. Reich, Marcia J. Citron, Suzanne Cusick, Susan McClary, Judith Tick, and Jane Bowers during the 1980s and '90s. The publication of Aaron I. Cohen's *International Encyclopedia of Women Composers* in 1981 (revised and enlarged in 1987 through collaboration with the International Council of Women),[2] followed by *The New Grove Dictionary of Women Composers*, edited by Julie Anne Sadie and Rhian Samuel, in 1994,[3] and *The Pandora Guide to Women Composers: Britain and the United States 1629–Present*, by Sophie Fuller, in 1994,[4] marked a new level of recognition for women composers. Meanwhile, the work of such trail-blazing scholars as Sheila Whiteley increased awareness of the centrality of gender and sexuality within popular music studies.[5] Like women's history itself, however, the development of women in music studies has been non-linear. Once the initial activity of the 1980s and '90s – a period which I like to refer to as the first wave of feminist musicology – subsided, research interests in women musicians seemed to drop off somewhat around the turn of the twenty-first century. Working upon a doctorate on women musicians in interwar France in the late 2000s, I sometimes felt as though I was pursuing a rather lonely research endeavour. In a 2017 article, Sally Macarthur, Dawn Bennett, Talisha Goh, and Sophie Hennekam perceptively referred to 'The Rise and Fall, and the Rise (Again) of Feminist Research in Music: "What Goes Around Comes Around"',[6] as we have recently seen something of a renaissance of interest in women in music studies. What I find so exciting about this second wave of feminist musicology is the broadening out of the field, away from a focus upon composers – which could be seen as being in danger of replicating patriarchal historiographical tendencies to focus upon the lives of 'great' individuals – to a more inclusive view of women's work in music, encompassing, amongst others, roles such as performers, conductors, educators, songwriters, sound artists, as well as those, such as journalists, promoters, managers, and arts administrators, working in the music industries more broadly. The cross-genre focus of much of this more recent work, and a new willingness for scholars and practitioners to come together at a plethora of new conferences, festivals, performances, collectives, recordings, and publications, is equally exhilarating. The opportunity to edit this book, focused upon women's musical work specifically in the period since 1900 from a cross-genre perspective, is an honour.

It would be impossible to consider every single woman working in music since 1900 within one book. Rather, the women and topics covered here represent examples and case studies of the sorts of musical work which women have done and the lived experiences which they have had, covering as broad a range of professional fields and musical genres as possible. Each chapter concludes with suggestions for 'further reading' intended to direct the interested reader towards more information on each topic. The focus of this book is upon Western music since 1900, including classical music, popular music, music technology, and women's wider work in music. The vast contributions which women have made to non-Western musics in the same period deserve specialist consideration in a further volume. The authors brought together within this book have taken a wide range of approaches to their specialist topics, including broad surveys, archival research, and detailed ethnographic micro-studies. Each section ends with a shorter 'In Her Own Words' reflection written by a female practitioner active within the field which that particular part of the book covers.

Part I considers women working within classical music. The first four chapters cover the changing situation of female composers between the early twentieth century and the early twenty-first. In Chapter 1, Sophie Fuller considers the musical landscape which female composers working in the earlier twentieth century inhabited. From the early days of the twentieth century, when women were expected to concentrate upon song and small-scale piano works, to the wider opportunities which opened up during the interwar period, Fuller considers a wide range of composers, including, amongst others, Cécile Chaminade, Maude Valérie White, Ethel Smyth, Elizabeth Maconchy, Grace Williams, Ruth Crawford Seeger, and Germaine Tailleferre. Chapters 2 and 3 move on to consider women working professionally as composers during the Cold War period of the mid-to-later twentieth century. Chapter 2, 'Women in Composition during the Cold War in Music', focuses on women active in the West, where, for all the apparent government liberalism, in musical terms, composers had to face what could often, at the time, seem like the monolithic regime of total serialism. Through a range of case studies, including Williams, Maconchy, Elisabeth Lutyens, Thea Musgrave, Betsy Jolas, Louise Talma, Julia Perry, and Miriam Gideon, Rhiannon Mathias deftly considers the compositional strategies which women developed to respond to this musical environment. Chapter 3, 'Behind the Iron Curtain: Female Composers in the Soviet Bloc', turns to the situation of women composers working within the Soviet Bloc, where, despite the public advocation of gender equality by state-socialist regimes, more traditional constructs of gender difference actually tended to be propagated. With a particular focus on the careers of Galina Ustvolskaya and Sofia Gubaidulina in the USSR, Ruth Zechlin in the GDR, and Grażyna Bacewicz in Poland, Elaine Kelly probes the possibilities open to female composers working under state socialism. Chapter 4 discusses the situation of contemporary female composers and poses the question: to what extent are they 'still exceptional'? Ranging across a wide range of figures, Astrid Kvalbein considers how contemporary women, including, amongst others, Kaija Saariaho, Jennifer Walsh, Judith Weir, Olga Neuwirth, Du Yun, Unsuk Chin, and Gabriela Lena Frank, explore feminist themes and provide gender critiques through their works, the tendency for women to engage with wider societal issues, including environmentalism, and the strategies that women have adopted to respond to an increasingly globalised world. In Chapter 5, I turn to the situation of women conductors. Through a case study of Ethel Leginska, I consider the early women conductors of the twentieth century, the majority of whom founded and led their own women's orchestras. I explore how many of these lost opportunities following the Second World War, and examine their re-emergence in the later twentieth century, with a particular focus upon Marin Alsop. I conclude my chapter by discussing the important work that Alsop and others, notably Alice Farnham, are doing through mentoring and training the younger generation of women conductors through such initiatives as Alsop's Taki Concordia Fellowship and Farnham's Women Conductors programme at the Royal Philharmonic Society. Chapter 6 shifts the focus to female performers within the classical music industry. Francesca Placanica considers the increased opportunities which female performers gained throughout the twentieth and twenty-first centuries; not only in terms of being able to achieve star status, but also through being able to integrate into professional orchestras. Focusing upon the trumpeter Alison Balsom and percussionist Dame Evelyn Glennie, she considers the new opportunities that have developed over recent decades for women to maintain careers as virtuosa performers of instruments historically deemed unsuitable for women to play. Placanica also deftly probes the high degree of sexualisation which many contemporary performers, including Yuja Wang, Katherine Jenkins, and Vanessa Mae, face in the contemporary classical music industry and how this can be negotiated in a mediatised culture. Composer Elizabeth Hoffman concludes Part I with a searching consideration of how gender has affected her own career and how it continues to affect women within the academy.

Part II turns to the rich tradition of women in popular music. Chapter 7, 'Most of My Sheroes Don't Appear on a Stamp: Contextualising the Contributions of Women Musicians to the Progression of Jazz', considers the vital part that women – both vocalists and instrumentalists – made to the development of jazz, although they have tended to be excluded from standard historiographical narratives of the genre. With a focus on the development of jazz in the United States, Tammy L. Kernodle considers women jazz musicians' work from the early days of New Orleans jazz; through jazz in Chicago, New York, Kansas City, and Europe; to the emergence of women jazz singers, including Billie Holiday and Ella Fitzgerald; and to the all-girl swing bands of the 1940s. Chapter 8 turns to the girl groups of the 1960s. Although often not taken seriously, they were one of the most successful musical phenomena of the first half of the 1960s in the United States. Jacqueline Warwick skilfully unpacks 'girl culture', the intersection of the girl groups with the contemporaneous Civil Rights Movement, and key figures and groups of the era, such as the Shirelles, the Ronettes, the Shangri-Las, and the Supremes. Chapter 9 probes the 'women-in-music' trope through a rock music lens. Leah Branstetter deftly draws upon the work of Joanna Russ to examine how women have been marginalised within rock. She considers the tendency of historiographies of rock to construct female rock musicians as anomalies, to devalue their contributions, and to resist categorising their music as 'authentic'. In Chapter 10, Katherine Williams considers female songwriters, focusing upon singer-songwriters who write and perform their own material, as opposed to songwriters who compose material for other artists. Concentrating upon four case studies, Williams interrogates the music of Carole King, Joni Mitchell, Kate Bush, and Adele. Turning to folk music, in Chapter 11, Michael Brocken focuses upon the British folk revival to consider both the traditional marginalisation of women's voices and the recent emergence of a more open folk scene within which women's voices 'figure'. Blending an auto-ethnographic and an ethnographic approach, Brocken considers not only his own growing awareness of gender issues within the folk scene as a male researcher, but also draws upon interview material with folk musician Emily Portman and folk and acoustic music promoter Rose Price. Chapter 12 presents a discussion of female solo artists in the popular music industry, with a particular focus on the influence and lasting effects of MTV and superstar branding. Through considering the careers of Tina Turner, Sinéad O'Connor, Alanis Morrisette, and Fiona Apple, Kristin J. Lieb probes the recurring themes of the human sacrifice of being a pop star, the sharing of narratives about abuse and exploitation, the recasting of the hot mess as a survivor, and the exploration of taboo subjects and identities. Virginia Kettle concludes Part II through a reflection of her career as a folk musician.

Acknowledging that music technology was (and to an extent remains) one of the most male-dominated musical fields, Part III turns to the theme of women and music technology. Louis Niebur's Chapter 13, 'Case Studies of Women in Electronic Music: The Early Pioneers', considers a range of the earliest ground-breaking women working with electronic music, including Daphne Oram and Delia Derbyshire at the BBC's Radiophonic Workshop in the UK, and Wendy Carlos, Pauline Oliveros, and Suzanne Ciani in the United States. Moving forward to the later twentieth and early twenty-first centuries, Chapter 14 provides a survey of contemporary female and gender-non-conforming artists using electronics for music. Margaret Schedel and Flannery Cunningham highlight how greater access to affordable means to manipulate digital sound from the autonomy of personal computers – away from difficult-to-access studios staffed by technicians and equipped with complex technology, which were previously largely the domain of male 'experts' – has opened up electronic music to a wider demographic of people (in terms of gender, race, and class). Taking an ethnographic approach which draws upon survey material from twenty-four respondents variously identifying as composers, sound artists, instrument builders, and programmers, this chapter explores some of this diversity through the artists' own words. Electroacoustic composer Manuella Blackburn concludes this part through an exploration of how motherhood, and a new interest in domestic sound sources, inspired by prolonged time spent in the home during pregnancy and the early days of motherhood, changed her compositional practice.

Part IV broadens the scope to consider women's wider work in music. Chapter 15, 'Women and Music Education in Schools: Pedagogues, Curricula, and Role Models', surveys women's contribution to music education. Although women in music studies has gained a steady foothold in university and conservatoire education over the last two decades, music education at school level (this chapter's focus) has tended to remain fairly conservative. Robert Legg discusses women's access to the teaching profession, highlighting that, while it has always been relatively open to women, persistent barriers remain, including a lack of women in leadership roles, and the gender pay gap. He also critiques the body/mind dualist view of music education, the lack of female role models in many curricula, and recent pedagogical debates of the twenty-first century. Chapter 16, 'Women in the Music Industries: The Art of Juggling', considers the persistent male-dominated nature of the popular-music industry and the space which contemporary FIMAs (Female Independent Music Artists) have carved out within it to sustain portfolio careers. Clare K. Duffin also presents two detailed case studies of Glasgow-based FIMAs, Emma Gillespie and Carol Laula. Steph Powers concludes Part IV 'In Her Own Words' through an auto-ethnographic exploration of her own portfolio career, which combines work as a performer, composer, music examiner, and critic. In the Afterword, Victoria Armstrong turns to the working conditions of women in the contemporary UK classical-music industry. She draws upon her recent UK-based ethnographic study into the working lives of twenty-four professional, classically trained female composers, conductors, and performers to examine the concepts of 'good' and 'bad' work within the cultural industries through a gendered lens.

The final stages of editing this book happened during the 2020 Covid-19 pandemic. As the devastating effects of the virus, and the lockdowns which governments worldwide imposed in an effort to try to contain it, became more fully felt, it became apparent that the particular consequences for women seemed to represent in microcosm the wider gendered conditions which have shaped women's lived experiences for so long. Insidiously, domestic abuse and violence increased in lockdown, when victims found themselves trapped in homes with their abusers. Women often took on the brunt of childcare and other caring and domestic responsibilities. An analysis of the impact of the pandemic on working parents by the Institute of Fiscal Studies (UK) in May 2020 found that working mothers were more likely than working fathers to have lost their job or been furloughed; that their working hours had fallen more; and that their time was interrupted more often by childcare.[7] Women's loss of employment – and the lack of childcare (rendered more acute by childcare providers facing long-term financial crises) – has led to many women facing a future of economic insecurity. Women of colour often suffered the very worse impact of the pandemic, as the virus affected BAME communities to a disproportionately high degree. The lives of all the authors in this book were touched in one way or another by the pandemic. I hold each one in awe for being able to maintain their focus upon completing this project during that time. The words used by Elizabeth Hoffman in her practitioner contribution about valuing female friendships as a 'special category of relationship' often echoed in my own thoughts as regular online 'girls' nights' with my friends, musicologists Helen Julia Minors and Laura Watson and composer Manuella Blackburn, became the weekly glimmers of light which sustained me during that difficult time.

This book would not exist without Kate Brett at Cambridge University Press. Her enthusiasm for the topic and support throughout the project were truly tremendous. My thanks go also to Eilidh Burrett and Hal Churchman at CUP. I am also grateful to the agents of Marin Alsop and Dame Evelyn Glennie, and to Emma Gillespie and Carol Laula for allowing us to reproduce images. My thanks go to The Open University for supporting this project through study time, to my colleagues in Music and within the AHSENT team for their interest in the project, and especially to my Staff Tutor colleagues for providing cover for me while I was working upon writing and editing. My interest in women in music was first sparked by my Oxford tutor, Prof. Susan Wollenberg. I could not imagine a more inspiring role model. My heartfelt thanks go to my parents, Christine and Robert, for all their support and encouragement over many years, and also to my parents-in-law, Wauki and Anthony. I am deeply grateful to my husband, Mark, who provided tremendous support, not least through taking on a great deal of the work in our home, while I was engulfed in the final stages of editing this book during the lockdown period. My thanks as always go to my daughter, Clara, who makes me smile every day.

Notes

1. See https://prsfoundation.com/partnerships/international-partnerships /keychange/ (accessed 21 June 2020).
2. Aaron I. Cohen (ed.), *International Encyclopedia of Women Composers*, second revised and enlarged ed. (New York: Books & Music USA, 1987).
3. Julie Anne Sadie and Rhian Samuel (eds.), *The New Grove Dictionary of Women Musicians* (New York: Norton, 1994).
4. Sophie Fuller, *The Pandora Guide to Women Composers: Britain and the United States, 1629–Present* (London: Pandora, 1994).
5. See, in particular, Sheila Whiteley (ed.), *Sexing the Groove: Popular Music and Gender* (London and New York: Routledge, 1997), and Sheila Whiteley, *Women and Popular Music: Sexuality, Identity and Subjectivity* (London and New York, 2000).
6. Sally Macarthur, Dawn Bennett, Talisha Goh, and Sophie Hennekam, 'The Rise and Fall, and the Rise (Again) of Feminist Research in Music: "What Goes Around Comes Around"', *Musicology Australia*, vol. 39, no. 2 (2017), 73–95.
7. Alison Andrew, Sarah Cattan, Monica Costa Dias, Christine Farquharson, Lucy Kraftman, Sonya Krutikova, Angus Phimister, and Almudena Sevilla, 'How Are Mothers and Fathers Balancing Work and Family Under Lockdown?', Institute of Fiscal Studies Z (27 May 2020), available at www.ifs.org.uk/publications/ 14860 (accessed 14 June 2020).

Abbreviations

AR	Augmented Reality
BASCA	British Academy of Songwriters, Composers and Authors (UK)
BBC	British Broadcasting Corporation (UK)
CMOs	Collection Management Organisations
DAWs	Digital Audio Workstations
EFDSS	English Folk Dance and Song Society (England, UK)
EMPAC	Experimental Media and Performing Arts Centre (New York, US)
FIMAs	Female Independent Music Artists
GDR	German Democratic Republic (East Germany)
IRCAM	Institut de Recherche et Coordination Acoustique/Musique (Institute for Research and Coordination in Acoustics/Music, France)
ISME	International Society for Music Education
MENC	Music Educators National Conference (US)
MU	Musicians' Union (UK)
NAfME	National Association for Music Education (US)
NAME	National Association of Music Educators (UK)
NIMEs	New Interfaces for Musical Expression
PPL	Public Performance Licensing (UK)
PRS	Performing Right Society (UK)
RCM	Royal College of Music (London, UK)
RTF	Radiodiffusion-Télévision Française (France)
SARC	Sonic Arts Research Centre (Queen's University, Belfast, Northern Ireland)
SNL	*Saturday Night Live* (US)
TOBA	Theater Owners Booking Association (US)
VR	Virtual Reality
WIM	Women in Music Organisation (US)

PART I

The Classical Tradition

1 | Women in Composition before the Second World War

SOPHIE FULLER

The 'Great' Composer?

At the start of the twentieth century throughout much of the United States and Europe, fuelled by the enduring image of the 'new woman', *femme nouvelle*, and *neue Frau*, there were widespread media discussions about women's roles in society and culture – what these roles were and what they should be. The debates took place as more and more women of all classes and nationalities, refusing any longer to accept subservient domestic positions, were moving into many different areas of public life with increasing confidence, independence, and determination.[1]

In the British musical press, writers continued a particular debate that had been raging for several decades. Why were there no 'great' women composers? The February 1900 edition of *The Musical Times*, for example, contained a report on a paper, 'Woman as a Musician', given by Dr Henry Harding at the fifteenth annual conference of the Incorporated Society of Musicians at Scarborough. Harding (1855–1930), organist and choirmaster at St Paul's Church in Bedford, was a representative member of the British musical establishment, with qualifications from the Royal College of Organists and Trinity College of Music as well as an Oxford University BMus and doctorate.[2]

'We are told that there are women novelists, women artists and so on' said the lecturer: 'why not women composers? I say emphatically that there *are* women composers; they do actually exist.' He definitely stated their number to be 489; but no woman, he added, had ever taken a high position as a composer, although they had done so in literature and the sister arts. They were splendid executants; why had they not the genius to compose? One authority declared that woman's strength of body would hardly endure necessary strains of brain and nerve power to compose. He took strong exception to the objectionable use of the words 'feminine' and 'femininity', as applied to composers and to music; and after alluding to the alleged femininity of Schubert, he expressed the devout hope that if Schubert really was feminine, women would imitate him. Women as musicians had been prevented from coming to maturity for want of training and development.

3

Although there had not hitherto been a great composer found in the ranks of women, in these days, when woman was advancing so rapidly, there was no reason why she should not take a high place in the ranks of composers.[3]

Harding's views on the position of women as composers were typical of the musical establishment. Many commentators, like Harding, recognised that women had not previously had, and still did not have, equal access to musical education and professional opportunities, but felt that, given the broadening of women's access to conservatoires and to the music profession, it would not be long before they were recognised as successful, mainstream, maybe even 'great', composers.[4]

There were, however, as Harding suggests, still commentators who held firmly to the belief that a woman had never been and could never be a 'great' composer. For example, A. L. S., in the *Musical News* of the same year, 1900, wrote emphatically:

It is impossible to find a single woman's name worthy to take rank with Beethoven, Handel, Mozart, Rossini, Brahms, Wagner, Schubert; we cannot even find one to place beside Balfe or Sir Arthur Sullivan . . .

If we seek for what may be called the feminine element in music, we have to look for it among the works of men, for the simple reason that women have produced nothing that can be given serious consideration.[5]

What made a composer 'great' was almost never defined in these discussions, although an interesting warning note about the 'great woman composer' had been sounded by E. A. C., possibly the composer Elizabeth Amelia Chamberlayne (1869–1919), in a letter to *The Musical World* back in 1890:

Why should we be impatient? let us hope on, wait, she will come. And when she does come, after all this talk, shall we be prepared to meet her? Shall we give her the honour due to her name? or shall we ignore her as a thing incomprehensible?[6]

E. A. C. seems to imply that a 'great' woman composer's music would be so different from that of the 'great' male composers of the canon, that neither it nor its creator would or could be recognised as 'great'. The debate about whether women's music was in some way different from that of men was to be a part of the debate over women's contributions as composers for many years.

Femininity in Music

Returning to Harding's paper, what is perhaps most notable about his views, apart from the strangely precise assertion that there were 489 women composers in existence, is his 'strong exception' to the idea that the concept of femininity could be applied to music. While A. L. S. was happy to recognise femininity in male composers, for Harding, and increasingly for the generations that followed, femininity was becoming a problematic concept that had all too often been applied to music and its creators. There was a drive instead to promote British music in particular as manly and virile, something that can be seen in much of the reception and promotion of British composers such as Hubert Parry (1848–1918) or Edward Elgar (1857–1934).[7]

Commentators inevitably linked women to femininity, expecting that the music produced by women should and would reflect this essential aspect of their beings, and this would in some way account for its difference. When a woman's music, expected to take the form of songs or shorter piano pieces, could be described as dainty, graceful, or charming it neatly fulfilled this expectation while at the same time predictably making it a lesser kind of music, never 'great'. On the other hand, if a woman did produce bold, forthright, complex music, in larger forms such as sonatas or symphonies, she was somehow betraying her essential self in a troubling way. The reception of the music created by various women composers can be seen to reflect this problematic set of expectations from the late nineteenth century and throughout the first forty years of the twentieth century (and indeed beyond).

For example, in the early years of her career Ethel Smyth published and appeared in concert programmes using her initials rather than her full name. George Bernard Shaw's review of the 1892 premiere of one of her works reveals the audience's surprise that the ambiguously gendered composer of a powerful orchestral work could turn out to be a woman:

When E. M. Smyth's heroically brassy overture to Antony and Cleopatra was finished, and the composer called to the platform, it was observed with stupefaction that all that tremendous noise had been made by a lady.[8]

Over forty years later, critics were still unsettled by women composing music which did not reflect prevalent ideas of womanhood. Here are two critical reactions to a 1935 London concert at which avant-garde music by Elisabeth Lutyens (1906–83), Elizabeth Maconchy (1907–94), and Grace Williams (1906–77) was heard, providing an interesting example from the period shortly before the Second World War. William McNaught wrote in the *Evening News* that the concert was 'an interesting study of the young female mind of today. This organ, when it takes up composition, works in mysterious ways. No lip-stick, silk stocking, or saucily tilted hat adorns the music evolved from its recesses'.[9] And an advance notice of the concert in the *Glasgow Herald* claimed: 'Musicians . . . are beginning to wonder when a woman composer is going to write some music reminiscent of the sex as it used to be'.[10] As scholars such as Marcia J. Citron have pointed out, these views on women's essential femininity are just a part of the complicated set of circumstances, including the lack of a thorough musical education for most women, as well as female role models, that served to exclude women from the canon of great composers.[11]

New Century: Established Composers (Chaminade, White, Smyth, and Le Beau)

The media debates over women's abilities as composers were doubtless directly prompted by the increasing numbers of women at the turn of the twentieth century who were regarded, by themselves and by others, as composers and who were leading successful and rewarding careers. At the start of the new century, throughout Britain, the United States, and continental Europe, women were publishing and achieving performances of their music in all genres, from symphonies and operas to chamber music and songs. Many of these women were of the same generation as Harding, well-established, middle-aged composers such as Ethel Smyth (1858–1934), Adela Maddison (1862–1929), and Maude Valérie White (1855–1937) from Britain; Louise Adolpha Le Beau (1850–1927) from Germany; Amy Beach (1862–1944) from the United States; or Cécile Chaminade (1857–1944) from France.

In the early twentieth century, Chaminade and her well-crafted music, notably songs and piano pieces, were known and loved throughout Europe and the United States.[12] Chaminade's varied reception during her lifetime provides more evidence of the conflicted concept of femininity as applied to women composers. She gave her name to an expensive perfume, created by the British company, Morny Frères, and which was advertised in the press as follows:

> Perfume 'Chaminade' is most happily named, its light and dainty odours, always fresh and harmonious, suggesting the melodic beauties of the 'Air de Ballet' – a few bars of which, written and signed by Madame Chaminade, are in Morny Frères' possession, and are used on the labels as the registered mark for this series of perfumery.[13]

The association with a female composer must have seemed apt for a 'light and dainty' fragrance. Yet in his 1901 book *Songs and Songwriters,*

American critic Henry T. Finck wrote that: 'Mlle Chaminade's face is said to have "a boyish look", and there is no specific feminine tenderness in her songs – a trait which she shares with other female composers, who seem to lack both true femininity and the virile faculty of creating ideas.'[14] A few years later the American writer Arthur Elsen, in his book *Woman's Work in Music*, referred to Chaminade as an example of his belief that 'women's work in music will always show more of delicate grace and refinement than man's, and will be to some extent lacking in the broader effects of strong feeling', claiming that her songs 'are among the most delightful in the world to-day, yet they charm by delicacy rather than strength'.[15]

After 1890, Chaminade, who had produced orchestral and stage works in the 1880s, concentrated on composing and publishing songs and piano pieces.[16] Women who needed to make a living from their musical endeavours were excluded from many of the lucrative music-related positions that their male contemporaries were able to fill, from teaching composition at conservatoires and universities to conducting mainstream symphony orchestras.[17]

There were many practical reasons why women working as composers in the early twentieth century would concentrate on smaller genres such as song, including the comparative ease with which they could be performed in a variety of settings, the fact that through publication, songwriting in particular was one of the few potentially financially profitable forms of composition, and the limited access of some women to a thorough training in counterpoint or orchestration. Women were also socialised to communicate feelings and develop their instincts and emotions in ways that many people would have regarded as entirely inappropriate for men. In song, women found a genre which was entirely suited to a direct and crystallised expression in music of feeling, ideas, and emotions.

Maude Valérie White, who had studied at London's Royal Academy of Music, was primarily a songwriter and reached the height of her fame and critical acclaim in the 1890s.[18] She was an inveterate traveller and set texts in a wide variety of languages, from English and German to French, Italian, Spanish, and Swedish. At the start of the twentieth century, in the autumn of 1901, White decided to live in Sicily for the sake of her health and was never again to have a settled home in England. Her songs, such as her hauntingly sensual D'Annunzio setting 'Isaotta Blanzemano' (1904), became increasingly inventive and the concerts of her music that she organised continued to be well received and financially successful.[19]

Women often played central roles in musical salons throughout Europe, Britain, and the United States and a more nuanced consideration of exactly what is meant by the term 'salon music', a term often used in connection with the music created by women such as White or Chaminade, is long overdue.[20] At a time when women were just beginning to embrace public life, it is not surprising that many of them found a comfortable and welcoming place in the semi-public world of the salon, as composers, performers, hosts, and audience. The notable Parisian salon host Winnaretta Singer, the Princesse de Polignac (1865–1943), was an important figure in the lives of many early twentieth-century composers, including Claude Debussy (1862–1918), Igor Stravinsky (1882–1971), Ethel Smyth, Adela Maddison, and Germaine Tailleferre (1892–1983). The Princesse de Polignac commissioned a wide variety of music and, through the concerts at her salon, provided an invaluable performance space in which composers could gain a hearing for their latest works in all genres, from orchestral and choral works to piano pieces and songs.

Many of the women working at the turn of the twentieth century, such as Ethel Smyth or Louise Adolpha Le Beau, were eager to move beyond the world of song. Smyth studied in Leipzig, although privately, after a brief, unsatisfactory period at the conservatorium. She had fought in the late nineteenth century to gain a hearing for her orchestral work and then, nothing daunted, turned to creating one of the most complex and difficult to produce of all musical genres, opera. In 1902 her second opera *Der Wald* was premiered in Berlin, followed by *The Wreckers* at Leipzig in 1906,[21] *The Boatswain's Mate* in London in 1916, *Fête galante* in Birmingham in 1923, and *Entente cordiale* in London in 1925. *The Wreckers*, arguably her greatest achievement, is a gripping and poignant work, with a particularly intense and impassioned love duet between the two protagonists in the second act. Smyth was probably most widely performed and recognised in the 1920s, although by this time she was growing increasingly deaf and had turned to writing and broadcasting.[22] She produced a remarkable series of memoirs and essays, in which she created a memorable image of herself as a feisty, indomitable woman, raging against the male 'machine' in order to find a hearing for her music.[23]

As a composer, Le Beau was also known primarily for her large-scale orchestral and vocal works. As a writer, she produced much music criticism as well as an autobiography, *Lebenserinnerungen einer Komponistin* (Memoirs of a Composer),[24] in which, like Smyth, she detailed the problems and discrimination she had faced as a composer who was a woman. Like Smyth, Le Beau studied music privately. As she recounts in her memoirs, after deeming her Violin Sonata to be 'manly and not sounding as if composed by a woman', the composer Josef Rheinberger agreed to teach her, despite the fact that he did not usually accept women as students.[25] Also like Smyth, Le Beau found it hard to gain a hearing for her two operas *Hadumoth* (1888–91) and *Der verzauberte Kalif* (1901–3).

The Cosmopolitan Composer and Difficulties in Germany (Maddison and Poldowski)

The situation for women in Germany, particularly in the most conservative cities such as Berlin, does seem to have been particularly difficult for women who were trying to build careers as composers. Nevertheless, in the later nineteenth century and into the twentieth, studying in Germany, either privately or at a German conservatoire, was regarded as the best career choice for musicians from elsewhere in Europe and the United States, reflecting the high regard in which the Germanic canon was still held. Women from elsewhere followed their male contemporaries to go and study in various German cities, despite the fact that they were not always welcoming to women musicians. As a young woman, Smyth fought with her father to be allowed to study in Leipzig, although she only studied at the conservatorium there for a brief period. In 1902, the American composer Mabel Daniels (1878–1971)[26] described the Munich Conservatory, where she was studying, in a letter home:

> You know that five years ago women were not allowed to study advanced counterpoint at the conservatory. In fact anything more advanced than elementary harmony was debarred. The ability of the feminine intellect to comprehend the intricacies of a stretto, or cope with double counterpoint in the tenth, if not openly denied, was seriously questioned.[27]

The British composer Adela Maddison moved from London to Paris at the end of the nineteenth century, arguably to further her compositional career. In Paris she was acquainted with the Princesse de Polignac and found a supportive atmosphere for her music.[28] But in 1906, for unknown reasons, she moved to live and work in Germany, from where she wrote to her friend Delius that she could 'find no sympathetic soul in Berlin – they all have a contempt for anything done by a woman in the composition line!'[29]

The cosmopolitanism of composers in the first decade of the twentieth century is perhaps particularly striking as far as women are concerned. A good example is the composer Poldowski (1879–1932), pen name of Irene Wieniawska (or after her marriage, Lady Dean Paul). She was born in Belgium, daughter of the famous Polish violinist Henri Wieniawski, studied in Paris, and lived most of her life in London. She was best known, and highly critically admired, for her songs, in turn dissonant, humorous, and languorous, most of which were settings of French texts.

In a fascinating article in the progressive music journal *The Sackbut* in 1924, journalist Yvonne Pert grappled with ideas of femininity as applied to women composers. She dismissed Smyth as a composer whose work was 'conceived according to masculine models' but did discuss specific contemporary composers, including the Welsh composer Morfydd Owen (1891–1918),[30] whom she felt were reflecting an undefined femininity in their music. Pert focused on Poldowski, describing her as

probably the most spontaneously feminine composer up to the present. Her work is instinct with the feminine quality of moods, the feminine reaction to images and atmospheres, the feminine impulses expressed in new varieties of rhythm and harmonic colour, slight though these variations may seem ... She has probably taken the first clearly conscious and decisive step towards the realisation of femininity as an objective in musical art.[31]

For many of these women, the First World War ruptured the ease with which they travelled and worked in different European countries as well as thwarting other aspects of their careers. German productions of Smyth's operas were cancelled at the outbreak of war, while Maddison was forced to return to England when her German companion and probably lover, Marta Mundt, was dismissed by her employer, the Princesse de Polignac.

The Disruption of the First World War, Conservatoires, and Prizes (Canal, Leleu, Maconchy, and Williams)

The war also curtailed the movements of those composers who additionally worked as performers. Promoting their own music through performance was often a way that women worked around the establishment assumption that their music was not worth hearing. Le Beau, like Chaminade and Beach,[32] was a professional pianist, as well as a composer. Many younger women such as the British viola player Rebecca Clarke (1886–1979) or the French pianists Marguerite Canal (1890–1978) and Jeanne Leleu (1898–1979), who began to be known as composers in the years after the First World War, were also in demand as performers and frequently took the opportunity to promote their own work. Both Canal and Leleu were winners of the prestigious French *Prix de Rome*, in 1920 and 1923 respectively.[33] This prize rewarded the winner with a period working at the Villa Médicis in Rome as well as guaranteed media coverage, both leading to invaluable performance opportunities. The only previous woman to win this prize, in 1913, had been Lili Boulanger (1893–1918),[34] a composer who, like Owen, died in her twenties but who nevertheless left a formidable legacy of distinctive and imaginative music in a powerfully individual musical voice.

As the twentieth century progressed, it became more common for women to study composition at conservatoires, and to benefit from the opportunities these institutions provided, from performances to networking. Winning prizes was not always so easy though. As a student at London's Royal College of Music in the late 1920s, Maconchy was told that the judges had decided not to award her the Mendelssohn Scholarship for composition since she would only get married and never write another note of music.[35] Interestingly, White had won the Mendelssohn Scholarship back in 1879 and Maconchy's daughter Nicola LeFanu (b.1947) was to win it in 1972. The Mendelssohn Scholarship provided money for the holder to travel and study abroad. Maconchy and her close friend, the Welsh composer Williams, were both awarded somewhat less prestigious Octavia Travelling Scholarships by the Royal College of Music and did spend valuable time in Europe – Maconchy in Prague and Williams in Vienna.[36]

Class Conflict and Struggles with Men (Crawford Seeger, Barraine, Tailleferre, and Mahler)

The radical American composer Ruth Crawford Seeger (1901–53) studied at Chicago's American Conservatory and then privately with Charles Seeger who, in an echo of Le Beau's experience with her teacher Rheinberger, was initially reluctant to teach a woman. Teacher and pupil were later to be married. Crawford Seeger won a Guggenheim Fellowship and in 1930 travelled to Europe, where she spent most of her time in Berlin, a not-altogether-satisfactory experience, despite the opportunity to meet numerous musicians and composers. On her return to the United States Crawford Seeger became increasingly involved in left-wing politics, regarding music as an important part of the class struggle. She was to devote much of the rest of her life to working with American folk song.[37] A similar devotion to left-wing politics can be seen in the life and career of Elsa Barraine (1910–99) while Maconchy was active in the Worker's Musical Association, founded in 1936.

Not all composers travelled beyond their home country. The British composer Dorothy Howell (1898–1982) studied at London's Royal Academy of Music. She went on to have several works in a somewhat unadventurous late-Romantic idiom performed at the celebrated Promenade Concerts in the 1920s, such as her tone poem *Lamia* (1919), based on Keats's poem of the same name.[38] The African American composer Florence Price (1887–1953) studied at Boston's New England Conservatory and eventually settled in Chicago in the late 1920s. In 1932 she won first prize in the prestigious Wanamaker competition for her Symphony and Piano Sonata, both in E minor. In both works, Price deftly introduces melodic and rhythmic elements of African American vernacular music.[39]

Charles Seeger's attitude was not one taken by composition teachers elsewhere. At the Royal College of Music, Maconchy and Williams, together with fellow students such as Dorothy Gow (1893–1982), found an endlessly supportive teacher and mentor in Ralph Vaughan Williams.[40] Paul Dukas, at the Paris Conservatoire, was similarly supportive of his female composition students, such as Barraine, Claude Arrieu (1903–90), and Yvonne Desportes (1907–93).

The careers of many of the women who worked as composers in the first forty years of the twentieth century were affected by the attitudes of the men – fathers and husbands – in their lives. Several decades after Smyth or Chaminade had faced implacable fathers, numerous men still made it difficult for their daughters to study music at a conservatory, including those of Clarke and Tailleferre. While some women, such as Maconchy, had understanding husbands who encouraged and nurtured their careers, others faced considerable resentment or even prohibition. The best-known example from this time is probably Alma Mahler (1879–1964). The young Alma Schindler had thrown herself into composition. But her first husband, Gustav Mahler, famously wrote to her in 1901 before they were married to say 'The role of "composer", the "bread-winner", is mine; yours is that of a loving partner, the sympathetic comrade'.[41] Despite having previously written to a friend 'He thinks *nothing* of my art and much of his own. And *I* think *nothing* of *his* art and much of my own', Alma Mahler capitulated and stopped composing.

Women Organising Together and Embracing New Technologies

Another composer who survived notoriously difficult marriages to two husbands who both tried to stop her composing was Tailleferre.[42]

Tailleferre, however, continued to compose throughout her long life. She had first come to attention as a member of the group of young French composers know as Les Six and was supported and encouraged by both Erik Satie and the Princesse de Polignac. The importance of support networks was invaluable for many of the women working as composers in the period before the Second World War. Some groups were established by women specifically to support women musicians, such as the Union des Femmes Professeurs et Compositeurs de Musique (Union of Women Composers and Music Teachers), founded in 1906 in France,[43] and the Society of Women Musicians, founded in 1911 in Britain.[44]

Also notable at a slightly later date in Britain were the Macnaghten–Lemare concerts, an initiative set up by three women (violinist Anne Macnaghten, conductor Iris Lemare, and composer Lutyens) who denied having overt feminist ideals but who nevertheless provided vital performance opportunities for themselves and for their friends, such as Maconchy and Williams.[45] As scholars such as Martha Vicinus have shown, women have frequently found that by organising together, they have been able to overcome chauvinism and discrimination.[46]

Like so many women of their generation, Maconchy and Williams keenly embraced the opportunities offered by the relatively new technologies of broadcasting and recording. Throughout the 1930s, a decade of growing economic depression and political unrest, they both had numerous works played on the various radio stations of the British Broadcasting Corporation (BBC) and began to see their music reproduced as 'records', although it was to be many years before either owned a record player.[47] In the 1930s, Crawford began to work extensively with field recordings of American folk song.[48]

Back in 1900, a report in the *Lady's Pictorial* on Henry Harding's paper noted that he had claimed that 'there was every hope ... that a pioneer woman, a courageous, pure and noble artist, would arise, and compel us to regard her as a composer as well as a musician'.[49] Nearly forty years later, by the outbreak of the Second World War, Britain, Europe, and the United States had seen many courageous and noble women who had refused to let the prejudices they faced prevent them from working as composers. Often creating their own networks and opportunities, they built on very different educational opportunities and life experiences to compel recognition for their striking and varied musical voices.

Notes

1. See Sheila Rowbotham, *A Century of Women: The History of Women in Britain and the United States* (London: Viking, 1997), 7–9, for the idea of a second wave of 'new women' at the start of the twentieth century.

2. Anonymous, 'Dr H. A. Harding Honorary Secretary of the Royal College of Organists', *The Musical Times*, 49 (September 1908), 565–7.

3. 'The Incorporated Society of Musicians', *The Musical Times*, 41 (February 1900), 113.

4. See, for example, Ernest Newman, 'Woman and Music', *The Musical Times*, vol. 51 (June 1910), 359–61.

5. A. L. S., 'Women and Music', *Musical News*, vol. 19 (1900), 64.

6. E. A. C., 'The Female Composer' [letter], *The Musical World*, vol. 70 (23 August 1890), 676.

7. See, for example, Sophie Fuller, 'Elgar and the Salons: The Significance of a Private Musical World', in Byron Adams (ed.), *Edward Elgar and His World* (Princeton: Princeton University Press, 2007), 223–47.

8. George Bernard Shaw, *Music in London 1890–94*, revised ed. (London: Constable, 1932), 37.

9. William McNaught, *Evening News* (5 February 1935), n.p. (Iris Lemare archive).

10. Anonymous, *Glasgow Herald* (4 February 1935), n.p. (Iris Lemare Archive). It is interesting that this London concert series attracted press attention as far away as Glasgow.

11. See Marcia J. Citron, *Gender and the Musical Canon* (Urbana and Chicago: University of Illinois Press, 1993).

12. Marcia J. Citron, 'Cécile Chaminade', in Julie Anne Sadie and Rhian Samuel (eds.), *The New Grove Dictionary of Women Composers* (London: Macmillan, 1994), 112–15.

13. Anonymous, *The Sketch* (2 November 1910). It is interesting that this company had given itself a French name.

14. H. T. Finck, *Songs and Songwriters* (London: John Murray, 1901), 226.

15. Arthur Elsen, *Woman's Work in Music* (Boston, MA: L. C. Page & Co., 1904), 237.

16. Marcia J. Citron, 'Cécile Chaminade', 113.

17. Women did, of course, both teach and conduct, but were not accepted in the most financially rewarding or prestigious posts.

18. On White, see Sophie Fuller, 'Maude Valérie White' in 'Women Composers during the British Musical Renaissance, 1880–1918' (PhD thesis, King's College, University of London, 1998), 142–202.

19. See, for example, the review of a concert White gave at London's Bechstein Hall in 1905: Anonymous, *The Times* (4 December 1905), 11. White wrote of this concert

that 'from a financial point of view it was one of the most successful concerts I ever gave in London': Maude Valérie White, *My Indian Summer* (London: Grayson & Grayson, 1932), 118. 'Isaotta Blanzemano' was premiered by the singer Elsie Swinton at this concert. See David Greer, *A Numerous and Fashionable Audience: The Story of Elsie Swinton* (London: Thames Publishing, 1997), 74.

20. Examples of recent revisionist scholarship on salon culture include, Sylvia Kahan, *Music's Modern Muse: A Life of Winnaretta Singer, Princesse de Polignac* (Rochester, NY: Rochester University Press, 2003); Aisling Kenny and Susan Wollenberg, *Women and the Nineteenth-Century Lied* (Farnham: Ashgate, 2015); and Anja Bunzel and Natasha Loges, *Musical Salon Culture in the Long Nineteenth Century* (Woodbridge and Rochester, NY: The Boydell Press, 2019).

21. This opera had been originally written to a French libretto as *Les naufrageurs*; this was then translated into German as *Strandrecht* for the premiere and later to English as *The Wreckers*, which remains the title by which it is most frequently known.

22. On Smyth, see the many writings of Elizabeth Wood, such as 'Lesbian Fugue: Ethel Smyth's Contrapuntal Arts', in Ruth A. Solie (ed.), *Musicology and Difference: Gender and Sexuality in Music Scholarship* (Berkeley: University of California Press, 1993), 164–83 and the entry by Sophie Fuller in *The Grove Dictionary of Music and Musicians*.

23. See, in particular, Ethel Smyth, *Female Pipings in Eden* (London: Peter Davis, 1934).

24. Louise Adolpha Le Beau, *Lebenserinnerungen einer Komponistin* (Baden-Baden: Emil Sommermayer, 1910).

25. Judith E. Olsen, 'Louise Adolpha Le Beau: Composer in Late Nineteenth-Century Germany', in Jane Bowers and Judith Tick (eds.), *Women Making Music: The Western Art Tradition, 1150–1950* (Basingstoke and London: Macmillan, 1986), 284.

26. On Daniels, see Mary Ann McCabe, *Mabel Daniels: An American Composer in Transition* (Abingdon and New York: Routledge, 2017).

27. Quoted in Carol Neuls-Bates (ed.), *Women in Music: An Anthology of Source Readings from the Middle Ages to the Present*, 2nd ed. (Boston, MA: Northeastern University Press, 1996), 220.

28. On this period in Maddison's life, see Sophie Fuller, '"Devoted Attention": Looking for Lesbian Musicians in Fin-de-Siècle Britain', in Sophie Fuller and Lloyd Whitesell (eds.), *Queer Episodes in Music and Modern Identity* (Urbana and Chicago: University of Illinois Press, 2002), 85–7.

29. Letter from Maddison to Delius (11 February (before 1910)), Delius Trust.

30. On Owen, see Rhian Davies, *Never So Pure a Sight: Morfydd Owen (1891–1918): A Life in Pictures* (Llandysul: Gomer, 1994).

31. Yvonne Pert, 'The Woman in Music', *The Sackbut*, 5 (1924–5), 44–5. For further information on Poldowski, see Anon, *Miniature Essay: Poldowski*

(London: Chester, 1924) and Sophie Fuller, *The Pandora Guide to Women Composers: Britain and the United States, 1629–Present* (London: Pandora, 1994), 249–51.

32. On Beach, see Adrienne Fried Block, *Amy Beach: Passionate Victorian. The Life and Work of an American Composer 1867–1944* (New York and Oxford: Oxford University Press, 1998).

33. On Canal, Leleu, and other French women composers of their generation, see Laura Hamer, *Female Composers, Conductors, Performers: Musiciennes of Interwar France, 1919–1939* (Abingdon and New York: Routledge, 2018).

34. On Boulanger, see Léonie Rosenstiel, *The Life and Work of Lili Boulanger* (Madison, NJ: Fairleigh Dickinson University Press, 1978) and Caroline Potter, *Nadia and Lili Boulanger* (Farnham: Ashgate, 2006).

35. See Rhiannon Mathias, *Lutyens, Maconchy, Williams and Twentieth-Century British Music: A Blest Trio of Sirens* (Farnham: Ashgate, 2012), 28.

36. See Sophie Fuller and Jenny Doctor (eds.), *Music, Life, and Changing Times: Selected Correspondence between British Composers Elizabeth Maconchy and Grace Williams, 1927–77*, vol. 1 (Abingdon and New York: Routledge 2019), 7–8.

37. On Crawford Seeger, see Judith Tick, *Ruth Crawford Seeger: A Composer's Search for American Music* (Oxford and New York: Oxford University Press, 1997).

38. On Howell, see Vincent James Byrne, 'The Life and Work of Dorothy Howell' (MA thesis, University of Birmingham, 2015).

39. On Price, see Sophie Fuller, *The Pandora Guide to Women Composers: Britain and the United States, 1629–present* (London: Pandora Press, 1994), 254–6.

40. See Jenny Doctor, '"Working for Her Own Salvation": Vaughan Williams as Teacher of Elizabeth Maconchy, Grace Williams and Ina Boyle', in Lewis Foreman (ed.), *Vaughan Williams in Perspective: Studies of an English Press* (Illminster: Albion Press for the Vaughan Williams Society, 1998), 181–201.

41. Quoted in Cate Haste, *Passionate Spirit: The Life of Alma Mahler* (London: Bloomsbury, 2019), 89.

42. On Tailleferre, see Hamer, *Female Composers, Conductors, Performers*, 94–120.

43. See ibid., 18.

44. See Sophie Fuller, 'The Society of Women Musicians', in *The British Library – Discovering Music: Early 20th Century*, www.bl.uk/20th-century-music /articles/the-society-of-women-musicians.

45. See Sophie Fuller, '"Putting the BBC and T. Beecham to Shame": The Macnaghten-Lemare Concerts, 1931–7' *Journal of the Royal Musical Association*, vol. 138, no. 2 (2013), 377–414.

46. Martha Vicinus, *Independent Women: Work and Community for Single Women, 1850–1920* (London: Virago, 1985).

47. See Fuller and Doctor (eds.), *Music, Life, and Changing Times*, vol. 1.

48. Tick, 'Lomax Country', in *Ruth Crawford Seeger*, 247–67.

49. Anonymous, 'Bass Trombone', 'Musical Notes', *Lady's Pictorial*, 39
    (13 January 1900), 59.

Further Reading

Block, Adrienne Fried. *Amy Beach: Passionate Victorian: The Life and Work of an American Composer 1867–1944* (New York and Oxford: Oxford University Press, 1998).

Brown, Rae Linda, The Heart of a Woman: The Life and Music of Florence B. Price (Urbana, Chicago and Springfield: University of Illinois Press, 2020).

Hamer, Laura. *Female Composers, Conductors, Performers: Musiciennes of Interwar France, 1919–1939* (Abingdon and New York: Routledge, 2018).

Mathias, Rhiannon. *Lutyens, Maconchy, Williams and Twentieth-Century British Music: A Blest Trio of Sirens* (Farnham: Ashgate, 2012).

Tick, Judith. *Ruth Crawford Seeger: A Composer's Search for American Music* (Oxford and New York: Oxford University Press, 1997).

2 | Women in Composition during the Cold War in Music

RHIANNON MATHIAS

Following the sacrifices of the Second World War, the second half of the twentieth century witnessed enormous social and cultural changes. This was the era of the Cold War (*c*.1947–89), a period defined by political, economic, and ideological tensions between the United States and its Western allies, and the Soviet Union and countries in the Eastern Soviet Bloc (USSR).[1] Major steps forward for women in society were attained in this era, brought about by the women's movement of the 1960s and '70s (second-wave feminism). These steps were taken at a time when 'classical' music was undergoing radical, unprecedented change, in an age of new communications, when radio, television, the cinema, and sound technologies greatly expanded the audience for music of all genres from all periods.

This chapter focuses on a number of women composers – all born within the first three decades of the twentieth century – who made vital contributions to the post-war international music scene. These composers worked in a profession that was male-dominated, and engaged with the tumultuous musical events of the mid-century. Their music is permeated with the spirit of its time – in varying degrees of temperature – embodying the individual composer's own creative choices and very particular cultural and social environment. Each one succeeded in breaking through the Cold War's musical sound barrier.

A Lunar Landing and a Symphony

Post-war musical developments were certainly in the mind of Welsh composer Grace Williams (1906–77) when she wrote in 1973 about how listening to a 'way-out' electronic piece (after a Mahler Symphony) made her feel that she had 'left the earth and landed on the moon'. Warming to her space-age association, Williams argued that

In a way the anti-*avant-garde* musicians are similar to those who oppose the lunar landings. There are others – and they include me – who, though themselves would hate to go to the moon, accept the landings as inevitable.[2]

Such comments seem eminently reasonable but also reveal Williams's feelings of being outpaced and outmoded in the post-war musical race. She had been stung by a critic who had described her music as being 'eons removed from the world of the avant-garde', and frequently confessed to feelings of isolation.[3] As she stated:

> To continue composing in the post-war years without capitulating to Schoenberg's serialism was like being left behind in a backwater, when everyone else was swimming ahead with the tide.[4]

(For a discussion of Williams's pre-war career, see Chapter 1, 'Women in Composition before the Second World War'.)

Revolution had been in the air after the war. Intense tussles broke out between cohorts about the very nature of musical style and language, and questions about what form the 'music of the future' should take lingered on until the end of the twentieth century. The biggest explosion had been formed by a perceived crisis in the major–minor key system in Vienna in the century's early decades, and Schoenberg's replacement of that system with the twelve-note/serial method. Many of post-war Europe's most influential musicians, including René Leibowitz and Theodor W. Adorno, believed that this (Second) Viennese solution to an apparently exhausted tonality should now be applied to music as a whole, creating an international lingua franca for a new post-war age. Such a notion was debated and radicalised into variants (such as total serialism), principally by Pierre Boulez in France and Karlheinz Stockhausen in Germany, and was given credence by Stravinsky's own 'capitulation' to serialism in the early 1950s.

International music discourse was dominated for several decades by this intense preoccupation with the nature, shape, and form of musical language. Triggered by Boulez's inflammatory pronouncement in 1952 that 'every composer outside the serial experiments has been *useless*', the resulting Cold War in music created a peculiar situation for a time, in which new works were appraised (or measured) by the extent to which their music conformed to this new orthodoxy.[5] The advent of electronic music, spectral music, minimalism, and other styles would prove that there was more than one stylistic choice available for composers to make, but Williams's fears about being left behind in this strange new world were well founded. Music written in a broadly tonal idiom – in the 1950s and '60s, certainly – risked being dismissed as irrelevant or unoriginal by progressives advocating a complete break with the musical past in favour of new terrain. Most composers who were serious about their craft, whether traditionalist or progressive, felt compelled to justify their compositional choices.

Williams shared her anxieties with her friend, the Austrian composer Egon Wellesz (1885–1974), with whom she had studied for a year in Vienna after graduating from the Royal College of Music in the late 1920s. Wellesz had been a pupil of Schoenberg's, alongside Alban Berg and Anton Webern, and had a rare insight into, and admiration for, the radical musical innovations of his Second Viennese friends. He was not, however, an admirer of the post-war avant-garde. 'The noise-makers have the upper hand', he told Williams in August 1962, 'it is still a post-war neurosis and "angry young men" attitude which one must ignore.'[6]

Few could ignore the angry-young-men attitude at this time, but Williams discreetly focused instead on writing works which heralded a new dawn for Welsh music. Her quiet revolution began in the interwar period, when she first gained a public profile with a series of expertly crafted orchestral works, including the popular *Fantasia on Welsh Nursery Tunes* (1939/40). A woman making musical use of nursery tunes may have played into status quo stereotypes about women at this time, but Williams broke that particular mould in 1943 when she became the first Welsh composer to write a symphony ('Symphonic Impressions'). In the years immediately following the war Williams underwent a significant period of creative renewal, the original, declamatory style of *Penillion* for orchestra (1955) and the Second Symphony (1956) partly defined by her evocation of the sounds and cadences of the Welsh language in purely instrumental terms. She did use a twelve-note row as a passacaglia theme in the second movement of her Trumpet Concerto (1963), but cast it within a tonal framework. As she explained:

I have avoided things which were wrong for me such as serialism because it was not melodically suitable. But remember, every composer has his own series of notes which form his own idiom . . . we've all got a 'series', or there would be no style.[7]

Music on the Right and Left – *Plupart du Temps* (*Most of the Time*)

Although aeons removed from Williams in terms of musical idiom and style, a concern with melody and vocal and instrumental equivalents have also been fundamental to the music of the French composer Betsy Jolas (b.1926). Born in Paris, Jolas spent the war years in the United States and, after graduating in music from Bennington College, Vermont, returned with her family to France in 1946. She continued her studies at the Paris

Conservatoire with Simone Plé-Caussade, Darius Milhaud, and Olivier Messiaen at a time when distinctions between music of the past (tonal) and the future (serial) were starting to be fiercely debated. Recalling the particular atmosphere in Paris after the war, Jolas has stated that

> It was both disturbing and exciting. It was very much connected to the general situation at the time which was the Cold War. You had to take sides, it was very clear, you had to decide what kind of music you were going to write ... It was tyrannical ... there was the right and left in music as well as in the world.[8]

By Jolas's own admission, it took her 'a long time to know the kind of music I wanted to write'.[9] The lyrical music of Webern became a guiding light for her at this time, and she admired and acquainted herself with the radical experimentalism of Boulez, Stockhausen, and Berio, while attending events at Donaueschingen and Darmstadt in (West) Germany, and Domaine Musical concerts (in Paris). She did not share the enthusiasm of her peers for all the emerging avant-garde techniques (musical pointillism, for instance), however, and was never a disciple of serialism. She focused on forging a musical series of her own in these formative years, her compositional approach shaped as much by her (forbidden) love of tonal music – in particular, the Renaissance choral works of Perotin, Lassus, and Josquin she gained knowledge of during her early studies in the States – as by avant-garde techniques.

   Jolas's fascination with the relationship between words and music, and the expressive potential of the voice, is revealed in pieces such as the Reverdy song cycle, *Plupart du temps* for mezzo-soprano and piano (1949) and in her *Mots* for vocal quintet and ensemble (1963). In *Quatour II* for soprano and string trio (1964), the singer is balanced as an equal with the instruments, and articulates 'a flexible art of phonemes representing the vocal equivalent of bowings and tonguings'.[10] The quartet was commissioned by and premiered at one of Boulez's prestigious Domaine Musical concerts in 1966, and Jolas continued to explore new modes of vocal and instrumental equivalents in her *D'un opéra de voyage* for twenty-two instruments (1967), a piece also premiered by Domaine Musical performers. The essence of the melodic line, the accents and inflexions of language, and the spirit of experimentalism have remained central to Jolas's *oeuvre*, animating works such as the vocal *Sonate à 12* (1970) and the *11 Lieder* for trumpet and orchestra (1977) as well as her operas, *Le pavillon au bord de la rivière* (1975) and *Schliemann* (1990). A highly esteemed figure on the French musical scene, Jolas succeeded her teacher Messiaen as Professor of Analysis and Composition at the Paris

Conservatoire in 1975, and was elected a member of the American Academy of Arts and Letters in 1983.

An Angry Young Woman – *And Suddenly It's Evening*

Virgil Thomson once observed that France, the United States, and England tended to neglect their women composers, before going on to identify Jolas and Elisabeth Lutyens (1906–83) as two of the best.[11] Continental avant-garde ideas were not always clearly received across the Channel, and the English music establishment's hostility towards serialism in the immediate post-war years meant that recognition for Lutyens came late. Inspired, like Jolas, by hearing a performance of Webern's music, Lutyens had decided to start with twelve-note music in the late 1930s, and her Chamber Concerto No. 1 for nine instruments (1939–40) – the first piece by an English composer to use serial techniques – marked an important milestone. Wartime England was not in the mood, however, for a musical revolution associated with an Austrian (Schoenberg) and an angry young woman. Mocked and criticised for writing unladylike music and for adopting an 'un-English' musical method, Lutyens later confessed to being made to feel at this time 'like a Communist before the Committee for Un-American Activities'.[12] Significantly, her icy reception at home was in stark contrast to the warm welcome she received from young composers (including Boulez) in Paris, where, by 1947, 'twelve-tone music was ... completely accepted so that I lost the sense of utter isolation I had felt in England'.[13]

Lutyens continued, in her isolated position, to explore advanced musical terrain in her sensuous Rimbaud cantata, *O Saisons, O chateaux* (1946) and String Quartet No. 6 (1952). She took a *sui generis* approach to serial composition in these works, and made the decision to reject the pointillistic techniques and total serialism 'cul-de-sac' embraced by younger, avant-garde composers in the 1950s.[14] Her luminous Motet for unaccompanied chorus (1953), a setting of extracts from Wittgenstein's *Tractatus Logico-Philosophicus*, revealed her to be one of the finest polyphonists of the mid-century, and was responsible for igniting wider, serious interest in her music in Britain. The Motet was one of several of Lutyens's pieces that were commissioned by William Glock for his Dartington Summer School of Music. Glock was a seasoned champion of contemporary music, and many leading musicians (including Stravinksy, Boulanger, and Boulez) regularly visited Dartington, a safe retreat for contemporary music after the war. Glock was highly influential in raising the overall profile of contemporary music in Britain in the 1960s, and it was not a coincidence that many of Lutyens's most critically acclaimed pieces, including *And Suddenly It's Evening* for tenor and ensemble (1966) and *Essence of Our Happinesses* for tenor, chorus, and orchestra (1968), were commissioned by the BBC during his tenure there as Music Controller and Proms Director (1959–73).

Dramatic *Space Play* and La Boulangerie

The change in attitudes towards contemporary music in Britain came at the right time for Scottish composer Thea Musgrave (b.1928). Musgrave regularly attended Glock's Dartington in the 1950s and also studied in Paris and the United States at this time. Attuned to the various new cross-currents in music, she explored aspects of both neoclassical and serial styles in her music, but remained independent of any particular ideology or school of composition. Following the completion of her second opera, *The Decision* (1964–65), she began to develop what she termed a 'dramatic-abstract' approach to instrumental writing, composing a series of pieces which explored the inherent dramatic potential of concertante form from different angles. Her Chamber Concerto No. 2 (1966), a piece premiered at Dartington, included notated 'ad. lib' passages for the instruments in different *tempi*, and disruptive (Ivesian) collisions between highly chromatic music and popular tunes such as 'The Swanee River'. Musgrave expanded her concept to include different elements of physical theatre in her Clarinet Concerto (1968), Horn Concerto (1971), Viola Concerto (1973), and *Space Play* (1974). In *Space Play*, Musgrave specifies that the nine instrumentalists should all be physically separated on stage. In the Horn Concerto, the orchestra essentially assumes the traditional seating plan, but members of the orchestra's horn section are positioned offstage and move around the concert hall during the performance. In the Viola Concerto, the orchestra's viola section is placed where the 1st violins usually sit, and play standing up towards the end of the piece. The solo clarinet moves around different sections of the orchestra, meanwhile, in the Clarinet Concerto. The dramatic-musical aspects explored in these instrumental works went on to inform the series of operas she wrote after her move to the United States in 1972. Operas such as *Mary, Queen of Scots* (1977), *Harriet, the Woman Called Moses* (1984), *Simon Bolivar* (1992), and *Pontalba* (2003) have shown Musgrave to be one of the foremost opera composers of her generation.

Musgrave studied with Nadia Boulanger in Paris from 1950 to 1954, and became the first woman composer to win the Lili Boulanger Memorial Prize in 1952. Boulanger, one of the most renowned composition teachers of the twentieth century, was an advocate of neoclassicism and an ardent champion of the music of Stravinsky. Female members of her 'Boulangerie' included the American composers Marion Bauer (1882–1955), Louise Talma (1906–96), and Julia Perry (1924–79); the South African-British composer Priaulx Rainier (1903–86); Polish composer Grażyna Bacewicz (1909–69); and the Australian composer Peggy Glanville-Hicks (1912–90). Most of these composers used neoclassical principles as their starting points, but embraced new musical possibilities in their music from the 1950s onwards. In the case of Glanville-Hicks, her rejection in the late 1940s of both neoclassicism (defined by the composer as the '[pushing] around of musical rubble from the nineteenth century') and serialism ('a camouflage for the ungifted'), led her to formulate her own 'melody-rhythm' approach to composition, informed by an exploration of world musics.[15]

American Toccatas

Boulanger's influence on her many American students (including Aaron Copland) shaped the direction of contemporary music for a time in the United States. Like Copland, Louise Talma had studied with Boulanger at the Conservatoire Americain, Fontainebleau, and her neoclassic *Toccata for Orchestra* (1944) and jubilant *Alleluia in the Form of a Toccata* for piano (1945) were amongst the first pieces to bring her to public attention in America. Talma was the only female member of the so-called American 'Stravinsky School' in the early 1950s, along with Irving Fine, Lukas Foss, Harold Shapero, and Alexei Haieff, a group of composers recognised by many as being at the forefront of American music.[16] The ensuing battle for music which erupted on American soil in the mid-1950s, however, prompted a seismic shift in attitudes in favour of serialism.

Talma was acutely aware of Cold War rifts between progressives (serialists and ultra-modernists) and tonally oriented composers that were playing out in America at this time, but first became genuinely interested in serial possibilities when she heard her friend Irving Fine's use of the method in his String Quartet (1952).[17] Some of her earliest explorations in serial composition date from this time, and include her beautifully crafted Six Etudes for piano (1954), the Second Piano Sonata (1955), and her opera, *The*

Alcestiad (1955–58), which combines both serial and tonal elements.[18] Talma's own categorisation of the three periods of her work as 'neoclassical' (1925–52), 'serial' (1952–67), and 'non-serial atonal' (1967–96), serves as a useful guide to her compositional development, while also revealing the way in which she responded to mid-century challenges.[19] While a clear allegiance to extended tonality runs throughout her *oeuvre*, 'late' works such as the achingly poignant *13 Ways of Looking at a Blackbird* for tenor and instrumental ensemble (1979), and the evocative soundscapes of *The Ambient Air* for ensemble (1983), reveal that the different compositional methods Talma drew from enabled her to find a distinctive musical idiom which was both highly personal and of its time. She could have spoken for many composers when she stated in 1979 that

I like to use serialism as a tool and to incorporate it with the other forms in music. I see no reason for chopping off what's developed simply because something new has come along.[20]

Awards and Condemned Playgrounds

Talma was the first American woman composer to be awarded two Guggenheim prizes (in 1946 and 1947). Previously, only Ruth Crawford Seeger (1901–53), discussed in Chapter 1, one of the brightest lights on the interwar American modernist music scene, had been a Guggenheim recipient (1930), but in post-war years the names of more women composers began to appear more regularly in America's award lists. This was an important breakthrough and revealed that women of outstanding ability, particularly those who had benefitted from the right type of formal training in composition, were beginning to gain recognition from musical establishments. The African American composer Julia Perry is a case in point. While still in her twenties, Perry had, unusually, already gained an international profile for her radiant *Stabat Mater* (1951), widely performed in both America and Europe, and the two Guggenheim prizes she received (in 1954 and 1956) followed periods of study with Dallapiccola in Florence (from 1951) and Boulanger in Fontainebleau (1952).[21]

Two of Perry's pieces, both composed in 1952, particularly stand out: her beautiful spiritual 'I'm a Poor Li'l Orphan in This Worl'' for voice and piano, and the astringently neoclassical *Short Piece for Orchestra*, a work of vivid colours skilfully deployed in ensemble and tutti episodes. Contrasts of instrumental timbre was further developed in her *Homunculus, C. F.* for ten percussionists (1960), a magical rumination on the transformative possibilities of the chord of the fifteenth (the 'C. F.' of the title). J. Michele Edwards has suggested that Perry's later works, including twelve symphonies (1961–73) composed in the heat of the Civil Rights struggle, may have drawn the many musical strands in this fascinating composer's world together.[22]

Perry was the recipient of an award from the American Academy of Arts and Letters in 1964, and a decade later Talma became the first woman composer to be elected as an Academy member. She was followed into the Academy a year later by her friend, Miriam Gideon (1906–96). Gideon had not been a pupil of Boulanger, but had studied in New York with Roger Sessions (from 1935 to 1943), where she had worked alongside fellow students Milton Babbitt, Vivian Fine, and Hugo Weisgall. Although interested in serial techniques, Gideon preferred the freedom of composing without systematic scaffolding, and focused instead on devising her own personal musical language, built from motivic cells.[23]

Gideon's acute sensitivity to the word, and flair for sophisticated word-setting, is immediately evident in her early *The Hound of Heaven* for voice, oboe, and string trio (1945); and in the later cycle *The Condemned Playground* for soprano, tenor, and mixed ensemble (1963), she seamlessly combines texts in English with Latin (i. 'Pyrrha'), Japanese (ii. 'Hiroshima') and French (iii. 'The Litanies of Satan') to vivid effect. Gideon was the first woman composer to be commissioned to write music for the synagogue, and her *Sacred Service for Sabbath Morning* (1970) and *Shirat Miriam L'shabbat* (1974) are amongst her finest pieces. Composed for use in services, the music in these large-scale solo, choral, and instrumental works possesses a monumental quality which both reflects and transcends its time.

It would be interesting to know what the Senate Committee for Un-American Activities made of Gideon's music. Her third husband, the English scholar Frederic Ewen, became a victim of McCarthyism in 1952 when he was subpoenaed by the Senate Internal Security Subcommittee to account for his alleged communist sympathies. Although nothing was proven, as a result both he and Gideon – simply by association – lost their teaching posts at Brooklyn College, New York.[24] Reflecting simmering tensions between the United States and the Soviet Union, the Cold War witnessed a reignition of fears in America about the spread of communism, and the need for exposure of alleged supporters of that ideology at home reached panic levels under Senator Joseph McCarthy's direction in 1950–54. Many innocent Americans became victims, at a time when simply reading a copy of a left-wing magazine was enough to arouse suspicions. Gideon's teaching career was curtailed during these years of paranoia, but she continued to compose and to be supported by friends, and was reinstated as a music teacher at Brooklyn College in the 1970s. Research has revealed that the FBI kept the couple under surveillance – and that Gideon's file was still open in the early 1980s.[25]

A Lament for Prague

Cold War events also affected Elizabeth Maconchy (1907–94) in August 1968, when the hopes of the Prague Spring were abruptly quashed by the Warsaw Pact invasion of Czechoslovakia.[26] Maconchy (also discussed in Chapter 1) had studied in Prague with Karel Jirák (1891–1972) in 1929 after graduating from the Royal College of Music, and had remained in touch with Czech friends since that time. Her Piano Concertino (1928) was premiered in Prague and was one of several early works, including her orchestral suite, *The Land* (1930), and first string quartets (nos. 1 and 2, 1933 and 1936), to mark her out, in the eyes of many, as *the* frontrunner in British music in the 1930s; with Benjamin Britten, Lennox Berkeley, and Lutyens as laudable runners-up. Czechoslovakia, its music, its people, and the part it had played in launching her career remained precious to Maconchy ever afterwards. The brutality and violence of the Soviet occupation in August 1968 so dismayed her that the slow movement of the Ninth String Quartet she was writing became a 'threnody or lament' for Prague.[27]

Maconchy's thirteen string quartets comprise one of the most significant quartet series by a twentieth-century composer. She was drawn, like Musgrave, to the form's inherent dramatic potential; each quartet fulfils her belief that music should be an 'impassioned argument',[28] and her series reflects its time by revealing a gradual move away from tonality towards freer, more dissonant pastures. After completing seven quartets, she took a break from string writing in 1956 to focus on writing a trilogy of chamber operas, *The Sofa* (1957), *The Departure* (1958), and *The Three Strangers* (1961), as well as a Serenata Concertante for Violin and Orchestra (1962), and a *Nocturnal* for a cappella chorus (1965).

Maconchy's apparent failure to step in line with Webern, Boulez, and Stockhausen caused many to believe that she had become outpaced in the 1950s, but this was a misunderstanding of her position. She had, in fact, shown an awareness of twelve-note music as early as 1942 in her Quartet No. 4, but had rejected a strict use of the method because it 'seemed thematically to be an inhibiting rather than a liberating technique'.[29] Clear in her choices, Maconchy returned to the quartet medium in 1967, and her 'late' quartets (nos. 8–13, 1967–84) feature advanced (non-serial) harmonic language, formidably sharp contrasts of textures and sonorities and unsynchronised, *senza misura* passages for the instruments. Her position as a highly regarded leader in British music was endorsed when she became the first woman to be elected as Chairman of the Composers' Guild of Great Britain in 1959. She succeeded Britten as President of the Society for the Promotion of New Music in 1976, and was made a Dame of the British Empire in 1987.

Women and the Cold War in Music

Maconchy's independence, determination to pursue her own course, and ability to weather musical storms and fashions are personal qualities that are shared, in some shape or form, by all of the composers discussed in this chapter. Composition is a lonely, time-consuming, and demanding craft, and the right and left disputes of the Cold War in music presented stimulating and often taxing challenges for all composers, both male and female. There was, however, a stealthier, mid-century musical battle that was exclusively designed for women only. A lack of familiar, historic role models, together with a tradition of criticism pointing to women's inherent creative inferiority in music, meant that the 'Why No Great Women Composers?' debate (also discussed in Chapter 1) was still raging for composers working in the 1950s.[30] Noting the novel appearance of music by five women composers (including Maconchy and Lutyens) in BBC radio programmes in April 1950, for instance, critic Harold Rutland commented that although women composers were 'now making their presence felt', the rarity of women composers was surely because

most women have quite enough to do, to keep the world going, without their being expected to indulge in fantasies, or the concentrated thought and feeling that brings these fantasies to fruition as works of art.[31]

Electroacoustic music pioneer Pauline Oliveros (1932–2016) connected historic women composers' exclusion from the canon to the fact that 'being female was a unique qualification for domestic work'. But even in 1970, she argued, stereotypical perceptions of gender in society meant that a woman could not 'escape being squashed in her efforts – if not directly, then by subtle and insidious exclusion by her male counterparts'.[32] (For an in-depth discussion of Oliveros, see Chapter 13, 'Case Studies of Women in Electronic Music: The Early Pioneers'.) Pondering this issue further, Musgrave turned the spotlight on her generation's dilemma when she stated that

The very fact that there have been so far rather few women composers makes it that much harder for a woman . . . [I]t's very hard in any case to master the craft and the art of composition without having to fight at the same time the battle against self-consciousness and one's right to do it at all.[33]

Jolas confessed to frequently asking herself if she was 'really a composer?' adding with a smile that 'only a woman would ask that question – not a man'.[34]

As discussed in the preface, since the 1980s there has been a concerted effort to include women composers. Pioneering research by scholars, together with a belated awareness within the academy of excluded herstories, has resulted in more women composers (both historic and contemporary) gaining their rightful places in music textbooks, lecture rooms, conferences, and concert halls. Ellen Taaffe Zwilich (b.1939) became the first woman composer to win the Pulitzer Prize for Music (established in 1943) with her First Symphony in 1983, and Joan Tower (b.1938) became the first female recipient of the Grawemeyer Music Award in 1990 for *Silver Ladders*. Tower's inspired *Fanfares for the Uncommon Woman* (nos. 1–6, 1986–2017) are dedicated to 'women who take risks'.[35]

Is the Cold War for women composers finally over? Today, composers from the generation born mid-century – the long list includes Rhian Samuel (b.1944), Nicola LeFanu (b.1947), Kaija Saariaho (b.1952), Chen Yi (b.1953), Judith Weir (b.1954), Elena Kats-Chernin (b.1957), and Chaya Czernowin (b.1957) – are writing music in the knowledge that, although music by women remains under-represented in concert halls,[36] they will get a fair hearing. After all, Oliveros was surely right in thinking that 'the greatest problems of society will never be solved until an egalitarian atmosphere utilising the total creative energies exists among all men and women'.[37]

Notes

1. The seven European states that comprised the Eastern (Soviet) bloc were Poland, Hungary, Czechoslovakia, Romania, Bulgaria, Albania, and the German Democratic Republic (GDR, East Germany).

2. Grace Williams, 'How Welsh Is Welsh Music?', *Welsh Music*, vol. 4 (Summer 1973), 12.
3. Grace Williams, 'Composer's Portrait' (1967), printed in *Welsh Music*, vol. 8, no. 5 (Spring 1987), 11.
4. Williams, 'Composer's Portrait' (1976), printed in ibid., 15.
5. Pierre Boulez, 'Schoenberg Is Dead' (1952) reprinted in Pierre Boulez, *Notes of an Apprenticeship*, collected by Paul Thevenin, trans. Herbert Weinstock (New York: Knopf, 1968), 274.
6. Egon Wellecz, letter to Grace Williams (6 August 1962), private collection (reproduced with permission).
7. Grace Williams cited in Heward Rees, 'Views and Revisions: Grace William in Interview with Heward Rees', *Welsh Music*, vol. 5, no. 4 (1976–1977), 14.
8. Betsy Jolas, interview with Samuel Andreyev (18 November 2018), available at: www.youtube.com/watch?v=DHTGOayU1DQ (accessed 11 December 2020).
9. Betsy Jolas, quoted in Joan Peyser, *The Music of My Time* (New York & London: Pro/Am Music Resources, 1995), 224.
10. Betsy Jolas, note in the score of *Quatour II* (Paris: Heugel, 1964).
11. Virgil Thomson, 'Elisabeth Lutyens', *Grand Street*, vol. 2, no. 4 (Summer 1983), 182–3.
12. Elisabeth Lutyens, *A Goldfish Bowl* (London: Cassell, 1972), 167–8.
13. Ibid., 165.
14. Lutyens in interview with Stephen Plaistow, BBC Radio 3 (5 July 1971), National Sound Archive, catalogue no. P654R BD1, British Library.
15. Peggy Glanville-Hicks, quoted in Victoria Rogers, *The Music of Peggy Glanville-Hicks* (Farnham and Burlington, VT: Ashgate, 2009), 87. Rogers has argued that Glanville-Hicks's exploration of rhythm and 'world musics' was informed by the innovations of Edgard Varèse (1883–1965), John Cage (1912–92), Harry Partch (1901–74), Colin McPhee (1900–64), Alan Hovhaness (1911–2000), Lou Harrison (1917–2003), and Paul Bowles (1910–99), 89–96.
16. See Arthur Berger, 'Stravinsky and the Younger American Composers', *The Score*, no. 12 (June 1955), 39–40.
17. See Joseph N. Straus, 'The Myth of Serial "Tyranny" in the 1950s and 1960s', *Musical Quarterly*, vol. 83, no. 3 (1999), 301–43, and Anne C. Schreffler, 'The Myth of Empirical Historiography: A Response to Joseph N. Straus', *Musical Quarterly*, vol. 84, no. 1 (2000), 30–9.
18. For an insight into Talma's use of serialism in her opera *The Alcestiad*, see Kendra Preston Leonard, *Louise Talma: A Life in Composition* (Aldershot: Ashgate, 2014), 155–95.
19. Louise Talma, interview with Luann Dragonie (21 January 1995) *Louise Talma Society Website*; available at http://web.archive.org/web/20060816030109/ http://www.omnidisc.com/Talma/Biography.html (accessed 11 December 2020).

20. Louise Talma, cited in Richard M. Braun, 'Louise Talma at 72', *SoHo News* (25 January 1979), 29.
21. For an account of Perry's life and work, see Helen Walker-Hill, *From Spirituals to Symphonies: African-American Women Composers and Their Music* (Champaign, IL: University of Illinois Press, 2015), 93–140.
22. J. Michele Edwards, 'Julia Perry', *Grove Music Online* (2001).
23. Ellie Hisama has applied the concept of 'motivic saturation' to Gideon's pieces. Ellie Hisama, *Gendering Musical Modernism: The Music of Ruth Crawford, Marion Bauer and Miriam Gideon* (Cambridge: Cambridge University Press, 2001), 152.
24. This committee was 'the Senate equivalent to the House Un-American Activities Committee'. See Brooklyn College, 'Senate Internal Security Subcommittee 1952–1953', City University of New York (online); available at http://academic.brooklyn.cuny.edu/english/melani/bc/senate_1952/index.html.
25. Mary Robb, 'The Music of Miriam Gideon during the McCarthy Era, Including a Complete Catalogue of Her Works' (PhD thesis, University of Edinburgh, 2012), 74–5. Robb has suggested that Gideon's experience of brutal anti-communist practices in the early 1950s caused the composer to withdraw from society and to enter a state of inner exile.
26. In May 1955 the Soviet Union signed a treaty (the Warsaw Pact) with the seven European countries that formed the Soviet Bloc, which amalgamated military forces under one (Soviet) command. Czechoslovakia was one of the countries in the Soviet Bloc, but its ruler, Alexander Dubcek, had begun to introduce liberal reforms in 1968 (the Prague Spring), which the Soviet authorities rejected. The August invasion of Czechoslovakia was undertaken by Warsaw Pact forces taken from the Soviet Union, Poland, Bulgaria, and Hungary.
27. Elizabeth Maconchy, note to String Quartet No. 9 in booklet accompanying the CD collection *Elizabeth Maconchy: Complete String Quartets 1–13*, Regis Records/Forum, FRC 9301 (1989), 15.
28. Elizabeth Maconchy, *The Composer Speaks*, BBC Radio 3 (October 1971).
29. Elizabeth Maconchy, *Composer's Portrait*, BBC Third Programme (June 1966).
30. See George Upton, *Woman in Music* (Boston, MA: J. R. Osgood, 1880) and Carl E. Seashore, 'Why No Great Women Composers?' *Music Educators Journal*, vol. 26, no. 5 (March 1940), 21–88.
31. Harold Rutland, 'Music Diary', *The Radio Times* (7 April 1950), 11.
32. Pauline Oliveros, 'And Don't Call Them "Lady" Composers' (*New York Times*, 1970), reprinted in Oliveros, *Software for People: Collected Writings 1963–80* (Baltimore, MD: Smith Publications, 1984), 49.
33. Thea Musgrave in *Women as Composers*, BBC Radio 3 (2 August 1973), catalogue no. 60417 (1), National Sound Archive, British Library.
34. Betsy Jolas interview (November 2018).
35. Joan Tower, note to *Fanfare for the Uncommon Woman*; available at www.musicsalesclassical.com/composer/work/33991 (accessed 11 December 2020).

36. See 'Inequality in Music: Women Composers by Numbers', *Donne: Women in Music* (n.d.). www.drama-musica.com/stories/2018_2019_orchestra_seasons .html (accessed 11 December 2020).

37. Oliveros, *Software for People*, 49.

Further Reading

Gideon, Miriam and Judith Shira Pinnolis. 'A Conversation with Miriam Gideon (1906–1996).' *Musica Judaica*, vol. 17 (June 1977), 106–41.

Jolas, Betsy. *Molto Espressivo* (Paris: L'itineraire, 1999). Collected writings (in French).

Mathias, Rhiannon. *Lutyens, Maconchy and Williams and Twentieth Century Music: A Blest Trio of Sirens* (Farnham: Ashgate, 2012).

Musgrave, Thea and Frank J. Oteri. 'Thea Musgrave: Where the Practicality Comes In', *NewMusicBox*, New York (December 2017); available at https://nmbx .newmusicusa.org/thea-musgrave-where-the-practicality-comes-in/ (accessed 11 December 2020).

3 | Behind the Iron Curtain: Female Composers in the Soviet Bloc

ELAINE KELLY

Working as a Female Composer in the Soviet Bloc

One of the strongest manifestations of the societal progress promised by Marxist Leninist ideology was the advocation of gender equality by state-socialist regimes. Article 122 of the 1936 Soviet Constitution declared that 'women in the USSR are accorded equal rights with men in all spheres of economic, state, cultural, social and political life', and asserted that the possibility of exercising these rights should be ensured via 'state protection of the interests of mother and child, prematernity and maternity leave with full pay, and the provision of a wide network of maternity homes, nurseries and kindergartens.'[1] This idealism was reflected in the changing demographics of the Soviet workforce in the 1930s. Women entered the workplace en masse to fulfil the demands of Stalin's ambitious economic plans, often undertaking jobs involving heavy manual labour, which confounded traditional gender divisions. Indeed, such was the transformation of the position of women in the public sphere that images of the 'new Soviet woman' became synonymous, as Susan Reid has documented, with 'the emancipation and rising living standards of the working people as a whole'.[2]

In the period after the Second World War, as Soviet-supported regimes consolidated power across Eastern Europe, the linking of gender equality with socialist progress continued apace. Women constituted 46 per cent of the workforce in the Soviet Union, for example, in 1956, and 49 per cent in 1964; in 1964 they also made up 53 per cent of students graduating from higher education.[3] Epitomising this trend was Valentina Tereshkova's successful bid to be the first woman in space in June 1963. As Nikita Khrushchev declared at the celebrations in Moscow's Red Square to mark her triumphant return to earth, Tereshkova was evidence 'that women raised under socialism walk alongside men in all the people's concerns, both in self-sacrificing labour and in heroic feats which amaze the world'.[4]

The biographies of some female composers from the Soviet Bloc can be read in terms of this narrative of emancipation. The East German composer Ruth Zechlin (1926–2007) is a case in point. Zechlin graduated from the Leipzig Conservatory in 1949, and was appointed the following year to teach composition, musicianship, and harpsichord at the newly founded music conservatory in East Berlin. She later recalled that this position had come her way because the men had either 'fallen in the war', were imprisoned, or had been prevented by conscription from studying and were thus not suitably qualified.[5] If she owed the launch of her career to the wartime decimation of East Germany's working-age male population, her subsequent trajectory reflected the possibilities open to women under state socialism. Over the course of the 1950s and 1960s, Zechlin established herself as one of the GDR's foremost composers, and in interviews given later in her life was adamant that she had never experienced gender discrimination. As she remarked in 1992: 'My musical education was identical to that of a man. I did not have to accept any restrictions as a result of my gender. The living and working conditions for me as professor and composer were also completely similar to those of men.'[6] Zechlin was awarded the Kunstpreis der DDR (Art prize of the GDR) in 1965 and the prestigious Hanns-Eisler-Preis for her composition *Gedanken über ein Klavierstück von Prokofjew* (Reflections on a piano piece by Prokofiev, 1967) in 1968, and in 1969 she was promoted to a professorship at the conservatory, an appointment of which, as West German composer Erna Woll noted, 'female composers in the Federal Republic of Germany could only dream'.[7] Zechlin's place in the GDR's cultural pantheon was assured in 1970, when she was made a member of the East German Academy of the Arts and director of a masterclass of composition there.

Other female composers enjoyed similar successes within the socialist system. Grażyna Bacewicz (1909–69) deftly navigated the imposition of socialist realism in post-war Poland and was a central figure in the vibrant new music scene that emerged there during the 1950s, while Aleksandra Pakhmutova (b.1929) took a different route; after graduating from Vissarion Shebalin's masterclass in composition at the Moscow Conservatory, she embraced the role of state artist and emerged to prominence – she was purportedly Leonid Brezhnev's favourite composer – by writing official music to celebrate every conceivable achievement of the Soviet state. Yet if paths to a career in composition were more accessible to women in the Soviet Bloc than to their Western counterparts, such paths were by no means free of obstacles. The narratives of equality so central to socialist discourse often belied the perpetuation of more traditional constructs of gender difference.

The acceptance of women into the labour force did not, notably, lead to any significant feminisation of the public sphere. The new socialist personality was implicitly masculine; the images of women driving tractors and working in mines that proliferated in the 1930s were not accompanied by counter-images of men engaging in domestic labour. Moreover, in the workplace women continued, by and large, to be perceived as second-class citizens, with figures such as Tereshkova the exception rather than the rule. Women, as Donald Filtzer notes, 'formed the overwhelming majority of auxiliary workers doing heavy, manual and usually unskilled or semi-skilled labour'.[8] They were excluded from the upper echelons of power and decision making in politics, and were predominantly confined to lower and mid-range roles in professional occupations. Fundamentally, the ideal of the politician, the university professor, and the scientist continued to be conceived in the image of man. This trend was conspicuous where art was concerned; the romantic construct of the genius artist devoting himself exclusively to the production of great artworks was an enduring one.

Female composers were regularly confronted with, and also sometimes internalised these norms. The Russian composer Galina Ustvolskaya (1919–2006) recalled how she was permitted to enter Shostakovich's masterclass at the Leningrad conservatory in 1940 'despite the rumour that Shostakovich usually does not accept young women in his class as he does not believe in their creative abilities'.[9] Ustvolskaya, in turn, appears to have replicated this conviction, purportedly preferring to teach male students in her own composition classes.[10] Zechlin welcomed both male and female students in her masterclasses; in an interview published in 1979, however, she claimed that her female students, despite their musicality, 'fail at a very particular point'. It becomes problematic, she claimed, 'when they have to bring what they have learned into a musical statement of their own'.[11] The reasons for this, she argued, were 'physiological': composition demanded a form of masculine intelligence that was alien to most women.[12] Speaking of her own abilities, which she believed she had inherited from her father, Zechlin explained: 'I consider this form of thinking, which I have not found so pronounced in any other woman, to be a masculine talent.'[13]

Compounding stereotypes of the male composer was the fact that socialist gender equality had not liberated women from the binds of domesticity. The failure of Soviet Bloc countries to account effectively for the labour of child-rearing and housework meant that many women found themselves performing two roles in society, the so-called double burden. The shortage of state-funded childcare was a continuous complaint, and the labour that women were expected to perform in the home impeded their advancement in the workplace. Moreover, the continued association of women with domesticity perpetuated the construct of a masculine public sphere within which women were cast in the role of other. Women composers had to work hard and often make significant personal sacrifices to succeed in this climate. Ustvolskaya had no children and shunned housework altogether; her husband Konstantin Bagrenin recalled that 'she never cooked and had no interest in any form of domesticity'.[14] Others managed in various ways to combine their creative lives with family. Bacewicz, who gave birth to a daughter in 1942, pondered how female composers might reconcile the labour of motherhood with creative work and concluded that she was fortunate in being in possession of 'a small, invisible motor which allows me to do in ten minutes what takes others an hour to do'.[15] 'A woman with composing abilities', she continued, 'can be a serious composer, can marry, have children, travel, and have adventures, and so on, on the condition she is in possession of this little motor. If, on the other hand, she does not have one, she needn't bother trying.'[16] Bacewicz's internal motor was notably assisted by her capacity to employ a housekeeper.[17] Zechlin, who also had one daughter, did likewise. Sofia Gubaidulina (b.1931), in contrast, did not have such resources at her disposal when she gave birth to her daughter Nadia while a student at the Moscow Conservatory in 1959. She suspended her composition work for the first year of her daughter's life and looked after her in a wooden house without running water in the Moscow outpost of Tomilino. At the end of the year, however, she returned to her dormitory in the conservatory while her parents brought Nadia up at their home in Kazan.

Decentring Socialist Aesthetics: Grażyna Bacewicz and Ruth Zechlin

The masculine orientation of the socialist public sphere was replicated in the aesthetics of socialist realism. Socialist realism, as Nina Noeske has detailed, retained the gendered norms of nineteenth-century romanticism and infused them with an additional layer of military rhetoric. Composers were encouraged to draw on the heritage of the revolutionary Beethoven rather than the feminine traditions of bourgeois domesticity, and to express their support for the socialist fight in large-scale 'public' forms depicting heroic struggle, or rousing mass songs.[18] Female composers were more than capable of contributing to this civic effort, and many did.

Ustvolskaya, for example, produced some textbook examples of socialist realism early in her career with works such as *Son Stepana Razina* (*The Dream of Stepan Razin*) for bass and orchestra, which was premiered by the Leningrad Philharmonic in 1949, and her Poem No. 1 ('The Hero's Exploit') for orchestra of 1959. *Stepan Razin*, which was written shortly after Zhdanov's formalist decree of 1948, celebrates with rousing folk tunes and heroic lyrical melodies the exploits of the seventeenth-century Cossack folk hero Stepan (or Stenka) Razin, who led Cossack and Russian peasants in a revolt against the aristocracy. Yet, while figures such as Ustvolskaya could write very effective music in state-approved models, it is perhaps unsurprising that the female composers who emerged most prominently from the Soviet Bloc, Ustvolskaya included, largely eschewed socialist realism in favour of more idiosyncratic, individual modes of expression.

Bacewicz is an interesting example in this regard. The oldest of the composers under discussion here, she was in her thirties by the time Poland came under Soviet occupation and had already been exposed to a wide variety of musical influences, French neoclassicism in particular. She studied composition at the Warsaw Conservatory with Kazimierz Sikorski, who was a student of Nadia Boulanger, and in 1932 she travelled to Paris to take lessons with Boulanger herself. A prodigious violinist and pianist, Bacewicz also studied violin with André Touret and Carl Flesch while in Paris, and returned to Poland in 1936 to take up the role of principal violinist of the Polish National Symphony Radio Orchestra. Over the course of the Second World War as performance opportunities became scarce, she focused increasingly on composition, and ceased performing in public altogether after suffering serious injuries in a car crash in 1954. By the time socialist realism was introduced to Poland in 1948, Bacewicz had already established herself as one of the country's foremost composers alongside Witold Lutosławski and Andrzej Panufnik. The imposition of Zhdanovian aesthetics from the Soviet Union did little to quash this trajectory. Indeed, the years between 1948 and 1955, when socialist realism was at its height in Poland, were the most productive of Bacewicz's career. Her Symphonies nos. 2–4, Concerto for String Orchestra, Violin Concertos nos. 3–5, Piano Concerto, Cello Concerto no. 1, String Quartets nos. 4–5, Quartet for 4 Violins, Piano Quintet no. 1, Violin Sonatas nos. 4–5, and Piano Sonatas nos. 1–2 all date from this period.

In many ways, the musical language that Bacewicz had evolved in the 1930s and early 1940s lent itself to socialist-realist expression. Her predilection for traditional forms and neoclassical sound worlds mapped well onto Zhdanovian ideals, as did her penchant for deploying folk tunes and folk-inspired melodies and inflections. Yet, as Adrian Thomas observes, these traits, rather than miring her in a world of musical propaganda, enabled her to steer 'an overtly non-programmatic path through the mine-field of socialist realism'.[19] Bacewicz inscribed to some extent in her symphonies the heroic tropes of struggle and overcoming so beloved of socialist regimes. In her chamber music, however, she explored intimate sound worlds that sat incongruously with the public rhetoric of the socialist collective.

A striking example of Bacewicz's capacity to bring the private into the public sphere and write music that could speak simultaneously to different audiences is her fourth String Quartet. The work was commissioned by the Polish Composers' Union for submission to the annual international string quartet competition in Liège in 1951; Bacewicz won first prize in the competition, and was subsequently awarded a Polish state prize for the quartet in 1953. That her quartet had resonances both for the Western jury and Polish officials is a testament to the extent to which she maintained an idiosyncratic musical language within the tightening confines of post-war socialist realism. The first movement of the quartet is a case in point. It unfolds in what is essentially a traditional sonata-form structure and draws on folk music for its thematic content; yet it repeatedly subverts the sonata-form characteristics that were idealised within socialist-realist aesthetics. Its first theme has, as Thomas observes, 'all the appearance of a traditional second subject'.[20] Emerging out of an introspective andante introduction, it is a lyrical folk melody, which is presented in canon. This theme stands in stark contrast to the strident dissonant chordal passages that follow at various points in the movement. Bacewicz does not, however, reconcile these sound worlds, eschewing the expected dialectical resolution of sonata form.

Bacewicz's prominence in the early Polish People's Republic can be ascribed to a number of factors. Her status as a composer was undoubtedly augmented by her visibility as a performer; she was able to draw on a large network of colleagues to ensure her music was played, and she premiered many of her works herself. It was also arguably the case that her music represented an acceptable model for the output of a female composer. Her compositions are conservative for the 1950s, favouring traditional forms and structures; even her most dissonant works contain lyrical moments; and her compositional processes are generally free-form (instinctual) rather than rigorously controlled (rational). She followed her younger Polish colleagues in exploring serialism towards the end of the 1950s and early 1960s, but it was her experiments in timbre that resulted in the most distinctive music of her later years. Works such as *Pensieri notturni* (Night thoughts, 1961) employ unusual instrumental combinations and extended techniques to create shimmering textures not dissimilar to Bartók's night music.

Standing in many ways at the opposite end of the spectrum to Bacewicz was Zechlin, who perceived the practical manifestation of her 'masculine' composition gifts in her ability to control rigorously the sounds she produced. Of her approach, Zechlin explained: 'During the process of composing, I think predominantly linearly, although the harmonic intervals result by no means accidentally. They are planned and intended. This also applies to the orchestration . . . [the instruments are chosen for their] individually coloured sounds that do justice to my need for expression.'[21] This preoccupation with parameters of control reflects Zechlin's training as a harpsichordist and organist. She counted J. S. Bach amongst her foremost influences and frequently deployed polyphonic techniques, canons in particular, in her music. At the same time, her music was inherently experimental. Her compositions from the late 1960s onwards incorporate extreme dissonances, aleatory, and extended techniques. Moreover, her desire for control did not come at the expense of expression. On the contrary, the extent to which she controlled her material was paradoxically liberating, resulting in musical statements that could be profoundly lyrical, dramatic, and, occasionally, outright confrontational. Nowhere is the latter more evident than in her short organ piece, *Wider den Schlaf der Vernunft* (Against the sleep of reason), which she wrote to perform at an event in East Berlin's Erlöserkirche in October 1989 that was organised by leading members of the GDR's intelligentsia in support of the mass demonstrations that precipitated the fall of the Berlin Wall a month later. (Zechlin notably never paid with party membership for her compositional success in the GDR.) The piece takes its title from the Goya painting *The Sleep of Reason Produces Monsters*, and is characterised by a barrage of oppressive and insistent chord clusters. It is, as Zechlin herself explained, 'a very aggressive piece', intended 'to shake up and remind [listeners] that one must be wide awake now so as to ensure that the whole thing doesn't go in the wrong direction again'.[22]

Liminal Spaces: Galina Ustvolskaya and Sofia Gubaidulina

The disciplined expression of Zechlin's music finds certain parallels in the uncompromising mature aesthetic of Ustvolskaya. Ustvolskaya herself not only rejected any categorisations of her as a 'female' composer; she also confounded critics by positing a complete break – effectively a performance of patricide – between her and her male forefathers. She repeatedly renounced the influence of her own teacher Shostakovich and claimed to have evolved a musical language that was untouched by the legacy of earlier composers.[23] Certainly, her mature works, marked by pounding dissonances and incongruous instrumental combinations, owe little to socialist-realist traditions. Her music is loud, but it is the loudness of nihilism rather than heroism. Ustvolskaya's final decades in the Soviet Union were spent in self-imposed isolation. She retired from her teaching post at the Professional School of Music as soon as she reached the pensionable age of fifty-five in 1977, and withdrew into a life of reclusivity that challenged not only Soviet norms but also the gendered expectations of her Western critics. Dealing with the outside world through a small circle of supporters, including her husband Bagrenin, the composer and editor Viktor Suslin, and the pianist Oleg Malov, she refused to give interviews, often shutting down requests abruptly, and maintained extraordinarily tight control over performances of her music and the construction of her image.

Like many composers in the late Soviet Bloc, Ustvolskaya conceived of her music in the 1970s and 1980s as a form of spiritual expression; all of her works from this period, apart from the Piano Sonatas nos. 5 and 6, bear religious inscriptions. Her spirituality was not a refuge; this music speaks neither of consolation nor redemption. Ustvolskaya's god, with whom – eschewing the patriarchal conventions of organised religion – she claimed to commune directly, was clearly a wrathful god, standing in judgement rather than granting mercy. Characteristic is her Composition no. 2 'Dies irae', which she wrote between 1972 and 1973 and scored for the unsettling combination of piano, eight double basses, and a custom-made wooden cube struck by a hammer. The work consists of ten short sections, which offer little in the way of contrast or change of pace. The listener is bombarded throughout by a relentless march of piano clusters, *tutti* double-bass attacks, and ominous shotgun-like strikes of the hammer on the wooden cube.

Ustvolskaya argued that her ensemble music should not be considered as 'chamber music' in the conventional sense.[24] Indeed, in works such as Composition no. 2, there is little sense of concerted playing. She juxtaposes starkly opposing instruments – Composition no. 1 'Dona nobis pacem' (1970–1) is scored for piccolo, tuba, and piano, and Composition no. 3 'Benedictus, qui venit' (1974–5) for four flutes, four bassoons, and piano – and is not interested in finding resonances between them. On the contrary, each instrument or instrument grouping ploughs its own path, seemingly oblivious to the other sounds being made around it. Her five symphonies equally defy the ideals of coming together synonymous with the genre. Symphony no. 2 'True and Eternal Bliss!' (1979), for example, which is scored for choirs of six flutes (one doubling piccolo), six oboes, and six trumpets, is similar to Composition no. 2 both in its scoring of disparate instruments and in its treatment of these. Again the musical language is characterised by passages of rigidly paced pounding chords, clusters, and drum beats, which in this work alternate with a series of tense recitations. In the first three recitations the speaker releases guttural cries – a 'scream into space' as Ustvolskaya wrote on the autograph score of the work – and shouts the word 'Gospodi' (Lord). The fourth recitation starts similarly, but then the speaker begins to utter the words from Hermannus Contractus's 'De sanctissima Trinitate' that give the symphony its title: '*istinnaya i blagaya vechnost, vechnaya zhe i blagayu istina, istinnaya i vechnaya blagost*' ('true and blissful eternity, eternal and blissful truth, true eternal bliss'). Against these words, the instruments finally begin to function as an ensemble, coming together to form long sustained chords with a timbral quality akin to that of an organ. The evocation of eternal bliss is transitory, however. The speaker returns at the end to his cries into the abyss for 'Gospodi'. The only response is an echo, a gently wailing piccolo line, which along with solitary piano notes, brings the piece to a close.

Ustvolskaya drew again on Hermannus's text in each of her subsequent symphonies, which she titled 'Jesus, Messiah, Save Us!' (Symphony no. 3, 1983), 'Prayer' (Symphony no. 4, 1985–7), and 'Amen' (Symphony no. 5, 1989–90) respectively. An eleventh-century monk, mathematician, and music theorist, Hermannus was paralysed and could speak only with difficulty, a state of existence that possibly resonated with Ustvolskaya's own self-imposed isolation. The tortured soundscapes of her late works have been explained in various ways by music critics: they are the response of a 'victim' of Soviet oppression, a response to the collective trauma of Soviet history, or to the failed ideals of socialism.[25] Ustvolskaya herself had little to say about politics. She did, however, describe her works as 'the fruit of my tormented life',[26] a statement that has particular resonances in the context of the penultimate composition in her catalogue, her Piano Sonata no. 6 (1988). The sonata is a terse, one-movement work in which tightly controlled blocks of material, made up of carefully prescribed piano clusters, are subject to motoric permutations and repetitions. The rigid compositional processes driving the work are notably countered by the visceral somatic discomfort that the piece induces both in the listener and, in particular, the performer, who has to play the barrage of clusters at four and five *forte* markings throughout. Ustvolskaya, as Maria Cizmic insightfully observes, creates 'a music space in which pain becomes visibly known'.[27]

Gubaidulina's compositions similarly combine the rational and the irrational, the cerebral and the somatic. Like that of Ustvolskaya, her music is profoundly spiritual; she was baptised in the Orthodox Church in 1970 and has frequently since composed works on religious themes. Her spirituality is not, however, as cataclysmic as Ustvolskaya's; her music suggests the possibility of redemption and peace. Ustvolskaya and Gubaidulina are examples of the very different ways of being – on personal and musical levels – that were possible in the more individualised societies of the late Soviet Bloc. Neither composer was dissident; both, however, forged distinctive aesthetics that were opposed – in quite distinct ways – to the collective ideals of state socialism. Like many of her Soviet contemporaries, Gubaidulina began experimenting with serialism and other formal compositional processes in the 1960s, when the grip of socialist realism loosened its tenacious hold on the state. She did not, notably, associate systematic compositional processes with rational expression. Serialism, for Gubaidulina, represented freedom rather than constraint; as Peter Schmelz observes, serialism was synonymous for her with 'the perfect, limitless order of the beyond'.[28] Gubaidulina adopted formalistic processes, which included operations involving rhythm and duration, not as an abstract means of control but as a way of evoking contrasts between sacrifice and redemption, between the worldly and otherworldly. Her concerto for violin and orchestra, *Offertorium* (1980), is a case in point. It opens with the theme of Bach's *Musical Offering*, which is presented initially in D minor and distributed pointillistically across individual instruments of the orchestra. All but the final note of the theme are sounded in this first statement. A series of variations then follows in which the theme is 'sacrificed'. A note is removed from the beginning and end of each statement until all that remains in the tenth variation is the E pitch from the centre of the theme. After an extended violin cadenza, the theme is gradually rebuilt in the third section of the piece, emerging redeemed in the process. It returns in full in the coda, notably stated now in retrograde and played in its entirety by the solo violin rather than being treated pointillistically.

Gubaidulina was particularly intrigued by the possibilities inherent in the Fibonacci sequence and the associated golden ratio. Discussing her use of it in an interview with Vera Lukomsky, she observed: 'I like this system because it does not deprive me of my freedom, does not limit my fantasy'.[29] She also perceived it to have restorative effects. With regard to her 1993 composition *Jetzt immer Schnee* (Now always snow), she noted: 'I experience the material [in this piece] as very aggressive substance ... I call this an illness. The material requires the artist to find a solution for healing the pain.' This solution, she claimed, could be found in the Fibonacci series; she could 'heal the material' by deploying it to resolve 'dissonance to consonance with regard to time proportions'.[30] A good example of how she applied the sequence in practice can be observed in her symphonic work *Stimmen ... Verstummen ...* (Voices ... fall silent ...) of 1986. This twelve-movement composition juxtaposes two diametrically opposed sound worlds. The odd movements nos. 1, 3, 5, and 7, which depict the 'eternal' and are characterised by shimmering, ethereal soundscapes that centre initially on a D-major triad, are composed according to the Fibonacci sequence. The 'earthly', meanwhile, is evoked by the even movements nos. 2, 4, 6, and 8, which are freely composed and full of chromatic writing, dissonance, and often harsh timbres. Over the course of the work, the heavenly visions grow progressively shorter as each successive odd-numbered movement decreases in length in proportion with the Fibonacci sequence: movement 1 lasts 55 quavers; movement 3 lasts 34 quavers; movement 7 lasts 21 quavers, and movement 7 lasts 13 quavers leading to an extended silence (zero quavers) in the ninth movement.[31] Conversely the earthly movements get successively longer, culminating in the 'apocalypse' of the eighth movement, which is replete with aleatoric passages and intrusive polytonal chords. The silence that follows in the ninth movement instigates a rebirth of the eternal. The conductor gesticulates throughout the silence, following a choreography of arm patterns that are determined, again, by the Fibonacci sequence and lead to a G-major triad on the organ, which evokes 'eternal light'.[32] The alternation of eternal and earthly returns in movements 10 to 12. Now, however, the even rather than odd movements are eternal, and the work closes with a return to the shimmering D-major chord of the opening.

Unlike that of Ustvolskaya, Gubaidulina's spirituality did not involve a rejection of the world around her. Her existence in the late Soviet Union was in many ways a liminal one; as was the case with her close colleagues Alfred Schnittke and Edison Denisov, few of her works were performed in state-sanctioned venues. Yet, she was far from isolated, playing an active role in Moscow's lively unofficial music scene. She was a founding member of the improvisation ensemble Astreya, together with Suslin and Vyacheslav Artyomov. She was also acutely attuned to the gendered norms of socialist politics and aesthetics. She saw advantages in her status as a female composer. As she explained to Gerald McBurney, she had more freedom to experiment than figures such as Schnittke: 'Nobody took much notice of me. They could always dismiss what I did as simply female eccentricity. It was much harder for the men.'[33] Yet she also sought to confront the hegemony of masculine tropes in socialist realism and Western art music more generally. She viewed as anachronistic, for example, the traditional opposition in concertos of soloist and orchestra, with the soloist as hero leading the orchestra (the 'crowd' or 'army') to victory. In reality, she explained, 'the hero is disappointed in everything, nobody knows what the truth is'.[34] Accordingly, in her own piano concerto, *Introitus* (1978), she wrote a solo part that 'is purely meditative, completely deprived of virtuosity'.[35] She likewise exposed the Soviet fallacy of the collective or crowd as an inherently positive force. In *Chas Dushi* (Hour of the soul), which she composed for wind orchestra and mezzo soprano in 1974 and later revised for percussion, orchestra, and mezzo soprano, she invoked the suppression of the poet Marina Tsvetaeva (1892–1941), who committed suicide after being ostracised by the Soviet state. Tsvetaeva's soul is represented in the work by the solo percussion part, written for Mark Perkarsky, which dominates the first section of the piece. This is opposed midway by a polystylistic section, in which Gubaidulina quotes snippets of what she describes as 'popular and patriotic songs, representing vulgarity and the aggressiveness of the common crowd as bred by the Soviet system'. 'Vulgarity and aggressiveness', she expounds, 'are the murderers that killed the poet.'[36] Notably, Gubaidulina sees the percussion as depicting the 'dominant masculine, side' of Tsvetaeva's personality.[37] The poet's feminine side appears only at the end of the work, after her death via polystylism, when the mezzo soprano, who has been hiding in the orchestra until this point, emerges to sing Gubaidulina's setting of the poem that gives the work its title. The expression of femininity was possible only when the socialist collective had been silenced, in this case via an extensive tom-tom solo.

Conclusion

Ultimately, the silencing of the socialist collective was not a prerequisite for the emergence of female composers in the Soviet Bloc. If the realities of female emancipation did not live up to the utopian ideals that were promised by state-socialist regimes, the opportunities that were created for women, and the expectations across the Soviet Bloc of what women could achieve, surpassed those in the West. Female composers were confronted continuously in the Soviet Bloc by an aesthetic discourse and sociopolitical values from which they were excluded by virtue of their gender. This confrontation was at times oppressive. Yet, as the women in this chapter demonstrate, it could also inspire profound creativity. Inadvertently, the hyper-masculine climate of socialist realism set the scene for a host of distinct female musical voices to emerge.

Notes

1. Available at www.marxists.org/reference/archive/stalin/works/1936/12/05 .htm (accessed 11 December 2020).
2. Susan E. Reid, 'All Stalin's Women: Gender and Power in Soviet Art of the 1930s', *Slavic Review*, vol. 57 (1998), 137.
3. Melanie Ilič, 'Women in the Khrushchev Era: An Overview', in Melanie Ilič, Susan E. Reid, and Lynne Attwood (eds.), *Women in the Khrushchev Era* (New York: Palgrave Macmillan, 2004), 7–8.
4. Cited in Sue Bridger, 'The Cold War and the Cosmos: Valentina Tereshkova and the First Woman's Space Flight', in Melanie Ilič, Susan E. Reid, and Lynne Attwood (eds.), *Women in the Khrushchev Era* (New York: Palgrave Macmillan, 2004), 231.
5. Beate Philipp, *Komponisten der neuen Musik* (Kassel: Furore-Verlag, 1993), 135.
6. Ibid., 134.
7. Ibid., 73.
8. Donald Filtzer, 'Women Workers in the Khrushchev Era', in Melanie Ilič, Susan E. Reid, and Lynne Attwood (eds.), *Women in the Khrushchev Era* (New York: Palgrave Macmillan, 2004), 30.
9. Elena Nalimova, 'Demystifying Galina Ustvolskaya: Critical Examination and Performance Interpretation' (PhD thesis, University of London, Goldsmiths, 2012), 57.
10. Ibid., 100.
11. Ursula Stürzbecher, *Komponisten in der DDR: 17 Gespräche* (Hildesheim: Gerstenberg Verlag, 1979), 151.
12. Ibid., 153.
13. Ibid., 155.
14. Cited in Nalimova, 'Demystifying Galina Ustvolskaya', 227.
15. Grażyna Bacewicz, trans. Anna Clarke and Andrew Cienski, *A Distinguishing Mark* (Orleans, Ontario: Krzys Chmiel, 2004), 21.
16. Ibid., 22.
17. Ibid., 56–7.

18. Nina Noeske, 'Gender Discourse and Musical Life in the GDR', in Elaine Kelly and Amy Wlodarski (eds.), *Art Outside the Lines: New Perspectives on GDR Art Culture* (Amsterdam and New York: Rodopi, 2011), 179–82.

19. Adrian Thomas, *Polish Music since Szymanowski* (Cambridge: Cambridge University Press, 2005), 71.

20. Ibid., 73.

21. Philipp, *Komponisten der neuen Musik*, 129.

22. Gabriele Mittag, '"Also, bestimmte Dinge . . . waren einfach verboten": Interview mit der Komponisten Ruth Zechlin', *TAZ*, 3 February 1990, 33; available at https://taz.de/!1782000/(accessed 11 December 2020).

23. See, for example, Thea Derks, 'Galina Ustvolskaya: "Sind Sie mir nicht böse!" (Very Nearly an Interview)', *Tempo*, vol. 193 (1993), 33.

24. See http://ustvolskaya.org/eng/creativity.php (accessed 11 December 2020).

25. For an overview of this critical reception, see Simon Morrison, 'Galina Ustvolskaya: Outside, Inside, and Beyond Music History', *Journal of Musicology*, vol. 36 (2019), 96–129.

26. Available at http://ustvolskaya.org/eng/creativity.php.

27. Maria Cizmic, *Performing Pain: Music and Trauma in Eastern Europe* (New York: Oxford University Press, 2012), 93.

28. Peter Schmelz, *Such Freedom, If Only Musical* (New York: Oxford University Press, 2009), 264.

29. Vera Lukomsky, '"Hearing the Subconscious": Interview with Sofia Gubaidulina', *Tempo*, vol. 209 (1999), 30.

30. Ibid., 29.

31. See Lukomsky, 'Hearing the Subconscious', 30–1.

32. Ibid., 31.

33. Gerald McBurney, 'Encountering Gubaydulina', *The Musical Times*, vol. 129 (1988), 121.

34. Vera Lukomsky, '"The Eucharist in My Fantasy": Interview with Sofia Gubaidulina', *Tempo*, vol. 206 (1998), 29.

35. Ibid., 30.

36. Ibid., 31.

37. See Claire Polin, 'Conversations in Leningrad, 1988', *Tempo*, vol. 168 (1989), 19; and Lukomsky, 'The Eucharist in My Fantasy', 31.

Further Reading

Lukomsky, Vera. '"The Eucharist in My Fantasy": Interview with Sofia Gubaidulina.' *Tempo*, vol. 206 (1998), 29–35.

Lukomsky, Vera. '"Hearing the Subconscious": Interview with Sofia Gubaidulina.' *Tempo*, vol. 209 (1999), 27–31.

Morrison, Simon. 'Galina Ustvolskaya Outside, Inside, and Beyond Music History.' *Journal of Musicology*, vol. 36 (2019), 96–129.

Noeske, Nina. 'Gender Discourse and Musical Life in the GDR', in Elaine Kelly and Amy Wlodarski (eds.), *Art Outside the Lines: New Perspectives on GDR Art Culture* (Amsterdam & New York: Rodopi, 2011), 175–91.

4 | Still Exceptional? Women in Composition Approaching the Twenty-First Century

ASTRID KVALBEIN

In December 2016 the curtain rose for Kaija Saariaho's *L'Amour de loin* (Love from afar, 2000, libretto by Amin Maalouf) at the Metropolitan Opera in New York. This was the first opera composed by a woman to be staged at the prestigious American opera house in 113 years, since Ethel Smyth's *Der Wald* in 1903. *L'Amour de loin*, which premiered at the Salzburg Festival in 2000, was, at the time, one of the most successful operas by a contemporary composer in the Western world, having already been performed in Paris, London, Toronto, Helsinki, and elsewhere. When the Met eventually staged it, it was regarded as a milestone, not only for female composers, but also for the institution's willingness to stage new works.

Saariaho (b.1952) has refined her vocal, orchestral, and electronic sound palette since her studies at IRCAM (Institute of Research and Coordination in Acoustics/Music) in the 1980s. As a student in Paris, as well as in Helsinki, Freiburg, and Darmstadt, Saariaho was very often the only young woman, and she fought to find the confidence to compose in an environment lacking female role models. But she persisted.[1] In interviews on the occasion of the premiere of *L'Amour de loin* at the Met, Saariaho was asked to comment on the apparent lack of female composers in the operatic world. On US National Radio, she responded that: 'It's kind of ridiculous ... I feel that we should speak about my music and not of me being a woman'. However, Saariaho also observed young women battling the same barriers as she did more than thirty years earlier: 'Maybe we, then, should speak about it, even if it seems so unbelievable ... You know, half of humanity has something to say, also.'[2]

After *L'Amour de loin*, Saariaho continued the collaboration with Maalouf. The oratorio *La Passion de Simone* (2006) is based on the writings of the philosopher and left-wing activist Simone Weil (1909–43), while the opera *Adriana Mater* (2005) tells the story of a woman who is raped and becomes pregnant during a cruel war, and *Emilie* (2008) explores the character of the passionate and intelligent noblewoman and scientist Émilie du Châtelet (1706–49). Two decades into the twenty-first century, from her position as one of the most successful composers of her generation, Saariaho seems more politically engaged in her operas than ever before, often explicitly taking a woman's point of view.[3]

As a visiting professor she is also a sought-after role model for students at universities and conservatoires throughout the USA and Europe. Although women are still a minority in such positions, the numbers are increasing. Composing women also stand out as exceptional in terms of originality, reputation, and quality, and receive prestigious prizes, commissions, and other tokens of recognition. In this chapter a selected few of them will be introduced – from across the globe but, because of the author's background, with some prominence given to examples from north-western Europe – in an attempt to draw an outline of the situation at the beginning of the twenty-first century.

women still minority in music, esp. composers

To begin with, emphasis is placed on opera and music drama, in particular works that highlight social and political issues, including gender. Other topics include how women composers and their works are present in a globalised world, how new musical 'ecosystems' are explored in the face of an emerging climate crisis, and how new aesthetics find their way into different venues, from traditional concert halls and opera houses to old and new avant-garde festivals.

emphasis is on operas & musical dramas focused on social & political issues

Socially Engaged Opera and Music Drama

Concerns for social and political issues come to the fore in a range of operas at the beginning of the twenty-first century. For British composer Judith Weir (b.1954), who wrote her first opera in her mid-twenties, music drama has provided fertile ground for experimentation since *King Harald's Saga* (1979), a ten-minute, one-woman show involving eight acting roles, including St. Olaf, an Icelandic sage, and the Norwegian army. Her catalogue includes a range of instrumental and vocal works in which the composer combines musical 'storytelling' with the subtle utilisation of folk music, drawing on her Scottish heritage, such as bagpipe practices of the Scottish Highlands, and, in the opera *The Vanishing Bridegroom* (1990), Gaelic songs. She has brought in elements of Chinese opera and placed material from older Western art music in new settings. Weir is a highly respected composer, and in 2015 she became the first woman to be appointed Master of the Queen's Music, succeeding Peter Maxwell Davis (1934–2016) after a succession of twenty male musicians and composers. Her most recent opera *Miss Fortune* (2011) sets the story of a Sicilian folktale *Sfortuna* (Misfortune) in a modern context: the main character falls victim to the financial crisis and lives a miserable life, constrained to a sweatshop and surrounded by urban riots.[4] This production, for which Weir wrote the libretto herself, seems to represent, as in the case of Saariaho, a recent move towards addressing current societal issues more explicitly.

Austrian composer Olga Neuwirth (b.1968) has always used music drama as a vehicle for social critique. She started working with author, playwright, and 2004 Nobel Literature Prize laureate Elfriede Jelinek (b.1946) in her twenties, and the collaboration has stirred up both enthusiasm and controversy. Neuwirth has set to music the topics that Jelinek has dealt with throughout her career: totalitarianism, fascism, and dysfunctional families in bourgeoisie cultures, some of which are exposed in the renowned novel *The Piano Teacher* (*Die Klavierspielerin*, 1983, which was adapted into the French-language film *La Pianiste* by Michael Haneke in 2001).

Neuwirth and Jelinek's opera *Bählamms Fest*, which premiered at the Wiener Festwochen in 1999, was recognised as an imaginative take on a 'perverted family dynasty', based on a surrealistic drama by Leonora Carrington.[5] The two also collaborated on an opera based on the TV and film director David Lynch's *Lost Highway* (2003), which includes pre-recorded material in which images, film, and electronic soundtracks play important roles. A third opera was commissioned by the Salzburg Festival and Paris National Opera for the Mozart Anniversary in 2006, but *Der Fall Hans W.* – which in its first version was set in a Second World War euthanasia clinic for children, but later took as its subject a recently convicted murderer and child molester – was first postponed, and eventually rejected. The commissioners argued that the quality of the libretto was inferior and the topic of paedophilia already exhausted. The incident led Jelinek to declare that she would never write an opera libretto again.[6]

Neuwirth, meanwhile, has kept on writing for stage as well as instrumental music. Her compositional palette is inspired by continental modernists such as Luigi Nono, Hans Werner Henze, and Adriana Hölzsky, and she often designs lively patchworks of quotes, samples, and references from a range of sources. The trumpet concerto ... *miramondo multiplo* ... (2006) references, amongst others, Gustav Mahler, Miles Davis, and Igor Stravinsky. The opera *American Lulu* (2012) is a jazzed-up version of Alban Berg's work, set in the American South, and aims to interpret Lulu's story from a female perspective. *The Outcasts* (2009–11), a tribute to Moby Dick's creator Herman Melville, holds a different take on gender issues: here Ishmael is depicted as a woman. *Orlando* (2019),

[handwritten margin note: Olga Neuwirth worked w/ Elfriede Jelinek to critique social issues that often stirred controversy]

based on Virginia Woolf's novel, portrays a poet who changes sex from male to female. This was the first opera ever to be commissioned by the Vienna State Opera from a female composer. The lush score, with references 'from Elizabethan vocal polyphony to post-punk assault' impressed the critics,[7] as did the adaptation of Woolf's novel in Act One. But Act Two, which brought in issues from the Holocaust up to 2019 was deemed, by many, too 'overcrowded' with ideas.[8]

While a marginal, if increasing, number of operas by contemporary women composers are being mounted on the main stages of the grand opera houses, new music often finds its way to alternative venues. For instance, Tansy Davies' (b.1973) *Between Worlds* (2014) – which commemorates the events of 9/11 – was commissioned by the English National Opera, but produced at a smaller, more flexible stage at the Barbican Centre. Davies' and writer Nick Drake's second opera *Cave* (2018) was staged by the Royal Opera in an abandoned industrial warehouse. The drama, set in a cave where a man searches for his daughter after an environmental disaster, comprised only two singers and a small ensemble, in addition to electronics.

Political issues appear in many chamber operas in the early 2000s. The last words of men sentenced to death make up the libretto of *Dead Beat Escapement* (2008) by the Norwegian Cecilie Ore (b.1954), and her *Adam & Eve – a Divine Comedy* (2015) depicts violence against women in the name of religion. Consequences of racism are highlighted in *Jean-Joseph* (2015) by Swedish composer Tebogo Monnakgotla (b.1972), which tells the story of the Madagascan poet Jean-Joseph Rabearivelo who committed suicide when rejected from attending the world exhibition in Paris in 1937, while Finnish composer Lotta Wennäkoski's (b.1970) monodrama *Lelele* (2010–11) quotes documentary reports about trafficking and forced prostitution.

Apparently, many composers put gender issues on the agenda with increasing intensity after having gained a certain professional reputation. For Wennäkoski's part it started with the more light-hearted *Life and Love of a Woman* (2002–03), in which new poetry on motherhood is set to music in dialogue with Robert Schumann's famous cycle *Frauenliebe und Leben* (1841). In contrast to the idealised world of the nineteenth-century songs, Wennäkoski's music – shifting between atonal phrases, sounds, and quotes from many genres – is set to poems about everyday exhaustion and mess, the ovum waiting for the moment in which it will drop, and animal-like maternal instincts.

Whether or not thematising parenthood is a feminist strategy or merely an exposure of human experience, several new works are set in the

[Handwritten margin notes:] early 2000s political issues also voiced w/ death penalty, violence of women, & suicide & human trafficking

[Handwritten margin notes:] many composers focus on gender issues

[Handwritten margin notes:] Wennäkoski wrote of motherhood and the stress & everyday exhaustion w/ atonal elements

domestic sphere – which has traditionally been considered feminine. Amongst them are *Emil* (2001) for solo voice by Carola Bauckholt (b.1959), which imitates a baby's babbling, and the subsequent *Emil will nicht schlafen* (Emil doesn't want to sleep, 2010) for singer and ensemble, in which the German composer mixes theatrical elements and playful composing with sound in a characteristic manner. A personal account of the effects of motherhood on composing is also provided by electroacoustic composer Manuella Blackburn in 'In Her Own Words 3'.

Women Composers in a Globalised World

A different conception of playfulness is staged in *Alice in Wonderland* by Berlin-based South Korean composer Unsuk Chin (b.1961), which premiered at the Bavarian State Opera in 2007. The opera depicts a dream-like, partly grotesque, version of Lewis Carroll's tale. Like Saariaho, Chin holds a special interest in the female voice and in the blending of electronic and acoustic sounds. Chin's breakthrough work, the *Akrostichon-Wortspiel* (1991/1993), is a vocally acrobatic piece for high soprano and ensemble that comprises seven scenes from fairy tales in which the words are used as much as tools for playing with sounds as to tell a story. Her output is carnivalesque in its rapid shifts between modernist soundscapes and references to jazz and other genres. The influence of Chin's teacher György Ligeti is evident, as are the skills acquired in the electronic music studios in Berlin and Paris (IRCAM).

Chin, who moved from Seoul to Hamburg to study in the mid-1980s, has been a prominent figure on the contemporary music scenes of Europe. Her works, such as *Double Bind* (2007) for solo violin and electronics, have been performed by a range of renowned soloists and ensembles. Influences from her native East Asian region have been scarce, as she has feared that her music might be conceived as exotic; that is, considered to be attractive due to its colourfulness and strangeness in relation to dominant Western idioms. But she did eventually compose a concerto, *Šu*, in 2009, for Wu Wei, a virtuoso on the Chinese mouth organ, the sheng.[9] However, the concerto does not cite traditional music from either China or Korea, and it is only one in a series including cello, clarinet, and piano concertos with Western symphony or chamber orchestras.

In an increasingly globalised world, elements from different native and national cultures find their way into contemporary music in a variety of styles and forms. While some composers, such as Chin, are sceptical of the

[handwritten margin note: Chin has created many works & become popular in Europe, but feared her native East Asian music may be viewed as exotic → this is common for composers]

threat of exoticism, others draw more willingly on the resources of musical multiculturalism. For Gabriela Lena Frank (b.1972) – born in California to Chinese-Peruvian and Lithuanian-Jewish parents – exploring her mixed ancestry has been crucial. She has conducted close-up studies of Andean music in particular, and her work titles display her South American influences: *Leyendas* (Legends, for string orchestra, 2001), *La Llorona* (The crying woman; tone poem for viola and ensemble, 2007), and an opera on the relationship between two iconic Mexican artists, *El último sueño de Frida y Diego* (The last dream of Frida [Kahlo] and Diego [Rivera]), commissioned for the Fort Worth Opera in 2021. Frank has also composed for indigenous instruments in *Compadre Huashayo* (2012).

[handwritten margin note: examples of using one's culture in music]

Her practice, which also involves community work and running her own creative academy of music encouraging young female composers in particular, has been described as a kind of musical anthropology.[10] Frank herself states that her approach is typically American: 'We bring in a lot of cultures, eat it up and make it into something new'.[11] The composer nevertheless calls herself 'old-fashioned' in the sense that she primarily writes for acoustic instruments and traditional classical formats, and is inspired by earlier twentieth-century composers who mixed new music with old folkloristic elements, such as Béla Bartók and Alberto Ginastera.

[handwritten margin note: sees herself as old fashioned b/c of the use of acoustic instruments & traditional classical formatting]

Eastern European traditions are also vital to Roxanna Panufnik, daughter of composer Andrzej Panufnik, who fled to Britain from Poland in the 1950s. But her spiritual interests imply utilising sources from a greater world, in works comprising elements from Byzantine and Western chant, Jewish shofar, Islamic calls to prayer, Spanish Sephardic music, and Greek bouzouki scales. Her *Unending Love* (2017), based on a poem by Rabindranath Tagore, is scored for double choir, Carnatic singer, and various Indian instruments.

Regardless of geographical points of connection, Panufnik's and Frank's tonal languages are fundamentally harmonic. Liza Lim (b.1966), who grew up in Brunei and Australia with Chinese parents, and who also integrates elements from various cultures in her works, resides on the more experimental side. Like Chin, she holds a strong position within the Western avant-garde. Lim is an advocate for transculturalism: the idea that certain phenomena – such as time, beauty, and nature – might transcend cultural differences by deep, ecological connections. In a programme note on her 2016 work *How Forests Think* for sheng and ensemble, she compares the forms with plants 'growing toward light and water; like mycelial strands entwining with tree roots in a co-evolving internet of plant-life'.[12] Transcultural and ecological ideas, Lim states, 'have enabled me to think about composition as a way of populating musical spaces with "creatures" rather than structural forms'.[13] In her creating, she states, (human) musicians and (non-human) musical instruments join 'fictional composites of plants, animals, elements, spirits and all kinds of cultural ideas' in a speculative play, resulting in something that is hard to define in standard musicological terms.[14] Lim is thus not merely an advocate for multi- or transculturalism. She also searches for new models by which one can understand forms and structures by looking away from traditional Western musicology and turning towards indigenous cultures, as well as ecosystems at work in nature.

New Ecosystems in Music

Nature, in details and vast landscapes, has been a source of inspiration for artists of all times. But at the start of the twenty-first century the threat of an environmental crisis has made it a particularly urgent topic. At the same time, new technologies have been driving forces in the development of contemporary soundscapes. British-Norwegian Natasha Barrett (b.1972), who grew up amongst her father's vinyl albums of Claude Debussy's music and the evolving synthesiser technology of the 1980s,[15] was awarded the 2006 Nordic Council Music Prize for . . . *fetters* . . . (2002), which is inspired by microsystems in nature; the physical laws for the motions of molecules in a limited space whose energy eventually makes the space explode into a new space. Barrett, a leading composer and researcher within electronic music, has since developed advanced techniques for three-dimensional acousmatic soundscapes, with precise renderings of recorded sounds and artistic ideas alike.

Many composers utilise new technology to enhance our ability to listen to our environment, such as sound artist Jana Winderen (b.1965), who is fascinated by the interplay between human artefacts, technology, and nature. A recurring element in her works is recordings from the Arctic regions both above and below water, of whale song and what disturbs it: noise from cruise ships and seismic blasting. In the composition *Classified* (2017), commissioned by the Borealis Festival, such material was conveyed by way of multiple loudspeakers in a huge storage building for fishing equipment in Bergen.

Music from the Nordic region risks becoming trapped in its own brand of exoticism in the sense that listeners 'hear' cold or Arctic landscapes in it, whether intended or not on the part of the composer. Icelandic Anna

Thorvaldsdottir (b.1977) often points to the wild and barren nature of her home country as a source of inspiration and her music is promoted as 'an ecosystem of sounds, where materials continuously grow in and out of each other' in continuous processes of growth and transformation.[16] But, although she brings in ideas and material from nature, she emphasises their abstract and technical qualities in the compositional process. For instance, Thorvaldsdottir thematises time, texture, and motion in *Aion* and *Dreaming* for symphony orchestra, and in chamber works such as *In the Light of Air* (2013/2014) and *Fields* (2016), as well as in the chamber opera *UR* (2015). The inspiration from nature is not to be taken too literally. She has stated that: 'when I am inspired by a particular element that I perceive in nature, it is because I perceive it as musically interesting'.[17] Nature thus inspires sound worlds, from electroacoustic and site-specific compositions to meditative, orchestral landscapes, and, in the case of Japanese-American composer Karen Tanaka (b.1961), poetic, minimalist pieces with titles such as *Water and Stone, Silent Ocean, Tales of Trees*, and *Crystalline*, combining sophistication and simplicity in an accessible musical language.

Reaching Out for Broader Audiences

The different currents in the field of contemporary music reach different audiences, some larger than others. On the one hand, new works are presented at forums and festivals for cutting-edge experimental repertoire – such as in Donaueschingen, Darmstadt, and Huddersfield. On the other hand, composers collaborate with the established institutions and have their works performed in the concert halls of symphony orchestras as well as in chamber music series and at festivals all over the world. One of the most successful composers in the realms of traditionally oriented symphonic music is the American Jennifer Higdon (b.1962). Her *Blue Cathedral* has been performed hundreds of times since its premiere in 2000.

Higdon is an eager communicator both in her collaborations with performers and in relation to audiences. She often gives interviews and pre-concert talks, and she provides the listeners with programme notes that give an insight into the stories behind the music. *Blue Cathedral*, for instance, was written in memory of her late brother, and she imagined the cathedral as a place for 'beginnings, endings, solitude, fellowship, contemplation, knowledge and growth'. Here she 'saw the image of clouds and blueness permeating from the outside' and imagined the listener entering 'from the back of the sanctuary, floating along the corridor among giant crystal pillars'.[18]

Higdon's music bears witness to inspiration from film and popular music, and her *Violin Concerto* has been described as a 'showpiece' in which 'chromatic neo-Romanticism and inventive orchestration keep the piece lively and surprising'.[19] The concerto, which was written for Hilary Hahn, was awarded the 2010 Pulitzer Prize the year it premiered, with the prize committee calling it 'a deeply engaging piece that combines flowing lyricism with dazzling virtuosity'.[20]

Communication, musical craftswomanship, and emotional intensity are also at the heart of the works of Augusta Read Thomas (b.1964). A professor of composition at the University of Chicago and a sought-after, prolific composer, she draws on influences from Bach via Mahler, Stravinsky, and Debussy to jazz.[21] *Radiant Circles* (2010) evolves around the colours of the different instrument groups in the symphony orchestra in one twelve-minute-long crescendo with particularly virtuosic parts for trumpet and timpani. Her 2019 opera *Sweet Potato Kicks the Sun* has a quite different temperament, featuring the artist Nicole Paris in a key role beatboxing.[22]

The musical life of the USA apparently provides a fertile environment for emotionally intensive, tonally rooted works in traditional formats, as well as for the blending in of elements from popular music. Amongst the younger generation, Missy Mazzoli (b.1980) mixes groovy sections with lyrical melodic lines and soft harmonies in a personal brew of a minimalist language. Her opera *Breaking the Waves,* based on Lars von Trier's film of the same name and premiered at Opera Philadelphia in 2016, was described as supporting the dynamic of the tragic story 'by wedding strong lyric invention to an unsettled, insidiously dissonant chamber-orchestra texture that evokes the jagged beauty both of [the Isle of] Skye and of Bess's inner landscape'.[23]

Symphony orchestras and opera houses can be uneasy partners for contemporary composers, given the history and the inherent expectations they carry with them. Sarah Kirkland Snider (b.1973) explains that when thinking about classical institutions and 'their values, their history',[24] it brings out something different than when she composes for musicians who are comfortable in both classical and popular music. Herself manoeuvring in what she calls 'the cracks between' these worlds, she stresses how individual performers are often crucial to the making of her music. Amongst them is Shara Worden, for whom she has composed the cycles *Penelope* and *Unremembered* for singer and orchestra.

Intimate collaborations between musicians and composers are, if not *[handwritten: musicians and composers are now working much closer]* new in a historical perspective, characteristic for several contemporary music projects. At times the division between composer and performer is fully erased. Lera Auerbach (b.1973), who defected to the USA from the Soviet Union in 1991, has collaborated intimately with high-profile musicians such as the violinists Gideon Kremer and Leonidas Kavakos. But she also conducts and plays her own music on the piano. Her output is *[handwritten: is new to the 21st & 20th century]* voluminous, passionate, often meditative, inspired by dreams and visions, and draws on input from classical sources from Beethoven to Shostakovich and Schoenberg. She is an outspoken advocate for tonality and writes mostly in traditional chamber, orchestral, and operatic formats, including *[handwritten: also now composer & performers]* her 2012 *Requiem (Dresden. An Ode to Peace)*. She is also a poet, painter, and sculptor.

Various forms of artistic multitasking are practised by many, including the younger composer-conductor Sara Caneva (b.1991). However, blurring the distinctions between composing and performing can involve more than just mastering different disciplines. It can also be considered an act of intervention in the norms inherent in the Western tradition since the romantic era, in particular in the tendency to give the composer's 'abstract' ideas and the authoritative score prominence over the physical practice of performance.

Challenging the Composer–Performer Division

In 2016, Jennifer Walshe (b.1974) presented a manifesto for a new school which she names The New Discipline.[25] Referring to historical avant-garde *[handwritten: works on composers also performing]* movements such as Dada and Fluxus, as well as contemporary colleagues, the Irish composer and singer promotes a practice in which she not only provides scores and instructions, but also takes part in the directing, choreographing, and performing of her works. The New Discipline appreciates 'composers being interested and willing to perform, to get their hands dirty, to do it themselves, do it immediately'.[26] Walshe's manifesto might be seen as a response to the critique musical modernism has encountered throughout the last century; of being too cerebral, too detached from sensuous pleasure and pain – that is, the body – and thus, perhaps, all the harder for women to relate to.[27]

An outspoken feminist, Walshe has toured European contemporary music scenes with the chamber opera *XXX Live Nude Girls* (2003).[28] Performed by two female singers, an instrumental ensemble, and two puppeteers, it is set in a doll's house inhabited by Barbie characters – projected on video screens – who experiment with sex in their otherwise rather miserable lives. For the 2019 project *Time Time* Walshe joined forces with philosopher Timothy Morton in exploring time in an ecological, astronomical, and bodily sense (such as ageing). 'We call it an opera, but it's not an opera in the conventional sense', Walshe stresses.[29] It deals with time as a phenomenon, but as much as that, it explores what might happen between a composer, free improvising musicians, and audiovisual elements in the moment, on stage.

Maja Ratkje (b.1973) also draws upon her resources as an improvising singer and noise musician, blending acoustically and electronically pro-duced sound. The Norwegian composer launched her solo album *Voice* (2003) shortly after having collected prizes for the instrumental ensemble works *Waves I* and *Waves II* (both 1997). *Crepuscular Hour* (2010) was co-commissioned by the Huddersfield and Oslo Contemporary Music Festivals, and is scored for no fewer than six noise musicians, three choirs, and church organ. Ratkje also raises her voice about political issues and the environmental crisis in particular. She declines sponsorships from compa-nies within the petroleum industry, and the orchestral work *§ 112* (2014) thematises a constitutional clause about the state's responsibility for the environment and the health of its citizens.

Societal issues are also brought to the fore by Chinese composer, multi-instrumentalist, and performance artist Du Yun (b.1977). When awarded the 2017 Pulitzer Prize, her opera *Angel's Bone* (libretto by Royce Vavrek) was reviewed as a work 'that integrates vocal and instrumental elements and a wide range of styles into a harrowing allegory for human trafficking in the modern world'.[30] In the 2019 concert project *Where We Lost Our Shadows*, Du collaborated with film-maker Khaled Jarrar in depicting the challenges of migration and the refugee crisis. The work zooms in on individual faces on screen and individual musicians on stage; vocalists using extended techniques, soloists in music from East Asia and the Middle East, and musicians in a European contemporary music ensemble. Crossover is characteristic for Du Yun, who is likely to offer a concert with her pop art band Ok Miss on the same night as works such as *Where We Lost Our Shadows*.

Walshe, Ratkje, and Du Yun are all composers who 'get their hands dirty' by performing and improvising and by loosening their artistic con-trol through letting others experiment with their material, often in colla-borative practices. They also operate, alongside artists such as Juliana Hodkinson (b.1973) and Mirela Ivičević (b.1980), in environments where

[handwritten margin note: also blending of sounds]

utilising and developing new technology is customary, and where the distinctions between opera, music drama, performance, sound art, composition, and improvisation are continuously challenged. Such creative spaces seem to hold a potential for composers with ambivalent feelings towards the established musical institutions, and their inherent conventions and traditions, in which the somewhat distant male composer of scores is still the norm. However, this does not imply that avant-garde and new music arenas are exemplary in terms of gender balance.

Avant-Garde Activism and Optimism

In the second decade of the twenty-first century, several measures were taken to promote women composers of the past and present, such as the PRS Foundation's 50:50 Keychange campaign, as discussed in Chapter 16, 'Women in the Music Industries: The Art of Juggling'. In contemporary music one important initiative emerged at the Darmstadt summer course and festival in 2016. The American composer Ashley Fure (b.1982) presented statistics showing a significant gender imbalance at the festival, which alongside the one in Donaueschingen has been a defining force in continental modernism since the later 1940s. Subsequent discussions concluded that more action was required and led to the founding of the Gender Relations network in Darmstadt (GRiD), which soon expanded its scope to Gender Relations in New Music (GRiNM).[31]

The statistics revealed that the average percentage of female composers in Darmstadt in the years 1946 to 2014 was only seven, rising to around eighteen when counting from 1990 to 2014. Moreover, the most frequently performed male composers had their works programmed about four times as often as the top ten female composers.[32] Amongst the most performed women composers were Olga Neuwirth, Kaija Saariaho, Jennifer Walshe, and Liza Lim. Also on the list are prominent names such as Youngi Pagh-Paan (b.1945), Chaya Czernowin (b.1957), Isabel Mundry (b.1963), and Misato Mochizuki (b.1969). The youngest is Swedish Malin Bång (b.1974), whose music often involves acoustical objects in addition to traditional instruments, bearing witness to an affinity for intimate sounds and noises, at times very quiet, although laid out in contrast to more dramatic, abrupt gestures. Bång can be said to be developing and refining continental post-Second-World-War Modernist aesthetics, as defined by composers such as Helmut Lachenmann, Wolfgang Rihm, and subsequently Rebecca Saunders (b.1967).

Saunders – British-born, but based in Berlin, and also on the Darmstadt top ten list– typically composes with the 'shadows' and noises of the sounds of instruments, as much as with the sonorous timbres idealised in the romantic era. The Ernst von Siemens Music Prize was awarded to her in 2019 for 'an oeuvre which leaves its visible and meaningful mark on contemporary music history through its astonishingly nuanced attention to timbre, and her distinctive and intensely striking sonic language'.[33] On this occasion, Saunders was the first woman to be awarded the main prize for composition. Only a few other women had won the lesser composers' prize, and violinist Anne-Sophie Mutter the main prize, in 2008, for her musicianship. Saunders, whose music had been performed regularly at the most prestigious contemporary music festivals in Europe, called it 'tragic' that her gender thus made headlines in 2019. But she also found it 'understandable' considering the many women in her generation who had not pursued their careers as composers. She did, however, also observe a 'wealth of very talented, strong, confident female composers who are at last being publicly recognised and becoming increasingly visible'.[34]

Two decades into the twenty-first century, women composers are still exceptional, to an extent that spurs timely activism. But there is also a sense of optimism in the field. Although not representative in numbers, the female 'half of humanity' – to quote Saariaho again – demonstrates that it has 'something to say' by being 'all over the place' with artistic outputs in a wide variety of styles, genres, forms, and formats. The composers discussed in this chapter relate to the issue of being female in a male-dominated profession in very different ways, some uttering fierce critique of suppressive systems, others claiming that they do not have to address the issue at all. But whether they thematise it or not, they all contribute to change by being heard and seen; at concerts and festivals, in clubs, opera houses, and orchestral venues, and not least, streamed through an infinite number of digital channels.

Notes

1. Pirkko Moisala, *Kaija Saariaho* (Urbana: University of Illinois Press, 2009).
2. Jeff Lunden, '"Half of Humanity Has Something to Say": Composer Kaija Saariaho on Her Met Debut', *NPR* (3 December 2016), available at www.npr.org /sections/deceptivecadence/2016/12/03/503986298/half-of-humanity-has-something-to-say-composer-kaija-saariaho-on-her-met-debut (accessed 5 November 2019).

3. See https://saariaho.org/works/ (accessed 5 November 2019).

4. Fiona Maddocks, 'Miss Fortune – Review', *The Guardian* (18 March 2012), available at www.theguardian.com/music/2012/mar/18/miss-fortune-opera-house-review (accessed 5 November 2019).

5. Barbara Basting, 'Drastische Töne: Die Komponistin Olga Neuwirth und ihre Zusammenarbeit mit Elfriede Jelinek', *Du: Die Zeitschrift der Kultur*, 59 (1999–2000), 22–5.

6. Anonymous, 'Jelinek-Neuwirth-Oper zum "Fall Wurst" abermals vor dem Scheitern', *NEWS* (30 June 2004), www.news.at/a/news-jelinek-neuwirth-oper-fall-wurst-scheitern-85710 (accessed 5 November 2019); Anonymous, 'Holender lehnt Produktion von Jelinek-Libretto ab', *Der Standard* (20 October 2004), available at www.derstandard.at/story/1831725/holender-lehnt-produktion-von-jelinek-libretto-ab (accessed 27 March 2020).

7. Alex Ross, 'Opera Against the Patriarchy', *The New Yorker* (6 January 2020), available at www.newyorker.com/magazine/2020/01/06/opera-against-the-patriarchy (accessed 1 April 2020).

8. Ljubiša *Tošic*, 'Epische Geschlechterreise: Olga Neuwirths neue Oper "Orlando"', *Der Standard* (9 December 2019), available at www.derstandard.at/story/2000112059895/epische-geschlechterreiseolga-neuwirths-neue-oper-orlando (accessed 1 April 2020).

9. For Details of *Šu*, see www.boosey.com/pages/cr/catalogue/cat_detail?sl-id=1&musicid=52419 (accessed 15 November 2019) and on Wui Wei, see 'Sheng Player Wu Wei: 'My Goal Is to Open and Widen the Repertoire for my Instrument', ICMA website (11 September 2015), www.icma-info.com/sheng-player-wu-wei-my-goal-is-to-open-and-widen-the-repertoire-for-my-instrument/ (accessed 27 March 2020).

10. See biography at Wise Music Classical website, www.wisemusicclassical.com/composer/2388/gabriela-lena-frank/ (accessed 11 December 2020).

11. Dayton Hare, 'Life Outside the Golden Cage: Composer Gabriela Lena Frank in Profile' in *The Michigan Daily* (11 October 2017), available at www.michigandaily.com/section/arts/life-outside-golden-cage-composer-gabriela-lena-frank-profile (accessed 11 November 2019).

12. See 'How Forests Think', *Lim Programme Notes* (n.d.) https://limprogrammenotes.wordpress.com/2016/02/06/howforeststhink/ (accessed 5 November 2019).

13. Ibid.

14. See composer website, 'Events', https://lizalimcomposer.com/concerts/ (accessed 5 November 2019).

15. Seth Colter Walls, 'Tickling the Ear With Sounds That Are Almost Tangible', *New York Times* (23 July 2019), available at www.nytimes.com/2019/07/23/arts/music/natasha-barrett-3d-audio-empac.html (accessed 5 November 2019).

16. See 'Bio', composer's website, www.annathorvalds.com/bio (accessed 5 November 2019).

17. See 'Aion', composer's www.annathorvalds.com/aion (accessed 5 November 2019).

18. Jennifer Higdon, programme notes for 'Blue Cathedral', www .jenniferhigdon.com/pdf/program-notes/blue-cathedral.pdf (accessed 5 November 2019).

19. Allan Kozinn, 'Sound That's Lush and Slow, Speedy and Precise' *New York Times* (16 February 2011), available at www.nytimes.com/2011/02/17/arts/ music/17curtis.html (accessed 5 November 2019).

20. See 'Violin Concerto, by Jennifer Higdon (Lawdon Press)', The Pulitzer Prizes website, www.pulitzer.org/winners/jennifer-higdon (accessed 5 November 2019).

21. Jennifer Kelly, 'Augusta Read Thomas', in *In Her Own Words: Conversations with Composers in the United States* (Urbana: University of Illinois Press, 2013).

22. See 'Sweet Potato Kicks the Sun', composer's website, www .augustareadthomas.com/composition/sweet-potato/sweet-potato-NicoleParis.html (accessed 15 November 2019).

23. Alex Ross, 'Prototype Festival's Striking Heroines', *The New Yorker* (29 December 2016), available at www.newyorker.com/magazine/2017/01/09/ prototype-festivals-striking-heroines (accessed 17 October 2019).

24. New Music USA, 'Sarah Kirkland Snider: The Full 360', *YouTube* (1 September 2015) www.youtube.com/watch?v=0bCF5-7-Em4 (accessed 5 November 2019).

25. See 'The New Discipline: A Compositional Manifesto by Jennifer Walshe', Borealis Festival website (n.d.) www.borealisfestival.no/2016/the-new-discipline-a-compositional-manifesto-by-jennifer-walshe-2/ (accessed 1 April 2020).

26. See 'The New Discipline', Borealis Festival website (n.d.) www .borealisfestival.no/the-new-discipline-4/ (accessed 11 November 2019).

27. Susan McClary, 'Terminal Prestige: The Case of Avant-Garde Music Composition', *Cultural Critique*, no. 12 Discursive Strategies and the Economy of Prestige (1989), 57–81.

28. Andrew Clements, 'XXX Live Nude Girls', *The Guardian* (17 November 2003), available at www.theguardian.com/music/2003/nov/17/ classicalmusicandopera (accessed 11 November 2019).

29. Michael Dervan, 'Men Just Get Away With Being Composers. We Have to Do This Activism and Keep Composing', *The Irish Times* (25 February 2019), available at www.irishtimes.com/culture/music/men-just-get-away-with-being-composers-we-have-to-do-this-activism-and-keep-composing-1 .3801540 (accessed 11 November 2019).

30. See 'Angel's Bone, by Du Yun', The Pulitzer Prizes website, www.pulitzer.org /winners/du-yun (accessed 11 November 2019).

31. See GRINM website, https://grinm.org/ (accessed 11 November 2019).

32. See 'GRID: Gender Research in Darmstadt', https://griddarmstadt
    .files.wordpress.com/2016/08/grid_gender_research_in_darmstadt.pdf
    (accessed 11 November 2019).
33. Mark Brown, 'British Composer Rebecca Saunders Wins Ernst von Siemens
    Music Prize', *The Guardian* (17 January 2019), available at www
    .theguardian.com/music/2019/jan/17/british-composer-rebecca-saunders-
    wins-ernst-von-siemens-music-prize (accessed 11 November 2019).
34. Ibid.

Further Reading

Kelly, Jennifer. *In Her Own Words: Conversations with Composers in the United
        States* (Urbana: University of Illinois Press, 2013).
Macarthur, Sally. 'The Woman Composer, New Music and Neoliberalism.' *Musicology
        Australia*, vol. 36, no. 1 (2014), 36–52.
Moisala, Pirkko. *Kaija Saariaho* (Urbana: University of Illinois Press, 2009).
Rutherford-Johnson, Tim. *Music After the Fall: Modern Composition and Culture
        since 1989* (Oakland: University of California Press, 2017).

5 | On the Podium: Women Conductors

LAURA HAMER

Introduction

Orchestral conducting is one of the most male-dominated musical areas. A number of high-profile gaffes from prominent male conductors in recent years – in 2013 Vasily Petrenko claimed that orchestras 'react better when they have a man in front of them' and that 'a cute girl on a podium means that musicians think about other things',[1] while in 2017 Mariss Jansons quipped that women conductors were not his 'cup of tea'[2] – suggest that cultural perceptions that conducting just isn't natural for women remain. Against this, however, women have also made significant inroads onto the conductor's podium. Just a few days after Petrenko's comments, Marin Alsop became the first woman to conduct the Last Night of the BBC's Proms (7 September 2013). Today, a whole raft of women, including Alsop, JoAnn Falletta, Simone Young, Alice Farnham, Xian Zhang, Jessica Cottis, and Ariane Matiakh, to name but a few, number amongst the most celebrated in the profession. Alongside this, a significant number of historical female conductors, such as Nadia Boulanger, Ethel Leginska, Veronika Dudarowa, Antonia Brico, and Frédérique Petrides, featured prominently on the podium earlier in the twentieth century. This chapter discusses the situation of women conductors and women's orchestras in the first half of the twentieth century, paying particular attention to the career of Leginska as an instructive case study. It also discusses the re-emergence of women at the heads of orchestras in more recent decades, focusing upon the career of Alsop. The chapter concludes with a look at the current situation of women conductors, and the various mentoring and training schemes that have developed to support them.

A Golden Age of Women's Orchestras and Conductors

Many of the most successful women conductors of the first half of the twentieth century forged their careers working with women's orchestras.

The music conservatoires which were founded throughout the nineteenth century admitted large number of female instrumentalists and trained them to a professional level. Most contemporary orchestras, however, refused to admit women. The first women's orchestras were formed in direct reaction to this. The earliest women's orchestra, the Wiener Damenorchester, was founded by Josephine Amann-Weinlich in Vienna in 1868; the Los Angeles Woman's Orchestra, the first American women's orchestra, was established in 1893. Many similar ensembles were created across Europe and North America throughout the final decades of the nineteenth century and early ones of the twentieth. Before the mid-twentieth century, women were strongly discouraged from learning wind or brass instruments, as the physical effort required to play these was considered unsightly. Similarly, the double bass and percussion were also considered unfeminine. Thus, women's orchestras often struggled to find women to fill all the parts. Some women's orchestras, such as the British Women's Symphony Orchestra (founded in London in 1922), overcame this by hiring male players.

As Carol Neuls-Bates has discussed, women's orchestras were a particularly marked feature of American concert life during the interwar period.[3] The cultural expansion which accompanied the post-First-World-War economic boom led to a marked development in orchestral life: more concert halls were built, the concert season was lengthened, and new symphony orchestras were established throughout the country. At the time, however, most American symphony orchestras were largely staffed by European-born men. Both women and men born and trained in America faced discrimination. Female instrumentalists faced a double layer of discrimination, however, as, except for harpists, the major American orchestras refused to hire them. Thus, around thirty American women's orchestras – many with a full complement of at least eighty players – were founded.[4] The first of these were established in the largest cities, including Philadelphia (the Philadelphia Women's Symphony Orchestra, 1921), Chicago (the Chicago Women's Symphony Orchestra and Women's Symphony Orchestra of Chicago, both 1924), and New York (the American Women's Symphony Orchestra, 1924). As American women were more inclined to learn a wider variety of orchestral instruments than Europeans, their women's orchestras were less reliant upon male players. The Women's Symphony Orchestra of Chicago, which was strongly committed to raising the profile of women as orchestral musicians, managed to eliminate the reliance upon male players altogether within just a few years. They offered scholarships to female pianists and violinists in return for them re-training on the oboe, French horn or trombone (the only instruments which they had initially hired men to play) and to female high school students studying winds and brass. They also particularly promoted the music of American female composers.[5]

Pioneer on the Podium: Ethel Leginska

Ethel Leginska (born Liggins, 1886–1970) was one of the most successful and pioneering women conductors of the first half of the twentieth century. British by birth, Leginska made the USA her home from 1913, and it was there, despite numerous appearances as a guest conductor with major European orchestras, that her conducting career unfolded. Leginska had already established herself as an internationally acclaimed concert pianist, and achieved some success as a composer, before she turned her attention to conducting in the early 1920s, seeking instruction from Robert Heger and Gennaro Papi between 1920 and 1922.

Her reputation as a leading concert pianist enabled her to secure opportunities to appear as a guest conductor with a number of major European and American orchestras, usually through agreeing to perform a piano concerto as part of the programme. By appearing as a conductor-pianist, Leginska revived the tradition of directing from the keyboard, which had dropped out of fashion in the nineteenth century. Thus, she was a pioneer not only as a woman conductor, but also as a conductor-pianist.

In November 1924, Leginska appeared as a guest conductor with the London Symphony Orchestra, Berlin Philharmonic, and Munich Konzertverein. In January 1925 she became the first woman to conduct at Carnegie Hall, when she made her American conducting debut leading the New York Symphony Orchestra. This was followed in April 1925 by an appearance with the People's Symphony Orchestra of Boston. In August 1925, she conducted the Los Angeles Philharmonic Orchestra at the Hollywood Bowl. Despite facing hostility from some male orchestral players and critics, these concerts were generally well received and Leginska sought a permanent position. Women conductors tended to be viewed as novelties in the early twentieth century, however. So, although her status as a leading concert pianist enabled her to secure guest appearances, it is highly unlikely that she would have been appointed as a principal conductor with a leading orchestra at the time.

Undeterred, Leginska formed her own orchestra, the Boston Philharmonic Orchestra, in 1926. Except for herself, the harpist, and the pianist, all the members were men. With the Boston Philharmonic Orchestra, Leginska intended to open up classical music to all. Thus, standing admission to their concerts cost just 25 cents, with seats costing from 50 cents. Although the Boston Philharmonic Orchestra was an artistic success, it proved to be financially inviable, and disbanded after only one season of six concerts.[6]

Between 1927 and 1930, Leginska worked with women's orchestras. In so doing, we can see her fitting within the wider trend of women conductors founding and directing their own women's orchestras during the earlier twentieth century. Prominent examples of other contemporary women conductors who formed their own women's orchestras include Jane Evrard, who formed her Orchestre féminin de Paris in 1930;[7] Frédérique Petrides, who formed her Orchestrette Classique in New York in 1933; and Antonia Brico, who formed her Women's Orchestra of New York in 1934. Leginska founded her Boston Women's Symphony Orchestra in 1927. Forming her own women's orchestra also enabled Leginska – who selected and trained each of the members herself – to champion women as orchestral players. The Boston Women's Symphony Orchestra proved to be very successful. Over a three-year period, they gave over two hundred concerts, and undertook two tours. The orchestra was, despite some comments of a gendered and patronising nature, generally well received. A review which appeared in *The Boston Herald* in 1929 commented on the good job that Leginska had done in training the instrumentalists:

Once more, yesterday afternoon, Ethel Leginska and her orchestra played before Jordan Hall sold-out. Whether the public went to the hall in support of feminism, out of personal regard for Miss Leginska, or, let us hope, in the mere wish to hear good music, does not matter. A large company did at all events hear an excellent programme, admirably performed, and derived . . . rare pleasure . . . Miss Leginska has at her command an able body of players . . . Her basses, especially, she has bettered, so much so that their tone is at times of a genuine loveliness . . . She has brought her orchestra to a pass when they can do work technically, musically, and emotionally admirable. And she has developed a public eager to hear her.[8]

The difficult economic conditions caused by the Wall Street Crash (1929) forced the orchestra to disband in 1930.

The Boston Women's Symphony Orchestra was not the only women's orchestra that Leginska was associated with. Following a guest appearance, she was also appointed as conductor and director of the Women's Symphony Orchestra of Chicago in 1927, a post which she held, on a part-time basis, until 1930. She formed one final women's orchestra, the

National Women's Symphony Orchestra, based in New York, in 1932. The continuing tough economic conditions of the Depression also prevented this from being financially feasible in the long term. It disbanded after just a few months. Leginska did not form any further orchestras. From 1933 she made only guest appearances as a conductor.

J. Michele Edwards has described Leginska as a 'New Woman', arguing that she 'shared traits with others identified as "new women" during the 1910s and 1920s: bobbed hair, concert attire modelled on men's formal wear, outspokenness about feminist issues, and a serious focus on work and career'.[9] Leginska adopted her signature look of a dark suit (jacket and skirt) with white blouse, collar, and cuffs, and 'bobbed' hair for her appearances as a concert pianist as early as 1915. At a time when concert halls were often very cold, this ensemble kept her warm while also allowing her plenty of arm and shoulder movement. Leginska described this practical attire as 'always the same and always comfortable, so that I can forget my appearance and concentrate on my art'.[10] She retained this distinctive look for her work as a conductor in the interwar period (see Figure 5.1).

Appearing on the podium in a suit consciously modelled on men's formal wear allowed Leginska to underline the fact that, not only had she taken what was traditionally a man's place upon the conductor's podium, but that she had also taken his clothes in which to do it. Leginska was a trailblazing pioneer, not only as one of the most prominent women conductors of the later 1920s, but also through reviving the practice of the conductor-pianist, and via her work championing women orchestral players. With the arrival of the Second World War, opportunities for her to conduct dried up. Throughout the final decades of her life she maintained a large private studio of piano pupils in Los Angeles.

An Exceptional Career: Nadia Boulanger

Nadia Boulanger (1887–1979) became arguably the most successful woman conductor to emerge during the 1930s. Between 1933, when the Parisian arts patroness the Princesse Edmond de Polignac launched Boulanger's conducting career through a gala concert in her salon, and the end of the decade, she had become the first woman to conduct the Royal Philharmonic Society, the National Symphony, and the orchestras of Boston and Philadelphia. In addition, she had also directed dozens of orchestras in France, Belgium, the UK, and the USA. Boulanger's career must be regarded as exceptional amongst those of women conductors of

Figure 5.1 Ethel Leginska, English pianist, conductor and composer, 1935. Photo credit: Tully Potter/Bridgeman Images

the first half of the twentieth century, however, because, unlike most others, she did not make her career through founding and working with her own women's orchestra. In fact, as Jeanice Brooks has discussed, Boulanger went to get lengths to downplay her femininity upon the podium.[11] Boulanger claimed that her conducting was an extension of her teaching – a much more socially accepted musical role for women – rather than a result of ambition (although her earliest forays onto the podium actually date from 1912 to 1913). In rehearsals and in interviews she consistently constructed herself as serving the music's higher purpose, rather than emphasising her own agency as the conductor. Always dressed plainly, she even chose to conduct without a baton, the outward symbol of a conductor's authority, and, as Brooks has identified, a potential phallic symbol.[12] Thus, Boulanger was very careful not to present herself as a threat. While Boulanger's performative strategy enabled her to succeed as a conductor, it did not, as Edwards has observed 'open a door for subsequent generations of women conductors'.[13]

Mid-Century Retrenchments and the Exception of Veronika Dudarowa

The golden age of women's orchestras that had flourished during the first half of the twentieth century was brought to an abrupt end by the arrival of the Second World War. Although male military conscription opened up desks for women in the previously all-male orchestras, most women's orchestras were so depleted that they were forced to disband. Very few survived the war, and even fewer reformed afterwards. Although it may initially appear curious – disloyal even – that so many women left the women's orchestras to take up posts in male-dominated ensembles, there are a number of possible reasons for this. Firstly, most women's orchestras had always suffered financial insecurities. Even during wartime, the top professional orchestras retained relative financial security. On a related point, members of the women's orchestras tended to be paid significantly less than members of male or mixed ensembles. Secondly, the previously all-male orchestras were considerably more prestigious, so it is perhaps not surprising that women seized opportunities to join them.

Linda Dempf has commented that: 'It was not that women were suddenly accepted into male-dominated orchestras, but that the women's orchestras had served a purpose of giving women an opportunity to play and learn the orchestral repertoire ... Thus the all-women orchestra provided a training ground and was an important step for women orchestra players.'[14] New opportunities for female instrumentalists ironically also created decreased opportunities for female conductors, the majority of whom had worked with women's ensembles. With these gone, opportunities for women conductors decreased rapidly in the period following the Second World War, and this situation did not begin to improve (for most women) until the final decades of the twentieth century.

Although the decades immediately following the Second World War afforded only very few professional conducting opportunities for women, the career of Veronika Dudarowa (1916–2009) in the USSR is an important exception. Dudarowa, who studied conducting at the Moscow Conservatory, became a junior conductor of the Moscow State Symphony Orchestra in 1947. She was promoted to principal conductor in 1960, becoming the first

Russian woman to hold such a position. She retained this post until 1989. In 1991, following the fall of communism, she founded the State Symphony Orchestra of Russia. She led this orchestra until 2003 and remained as its artistic manager until her death. Although not well known outside Russia, Dudarowa was one of the most important Soviet and Russian conductors of the twentieth century. As Tim McDonald has commented: 'in her own country, she was a giant'.[15]

Re-emergence

In the West, women conductors did not begin to re-emerge on the podium until the 1980s. In 1984, Sian Edwards won the first Leeds Conductors' Competition, making her London debut with the Royal Philharmonic Orchestra in 1985; also in 1984, Odaline de la Martinez became the first woman to conduct a BBC Proms Concert; and in the USA, JoAnn Falletta was appointed Musical Director of the Long Beach Symphony in 1989. Although male conductors still outnumber female, particularly at the top of the profession, there are now a significant number of high-profile women conductors active. Alongside Edwards, Martinez, and Falletta, Claire Gibault, Jane Glover, Simone Young, Xian Zhang, and Ariane Matiakh, to name but a few, have all carved out leading, international careers.

A striking feature of women's participation in professional conducting is the number – such as Margaret Hillis, Sarah Caldwell, Judith Somogi, Glover, Edwards, Young, and Laurence Equilbey – who have excelled as opera and choral conductors. Although this is obviously positive, two gendered reasons for the relative success of women conductors in the world of opera and choral music suggest themselves. Firstly, in opera the conductor is hidden in the pit; so it is not immediately obvious to the audience that the music is being directed by a woman. J. Michele Edwards has gone so far as to speculate that because 'the conductor works in the pit rather than in the spotlight ... this may have been more acceptable to audiences, orchestras, and even conductors'.[16] She quotes Glover revealing that 'maybe that's why I like it because I'm out of sight'.[17] Secondly, many opera and choral conductors begin their careers as piano répétiteurs. The supportive nature of this could be seen as reinforcing nurturing roles for women. Fiona Maddocks has suggested that women conductors have made particular progress in choral music because it 'requires the kind of collegiate powers at which women excel'.[18]

Pioneer, Leader, and Many Firsts: Marin Alsop

Marin Alsop (b.1956) has become one of the most successful and well-known conductors active anywhere in the world today. In a highly competitive field, she has carved out a remarkable international career, which has been distinguished by many firsts. She is the first woman to have become the principal conductor of a British orchestra (Bournemouth Symphony Orchestra, 2002), music director of a major American orchestra (Baltimore Symphony Orchestra, 2007), music director of a Brazilian orchestra (São Paulo Symphony Orchestra, 2012), and chief conductor of a Viennese Orchestra (Vienna Radio Symphony Orchestra, 2019). She became the first woman to conduct at the Teatro alla Scala in Italy (2011) and to conduct the Last Night of the BBC Proms (2013). Additionally, amongst many prestigious awards, she became the first conductor ever to receive a MacArthur Fellowship in 2005.

Alsop is the only daughter of professional musicians. Her father, LaMar Alsop, was concertmaster of the New York City Ballet Orchestra; the orchestra in which her mother, Ruth Alsop, was a cellist. At the age of nine, her father took her to hear one of Leonard Bernstein's Young People's Concerts with the New York Philharmonic, and the experience motivated her to become a conductor herself. Displaying a precocious musical talent from a very young age, Alsop entered the Juilliard Pre-College at the age of seven. She enrolled at Yale University in 1972, but later transferred to the Juilliard School, where she graduated with Bachelor's and Master's degrees in violin performance (1977 and 1978). During her early career, she worked as a freelance violinist in New York City. She began conducting studies with Carl Bamberger in 1979, later studying with Harold Farberman in 1985. Not unlike the pioneering women conductors of the early twentieth century, Alsop gained her first conducting experiences by founding her own ensembles. She founded the all-woman swing band String Fever in 1981 and established the Concordia Orchestra in 1984.

In 1989 Alsop became the first woman to win the Koussevitsky Conducting Prize at the Tanglewood Music Center, where she became a conducting student of Bernstein, who would become her mentor, Gustav Meier, and Seiji Ozawa. From the late 1980s and throughout the '90s, she moved through a succession of prestigious formative appointments. She was appointed associate conductor of the Richmond Symphony (Virginia) and music director of the Eugene Symphony Orchestra in 1989; Music Director of the Cabrillo Festival of Contemporary Music in 1992;

music director of the Colorado Symphony (Denver) in 1993; creative conductor chair with the St. Louis Symphony Orchestra in 1994; and principal guest conductor of the Royal Scottish National Orchestra in 1999.

Alsop achieved a major appointment in 2002, when she became principal conductor of the Bournemouth Symphony Orchestra. In 2007, she became music director of the Baltimore Symphony Orchestra. Under her leadership, the Baltimore Symphony Orchestra became particularly known for its outreach activities with the local community. In 2008, she founded OrchKids, which provides music education, instruments, performance opportunities, academic instruction, healthy meals, and mentorship at no cost for underprivileged children and teenagers in Baltimore City. The project has been described as 'an acknowledged leader in the El Sistema and social-change through music movement'.[19] Alsop became principal conductor of the São Paulo Symphony Orchestra in 2012. With her, the orchestra became the first Brazilian orchestra to appear at the BBC Proms in August 2012. In 2015, she succeeded her teacher Meier as director of graduate conducting at the Peabody Institute at Johns Hopkins University.[20] Alsop also has an extensive discography. Although she is particularly well known for her recordings of twentieth-century American music, especially Barber and Bernstein, she has recorded a very wide range of music, which also includes works by Brahms, Dvořák, Mahler, and Bartók. In 2010, her recording of Jennifer Higdon's Percussion Concerto with the London Philharmonic Orchestra and Colin Currie won a Grammy Award for Best Classical Contemporary Composition.

Alsop is aware of the gender issues surrounding her position on the podium. She has opined that: 'People aren't comfortable with seeing women in these roles, because there aren't any women in the roles . . . When you're the only one, you're always a target . . . Women have so few opportunities, comparatively speaking, that the pressure is enormous.'[21] This translates into an acute awareness of how body language and gesture are interpreted through a gendered lens. As she has explained:

The thing about conducting is it's all body language . . . our society interprets gesture very differently from men or from women . . . A delicate touch from a woman, for example, is often seen as weakness, when the same gesture from a man is seen as sensitive . . . Unlike men, women conductors are required to think twice about gesture because it's not just the gesture, it's how the musicians interpret the gesture.[22]

This awareness of body language and gesture also extends to how she comports herself during rehearsals: 'Everything sends a message . . . If

Figure 5.2 Marin Alsop. Photo credit: Grant Leighton

I sit down, the message is that either I'm tired, or that it's casual, or it's too much effort.'[23] Visually Alsop cuts a professional and authoritative figure on the podium. Not unlike Leginska, she also favours smart suits which allow plenty of shoulder room. Her signature look has become a black tailored suit, often accompanied with a red blouse (see Figure 5.2).

Although proud to have been the first woman to achieve many things in the world of conducting, Alsop has frequently expressed her astonishment that this can still be the case in the early twenty-first century. In conversation with Michael Cooper, the classical music critic for *The New York Times*, she has commented that 'I've been the first woman to do a lot of things, and I'm really proud, but I also think it's absolutely pathetic.'[24] In a similar vein, Alsop used her speech at her Last Night of the BBC Proms concert to observe that:

Quite a lot has been made of me being the first woman to conduct the Last Night of the Proms. I'm incredibly honoured and proud to have this title, but I have to say

I'm still quite shocked that it can be 2013 and there can be firsts for women. Here's to the seconds, thirds, fourths, fifths, hundredths to come.[25]

Mentors, Role Models, and All-Women Training Schemes

Alsop has used her position as a leading female conductor to enable these 'seconds, thirds, fourths, fifths, hundredths'. As Maddocks has observed, 'if she [Alsop] once resisted tiresome gender questions, now she accepts her duty as spokesperson'.[26] Alsop established her Taki Concordia Conducting Fellowship specifically for women in 2002. Currently worth $7,500 for Fellows and $5,000 for Associate Fellows, the awards offer talented young women conductors two years of intensive coaching and mentoring from Alsop.[27] On her official website, she has described her motivation for establishing the fellowship thus:

When I started conducting professionally over thirty years ago, I naively assumed there would be more and more women entering the field but, five years passed, then ten, then fifteen and I thought: 'Why aren't there more women?' and 'if I don't do something to change this landscape, who will?'

In 2002 I started the Taki Concordia Conducting Fellowship to create opportunities for talented young women conductors. I named the fellowship after my non-musical mentor, Tomio Taki, who helped me start my very first orchestra, Concordia, in 1984. Mr. Taki believed in me and wanted to be part of enabling a woman to break the glass ceiling in the conducting world. This fellowship was established in his honour and to thank him for his life-changing support.

To date (2019) we have had eighteen awardees and they are all doing extremely well. An unexpected and wonderful result of the Taki Fellowship is the community of women conductors that has been created. These gifted women have each other as resources, to act as sounding boards, offer advice and be a support system.[28]

Alsop's pioneering mentoring and training scheme has since inspired similar projects elsewhere. In 2014, Alice Farnham also launched a training programme for aspiring women conductors aimed at addressing the lack of women on the podium, with Andrea Brown, at Morley College. Since 2016, Farnham's Women Conductors programme has found a home at the Royal Philharmonic Society.[29] The programme provides dedicated workshops for emerging and student women conductors throughout the UK, and many leading senior female conductors have contributed to it. Reflecting on its importance, Farnham has commented in *The Guardian* that: 'If we are to encourage more women to become conductors they need both hands-on experience and inspirational role models.'[30] Beyond enabling young women conductors to meet and be trained by senior, female role models, these training workshops are essential for creating safe places within which student women conductors can practise and refine their skills. As Farnham has further commented:

> Training to be a conductor is tough, because the real practical experience is so public. Conductors have to spend hours learning scores in private, and a certain amount of work can be done on baton technique. But actually practising your 'instrument' (the orchestra) has to be done in front of lots of people. When it goes wrong – which it will – there's no hiding. Are women more reluctant to make mistakes in public than men are? Do they judge themselves, and are they judged by others more harshly? These may be generalisations, but perhaps there's some truth there . . . These workshops offer a safe place to have a go.[31]

A number of similar training programmes have emerged in recent years. Prominent examples include the Sorrell Women's Conducting Programme at the Royal Academy of Music (UK); the Female Conductor Programme at the National Concert Hall, Dublin (Republic of Ireland); Dirigent Musik i Väst (Sweden); and the Hart Institute for Women Conductors at the Dallas Opera (USA).

Conclusion

Although it is undeniable that women continue to be underrepresented on the conductor's podium, particularly at the highest level of the profession, there are now leading women conductors active throughout the world. The women-only conducting training programmes which have sprung up in recent years offer particular grounds for hope, as they have already proved tremendously beneficial in terms of diversifying the world of conducting and increasing the number of women professionally active. Karina Canellakis, the 2013 Taki Concordia Fellow, became chief conductor of the Netherlands Radio Philharmonic in 2019 and the first woman to conduct the First Night of the BBC Proms on 19 July 2019; Valentina Peleggi, the 2015 Taki Concordia Fellow, is principal conductor of the São Paulo Symphony Chorus; Lina Gonzalez-Granados, the 2017 Taki Concordia Fellow, is founder and artistic director of the Unitas Ensemble.[32] In the UK, meanwhile, Tianyi Lu became Welsh National Opera's first Female Conductor in Residence in August 2019. The scheme 'aims to equip aspiring female conductors with the necessary training and experience to pursue conducting careers'.[33] As part of her award, Lu will be mentored for eighteen months by Farnham. It is very much to be hoped that these schemes will contribute to what Alsop referred to in her Last Night speech at the 2013 BBC Proms as 'a natural progression towards more inclusion in classical music'.[34]

A wave of appointments of women to positions as music directors or principal conductors of major European and American orchestras also appears to point in this direction. The year 2016 marked three women conductors taking up principal conductor posts with major American and European orchestras: Chinese-American conductor Xian Zhang became musical director of the New Jersey Symphony Orchestra; Lithuanian conductor Mirga Gražinytė-Tyla was appointed music director of the City of Birmingham Symphony Orchestra; and Finnish conductor Susanna Mälkki became chief conductor of the Helsinki Philharmonic Orchestra. Mexican conductor Alondra de la Parra became music director of the Queensland Symphony Orchestra in 2017, meanwhile. It is to be hoped that these appointments signal a profound change. Alsop concluded her 2013 Last Night of the Proms speech by appealing to young women to 'believe in yourselves, follow your passion, and never give up, because you will create a future filled with possibility'.[35] It is greatly to be hoped that the growth in training and mentoring opportunities for aspiring women conductors, and the recent spate of appointments of women to high-profile conducting positions, hint that such a future is within grasp.

Notes

1. Charlotte Higgins, 'Male Conductors Are Better for Orchestras, Says Vasily Petrenko', *The Guardian* (2 September 2013), available at www .theguardian.com/music/2013/sep/02/male-conductors-better-orchestras-vasily-petrenko (accessed 24 May 2019).
2. Ivan Hewett, 'Mariss Jansons: "Women on the Podium Are Not My Cup of Tea"', *The Telegraph* (23 November 2017), available at www.telegraph.co.uk /music/concerts/mariss-jansons-women-podium-arenot-cup-tea/ (accessed 24 May 2019).
3. Carol Neuls-Bates, 'Women's Orchestras in the United States, 1925–45', in Jane Bowers and Judith Tick (eds.), *Women Making Music: The Western Art Tradition, 1150–1950* (Urbana and Chicago: University of Illinois Press, 1986), 349–69.
4. See Carol Neuls-Bates, 'Women's Orchestras in the United States, 1925–45', 351–3.

5. Ibid., 354.

6. For a detailed study of Leginska's conducting career, see Marguerite and Terry Broadbent, *Leginska: Forgotten Genius of Music, the Story of a Great Musician* (Wilmslow: The North West Player Piano Association, 2002); particularly chapter 13, 'Leginska's Orchestras', 180–206.

7. On Jane Evrard and the Orchestre féminin de Paris', see Laura Hamer, 'On the Conductor's Podium: Jane Evrard and the Orchestre féminin de Paris', *The Musical Times*, Vol. 152, No. 1916 (Autumn 2011), 81–100.

8. Anonymous, *The Boston Herald* (14 October 1929); cited from Marguerite and Terry Broadbent, *Leginska: Forgotten Genius of Music*, 198–9.

9. J. Michele Edwards, 'Women on the Podium', in José Bowen (ed.), *The Cambridge Companion to Conducting* (Cambridge and New York: Cambridge University Press, 2003), 223.

10. Marguerite and Terry Broadbent, *Leginska: Forgotten Genius of Music*, 89.

11. Jeanice Brooks, '*Noble et grande servant de la musique*: Telling the Story of Nadia Boulanger's Conducting Career', *Journal of Musicology*, vol. 14, no. 1 (Winter 1996), 92–116.

12. Ibid., 98.

13. J. Michele Edwards, 'Women on the Podium', 227.

14. Linda Dempf, 'The Woman's Symphony Orchestra of Chicago', *Notes*, Second Series, vol. 62, no. 4 (June 2006), 871.

15. Tim McDonald, 'Veronika Dudarowa: No-Nonsense Russian Conductor Revered in her Own Country', *The Guardian* (6 April 2009), available at www.theguardian.com/music/2009/apr/06/obituary-veronika-dudarova (accessed 1 November 2019).

16. J. Michele Edwards, 'Women on the Podium', 234.

17. Jane Glover cited in ibid., 234.

18. Fiona Maddocks, 'Marin Alsop, Conductor of Last Night of the Proms, On Sexism in Classical Music', *The Guardian* (6 September 2013), available at www.theguardian.com/music/2013/sep/06/marin-alsop-proms-classical-sexist (accessed 28 June 2019).

19. See OrchKids website, http://orchkids.org/ourprogram/ (accessed 27 February 2020).

20. For detailed information on Alsop, see her website: www.marinalsop.com/ (accessed 26 February 2020).

21. Caroline Crampton, 'Marin Alsop on Conducting: "You're Not There to Be Liked"', *New Statesman* (6 April 2017), available at www.newstatesman.com/culture/music-theatre/2017/04/marin-alsop-conducting-you-re-not-there-be-liked?fbclid=IwAR2UCtO-8XcWxI3G4bCeOAxSQ4I2LOXti_A5dpFQDaQyCqXgHNydef6YMTc (accessed 25 February 2020).

22. Maya Salam, 'Marin Alsop Raises the Baton for Women Conductors', *The New York Times* (17 June 2019), available at www.nytimes.com/2019/06/17/arts/marin-alsop-women-conductors.html (accessed 25 February 2020).

23. Caroline Crampton, 'Marin Alsop on Conducting: "You're Not There to Be Liked"'.

24. Maya Salam, 'Marin Alsop Raises the Baton for Women Conductors'.

25. Marin Alsop, Last Night of the Proms, Royal Albert Hall (7 September 2013); full speech available at www.bbc.co.uk/events/edrnc8/play/ax938g/p01g9vrw (accessed 28 June 2019).

26. Fiona Maddocks, 'Marin Alsop, Conductor of the Last Night of the Proms, On Sexism in Classical Music'.

27. On the Taki Concordia Conducting Fellowship, see https://takiconcordia.org /about-tccf/about-the-fellowship/ (accessed 1 July 2019).

28. Marin Alsop, www.marinalsop.com/qa/ (accessed 25 February 2020).

29. See https://alicefarnham.com/pages/women-conductors (accessed 4 December 2020).

30. Alice Farnham, 'Not Just a Cute Girl on a Podium: How to Get More Women Conducting', *The Guardian* (10 September 2015), available at www .theguardian.com/music/2015/sep/10/how-to-get-more-women-conducting-morley-college-alice-farnham (accessed 15 March 2020).

31. Ibid.

32. See https://takiconcordia.org/ (accessed 28 February 2020).

33. See 'Tianyi Lu Joins WNO as First Female Conductor in Residence', WNO website (16 August 2019), https://wno.org.uk/press/tianyi-lu-joins-wno (accessed 28 February 2020).

34. Marin Alsop, Last Night of the Proms, Royal Albert Hall (7 September 2013).

35. Ibid.

Further Reading

Brooks, Jeanice. '*Noble et grande servant de la musique*: Telling the Story of Nadia Boulanger's Conducting Career.' *Journal of Musicology*, vol. 14, no. 1 (Winter 1996), 92–116.

Edwards, J. Michele. 'Women on the Podium', in José Bowen (ed.), *The Cambridge Companion to Conducting* (Cambridge and New York: Cambridge University Press, 2003), 220–36.

Hamer, Laura. 'On the Conductor's Podium: Jane Evrard and the Orchestre féminin de Paris.' *The Musical Times*, vol. 152, no. 1916 (Autumn 2011), 81–100.

Neuls-Bates, Carol. 'Women's Orchestras in the United States, 1925–45', in Jane Bowers and Judith Tick (eds.), *Women Making Music: The Western Art Tradition, 1150–1950* (Urbana and Chicago: University of Illinois Press, 1986), 349–69.

6 | Soloists and Divas: Evolving Opportunities, Identity, and Reception

FRANCESCA PLACANICA

The 2014 Glyndebourne production of *Der Rosenkavalier* sparked controversy,[1] when a number of notorious British critics lambasted the visual appearance of the young mezzo-soprano interpreting Octavian, Irish rising star Tara Erraught (b.1986). The remarks mainly addressed her physique, which the critics claimed detracted from the sensual flair of the extremely luscious *mise en scène*. Writing in *The Financial Times*, Andrew Clark referred to her as 'a chubby bundle of puppy fat'; Andrew Clements described her as 'stocky' in *The Guardian* and Rupert Christiansen as 'dumpy' in *The Telegraph*; Michael Church jibed that Erraught's Octavian had 'the demeanour of a scullery maid' in *The Independent*; and Richard Morrison called her 'unbelievable, unsightly and unappealing' in *The Times*.[2] The backlash that followed this plethora of comments forced the artistic and academic world to look at the operatic scene with disenchanted eyes, questioning the working conditions of women performers in a realm where 'fat-shaming' and sexism could still be applied with such nonchalance.[3] After all, this was unfortunately not a first. In 2004, soprano star Deborah Voigt (b.1960) was fired from a Royal Opera House production of *Ariadne auf Naxos* because of her weight, which apparently hindered the production's envisaged embodiment of Ariadne.[4] Rather than seizing the opportunity to become a fierce voice of dissent against the evil affecting the business, Voigt came back to the scenes after the formidable weight loss of over 9.6 stone (135 pounds), thereby reacquiring in full her diva status, yet submitting to the 'rules of engagement' of the operatic market. In 2018, the #MeToo movement turned the heat of the debate on the even more appalling issue of sexual harassment in the opera business.[5]

These ordeals are eloquent testimonies to the often-unspoken struggle that female performers inhabiting the world of opera and classical music more broadly face, and share with women facing sexist behaviours in other work environments. Evidently, twenty-first-century female performers populate the classical and recording industry in ways and with a 'weight' that was unimaginable only a hundred years ago. Yet, the business is probably still not mature enough to allow the integration of women into the classical music industry without presenting a number of ominous resistances. It is on the intrinsic contradictions characterising the work and lives of female soloists in the twenty-first century that this chapter turns the spotlight, addressing the evolving career opportunities acquired by women performers, and observing the ingrained mechanisms governing notions of identity, reception, sexualisation, and marketing in the classical music business.

Evolving Opportunities and Strenuous Resistances

An increasing number of female classical music practitioners – both instrumentalists and singers – are now the face of recording labels and managing agencies. These advancements were made possible in the twentieth century thanks to a slow, yet progressive, assertion of women's rights, which mirrored in music what was happening at a societal level. The post-1968 cultural revolution was followed by a surge of feminist ideology in music and music studies, and the female soloist began to acquire greater territory in the live concert and recording industry. Although this trend reveals an improvement in terms of opportunities, it is far from representing a radical revolution within the classical music industry as a whole. In fact, the increase of female performers starring as soloists in prestigious concert seasons is not matched by a concurrent growth in the numbers of female instrumentalists within European and American orchestras, where the number of women is still very limited, and the resistance they face during the recruitment process as orchestral players and as board members is still apparent.[6] It should be noted, though, that instrumentalists and singers have always experienced quite different public statuses. The status of the star solo singer has been recognised since the development of monody in the sixteenth and seventeenth centuries, although the cultural burden born by singers is exemplified through the negative (and gendered) connotations associated with the very terms *diva* and *primadonna*.

As music criticism developed throughout the nineteenth century, accounts tended to focus upon female musicians' private and public appearance, rather than their musicianship. Musical professionalism often related to a specific social standing, as an opportunity only reserved to lower middle-class women belonging to musical lineage.[7] This was exacerbated by the essentially patriarchal culture of Romantic aesthetics, and its male-dominated bourgeois social structure, which often relegated female performers to the salon, where women – specifically wives – were admitted and 'tolerated', but annihilated in their aspirations to reach the public eye. An often-cited exception is Clara Wieck Schumann (1819–1896), one of the most accomplished and popular concert pianists of the nineteenth century. Lesser known names, such as the violinists Camilla Urso (1842–1902) and Wilma Norman-Neruda (1838–1911), were hired by orchestras to play as guest soloists, although their engagements often depended on their willingness to appear in very distinctive attires.[8]

In general, throughout the twentieth century, the societal changes demanded by women in everyday life and in the workplace determined a progressive shift in the way musical education and professionalism evolved. Not without resistance, female performers were able to access a wider range of instruments that were traditionally considered inappropriate for women to play (including woodwind, brass, percussion, and the larger strings). More women could enter music education up to conservatoire and university level, while the work of female composers and educators such as Nadia Boulanger in France, Ruth Crawford Seeger in the United States, and Elisabeth Lutyens in Britain left an indelible mark. The way soloists began to access greater work in British, German, and French music societies and orchestras also became a sign of the changing times. This was partly due to the opportunities created by all-female consorts and orchestras in the early twentieth century, often in response to gender discrimination.[9] (See Chapter 5 'On the Podium: Women Conductors' for a discussion of women's orchestras in the earlier twentieth century.) Most importantly, and as time progressed, female instrumentalists became able to enter the professional market and compete with men on a more equal basis. Perhaps the most eloquent testimony to the shift in recognition of women musicians was the birth of academic studies related to the female presence in music history, which originated in the wake of women's studies between the 1960s and 1970s, and critically developed in the 1980s and 1990s through the word of such scholars as Marcia J. Citron, Suzanne Cusick, Susan McClary, Judith Tick, and Jane Bowers (as discussed further in the Preface of the current volume).[10] Although still predominantly dominated by women scholars, the field has impacted on the conventional historical narrative underpinning the canon and has significantly paved the way to introducing a gender discourse in music. Pursuing the feminist perspective, the field has recently branched out to performers and performance studies: it is from this newly forged critical angle that this study stems.

A Question of Identity

My observations of the performance image of female soloists commence from an overview of different understandings of a performer's identity, drawing on a synthesis of some of the definitions attempted by musical performance and philosophy studies. I start with Philip Auslander's assertion that 'what musicians perform first and foremost is not music, but their own identities as musicians, their musical personae'.[11] To define the transitional 'entity that mediates between musicians and the act of performance', Auslander borrows the concept of personage from theatre studies.[12] According to this concept, musicians embody a version of themselves fashioned to the aim of performing in precise conditions, inscribed within the 'frame', that is the main structure, of a musical event.[13] Performance as a 'form of self-presentation' entails that, while some presentations may reach the viewer as a direct prolongation of one's personality, others may be more laborious or even the result of multi-agential constructions.[14] This self-shaping act concurs with 'the expressive equipment of a standard kind intentionally or unwittingly employed by the individual during her performance' to recreate the performer's front.[15] The front manifests the specifics of each performer – not only their techniques and artistry, but their own appearance and physicality – in ways that veer from the conventional conceptions of performance as the projection of a composer's work. From this performer-centred standpoint, musical performances are de facto social interactions, apt to establish communication codes; not only amongst musical collaborators, but also between performers and receivers. For Cusick, the receiving act of the audience is as 'performative' as the musicians' execution; therefore, 'all performances are ensemble pieces', entailing both the presence of audience and performers at a live event, but also their absence in the case of a remote performance experienced through recording.[16] The performer's identity, therefore, is a complex negotiation saturated with all the elements that concur to construct the 'social realm', where such identity is projected and where the spectator-consumer plays an active part as the receiver of this sophisticated communication act. Focusing particularly on the star status of pop performers, Jane Davidson similarly posits the identity of the performer as a multilayered entity, composed by multiple personae: the character of the person performing and asserting their iconic roles through their annexed stage etiquette. Finally, the more-or-less known subjective features of their off-stage personality, now, more than ever, widely spread through the interactivity allowed by social media, which allows an unprecedented proximity to one's favourite star.[17]

Voyeurism and Gaze

The voyeuristic insight into the private life of stage personae allowed by current forms of communications inform the audience's expectations to an even greater extent, even when the performer is not complicit in this mechanism through their online presence. These tensions are not limited to musicianship only; for instance, performers are, likewise, scrutinised for their looks, which is an issue for both female and male performers. However, women are generally more subjected to criticism related to their looks and private lives (especially when they also happen to be mothers and/or wives). On some occasions, even personal choices become targets for negative judgement. For instance, Erraught was not the only performer in the (now notorious) 2014 Glyndebourne production of *Der Rosenkavalier* who was attacked in the press. In addition to ridiculing Erraught's physique, Christiansen was also scathing in his judgement of Kate Royal's (b.1979) performance as Marschallin, describing her as 'short of her best and stressed by motherhood'.[18]

The body-centred mechanisms of musical performance agree with the concept of 'impersonation', which underpins both the agency of the performer and of the consumer.[19] John Rink centres the performer's and listener's corporeality as another foundational element of performance: 'Performers and listeners humanise music – *impersonate* music – by projecting themselves onto it and imagining themselves in it. That is not only why we make "the music": we are playing or listening to what we want it to be, but also why we have the potential to "become" the music as we interact with it.'[20] The desire mechanisms triggered by the immersive power of music as performed are channelled in an encompassing projection of the spectator's self into the idolisation of the source of that experience, the performer's body. As Robert Stam and Roberta Pearson have commented, 'Voyeurism renders desire as a purely visual activity . . . [The voyeur's] invisibility produces the visibility of the objects of his gaze.'[21] In twenty-first-century classical music performance consumerism, the paradox is that the visual surpasses the aural. In film studies, Laura Mulvey dissects the reception act of mainstream film spectatorship through psychoanalytical lenses determining that the conventions conveying pleasure are the result of a sexual tension produced by the active male gaze.[22] The ensuing power dynamics determine the objectification of women's bodies, their dismembering or fetishism into sexual representations fashioned to satisfy the male spectator. This encompassing theory is applied to the wide range of representations of women in performance, where their image is seemingly shaped to satisfy the male receiver. At the same time, by virtue of the mechanisms leading to the reflexive mechanism of impersonation, 'women become erotic objects for spectators within the auditorium, where they become objects of sexual interest and narcissistic pleasure for the spectator's identification with other people'.[23] Mulvey's reading fully applies to the subtle marketing conventions of the current classical music scenario, where female performers' appearances are meticulously packaged to meet the cultural canon of beauty and youth as foundational factors of success.

This type of representation of women in the arts and media is certainly not new to the twenty-first century. The notion of female musicianship as a bodily expression has existed in Western culture since at least the Renaissance. The association of body-musicianship has mainly been conferred on vocalists, with the notion of the voice as a prolongation of the body; however, female instrumentalists were not exempted from this kind of scrutiny, as iconography produced since the Middle Ages records. Throughout the centuries, with the exception of the 'paradox of the fat lady' for opera singers, the expectation that women musicians should project both a desirable look and a desirable sound perpetrated itself consistently; starting from the mid-twentieth century, these demands also eventually impacted heavily on the operatic world.[24] These trends were exacerbated by the emergence of the rock-and-roll scene in the 1950s, and of the pop music video industry in the 1980s and 1990s, which normalised the predominance of the visual over the aural in the leading marketing strategies of female performers and girls bands. (See Part II, 'Women in Popular Music', for a discussion of women's experiences in the popular music industry.) The images of women performers – often heavily sexualised both in song and appearance – were adapted to the expectations of younger audiences, who projected onto their favourite stars their own perspectives and desires. By the turn of the twenty-first century, art music was following the same trend, beginning to borrow marketing models from the competing pop industry, and thereby to promote the sexualised image of female performers. While, in most cases, their male counterparts were still portrayed in tuxedos and bow ties, marketing campaigns for women soloists, chamber music ensemble members, and opera stars began to buy into the advertising establishment that dictated that women should be garbed in revealing attire and adopt (sexually) provocative poses.

Contemporary Soloists in a Mediatised Culture

Over the past few decades, women have forged careers performing instruments which were deemed unsuitable for them until the mid-twentieth century. This is the case, for instance, of trumpeter Alison Balsom (b.1978), who has been awarded an Order of the British Empire (OBE) and two honorary doctorate degrees from Anglia Ruskin University and the University of Leicester. Balsom's recollection of her beginnings as a brass player flags exactly the type of gender bias surrounding the choice of a musical instrument on behalf of children and parents.[25] She has been vocal in denouncing gendered ideas about brass instruments not being appropriate for women and girls: 'I come from a family with no gender bias. I wanted to play the trumpet brilliantly and they encouraged me. It never occurred to me that other people found a female doing this surprising. So I'm aware of my novelty value: a blonde girl playing the trumpet. But a modern woman doesn't have to conform.'[26] Balsom blasts gender inequality in the classical music industry; she divides her time between a top-rank performance career and her work as an advocate for the rights of women working in the arts.[27]

Activism is a common trait of several leading women soloists, who are aware of being perceived as role models. This is also the case of percussionist Dame Evelyn Glennie (b.1965, see Figure 6.1), who defines herself as

Figure 6.1 Dame Evelyn Glennie. Photo credit: Caroline Purday, courtesy of Evelyn Glennie's managing team

'the first percussionist to pursue a career as virtuoso soloist'.[28] Her story is, in fact, unique, not only because of her capacity to build a career in a male-dominated environment, but also because she did so in spite of her profound deafness since the age of eight. Glennie experiences parameters such as pitch and frequency through vibration and an embodied cognition of tones and volumes. Drawing inspiration from her own life experiences, she pursues a busy schedule of activities, working as a speaker, consultant, performer, and composer aiming to teach the world 'how to really listen'.[29] On this, she believes: 'When we listen to music, we assume that it's all been fed through here (points to ears). This is how we experience music. Of course, it's not. We experience thunder, thunder, thunder. Think, think, think. Listen, listen, listen. Now, what can we do with thunder?'[30] She also strives to create new opportunities to access music for the hearing-impaired. As her online platform shows, the percussionist fully capitalises on her multitalented, yet accessible, persona to recruit and inspire her followers; from giving inspirational talks, to musical collaborations and performances, through selling her handmade jewellery, Glennie adapts swiftly to different modes of communication.

Two multifaceted talents of extremely different natures, Balsom and Glennie shape their personae as being very approachable and laid back. While Balsom cultivates the more classical appearance of a virtuosa recording artist for Warner House, Glennie maintains a more relaxed style consistent with her numerous collaborations, spanning classical, contemporary, pop, jazz, and rock repertoires. In both cases, their slick physical appearance, exuding elegance and rigour – although not likely to have been detrimental to their rise to success – is not a key factor in the marketing strategies that construct their personae. This is not the case for many other artists (and their managing teams) that bring physical appearance centre stage.

Within the capitalistic frame of the classical music industry, the survival of an emerging artist's star depends on their capacity to enlarge their fan bases by appealing to the language of mass consumerism. Opera singers have always been on the front line in these strategies. Mainly because of their inherent reliance on embodiment, they are more susceptible to buying into the idea that they must look as desirable as their voices sound. In the twenty-first century, there are numerous singers who engineer their public personae in ways that bring the fashion and cinematic industry close to the operatic world. This, perhaps, is in line with the example set by an iconic star who reached the status of a timeless idol, Maria Callas (1923–77). The cultural impact of Callas's persona is undoubtedly still alive in the twenty-first century, although her submitting to the burgeoning beauty canons of the contemporary fashion world by losing 5.7 stone (eighty pounds) between 1951 and 1953 inaugurated a trend amongst opera singers that subverted once and for all the caricatured stereotype of the fat soprano.[31] Callas's popularity relied on the alchemy of her voice and stage presence, which conferred on her a status of quasi-divinity. Nevertheless, she often paid a dear price in terms of privacy.

Nowadays the immediacy of social media facilitates an artist's negotiation between their private and public persona through the sharing of official and less-official accounts of their daily experiences on their platforms. The ultimate aim is to sell a pretended affinity with the audience member, thus, expanding the immersive mechanism of 'impersonation' to the private sphere. If the reward for complying with this trend is for classical performers to reach out of the traditionally secluded walls of art music and dive into the mass-media scene, the cost is that of succumbing to a rhetoric that encompasses many other aspects of the performance persona. This is the case, for instance, of piano sensation Yuja Wang (b.1987), who cultivates a highly sexualised image, through meticulous attention to fashions that capitalise on her petite body through revealing outfits, which are always complemented by high heels. One of the current faces of the Decca label, she fully invests in the visual construction of her performance persona to the point of identifying her music with her own style. 'If the music is beautiful and sensual, why not dress to fit? It's about power and persuasion. Perhaps it's a little sadomasochistic of me. But if I'm going to get naked with my music, I may as well be comfortable while I'm at it.'[32] Wang's metaphorical language is deliberately provocative and highly sexualised, perfectly tickling the consumerist mechanisms of desire. If music shows its seductive potential, so does the performer that embodies it without fearing to expose her corporeality. Her words could indeed be a clever factor of her marketing strategy; however, if this statement maintains some degree of authenticity, it would raise questions about the sense of self that the musician conveys by identifying her musical persona with her attire. By investing her sexualised image with an iconoclast attitude towards the stiff conventions of concert apparel, Wang entices a new generation of young classical performers to feel entitled to capitalise on their looks as well as on their artistry. Thanks to diligent use of the appropriate social-media platforms, where she promotes luxury brands and fashion firms, Wang reaches an idol status that takes her image well beyond the classical music scene; her looks are shared and promoted by the fashion firms she (or her marketing team) chooses for her recitals around the world.[33]

Many crossover artists fully invest in pop music marketing models, which inform the fashioning of both their image and their musical projects. This is certainly the case with violin prodigy Vanessa Mae (b.1978) and singer Katherine Jenkins (b.1980), who, besides careers as classical concert soloists, promote musical collaborations with pop and rock recording artists, while maintaining their respective popular images though high-level public engagement. While Jenkins cultivates her girl-next-door allure, featuring in television shows and bringing centre stage details of her private life through a clever use of press and social media, Mae's fierce display of her body promotes an over-the-top persona, while her multifarious talents and ability to switch smoothly from genre to genre throws critics into disarray. Engaged in a number of activities running parallel with their performance and recording careers – Jenkins is an Ambassador for Macmillan Cancer Society and well known for her performances for the British Forces Foundation; Mae is an Olympic skier and an actress – both artists have a large fan base, ranging from classical music aficionados to rock and pop listeners, and from television viewers to sports fans. Combining undisputed musical talent with their protean performance personae, their popularity matches their exposure to media to the point where even negative remarks further their popularity. In 2008, for instance, opera star Dame Kiri Te Kanawa (b.1944) attacked 'popera' stars. She diminished Jenkins and other artists' works, prophesying their inevitable artistic demise. Jenkins replied to her criticism, defining herself as being from a 'normal background' and as an advocate for the accessibility of classical music, as opposed to a conservative elite preoccupied with their own survival. 'I think that it's just obvious now that people really like that kind of music [crossover]. I think that it's become its own thing. It shows in the number of sales and I don't think people can ignore that.'[34] In this dynamic, 'sales' and the appreciation of 'the people' seem to determine the value of a musical endeavour.

Interestingly enough, it is difficult to find reports of Mae's work that do not make reference to her appearance. For instance, the criticism which her eclectic repertoire has attracted also addresses the way she uses her body in performance, almost as if her relaxed appearance necessarily equals a lack of musical identity. As Adam Sweeting has commented:

It isn't certain whether Vanessa Mae can succeed in pop, however. She looks the part, since her face and figure make her automatic pin-up fodder. She skipped out on stage wearing a sleeveless, backless sparkly top and hip-hugging pants, which the various lumps of electronic equipment dangling from her belt threatened to pull down at any moment. But it is difficult to take much of her material seriously.[35]

I would not be sure that a critic would refer to a man's work with similar vocabulary, yet this is the rhetoric used to describe Mae, who, needless to say, perhaps embraces it as an aid to further her fame. Certainly, a notable difference from the past is the following: if, once, a negative review or an inopportune digging into personal lives could break a career, nowadays, in the multifarious world of digital communication, negative critiques not only produce major visibility, but also then with the passing of time, become negligible pieces of information, easily overtaken by the frightening amount of material that keeps building up from different sources and media. The rapidity with which this information is absorbed by the media and thrown to the general public highlights new ways to generate popular content and to steer the fan bases for many of these artists. Most importantly, these mechanisms also determine new ways to conceive of popularity as a whole, not only as the fruit of successful mediation between artistic achievements and communication skills, but as the patchy result of good and bad responses to the performer's public personae, whereby negative remarks and personal attacks assume almost the same strategic importance as a positive reception. At any rate, the body of the performer remains the first and foremost element that is subjected to scrutiny, and torn apart on occasion.

In an ideal society that cherishes gender equality as an accomplished objective, the images of talented artists such as Wang, Jenkins, and Mae should be testimony to their empowerment and, even more so, to their freedom to fashion their image according to their personal taste; ultimately, the way they dress, move or age should be a negligible detail in the eyes of the general public and press. However, the harsh reality is that our society has failed to achieve equality and is currently even experiencing a regression in terms of civil rights. For this reason, the fear remains legitimate that the model represented by these artists might be absorbed into the consumeristic mechanisms of reification and mass-commercialisation of the female image that are so embedded in the current star system.

Conclusions

The number of women soloists with prominent roles in the classical music business has multiplied. From the 2000s on, leading female artists have become the faces of an increasing number of record labels; this has included historical brands such as Decca, Sony Classics, EMI, and Warner Classics, which have set an example for burgeoning independent labels. This is, perhaps, a consequence of the new marketing strategies adopted by classical labels, which, following the example of pop music labels, relinquished the paradigm of the white male master to begin to foster the work of younger women classical performers and attract minorities and younger audiences. This new generation of performers relies on the fashioning of their public image, communicated via a consistent online presence, through which they appeal to a large fan base. They often engage with parallel activities alongside their musical careers to voice their multiple talents and world views, and many espouse charitable causes.

These performers' public personae are often packaged according to marketing conventions that capitalise not only on their musical abilities, orientations, and collaborations, but also on their appearance; in many cases, putting this, rather than their sound, under the spotlight. The issue of the performer's identity is at stake here. Performance as the projection of a musician's persona within a social realm entails the interaction of multiple agencies, not least that of the spectator-consumer, who impose their desires onto the performer and her body, triggering an 'impersonating' act. What we witness is the construction of the performer's marketed identity through the active male gaze, which inscribes the work and life of these musicians within a patriarchal power dynamic. In short, if the twenty-first-century music industry sees women taking centre stage, its main structure and the rhetoric which derives from that structure still respond to an old-fashioned capitalistic scheme, which manufactures the performer's images in ways that con-solidate not only the male gaze but, especially, the male voice. This pervading filter often emerges through the sexist remarks of press and critics, or the statistics for the number of women hired in orchestras or present in the higher ranks of music establishments or within academia or the conservatoires. Ultimately, the male status quo remains unchallenged, despite an apparent acquiescence to female talent. In light of the luminous examples of some of the performers discussed in this chapter, if we still have to live with the presence of women soloists in the music industry as a concession, something is wrong with the classical music 'social realm' in ways that do not differ from many other work contexts.

Notes

1. Richard Strauss, *Der Rosenkavalier*; Richard Jones, director; Robin Ticciati, conductor, London Philharmonic Orchestra, Glyndebourne Opera House, 21 May–3 July 2014.

2. Andrew Clark, 'Der Rosenkavalier, Glyndebourne, East Sussex, UK – Review', *The Financial Times* (19 May 2014), available at www.ft.com/content/d135e9dc-dce3 -11e3-b73c-00144feabdc0 (accessed 28 May 2019); Andrew Clements, 'Der Rosenkavalier Review – New Glyndebourne Staging Lacks Emotion', *The Guardian* (19 May 2014), available at www.theguardian.com/music/2014/may/19/ der-rosenkavalier-review-glyndebourne-jones-ticciati (accessed 28 May 2019); Rupert Christiansen, 'Glyndebourne 2014: Der Rosenkavalier, Review', *The Telegraph* (19 May 2014), available at www.telegraph.co.uk/culture/music/ classicalconcertreviews/10839018/Glyndebourne-2014-Der-Rosenkavalier- review.html (accessed 8 June 2019); Michael Church, '*Der Rosenkavalier*, Glyndebourne, opera review: 'Perversely Cast', *The Independent* (19 May 2014), available at www.independent.co.uk/arts-entertainment/classical/reviews/der- rosenkavalier-glyndebourne-opera-review-perversely-cast-9395750.html (accessed 28 May 2019); and Richard Morrison, 'Der Rosenkavalier at Glyndebourne', *The Times* (19 May 2014), available at www.thetimes.co.uk/article/ der-rosenkavalier-at-glyndebourne-klm3mn7fkn2 (accessed 28 May 2019).

3. See, for instance, Anastasia Tsioulcas, 'In 2014, The Classical World Still Can't Stop Fat-Shaming Women', *National Public Radio* (20 May 2014), available at www.npr.org/sections/deceptivecadence/2014/05/20/314007632/ in-2014-the-classical-world-still-cant-stop-fat-shaming-women? t=1559992913450 (accessed 28 May 2019); Katie Lowe, 'Opera Reviewers: Forget the Body Shaming and Focus on the Singing', *The Guardian* (19 May 2014), available at www.theguardian.com/commentisfree/2014/may/19/ opera-reviewers-body-shaming-focus-singing-tara-erraught-glyndebourne (accessed 8 June 2019); I should point out that in my short overview most of the responses to these sexist remarks were, sadly enough, authored by female columnists only.

4. David Browning, 'Deborah Voigt: Off the Scales', *CBS News* (29 January 2006), cited by Julie C. Dunbar, *Women, Music, Culture* (New York and London: Routledge, 2010), 189.

5. For instance, the numerous reports of sexual harassment by Swedish opera singers in the wake of the '#MeToo' movement were cited as the main cause for the suicide of opera conductor Benny Fredriksson. See, for instance, Lia Eustachewich, 'Famed Opera Singer Blames Husband's Suicide on #MeToo Movement', *The New York Post* (31 July 2018), available at https://nypost.com /2018/07/31/famed-opera-singer-blames-husbands-suicide-on-metoo- movement/ (accessed 26 May 2019).

6. See Dunbar, *Women, Music, Culture*, 204–13.

7. Nancy B. Reich, 'Women as Musicians: A Question of Class', in Ruth A. Solie (ed.), *Musicology and Difference: Gender and Sexuality in Music Scholarship* (Berkeley and Los Angeles: University of California Press, 1995), 129–30.

8. Dunbar, *Women, Music, Culture*, 202.

9. Dunbar, *Women, Music, Culture*, 195–214.

10. Jane Bowers and Judith Tick (eds.), *Women Making Music: The Western Art Tradition, 1150–1950* (Urbana and Chicago: University of Illinois Press, 1987), 10.

11. Philip Auslander, 'Musical Personae', *The Drama Review*, vol. 50, no. 1 (2006), 102.

12. Auslander, 'Musical Personae', 102.

13. Auslander, 'Musical Personae', 108. Auslander also borrows the key terms of his analysis from Stan Godlovitch, *Performance Philosophy* (London and New York: Routledge, 1998).

14. Auslander, 'Musical Personae', 103.

15. Ibid., 108.

16. Suzanne G. Cusick, 'Gender and the Cultural Work of a Classical Music Performance', *Repercussions*, vol. 3, no. 1 (Spring 1994), 81.

17. Jane Davidson, 'The Solo Performer's Identity', in Raymond MacDonald, David J. Hargreaves, and Dorothy Miell (eds.), *Musical Identities* (Oxford: Oxford University Press, 2002), 111.

18. Rupert Christiansen, 'Glyndebourne 2014: *Der Rosenkavalier.*'

19. John Rink, 'Impersonating the Music in Performance', in Raymond MacDonald, David J. Hargreaves, and Dorothy Miell (eds.), *Handbook of Musical identities* (Oxford: Oxford University Press, 2017), 361.

20. Rink, 'Impersonating the Music in Performance', ibid.

21. Robert Stam and Roberta Pearson, 'Hitchcock's Rear Window: Reflexivity and the Critique of Voyeurism', in Marshall Deutelbaum and Leland Poague (eds.), *A Hitchcock Reader* (Oxford: Blackwell Publishing, 2009), 204.

22. Laura Mulvey, 'Visual Pleasure and Narrative Cinema', *Screen*, vol. 16, no. 3 (1975), 6–18.

23. Stephen Regan, 'Reception Theory, Gender and Performance', in Lizbeth Goodman and Jane De Gay (eds.), *The Routledge Reader to Gender and Performance* (London: Routledge, 1998), pp. 295-8.

24. Samuel Abel, *Opera in the Flesh* (Boulder, CO: Westview Press, 1996), 11-21.

25. See, for instance, Susan M. Tarnowski, 'Gender Bias and Musical Instrument Preference', *Update: Applications of Research in Music Education*, vol. 12, no. 1 (1993), 14–21. For more recent statistics, see Anonymous, 'People Still Show a Massive Gender Bias When It Comes to Musical Instruments', *The Irish News* (7 February 2017), available at www.irishnews.com/magazine/2017/02/07/news/people-still-show-a-massive-gender-bias-when-it-comes-to-musical-instruments-923487/ (accessed 24 May 2019).

26. Louette Harding, 'Alison Balsom: The Classical Soloist Who Has a Lot to Blow Her Trumpet About', *The Daily Mail Online* (11 December 2011), available at

www.dailymail.co.uk/home/you/article-2070684/Alison-Balsom-The-classical
-soloist-lot-blow-trumpet-about.html (accessed 24 May 2019).

27. Rick Burin, 'In the News: Alison Balsom Trumpets Gender Equality Ahead of Hall
    Show', *The Royal Albert Hall* (3 February 2017), available at www
    .royalalberthall.com/about-the-hall/news/2017/february/in-the-news-alison-
    balsom-trumpets-gender-equality-ahead-of-royal-albert-hall-show/ (accessed
    24 May 2019).

28. Evelyn Glennie, 'About', available at www.evelyn.co.uk/mission-statement/
    (accessed 24 May 2019).

29. Evelyn Glennie, 'Mission', www.evelyn.co.uk/mission-statement/ (accessed
    26 May 2019).

30. TED Conferences, 'Evelyn Glennie: How to Truly Listen', Monterey,
    California (February 2003), available at www.youtube.com/watch?
    v=IU3V6zNER4g (accessed 26 May 2019).

31. Arianna Huffington, *Maria Callas: The Woman behind the Legend* (Blue Ridge
    Summit, PA: Cooper Square Press, 2002), 221.

32. Fiona Maddocks, 'Yuja Wang: 'If the Music is Beautiful and Sensual, Why Not
    Dress to Fit?', *The Guardian* (9 April 2017), available at www.theguardian.com
    /music/2017/apr/09/yuja-wang-piano-interview-fiona-maddocks-royal-
    festival-hall (accessed 25 May 2019).

33. See Yuja Wang Instagram profile, available at www.instagram.com/yujawang
    .official/ (accessed 25 May 2019)

34. Hannah Furness, 'Katherine Jenkins: Why Classical Music Snobs Are Wrong',
    The Telegraph (20 January 2014), available at www.telegraph.co.uk/culture/
    music/music-news/10585261/Katherine-Jenkins-why-classical-music-snobs-
    are-wrong.html (accessed 26 May 2019).

35. Adam Sweeting, 'Vanessa Mae, Palladium, London', *The Guardian*
    (27 November 2001), available at www.theguardian.com/culture/2001/nov/27/
    artsfeatures5 (accessed 26 May 2019).

Further Reading

Auslander, Philip. 'Musical Personae.' *The Drama Review*, vol. 50, No. 1 (2006),
    100–19.

Davidson, Jane. 'The Solo Performer's Identity', in Raymond MacDonald, David
    J. Hargreaves, and Dorothy Miell (eds.), *Musical Identities* (Oxford: Oxford
    University Press, 2002), 97–115.

Mulvey, Laura. 'Visual Pleasure and Narrative Cinema.' *Screen*, vol. 16, no. 3
    (1975), 6–18.

In Her Own Words: Practitioner Contribution 1

ELIZABETH HOFFMAN

As I sit contemplating where my story as a practising, then aspiring, and finally professional woman composer begins, I immerse myself fleetingly in fragments of feminist Beat poet Diane di Prima's *Recollections of My Life as a Woman*. I am moved by her embodied flailings as she searches in the 1960s for 'what [womanhood] is [or, was]. How to do it. Or get through it. Or bear it. Or sparkle like ice underfoot'.[1] On my desk, too, is Suzanne G. Cusick's intricately researched portrait of seventeenth-century Medici court composer Francesca Caccini, and the 'circulation of power' that governed her personal and professional lives.[2] One passage from this book's Introduction catches a nerve, in sympathetic vibration: 'we do not so much need rooms of our own . . . as [we do] ways of being . . . that allow us to engage with the often immobilising and silencing effects of gender norms'.[3]

It's been at the professional level that such immobilisations – metaphorical brakes and roadblocks – have been a norm for me. I feel acclimated, but they drain energy. If, as Judith Butler contends, gender is constructed performance,[4] I hope I appear more like a drought-resistant tree than one with branches breaking under snow. It often feels like the latter. A thriving persona is hard to construct, since a tired battling of the elements is constant. The 'No-Exit-like' societal gaze never ends. This has fostered my empathy for others, and encouraged me to intervene in contexts that reinforce in- and out-group formation. Gender often seems an arbitrary marker; but sexism, like racism, has a distinct set of mechanisms and debilitating effects.

***

My earliest memories of musical aspirations still haunt me with complex feelings. I knew very young that my mom had given up music 'to have a family'. I learned later that she also gave up poetry and ballet. This made me angry since I wanted to tell her she shouldn't have. Despite this, it was my mom who instilled in me subtle musical sensitivity, and awe of music as a magical internal locus. And, yet, she lacked the confidence to coach me or to share her opinions at all. Perhaps my mom's own received messaging as a young adult was not unlike that conveyed to Cusick's Caccini, who 'would learn (by play) to lead a virtuous, chaste, industrious, and useful life'.[5] Both cathecting and rejecting, I was determined by the time I was eight or so not to lead a (purely) useful life.

I understood even then that the genders were somehow on opposite sides of a divide, but I didn't realise that music – its practice and creation – was tethered in the cavernous gap. How could something so beautiful be anything but transformative? I ridiculed my first piano teacher's assurance that women lacked the 'stamina' to concertise. (She was eccentric, had stamina, told me nuns had cracked rulers on her fingers, and didn't seem to like music much.) But, she wasn't alone in sharing opinions about musicking rules in a gendered world. Conservatory audition faculty told me that my Beethoven Op. 26 lacked 'masculinity'. Who trained or ordained them to assess performative gender quotients? Perhaps my nascent awareness of music's entanglement with feminism was galvanised then, since I did run to recover in a room of my own. Longer term, I internalised the experiential fact that I always had to prove myself. As a daily diet, if you are what you eat, this is constant malnourishment.

My education in college broadened but did not include women's music courses; there were none. I had to wait until the 1990s to ask the rhetorical Beethoven interpretation question above. I met Susan McClary in John Rahn's Feminist Music Theory class during graduate study. But I was unaware feminism had much left to do; rarely to that point had I felt 'exceptional' due to my class status as opposed to imagined personal deficits. I recall discomfort hearing the narrative of a housemate: she was a Chinese engineer receiving job nibbles given her qualifications and given the non-interference (it's easy to infer) of her gender-unclear first name. She never proceeded past the interview stages that followed the 'Dear Mr. . . .' letter invites. Still, in a hopeful bubble, I didn't see music as a male-dominated field. I felt at ease amidst ponytailed male computer programmers in grad school performing their own intervention in masculinity, and I was mostly validated by my professors. A sense of feminine handicap appeared later, as a shock, in my academic job context.

A sundry list of the workplace distractions I've navigated for decades would not be exceptional in itself, but the items newly unsettle me when clustered: (1) being asked to do the same job as a male colleague without equal compensation; (2) being told explicitly by numerous male colleagues of all ranks over a fifteen-year span that I am unsuited for leadership; (3) being routinely excluded from integral discussion of needs and solutions for a programme that I co-direct. I've heard of female colleagues told by administrators that their awards would be strategically omitted from mention to avoid overshadowing a male colleague. I was told as a first-year hire not to apply for a grant that a mid-level male faculty might also be competing for. I hear frequent tales of conference harassment. One recent story with a visual pathos: an unwanted public display of a tap on the rear by someone with a power differential, congratulating a presenter.

Yes, this is breathtaking from a foothold in the #MeToo era. The status quo hasn't changed much, so far as I've seen over my career. I'm happy to know that my hire into a composition programme was a productive event on the diversity front. I'm the first female in my department to have advanced from Assistant to tenured. Support from the university would have been welcome along the way; individuals isolated by discrimination deserve to have their challenges acknowledged by any system that is part of the dysfunction. Technology has become especially meaningful for me as a medium in which to question what creative tools mean, how they work, who makes them, and how it feels to use them in this gendered world. Especially since there's still few women full professors in music composition or technology, a trusted confidante for coping with layered aspects of power differentials is invaluable. Elainie and Meg are, for me, two pillars. So are former students, many now academics. Current students are equally savvy, though rarely see the whole landscape. I am glad about this, but finding ways to share, mentor, and yet protect is challenging. It is important to remember that official patriarchal narratives are not the only problems in musicological discourse; historiographies include the thoughts in our heads. It's important to note that women faculty may have steeper norms to circumnavigate than students, since students buttress narratives of dependence and colleagues generally don't. A hopeful caveat is that gender trouble does not lie under every unturned rock. Many male colleagues see women as people first, and many men are allies and supporters of women. The #MeToo and Bystander Intervention movements have provided new forms of camaraderie.

***

It's remarkable that music's comfort envelops a listener regardless of gender, colour, ethnicity, class. For me, attachment to music was immediate. I heard my mom play Chopin before I was born; I composed small pieces before I knew what composing was. A male college teacher took my composition activities seriously. For that last historical punctum, I'm grateful, since musicking is my life. If the music we write is a series of actions that embody instructions to recreate a set of actions, then our 'making a certain kind of music produces a certain kind of person'.[6] Increasingly, I believe that I compose my psychological wholeness – not through identification with the role of 'composer' or 'woman composer', but through self-discovery and affirmation. Mostly, I write music for its own sake, that is, for how it makes me feel in creating it, and for the sheer residual satisfaction of having used one's imagination reaching for a no-premises-involved creative thought. I cherish serendipitous discoveries with collaborators. In the face of dispiriting gender divides in the professional realm, making music and talking about it is, for me, a self-sustaining act, ideally, fancifully, a purifying force for good in the world.

How does one practise more applied forms of resilience through musical activity? In teaching I can set my own codes of professionalism and form my own assessments of what's best for a student despite the often-unwritten rules and layered agendas that shape much of what we do. I can interact with institutions or individuals as I choose, in response to their politics and values. Pre-empting gender-coded critiques is important. Men who don't show for meetings are more frequently de facto 'busy' academics, while women last to arrive are de facto 'cavalier'. This is familiar terrain that impacts our socialising and teaching. It is the adjudicating that is so harmful. We all are, after all, just people. Finding ways to be a pleasant irritant, dispassionately sharing passion rather than frustration in promoting awareness of gender-norm-laden behaviours seems a valuable skill. It's essential for women students to see this, since otherwise the – mostly subliminal – messaging around them will be set to repeat the cycles of marginalisation. Finally, the most gratifying act for me: I can write the music I wish to write. I hope to assure students through example that music doesn't need validation by the patriarchy or by an institution, usually patriarchal. The work–life balance message for women is a double-edged sword, since they are just as free to be obsessively focused on work as anyone. But for those who want balance, especially single moms, accommodation and support are deserved.

My essay's conclusion aspires towards positivity. For me, there exists a community of awe-inspiring women from whom I've derived strength for decades. They're vibrant role models, infinitely varied in their resistance to the status quo of subtle and overt exclusionary practices. I have shared rich conversation about sound and personal triumphs and tribulations with composers Annea Lockwood, Judy Klein, Daria Semegen, Diane Thome (my graduate advisor), Abbie Conant, Linda Dusman, Miya Masaoka, Lee Heuermann, Maria de Alvear, Linda Dusman, Yvonne Troxler, Shiau-uen Ding, Elizabeth Adams, Mara Helmuth, Laurie Spiegel, and others; and musicologists Gascia Ouzounian, Brigid Cohen, Annie Randall, and more; and, mea culpa, I am leaving out countless inspirational colleagues – including male friends and colleagues, and current and former students of all genders. Musicologist Suzanne Cusick, from whom I learn something even in the most mundane but literary emails: thank you. If challenges lead to tighter friendships, there is a silver lining in being a woman composer.

In figuring out 'how to do it, [... or at least how to] get through it',[7] I have come to value my female friendships as a special category of relationship. We can reclaim the value of gendered norms as we dismantle the rubric slowly. In my music I cultivate interconnected listening pathways, and sensorially weighted complexities; I write music that aspires to move in much the way that I like to converse with people who make me feel alive, and happy to be sharing time with them through conversation.

Hyper-sensitised to the trauma of living as a woman in our culture, I perceive within seconds whether someone sees me as 'woman' or as a 'person'. If the former, I brace myself, searching for creative modes of response, treating the interchange as research. Through it all (i.e. my stories of frustration) my dad now thumps his chest proudly, saying 'Me, Too, Me, Too' so routinely that I, too, feel pride, pleasure, and support from that simple performative gesture by someone who has come to understand. The challenges of being a woman in the world are becoming increasingly evident to those who care to see a future that is more inclusive in its distribution of power and resources, and in its allowances for those who wish to contribute, using our imagination and lived experience to prompt a better world in which music continues to be a profound part.

Notes

1. Diane di Prima, *Recollections of My Life as a Woman* (New York: Viking, 2001), 27.
2. Suzanne G. Cusick, *Francesca Caccini at the Medici Court: Music and the Circulation of Power* (Chicago: University of Chicago Press, 2009).
3. Suzanne G. Cusick, *Francesca Caccini at the Medici Court*, xxiv.
4. See in particular, Judith Butler, *Gender Trouble: Feminism and the Subversion of Identity* (New York and London: Routledge, 1990).
5. Ibid., 5.
6. Ibid., xxiv.
7. Diane di Prima, *Recollections of My Life as a Woman*, 27.

PART II

Women in Popular Music

Most of My Sheroes Don't Appear on a Stamp: Contextualising the Contributions of Women Musicians to the Progression of Jazz

TAMMY L. KERNODLE

In 1995 the United States Postal Service issued a new instalment in its American Music postage-stamp series. That same year I was gifted with a set of commemorative cards replicating these stamps. As I excitedly opened the package, I was surprised that the series featured no women musicians. While I was thrilled to see the beautiful images of Thelonius Monk, Errol Garner, John Coltrane, Charlie Parker, and several other influential jazz musicians, I was disappointed about the lack of representation as it related to women instrumentalists. It is hard not to view such omissions as the continued promotion of a historical narrative that privileges the intellectual contributions of men. Such omissions raise many questions. What would an inclusive survey of jazz's history read and sound like? Would promoting a more inclusive historical model radically disrupt our understanding of the cultural and sonic aspects of jazz? While I cannot exhaustively address these questions, in this essay I will survey how women musicians (instrumentalists and singers) contributed to the progression of jazz during the period when it shifted from the insular environment of New Orleans' black and Creole communities to the American leisure infrastructure that propelled cultural trends in the late nineteenth and early twentieth centuries.

[handwritten margin note: 1995: USPS issued new postage stamps w/ jazz musicians — but no female musicians ↓ even though women contributed heavily to the jazz movement as it shifted from New Orleans to American leisure infrastructure]

Mapping the Culture of Jazz

Jazz, by its musical practices and subculture perpetuates an 'underground', male-dominated community, that dictates a musical hierarchy based on one's ability to play harder, faster, and longer than the next person and one's ability to generate highly creative, spontaneous musical statements or solos. The importance ascribed to the solo in a jazz performance centres the music in intellectual labour that is not generally associated with women. Because it originates with musical and aesthetical values that eschew European conventions regarding masculinity and femininity, the public

[handwritten margin note: jazz has been a male-dominated community]

103

jazz in corperates many dif. cultures, but importantly for west africa

→

Unlike europe

and private, black women have been able to negotiate some, but not all of the politics of jazz more stealthily. Although jazz pulls from many different cultural and musical sources, most important is its link with West Africa. The musical traditions of this region differed significantly from those of Europe, as music not only served as an extension of everyday life but was also communal in practice. While there are specific gendered aspects to certain types of ritualised music, for the most part women actively and equally engaged in musical performances. This was the opposite of European traditions, which (largely) prohibited, until the nineteenth century, women from public performance unless within the church. It was not until the eighteenth and nineteenth centuries that women had full access to musical instruction. The roots of jazz are traced back to the musical practices that evolved out of cultural engagement between African slaves and Europeans within the milieu of early America.

reasons why women were not part of jazz

– environment
– idea women were not capable musicians
– gendered ideas of instruments

The music that came to be called jazz, or jass (the original spelling of the word), developed out of a number of cultural and social practices that excluded women: brass/military bands, rural blues, and ragtime. The confluence of these genres pervaded late-nineteenth-century New Orleans and quickly became an important part of the city's ritualistic life. There were a number of reasons as to why women musicians were not active in this early period. First, jazz was incubated in spaces that were generally deemed inappropriate for women of good reputation (e.g. streets, brothels, dance halls, the red-light district Storyville). The politics of respectability denoted that no self-respecting woman would perform outside of the home and for monetary profit. Second, there was the prevailing belief that women were not capable musicians or composers by virtue of their emotional and physical abilities. This also extended to gendered notions regarding instruments. Only instruments that did not compromise feminine graces (e.g. piano, harp, guitar, banjo) were acceptable. Thus, women were limited in their music making as well as in exposure to musical instruction.[1] These precepts did not, however, dissuade some women from performing in public and as the popularity of jazz increased, it provided options for working-class blacks to escape poverty.

Americans' growing infatuation with leisure culture in the late nineteenth century precipitated the mainstreaming of many forms of music that were initially heard primarily within the insular environment of Southern and Midwestern black communities. The integration of ragtime, blues, and spirituals into minstrel shows during this period enabled women performers to develop knowledge of the repertory and performance approaches that were to be identified as the early jazz aesthetic. The women who were able to penetrate the fraternal ranks of the early New Orleans scene did so because their talent was acknowledged and promoted by established male musicians or because they performed as part of familial units. In New Orleans during the early twentieth century, bandleaders like Oscar 'Papa' Celestin were important in recognising the talents of young female musicians. For almost two decades he led the house band at the Tuxedo Dance Hall. There were a number of female pianists that worked with the band during this period including Emma Barrett, the celebrated 'Bell Gal', and Jeanette Salvant Kimball. Domestic relationships, legal and common-law, also allowed women musicians to navigate the politics of respectability and the perils of the performing life.

Vaudeville and minstrel shows offered the first opportunities for black female performers. Segregation laws in the South and Midwest kept black and white performers separated, but many of the black performers managed to sustain successful careers. The Alabama Minstrels featured Mrs Henry Hart during the 1860s and 1870s. Lisetta Young, mother of famed saxophonist Lester Young, toured first with her family and later with her husband, Billy Young, during the first decade of the twentieth century.[2] Isabele Taliaferro Spiller travelled with the Musical Spillers, whose personnel included saxophonists Alice Calloway, Mildred Creed, Helen Murphy, Leora Meoux Henderson, and May and Mayda Yorke.[3] While these bands featured female brass and woodwind players, most of the professional female musicians during the late nineteenth and early twentieth centuries were pianists.

As one of the primary instruments taught to women of status, the piano became the centre of amateur female music making. Most women performed only in the home, but the transition of jazz into dance halls, jook joints, and tent shows provided opportunities for many black women. These women created a stomping, strong style of piano playing that became commonly known as 'gutbucket' or 'barrelhouse' piano. This style reflected a pianist's ability to capture the melodic, harmonic, and rhythmic aspects of the complete band within the full range of the piano. Gutbucket and barrelhouse piano styles were identified by their driving left-hand rhythm, which replicated the function of the drums and bass, and the improvised melodies played in the right hand. The melodies performed reflected a range of genres from the blues, to hymns, rags, and stomps.

Emma Barrett (1898–1982) was one of the first notable women to convey this style in early New Orleans jazz bands. Barrett learned to play by listening to street musicians. She became a member of Papa Celestin's famed Original Tuxedo Orchestra, and in 1923 became the first black female instrumentalist to record.[4] Like many of her peers, Barrett adapted a hard-driving approach to her playing that shattered the myth of a feminine approach to the piano. She bore the appellation the 'Bell Gal' because of her signature outfit; red dress, red garters, and jingling knee bells, which ornamented her playing.[5] After Celestin disbanded his group in 1928, she played intermittently with other bands for the next decade. She was an important part of the revival of New Orleans jazz during the post-Second-World-War years, performing weekly at the Happy Landing, a nightclub in Pecaniere, Louisiana. In 1961 Riverside Records released the album *The Bell Gal and Her Dixieland Boys Featuring Jim Robinson*, which provides strong sonic evidence of Barrett's piano playing. It also reveals the eclecticism of the post-war New Orleans repertory, as the remastered version includes bawdy blues tunes like 'I Ain't Gonna Give Nobody None of This Jelly Roll', standards including 'When the Saints Go Marching In', and original tunes such as 'The Bell Gal's Careless Blues' and 'Sweet Emma's Blues'. She would go on to record three more albums before suffering a stroke in 1968. Despite being partially paralysed, Barrett continued to perform with one hand until her death in 1983.

Migrations and the Birth of New Sounds

As America entered the First World War and continued the progression of the industrial revolution in the North, Southern blacks and whites began to migrate from the South in huge numbers. A parallel migration of jazz musicians brought considerable changes to the cultural life of cities like Chicago, Pittsburgh, Kansas City, San Francisco, and New York. It was in these spaces that New Orleans musicians interacted with a growing pool of proficient women musicians. The proliferation of music education within public school systems and the emergence of American conservatories during the last two decades of the nineteenth century significantly impacted the public and private music making of women. No longer relegated to the piano, harp, guitar, and banjo, a generation of brass and woodwind players emerged. Due to the connection between jazz and disreputable forms of leisure culture (e.g. prostitution, drinking, gambling, etc.), white female instrumentalists avoided the genre, opting to focus their attention on classical music and light dinner music. But for black women, the migration of jazz and blues provided opportunities for upward mobility.[6]

At a time when most working-class black women had limited economic choices (e.g. agricultural work, prostitution, domestic work), vaudeville circuits like the Theater Owners Booking Association (TOBA), speakeasies, and nightclubs provided more lucrative ways to make a living. The TOBA was the major booking agency for black vaudeville talent during the time. Despite the problems and hardships encountered by performers, it provided in most cases consistent employment and national exposure. Opportunities increased even more when Mamie Smith's 'Crazy Blues' in 1920 initiated a recording boom that fuelled America's thirst for black music during the height of the Jazz Age. While black women dominated this genre as singers, they also provided instrumental accompaniment.

The young black women that came to prominence in this historical period came from similar backgrounds. Most showed some musical promise at an early age and either developed that talent through formal training or on their own. The majority were born in the South and had either remained there or migrated to the North with their families during the years that preceded the First World War. They were raised in fundamental churches and left home during their adolescence to make a better life for themselves or to support their households. Regional music scenes such as those in Kansas City, St Louis, Memphis, New York, and Chicago boasted a roster of several active young women like saxophonist Irma Young and trumpeter Dolly Jones, who played in bands that performed in a variety of settings.

Chicago as Jazz's Second City

Chicago-based musicians took the foreground in introducing New Orleans jazz to Northern audiences. The genre became an important connection to home for many of the migrants, who discovered that the urban North was not as progressive in its social politics as they had hoped. Despite documented resistance against the proliferation of Southern culture in the North, jazz came to dominate the music scene in 1920s Chicago. One of the leading bands of the era, Joe 'King' Oliver's Creole Jazz Band, included one of Chicago's most talented musicians, Lil Hardin (1898–1971). Known as 'Jazz Wonder Child', Hardin's ability to read and write music made it possible for the unwritten 'head' arrangements that dominated the early New Orleans jazz aesthetic to be written down and preserved. Her piano playing, although sometimes very subtle, was featured on many of Oliver's early recordings, including the famous 'Dippermouth Blues', which became an early jazz standard.

In 1924 Hardin changed the course of jazz history when she married a young Louis Armstrong, urged him to pursue a solo career, and instructed him in music fundamentals. Although Armstrong would later deny the impact Lil had on his career, evidence of this influence can be found in his early post-Oliver band recordings. Lil composed a number of the group's repertory including the celebrated 'Struttin' With Some Barbeque', 'Brown Girl', and 'Hotter Than That'. These arrangements, as well as Louis' performances, were significant in shifting the performance aesthetic of jazz in the late 1920s. They served as a template for the music produced by the generation of musicians who were increasingly privileging solo improvisation over the collective improvisation of the early New Orleans style. As musicianship increased, the repertory that musicians played widened beyond the standards of the previous generation. Lil Hardin's arrangements became an important part of a new canon of songs. After the two separated in the 1930s, Lil continued to perform, recording with various all-female and male groups. Unfortunately, she would disappear from national attention during the height of the big band era, only to remerge during the Dixieland Revival of the 1950s.

Hardin's talent as an arranger was unmistakable, but she was not the only prominent female musician working Chicago's early jazz scene. Famed bandleader, arranger, and pianist Lovie Austin (1887–1972) started her career playing the vaudeville circuit of the 1920s. Later she led her own group, Lovie Austin and Her Blues Serenaders, directed her own musical shows, and served as the house pianist at Paramount Records. Her stint at Paramount earned her a place in both jazz and blues historiographies, as she provided accompaniment for and wrote arrangements for singers such as Ma Rainey, Ida Cox, and Ethel Waters. She worked with noted jazzmen such as Louis Armstrong, Johnny Dodds, and Kid Ory during these years. A number of historic recordings from the period bear Austin's name as pianist or arranger, including 'Downhearted Blues' and 'Travelin' Blues', which made her one of the few jazzwomen to profit from the growing popularity of jazz.

Jazz in a New York State of Mind

By the late 1920s New York was replacing Chicago as the city of music, and many musicians migrated east. The Harlem Renaissance and the proliferation of black dance bands and nightclubs drew musicians to New York. The popularity of these bands also marked the beginning of a new 'age' in jazz, cultivated by a new generation of players who attempted to validate the black experience with their music. Duke Ellington, Fletcher Henderson, Don Redman, and others gave America new sonic representations of jazz, sparked new dances, and provided new visual images of the jazz musician. Some of these bands consisted of black female musicians, not only as pianists, but also as brass and woodwind players.

The Fletcher Henderson band, which set the standard for thirties big band music, occasionally featured the bandleader's wife Leora Meoux (1893–1958). Leora played not only the trumpet, but also the saxophone. She met Fletcher while working on a riverboat and credits him and Louis Armstrong with teaching her how to play jazz.[7] She married Henderson, 'the architect of swing', in 1924 and took an active role as arranger, and road manager for the group. Occasionally she played sax and second trumpet in the band, but she was permanently aligned with the Musical Spillers, The Negro Women's Orchestral and Civic Association, Lil Armstrong's All-Girl Band, and her own group the Vampires.[8]

Kansas City, Here I Come: The Sound of the Southwestern Jazz Scene

Kansas City, Missouri, just like Chicago and New York, became an important cultural centre due to a burgeoning infrastructure of nightclubs, dance halls, brothels, and bars. The city quickly earned the distinction of being the 'Casbah of the Midwest' and served as the de facto 'capital' of the Southwestern jazz scene. In this region, which stretched into Texas, Oklahoma, Kansas, and as far west as Denver, Colorado, territory bands, along with pianists playing both ragtime and a blues-based piano style known as boogie-woogie supported a vibrant musical scene that catered to black and white listeners. A number of musicians, singers, and performers traversed this region, with many opting to remain in the city. Pianist Mary Lou Williams (1910–81) moved to the city in 1928 after her husband, saxophonist John Williams, was asked to join Andy Kirk's Clouds of Joy. She was one of a number of women musicians that worked in this vibrant scene. Williams, in her account of these early years, referenced two particular musicians; pianists Julia Lee and Mary Colston Kirk.[9]

Born in 1902, Julia Lee (1902–58) started piano lessons as a child. Her career included stints with groups that extended out of her family. She first worked with her father's string band, but came to prominence working in her brother's group, George E. Lee's Singing Novelty Orchestra. The band served as the training ground for a number of influential musicians, including Lester Young and Charlie Parker.[10] In 1933 Lee started a twenty-year residency at the Tap Room. There she cultivated a diverse repertory that included barrelhouse and boogie piano music, blues standards such as 'Trouble in Mind', and bawdy blues songs such as 'Gotta Gimme Watcha Got' and 'My Man Stands Out', which became her signature. For a time, she led her own band, Julia Lee and Her Boyfriends, which included musicians like Jay McShann, Vic Dickenson, Benny Carter, and Red Norvo. Unlike a number of her peers, Lee stayed in Kansas City all of her life, leaving only for recording sessions with Capitol Records in the 1940s.

Mary Colston Kirk (1900–90) studied music with Wilberforce J. Whiteman, the father of famed bandleader Paul Whiteman, during her formative years.[11] She displayed considerable talent, which eventually led to a stint with George Morrison's Jazz Orchestra. She was one of two female pianists that performed with the band. In 1925 she married tuba player Andy Kirk, and they moved for a short time to Chicago. After the birth of their son, Colson stopped performing publicly except for in church. Andy Kirk joined the band of Terrance T. Holder in the late 1920s, which brought the family back into the Southwestern jazz territory. By the time Mary Lou Williams arrived in Kansas City, Andy Kirk had assumed leadership of the group. Mary Kirk resumed her performing career in Kansas City, forming a trio, which included drummer Paul Gunther and a young Charlie Parker.[12] Later when the Kirks relocated to New York, Mary began teaching at a nursery and elementary school.

Mary Lou Williams was a consummate professional when she arrived in Kansas City in 1928. At a time when most young girls were playing with dolls, Williams, born Mary Burley, was travelling throughout the Midwest with some of the most notable bands of the period including McKinley's Cotton Pickers. She came to national prominence in 1929 when Kirk's regular pianist could not make an audition with an A&R man with Brunswick Records. Mary, at the urging of her husband John Williams, played the audition and aided the Kirk band in gaining a recording contract. She made her first solo recordings – the two original stride piano works 'Night Life' and 'Drag 'Em' – during these sessions. It was also during this session that the appellation 'Lou' was added to her name, largely because the engineer thought Mary was too common a name.[13] Her role in the band extended beyond that of pianist, as she became its primary arranger. Williams' arranging style was defined by her ability to synthesise the blues and other black folk practices like boogie-woogie into polished, swinging performances (such as 'Little Joe from Chicago').[14] She was also known for her unique instrument pairings (as exemplified, for example, through 'Walkin' and Swingin'") and innovative harmonic approaches (such as in 'Mary's Idea'). Williams remained with the band until 1942, but by that time her reputation of being an innovative arranger was set. Most of the big bands of that time had at least one of her pieces in their repertoire and she provided arrangements for some of the biggest bands of the period, including Benny Goodman ('Camel Hop', 'Lonely Moments'), Duke Ellington ('Trumpets No End'), and Jimmy Lunceford ('What's Your Story Morning Glory').

Women and the Globalisation of Jazz

In the years following the First World War, Europe offered some women jazz musicians opportunities that they were denied in the United States. For black musicians it offered freedom from the racial, economic, and cultural oppression they experienced daily in both the North and South. For black women that migrated there, Europe also presented some freedom from gender discrimination, as European audiences seemed enamoured with 'good' music regardless of the performer. Singer-dancer Josephine Baker, who arrived in Paris in the 1920s, set the stage for the migration of black women artists. Baker, with her audacious manner and highly charged performances, has come to personify what the French called *les années folles*.[15]

[handwritten margin note: Europe provided a place away from some prejudices]

Following Paris's acceptance of jazz, other European cities began cultivating the genre. Trumpeter Valaida Snow (1905–56) was one of the many jazzwomen who found fame and a cultured life in Europe. She arrived in England in the late 1920s, having already earned a reputation performing on Broadway. From 1926 until 1928 she toured the Far East, and returned to America in 1928. As she alternated between the United States, Russia, Europe, and the Middle East over the next few years, Snow's popularity increased. In the United States she recorded with Earl Hines' band, performed on Broadway, and appeared in several film shorts. In 1936 she settled in Europe (Paris and Scandinavia) and became a staple of the European jazz scene. The 'Queen of the Trumpet' or 'Little Louis', as she was commonly called, came to symbolise glamour and success. The latter was a reference to her musical prowess, which by testimony matched that of Louis Armstrong.[16] She is rumoured to have travelled 'in an orchid-coloured Mercedes Benz, dressed in an orchid suit, her pet monkey rigged out in an orchid jacket and cap, with the chauffeur in orchid as well'.[17]

While Europe offered a positive environment for black jazzwomen, it was not without its problems. The widening radius of Hitler's invasion of Europe prompted many black and Jewish performers to return to America, but Snow believed her celebrity would shield her. In 1940 she accepted an engagement in Denmark, which shortly thereafter fell to Nazism. She was imprisoned for eighteen months. The circumstances of that imprisonment were debated for many years, as Snow claimed to have been captured by the Nazis. Mark Miller, author of *High Hat, Trumpet, and Rhythm: The Life and Music of Valaida Snow*, believes she was taken into custody before the invasion to ensure her safety.[18] Although she attempted a comeback upon her release in the mid-1940s, Snow never fully regained the success she had before. In 1956 she died of a cerebral haemorrhage following a performance.

Jazz and the Making of the 'Girl'

As the popularity of big bands continued to grow, these larger aggregations became the defining paradigm in jazz from the mid-1930s until the mid-1940s. Although a number of women would find roles as instrumentalists in these groups, the female vocalists would greatly influence jazz traditions during this time. Before the 1930s the female jazz vocalist was an anomaly. That is largely because, before the late 1920s and early 1930s, there had not been a discernible jazz vocal tradition. However, when Louis Armstrong began singing wordless improvisations that extended his horn lines, a new vocal practice was born. The emergence of female jazz singers in the late 1920s and early 1930s paralleled the rise of the 'girl' as the persona situating the place of women in jazz. 'Girl' was a term used to market a context of youthfulness; a vibrancy that correlated with the politics of respectability, and destigmatised jazz. It was used to characterise female instrumentalists and singers regardless of biological age. The rebranding of jazz during this period significantly progressed the mainstreaming and whitening of its culture during the Depression years. The white female vocalist was essential in the early promotion of the image of the 'girl'.

As the big band rose in popularity many bandleaders sought ways in which to create diversity in their sound and image. At the centre of this change for many was the addition of the female jazz vocalist. Mildred Bailey (1903–51) first manifested this phenomenon when she joined Paul Whiteman's band in 1929. Bailey was born Mildred Rinker in Tekoa, Washington, but spent her formative years on the Coeur d'Alene

Reservation in Idaho. As a teenager she worked as a song demonstrator at Woolworth's department store. Bailey's sound was initially influenced by the shouting, percussive sound of vaudeville blues women, but it later evolved into a more nuanced, subtle aesthetic. During her career she was known by many different nicknames; 'The Rockin' Chair Lady' (a reference to a popular blues song she recorded with Whiteman) and 'The Queen of Swing'. Unfortunately, Bailey's career was hampered by health challenges, as well as her insecurities surrounding her weight. As the girl singer became more and more a part of the big band aesthetic, Bailey faded into obscurity.

The role of the early girl singer morphed into that of musical cheerleader and eye candy during the 1930s. Singers were often chosen more for their physical attributes than their musicianship, causing a rift between the male musician and the female vocalist. Most musicians viewed vocalists as 'canaries' or 'chirpers' who had no real knowledge of the music and were a waste of time. Bandleaders were no different in their assessments, as the early girl singer aesthetic developed into what I refer to as the 32-bar aesthetic. Most big band arrangements mirrored the 32-bar AABA formula that defined popular song form. Following the statement of the melody (AABA), most arrangements transitioned into cycles of melodic variation between sections, or the entire band and individual solos. Singers were generally restricted to singing the melody only, with the remainder of the performance focusing on the instrumentalists. Those 32 bars generally contained no improvisation or variation of melody or harmony. The replication of this formula by a number of bandleaders perpetuated the notion of a 'gendered' space for the girl singer that did not obstruct the 'real' work of male instrumentalists. It also reinforced the notion that girl singers lacked the intellectual and musical ability to perform jazz. The engagement between black bandleaders and black girl singers significantly shifted this paradigm. Billie Holiday (1915–59) and Ella Fitzgerald (1917– 96) were significant in expanding the repertory and agency of girl singers.

Holiday, born Eleanora Fagan (1915–59), learned to sing the blues listening to the records of Bessie Smith. When Count Basie hired her in 1935, it began a musical relationship that transformed the way in which she interpreted and performed the music. Holiday was significant in redefining the performance aesthetic of jazz. She modelled the performance approaches used by instrumentalists like her close friend, saxophonist Lester Young. The genius of Holiday's musicianship rested not so much in the size of her voice, but in her interpretation of the text and her ability to manipulate the melody in a manner that virtually milked the lyrics of every bit of emotional content. She expanded the jazz singer's repertoire to include original songs like the modern blues 'Fine and Mellow' or torch songs like 'Don't Explain' that reflected the often-troubled nature of her personal life. In 1938 Holiday reflected the growing connection between the black civil rights struggles and jazz when she debuted 'Strange Fruit', a song about the Southern practice of lynching, at the New York nightclub Café Society.

Ella Fitzgerald continued this progression of the girl singer aesthetic with her extensive range, amazing vocal control, and ability to create long, intricate vocal improvisations through scatting. Ella's career was launched when she won the Amateur Hour at the Apollo Theater and was adopted by 'Harlem's King of Swing', drummer and bandleader Chick Webb. Her first big hit was an interpretation of the famous nursery rhyme 'A-Tisket A-Tasket'. She would go on to be one of jazz's biggest selling artists, making a number of significant recordings, including a series of 'songbooks' that focused on the compositions of some of America's greatest songwriters (e.g. George Gershwin, Duke Ellington, and Jerome Kern). As the girl singer found more and more acceptance on bandstands and amongst the critics that served as the 'cultural gatekeepers', the female instrumentalist continued to battle for relevancy.

A Woman's Place Is in the Groove: The Birth of the All-Girl Band

The 1920s also marked the emergence of several all-female bands. Two major black women bandleaders that worked during this period were Marie Lucas (1880–1947) and Blanche Calloway (1903–78). Marie Lucas was the daughter of minstrel performer Sam Lucas and enjoyed wide recognition. Ellington, in his early career, saw her perform on various occasions at Washington's Howard Theatre, and later wrote of her band's abilities in his autobiography *Music Is My Mistress*.[19] Blanche Calloway, known as the 'Queen of Swing', was well known in many early jazz circles.[20] However, she never achieved the success of her younger brother Cab, who was backed by promoter Irving Mills and his promotion machine. Blanche's career, however, did consist of some successful stints with various all-female and all-male bands including Andy Kirk's Twelve Clouds of Joy, Chick Webb's Orchestra, and her own Blanche Calloway and Her Boy Toys.

Despite the successful stints of Mary Lou Williams, Lil Hardin, and a number of other women with all-male bands during the late 1920s and early 1930s, as the 1930s progressed, most women instrumentalists began to find it increasingly difficult to become members of the more established bands. All-girl bands provided an alternative, but some women resisted this format, believing male musicians would have to recognise their talents if they were juxtaposed with mediocre male players. Others believed the creation and success of all-girl bands would lead to true integration and acceptance of women into male bands and the mainstream jazz scene. As if gender was not limiting enough, race also impacted the treatment that all-girl bands received. White female bands generally received the more lucrative and prestigious jobs at theatres and hotels, but black bands were limited, for some time to the TOBA. White bands such as Phil Spitanly's Hour of Charm or Ina Ray Hutton and the Melodears received the attention of agents and record companies, while black bands were sustained economically through live performances. Despite these differences, neither kind of group were ever paid the same or as much as the most mediocre male groups. Many of the manufactured white bands relied on gimmickry and tricks to draw audiences. Unfortunately, this led to all-girl bands in general being viewed as novelty groups by critics. The seminal black bands of the thirties, the Harlem Playgirls and the Dixie Sweethearts, mirrored the performance aesthetic and repertory promoted by male bands. The popularity of these two groups served as the impetus for the creation of subsequent bands in the forties, which moved beyond the novelties and gimmicks.

In the book *Swing Shift: 'All-Girl' Bands of the 1940s*, scholar Sherrie Tucker explores how the 1940s became the 'golden age' for female jazz musicians as America's entrance into the Second World War and the diminishing number of available male musicians provided more performance opportunities for them. Colleges and secondary school music programmes became important aquifers for all-girl bands. The International Sweethearts of Rhythm, the Swinging Rays of Rhythm, and the Prairie View Co-Eds all evolved out of the segregated educational system of the South. Many high-school-aged girls left school and their families to join the professional bands that passed through their home towns.

The most famous of these groups was the International Sweethearts of Rhythm, which started as a fundraising initiative for the Piney Woods School for Girls in Piney Woods, Mississippi. The band's success was halted momentarily when its members defected from the school and resettled outside of Washington, DC. The next incarnation of the Sweethearts consisted of a number of important professional musicians including trumpeters Ernestine 'Tiny' Davis (1907–94) and Jean Starr, tenor saxophonist Viola 'Vi' Burnside (1915–64), and drummer Pauline Braddy (1922–96). This period marked the band's transition to a professional dance orchestra. Historically the Sweethearts were noteworthy not only because of their musical ability, which matched that of the most popular male bands, but also because they were one of the first interracial bands. They boosted members of white, Native American, and Asian descendent, and were the longest functioning all-girl band (c.1937–48).

From their premiere as a professional band at the famed Apollo Theatre in 1941, the Sweethearts distinguished themselves from other all-women bands of the time. In the 1940s they were frequently pitted against male bands in the 'Battle of the Sexes' series, toured Europe by invitation of Armed Forces radio, and were named one of the best bands of the period. The organisation, like many of the all-girl bands, had its share of problems. Hampered consistently by changing personnel and financial difficulties, the Sweethearts disbanded in 1948. Those members who chose to continue performing did so with regional, national, and international success.

Conclusion

By the time the Sweethearts split in 1948, the American jazz scene was shifting in sound and culture. The emergence of bebop aesthetically represented the black male's reclamation of jazz. For many, swing diluted the music, cutting off of its creative nature and making it possible for the most mediocre musician to circumnavigate their way through a jazz performance. Bebop, with its complex rhythmic and harmonic approaches, wove a musical language commensurate with the post-war male consciousness. The jazzwomen who had kept Americans entertained and dancing during the swing era quickly found themselves being forced back into the margins as bandleaders replaced them with returning male musicians, and all-women bands dissolved. These efforts to reclaim what had previously been a male terrain extended to every facet of life. The next seventy years of jazz's history were marked by fragmentation into various stylistic 'schools', ideological debates regarding what constitutes jazz, and the emergence of new influential voices. While you will find women musicians actively representing each of these substyles and cultural trends, there has been no significant change in attitude amongst critics, listeners, and musicians. Jazz continues to be equated with male intellectual work. Twenty-plus years after the release of the jazz postage-stamp series I referenced at the beginning of this essay, a number of women vocalists have been featured on stamps, but there has yet to be a stamp of a female jazz instrumentalist. The title of this chapter is a nod to a line from Public Enemy's 1990 song 'Fight the Power', during which rapper Chuck D references how the conventional narrative of the American hero is centred on the heteronormative lived experiences of white males. Black men, especially the radical and transgressive ones that Chuck D idolises, are excluded from this heroic framework. But through jazz, as well as blues, funk, soul, and hip-hop, black men found ways in which to insert their self-actualised sonic identities into this narrative. We have yet to see this with women musicians. However, like Chuck D's, my efforts to 'fight the power' involve challenging the perpetuation of this paradigm by 'decentring' the canonic presentation of jazz history in textbooks, museum exhibits, and anthologies with narratives such as the one presented here, that contextualise how women musicians collaborated *with* their male counterparts and each other to further the progression of jazz.

Notes

1. These views are discussed in detail in Judith Tick's chapter 'Passed Away Is the Piano Girl: Changes in American Life, 1870–1900', in Jane M. Bowers and Judith Tick (eds.), *Women Making Music: The Western Art Tradition, 1150–1950* (Urbana and Chicago: University of Illinois Press, 1987), 325–48.
2. Linda Dahl, *Stormy Weather: The Music and Lives of a Century of Jazz Women* (New York: Limelight Editions, 1984), 10.
3. D. Antoinette Handy, *Black Women in American Bands and Orchestras*, 2nd ed. (Lanham, MD: Scarecrow Press, 1998), 219–21.
4. Dahl, *Stormy Weather*, 16.
5. Dahl, *Stormy Weather*, 16.
6. Sally Placksin, *American Women in Jazz: 1900 to the Present: Their Words, Lives, and Music* (New York: Seaview Books, 1982), 69.
7. Handy, *Black Women in Bands*, 172.
8. Handy, *Black Women in Bands*, 172–3.
9. In 1954 Mary Lou Williams wrote a series of articles for the jazz periodical *Melody Maker* that surveyed her vast career and experiences. The eleven instalments have been coalesced in many different anthologies. They can easily be accessed through www.ratical.org/MaryLouWilliams/MMiview1954.html (accessed 11 December 2020).
10. Placksin, *American Women in Jazz*, 49.
11. Placksin, *American Women in Jazz*, 49.
12. Placksin, *American Women in Jazz*, 50.

13. Tammy L. Kernodle, *Soul on Soul: The Life and Music of Mary Lou Williams* (Boston, MA: Northeastern University Press, 2004), 62.

14. For a full study of Williams' arranging style and arrangements, see Theodore E. Buehrer (ed.), *Mary Lou Williams – Selected Works for Big Band*, Music of the United States of America, vol. 25. Recent Researches in American Music, Vol. A74 (Middleton, WI: A-R Editions, 2013).

15. *Les années folles* means the 'crazy years' in French. It is a reference to the cultural and artistic collaborations that took place during the 1920s. These were similar to those taking place in the context of the cultural movement that defined the Jazz Age in America.

16. Dahl, *Stormy Weather*, 81.

17. Dahl, *Stormy Weather*, 82.

18. Mark Miller, *High Hat, Trumpet and Rhythm: The Life and Music of Valaida Snow* (Ontario, CA: The Mercury Press, 2007), 116–22.

19. Handy, *Black Women in Bands*, 59.

20. Handy, *Black Women in Bands*, 61.

Further Reading

Taylor, Jeffrey. 'With Lovie and Lil: Rediscovered Two Chicago Pianists of the 1920s', in Nichole T. Rustin and Sherrie Tucker (eds.), *Big Ears: Listening for Gender in Jazz Studies* (Durham and London: Duke University Press, 2008), 48–63.

Tucker, Sherrie. 'Nobody's Sweethearts: Gender, Race, Jazz, and the Darlings of Rhythm.' *American Music*, vol. 16, no. 3 (Autumn 1998), 255–88.

Tucker, Sherrie. *Swing Shift: 'All-Girl' Bands of the 1940s* (Durham and London: Duke University Press, 2001).

Tucker, Sherrie. 'Telling Performances: Jazz History Remembered and Remade by the Women in the Band', *The Oral History Review*, vol. 26, no. 1 (Winter–Spring 1999), 67–84.

8 | Leaders of the Pack: Girl Groups of the 1960s

JACQUELINE WARWICK

It is a truth universally acknowledged that girls have terrible taste in music.[1] Indeed, this notion is held so fiercely as fact – in rock culture, anyway – that the mere taint of girl fans can sometimes be enough to impugn the reputation of an otherwise perfectly acceptable band of dudes. According to girl-hater logic, for example, the Beatles only became 'good' once they had shed the shrieking hordes of Beatlemaniacs and retreated into the recording studio to create the more serious, experimental work that would define rock in the 1960s and after. This view is predicated in clichés of girls as vapid, frivolous, and superficial: spoilt Daddy's girls; uptalking Valley Girls; mean Queen Bees; prissy bossy girls, and other stock characters of adolescent femininity.

In their way, these images correspond to the stereotypes of black femininity identified and theorised by Patricia Hill Collins – the mammy, the matriarch, the welfare mother, and the jezebel – as controlling images that perpetuate sexist, racist structures and assumptions. While all the stereotypes Collins confronts reduce African American women to their sexual and maternal functions, however, the clichés of teen girls hinge on narcissism, access to wealth, and immaturity – and tellingly, these images are overwhelmingly associated with whiteness, an exnomination that helps to force early maturity on non-white girls.[2] As scholars contributing to the growing literature on girl studies note, girls of colour are often perceived as older than their white age-mates, and these presumptions can have dangerous consequences for girls seen as women. But whether it is of the fond or predatory variety, the condescension that is aimed at girlhood has led some cultural critics to wonder what anxieties are masked by it; if patriarchal systems rely on girls becoming future helpmeets, wives, and mothers, then indeed 'it is the girl who is the most profound site of patriarchal investment, her unconstrained freedom representing the most fearsome threat to male control'.[3]

In relation to music, reductive stereotypes of girl fans as shallow and self-centred uphold an ideology of authenticity that limits girls and women to the roles of muse or of spectator, liking musicians for the wrong reasons and changing allegiances with fickle abandon. This ideology also helps to ascribe value to artists who themselves write the music that they perform, trivialising the creative work of performers of all genders, and debasing those genres of music that develop through collaborative processes with unseen contributors. Above all, it reifies rock as the most important style of popular music (to the point that it is called 'rockism'), and it invariably reinforces white male supremacy and heteronormativity along the way.

The ostensibly mindless hysteria of Beatlemaniacs, so irritating and ridiculous to those observers invested in codifying right and wrong ways to appreciate the Beatles, has since been theorised by feminists as a defiant rejection of restrictive expectations for girls and an important precursor of second-wave feminism.[4] For if we can see and hear girls without contempt, a different account of music in the 1960s emerges, and this girl-inclusive history can even allow us to appreciate the Beatles in new ways; after all, the Fab Four did record five cover versions of songs by girls on their first two albums: the Cookies' 'Chains', the Marvelettes' 'Please Mr. Postman', the Donays' 'Devil in Her (His) Heart' and the Shirelles' 'Boys' and 'Baby, It's You.' This is more than the songs by Chuck Berry and Little Richard they covered combined, and these choices surely suggest some respect for the musical tastes of girls. Since the 1960s was such a watershed decade for music and for youth culture, a reconsideration of girls in the music scenes of the decade can influence our perception of gendered participation in youth culture more broadly. In this chapter, I will focus principally on the girl group music of the early 1960s, and I will suggest that recognising this genre's importance can reinvigorate our understanding of how girls participate in youth music and youth culture, in that decade and beyond.

Girls, Boys, and Women

But to begin, it is useful to differentiate the social experience and function of 'girl' from those of both 'youth' and from 'woman', even while we acknowledge that girls constitute a market category that overlaps with both youth and women. In many contexts, girls constitute a particularised subset of youth, which is nominally gender-neutral but actually usually designates boys: storytelling about youth invariably centres on male experience, and female readers are expected to identify with male protagonists in ways that male readers are not encouraged to do with stories about female characters. Books about boyhood ranging from *Great Expectations* (Charles Dickens, 1861), *The Adventures of Tom Sawyer* (Mark Twain, 1876), and *The Jungle Book*

(Rudyard Kipling, 1894) to *The Catcher in the Rye* (J. D. Salinger, 1951) and the Harry Potter series (J. K. Rowling, 1997–2007) are held to be classics that will resonate with all readers, while *Emma* (Jane Austen, 1815), *Jane Eyre* (Charlotte Bronte, 1847), *Little Women* (Louisa May Alcott, 1868), *Anne of Green Gables* (L. M. Montgomery, 1908), and *The Bell Jar* (Sylvia Plath, 1963) are characterised as women's literature and not directed at male readers (many of whom read them anyway, of course!). In the cinematic world, films from 1946's *The Yearling* and 1967's *The Graduate* to 1986's *Stand by Me* and 2014's *Boyhood* present coming of age through the lens of white, American masculinity, but have nevertheless been embraced by audiences of all genders and nationalities.

In short; girls' stories are for girls, but boys' stories are for everyone. Because this assumption pervades so much of the media created for children, girls learn from an early age to perform a cross-gender identification in order to see themselves reflected in the stories presented to them, while boys are rarely encouraged to identify with anyone not like themselves. Furthermore, as John Berger told us in *Ways of Seeing*, 'from earliest childhood [a girl] has been taught to and persuaded to survey herself continually. And so she comes to consider the *surveyor* and the *surveyed* within her as two constituent yet always distinct elements of her identity.'[5] This is not unlike W. E. B. Du Bois's notion of double consciousness, articulated in his monumental *Souls of Black Folk* as the 'peculiar sensation [of an African American], this sense of always looking at one's self through the eyes of others, of measuring one's soul by the tape of a world that looks on in contempt and pity. One ever feels his two-ness, an American, a Negro: two souls, two thoughts, two unreconciled strivings.'[6] This kind of learned doubleness also shapes the listening habits of all girls, as they learn to recognise themselves as the subject of men's songs but also seek to empathise with and model themselves after male narrators and creators. Non-white girls exist at the intersection of both forms of marginalisation, as girls of colour are the least-depicted group in media made for children.[7] Small wonder, then, that Valerie Walkerdine considers that 'girls' fantasies are shaped entirely by the available representations: there are no fantasies that originate with girls, only those projected onto them'.[8]

Similarly, studies of childhood, youth, and adolescence have overwhelmingly presented masculinity as the norm, leading Angela McRobbie to predict in 1980 that 'questions about girls, sexual relations and femininity will continue to be defused or marginalised in the ghetto of Women's Studies'.[9] McRobbie was an important pioneer of studying girlhood within the broader landscape of popular culture studies, which was shaped by masculinist priorities in its early days as a scholarly field. Her lament points also to the often-uneasy position of girls in relation to women; because the term 'girl' has often been used to infantilise and trivialise adult women, many feminists and progressive folk prefer to avoid it. In white supremacist economies like the Southern United States at mid-century, for example, 'girl' was an acceptable way to refer to those black women who worked in the homes of white women – who expected to be called 'ladies' – and age was irrelevant to this distinction. First- and second-wave feminists seeking the dignity of equality with (white) men did not, unsurprisingly, want to align themselves with girls.

And yet, girls – and here I mean quite specifically adolescent and pre-adolescent females – were courageous activists and symbols of the Southern Civil Rights Movement. Long before she created hit recordings like 'Midnight Train to Georgia', and even before her fellow Atlantan Martin Luther King, Jr. took his first stand for justice, Gladys Knight earned the honour of a lifetime membership in the Atlanta chapter of the NAACP (National Association for the Advancement of Colored People) while still a child; aged eight in 1952, she won a national prize singing in the popular radio series *Ted Mack's Original Amateur Hour*, in spite of racist contempt for her participation.[10] Five years later, black civil rights activists in Little Rock, Arkansas, carefully chose six teenage girls (and three boys) to desegregate the city's Central High School. These community leaders reasoned that the necessary discipline of forbearance was already more familiar for girls than boys, as evidenced in the stunning composure of fifteen-year-old Elizabeth Eckford in photos of her attempts to enter the school, alone, in the face of a seething mob.[11] The four girls killed by murderous violence in the 1963 racist attack on the Sixteenth Street Baptist Church in Birmingham, Alabama became potent symbols of loss.

Girls and Girls' Voices

So, when I write about girl singers in this chapter, I choose my terms deliberately and advisedly, and with the utmost respect for girls and girlhood. Most singers in girl groups of the 1960s were audibly pubescent and even pre-pubescent, and their songs were explicitly about the experiences and concerns of female adolescence. Girl group music was a popular music phenomenon involving pre-teen and teen girls, especially prevalent in the United States during the early to mid-1960s, but with a significant echo in the 1990s with groups such as Destiny's Child and the Spice Girls. Girl groups are distinct from bands that involve girls as instrumentalists, and most groups comprised three to five members who generally dressed alike and performed simple choreography while they sang about themes of importance to girl culture. For the most part, songwriting credits on girl group records are attributed to professional songwriters, instruments are played by professional session players, and the songs treat such topics as crushes on boys, wedding fantasies, the strictness of parents, and the travails of adolescent romance, through songs like 'Beechwood 4-5789' (The Marvelettes, 1962), 'Chapel of Love' (The Dixie Cups, 1964), 'Party Lights' (Claudine Clark, 1962), and 'Da Doo Ron Ron' (The Crystals, 1963), amongst many more. Some of the best-known groups include the Shirelles, Ronettes, Chiffons, Little Eva, and Lesley Gore (the latter two associated with the genre although nominally solo artists). The Supremes and Shangri-Las are generally considered girl groups, although their chief popularity came after the main girl group phenomenon had ended, and it must be noted that from the very beginning of their success, the Supremes presented a sophisticated, aspirational version of femininity that aligned more with adulthood than adolescence. Between 1960 and 1964, girl group music dominated Top 40 radio in North America, an unprecedented and unrepeated instance of teenage girls taking centre stage of mainstream popular culture.

The first girl group songs began to circulate in the late 1950s in New York; these recordings all had distinctly different styles, and their popularity was generally limited to African American communities in north-eastern cities of the United States, so that they were not understood as representing a cohesive new style. Rather, these early records drew on musical styles such as doo-wop, jump blues, barbershop, and choral singing, and Tin-Pan-Alley-styled songs. These influences led to such diverse songs as the Chantels' 'Maybe', the Bobbettes 'Mr. Lee' (both 1957) and the Shirelles' 'I Met Him on a Sunday' (1958), all successful on the R&B charts. Sonically, these three songs have little in common beyond the use of young female voices; 'Maybe' uses a doo-wop harmonic progression, a 6/8 time signature, and a choral sound for backing vocalists to support seventeen-year-old Arlene Smith's ringing soprano, while 'Mr. Lee' is a rollicking twelve-bar blues with honking saxophone solo, walking bass, and precociously growling vocals from twelve-year-old Reather Dixon; and 'I Met Him on a Sunday', with its foregrounded handclapping and finger-snaps, simple, sing-song melody expressed by each girl in turn, and refrain of doo-wop syllables punctuating the story of a week-long romance, bears a strong resemblance to the handclapping and jump-rope songs so central to girls' play at mid-century.[12]

In the soundscape of the late 1950s, these three songs were embraced as part of the North American doo-wop style that was popular amongst urban youth, featuring teenage boys who developed their sound singing a cappella and filling in instrumental lines with nonsense syllables. While groups like Frankie Lymon and the Teenagers could roam their neighbourhoods and experiment with close-harmony singing in alleys and stairwells, however, the members of the Chantels, Shirelles, and Bobbettes had less freedom to wander the streets unchaperoned. Confined as they were by the restrictions of respectability and by their vulnerability to dangerous men, these girls gathered at supervised choir rehearsals, basketball practice, and glee club meetings to create songs that were at first derivative, but would eventually coalesce into a distinct, and distinctly girl-centred, new genre.

The Girl Group Era

In 1960, the Shirelles recorded Carole King and Gerry Goffin's composition 'Will You Love Me Tomorrow?', depicting a girl on the brink of her first sexual encounter, coincidentally in the same year that the US Federal Drug Authority approved the clinical use of the birth control pill for women. This record, which rose to the top position on the Billboard pop charts early the following year, is arguably the true start of the girl group phenomenon. The voices heard were audibly those of teenage girls, and the musical language and vocal style suggested that they were nicely brought up and respectable, as distinct from the womanly, raunchy blues queens who were more familiar discussants of female sexual desire. The Shirelles made it possible for 'nice' girls to talk about sex without disrupting society's preferred view of them as demure.

Songwriters King (b.1942) and Goffin (b.1939) were themselves teenagers, on the brink of a marriage triggered by an unplanned pregnancy, as they both worked tirelessly and enthusiastically to find their places in a newly professionalising rock 'n' roll music business.[13] As a songwriting duo, King and Goffin would become important architects of rock 'n' roll and youth culture in the early 1960s; as with other young songwriters such as Ellie Greenwich (b.1940), Jeff Barry (b.1938), Cynthia Weil (b.1940), Barry Mann (b.1939), Mort Shuman (b.1938), and Neil Sedaka (b.1939), Goffin and King were part of the Brill Building community of songwriters creating the soundtrack to adolescence just as baby boomers came of age.

(You can read more about Carole King's career as a songwriter in Chapter 10, "'(You Make Me Feel Like) A Natural Woman": Women in Songwriting'.) 'Will You Love Me Tomorrow?' provided a template for teens to talk about sex and love, and helped girls ask difficult questions of their boyfriends.

The record's style also set the standard for the girl group sound: a young, untrained voice, with backing vocals suggesting friends in dialogue with the lead singer, against a backing of pop instrumentation (i.e. piano or strings, not guitar) and rock 'n' roll rhythms and grooves. Over the next few years, the Marvelettes' 'Please Mr. Postman' (1961), Little Eva's 'The Locomotion' (1962), and the Crystals' 'Da Doo Ron Ron' (1963) adhered fairly closely to the style, presenting more examples of 'good' girls discussing their feelings and fantasies in candid, yet polite, ways. Often, the backing vocalists respond to the lead singer's statements with encouraging remarks such as 'go ahead, girl!' and songs like the Marvelettes' 'Too Many Fish in the Sea' (1964) address themselves explicitly to young women, with spoken phrases such as 'look here, girls, and take this advice'. This direct, spoken interpellation of girl listeners would be echoed in more explicitly feminist songs such as Laura Lee's 1971 'Women's Love Rights' and Madonna's 1989 'Express Yourself.'

Different musical versions of girl identity began to appear as the girl group phenomenon became more established. In 1963, a trio from New York's Spanish Harlem had spectacular success with 'Be My Baby', written for them by Brill Building songwriters Ellie Greenwich and Jeff Barry. This song seemed to articulate all of the dramatic intensity and heightened emotional state of adolescence, and the singers provided new models of girlhood for girl listeners to experiment with. The Ronettes, whose meteoric success in 1963–64 included five Top 40 hits and a UK tour with the Rolling Stones as their opening act, were a mixed-race group of two sisters and a cousin; as girls growing up under the watchful eye of their grandmother, they experimented with singing, dance, and fashion to create a striking look. Their distinct group style, provocative though it may have been, provided a measure of safety as they began to explore New York's club scene as teenagers, in that all three were marked as belonging together. It also helped them garner a following and the confidence to seek perform-ing opportunities; in this way they ultimately came to the attention of producer Phil Spector, who developed his famous 'wall of sound' produc-tion style around Ronnie Bennett's (later Ronnie Spector's) passionate vibrato.[14] Singer and producer went on to marry, and Ronnie discloses the abuse she suffered at his hands, and her difficulties leaving the marriage, in her autobiography *Be My Baby*.

Legacy of the Girl Groups

The Crystals and the Blossoms, in New York and Los Angeles respectively, were also acts produced by Spector, who recorded such girl group classics as 'Da Doo Ron Ron' and 'Then He Kissed Me' (both 1963 hits for the Crystals) and 'He's a Rebel', infamously recorded by the Blossoms in Los Angeles but then released as a single by the Crystals in 1962. Spector owned the names of both groups and decided that the Crystals needed a hit, while the Blossoms were more useful to him as a malleable group of session singers who could be paid studio session rates to provide backing vocals for an extraordinary range of artists, from Frank Sinatra to Betty Everett. The Blossoms' lead singer, Darlene Love, would eventually record 'Christmas (Baby Please Come Home)' with Spector, under her own name, and the Blossoms as a group earned overdue recognition in the 2013 documentary *20 Feet From Stardom*. By this time, the brilliant, tyrannical Phil Spector was midway through a prison sentence for the murder of Lana Clarkson, a reversal of fortunes that must have provided some sense of closure for the girl groups he produced after his exploitative and controlling treatment during their teen years in the 1960s.

Beginning in 1964, a tough, streetwise version of white girlhood issued from the Shangri-Las, whose songs, such as 'Leader of the Pack' (1964), were operatic in scope, narrating anguished tales of teenage death and tragedy. Listening to these records in the privacy and safety of her bedroom, a sheltered suburban girl could experiment with the tough, streetwise stance and seductive manner of the singers she heard, and she could give herself over to the powerful emotions enacted in the music. The navigation of dramatic conflicts between love and repressive social mores in Shangri-Las songs like 'I Can Never Go Home Anymore', 'Out in the Streets', and 'Past, Present and Future' (all 1965) ensured that these recordings were formative listening for teens such as Debbie Harry, who fronted a semi-ironic girl group called the Stilettos before co-founding the band Blondie in 1974 and, by extension, the New York punk rock scene. In her own career, Harry's performance of pretty blonde femininity was complex and subversive; by adopting some (but not all) of the conventions of attractiveness for the male gaze, she was able to poke apart easy assumptions about girls and women. Her blonde hair with deliberately visible dark roots foregrounded the artifice of beauty, and in her singing she similarly destabilised the tropes of girlhood, deploying textures ranging from breathy wistfulness in 'Sunday Girl' to predatory snarling in 'One Way or Another' (both from the 1978 album *Parallel Lines*).

Harry's ability to mimic the qualities of a girl's voice, well into her thirties, indicates both her canny understanding of girlhood as a costume and also her deep familiarity with the girl group records of her teen years.[15] The musical language created by girl groups in the 1960s had created an architecture of girlhood that would also shape the experiences of future generations of girls, as when the 1987 teen film *Adventures in Babysitting* introduced its central character, an archetype of 1980s suburban, white, American girlhood, via a bedroom lip-synch performance of the twenty-two-year-old song 'Then He Kissed Me'. In the twenty-first century, the brilliant singer-songwriter Amy Winehouse drew significantly from girl group sound and style, modelling the song structures and even production approaches to her recordings on the work of groups like the Shangri-Las, and encouraging thirteen-year-old Dionne Bromfield to make her recording debut, on Winehouse's label Lioness, with the Shirelles' 'Mama Said' in 2009.

Girl Singers and Boy Listeners

Male adolescent listeners have been equally enthralled and inspired by girl groups; Brian Wilson was moved to write a song for the Ronettes after hearing 'Be My Baby'. When Wilson took 'Don't Worry Baby' to his idol Spector, the more seasoned producer rejected it, so Wilson recorded the song in 1964 with his own group. The Beach Boys also recorded a cover version of a girl group song, transforming the Crystals' 'Then He Kissed Me' into 'Then I Kissed Her' in 1965. While Wilson and his bandmates switched gender pronouns in order to preserve 'proper' courtship patterns of active male and passive female, the possibility of adopting a girl's point of view through a song's persona did allow some boys and men to experiment with gender fluidity. This was particularly appealing during a time when expectations for boys and men were highly rigid, and writing songs for girls to sing allowed male songwriters to explore vulnerability and tenderness. Motown songwriter Eddie Holland observed that:

as a lyricist, I noticed that women were more interesting to write for. Women have a broader sensitivity to emotions than men, I think. We were taught coming up that you don't cry; you take it on the chin. We couldn't say we were hurt if we were hurt; we could only deal with those subjects through writing for women. That's why we liked working with girl groups so much.[16]

As part of the legendary Holland-Dozier-Holland songwriting team that wrote hits for Motown acts such as the Four Tops, the Isley Brothers, and

Marvin Gaye, as well as the Supremes and Martha and the Vandellas, Eddie Holland had ample opportunity to explore and express complex emotions through creating songs for male artists to sing: it is significant that he would value writing for girl singers.

Other male groups in the early 1960s found that singing girl group songs was the key to appealing to a female audience and earning massive popularity. Indeed, many of the British Invasion beat bands had their first North American hits with girl group songs; I have already noted that the Beatles recorded and performed numerous examples. What is more, the Fab Four's famously appealing androgyny derived in no small part from their ability to sing from the subject position of girls, demonstrated in many of their original songs (i.e. 'It Won't be Long' or 'You're Gonna Lose that Girl'). Herman's Hermits achieved international success in 1964 with their cover version of 'Something Good', a song that Carole King and Gerry Goffin had originally written as a solo effort for Earl-Jean McCrea of the Cookies earlier that year, and Manfred Mann recorded versions of the Exciters' 'Do-Wah-Diddy', Maxine Brown's 'Oh No, Not my Baby', and the Shirelles' 'Sha La La' in their contribution to the British Invasion of the mid-'60s. The appeal of girl group songs to young men continued, with male punk bands in the 1970s turning to songs like the Shangri-Las's 'Give Him a Great Big Kiss' (Johnny Thunders, 1978) and the Ronettes' 'Baby I Love You' (the Ramones, 1980), and Johnny Marr and Morrissey made their recording debut as the Smiths in 1982 with a rendition of the Cookies' 'I Want a Boy for my Birthday'.[17]

Conclusion

But the significance of girl groups to boys' music is not the only, nor even the most important, reason to celebrate them; girl groups gave voice to teenage girls at a crucial juncture in North American history, and their music provided models of racial integration. During the most active and revolutionary years of the Southern civil rights movement, girl group songs, created by teams of songwriters, musicians, producers, and singers from diverse ethnic backgrounds, were heard on Top 40 radio around the United States. Although the Marvelettes' 1960 'Please Mr. Postman' was issued with a drawing of an empty mailbox on the record cover for fear that a photograph of the black group would make it unmarketable to white listeners, by mid-decade the Supremes were icons of style and amongst the most visible African Americans in the world. Girl groups and their songs were emblematic of girl culture at the very moment when notions of youth identity, race identity, and female identity were in upheaval, and they played a central role in defining girlhood for decades to come.

In 2017, National Public Radio published a superb list of the 150 best albums by women, aptly named 'Turning the Tables' as it explicitly sought to overturn the hierarchies of taste that have excluded women's music making from canonical status. The Turning the Tables essays celebrated music from a wide range of genres and styles, honouring albums by girl groups like the Shangri-Las and the Ronettes, as well as work by Pauline Oliveros, Nina Simone, and Joni Mitchell; this approach allowed the list's curators to make room for joyful, exuberant pop songs alongside serious, introspective music. Listening to this broader soundscape and honouring the value of girls' music ensured that the list makers documented a history of girls and women in music that is both restorative and inspiring. In celebrating girls and their musical creations, we can help to build a world where girls and women raise their voices with confidence that they will be heard.

Notes

1. Some paragraphs of this chapter are lifted wholesale from my essay on 'girl groups' in the *Grove Dictionary of American Music* (New York: Oxford University Press, 2016). My thanks to editor Charles Garrett for allowing me to reprint this material. I have also articulated some of these ideas in my *Girl Groups, Girl Culture: Popular Music and Identity in the 1960s* (New York: Routledge, 2007) and elsewhere.
2. Patricia Hill Collins, *Black Feminist Thought: Knowledge, Consciousness, and the Politics of Empowerment* (New York: Routledge, 1990). See also Marcia Chatelain, *South Side Girls: Growing Up in the Great Migration* (Durham, NC: Duke University Press, 2015), and Monique W. Morris, *Pushout: The Criminalization of Black Girls in Schools* (New York: The New Press, 2016).
3. Frances Gateward and Murray Pomerance, *Sugar and Spice and Everything Nice: Cinemas of Girlhood* (Detroit, MI: Wayne State University Press, 2002), 13.
4. Barbara Ehrenreich, Elizabeth Hess, and Gloria Jacobs, 'Beatlemania: Girls Just Want to Have Fun', in Lisa Lewis (ed.), *The Adoring Audience: Fan Culture and Popular Media* (New York: Routledge, 1992), 84–106.
5. John Berger, *Ways of Seeing* (London: Penguin Books, 1972), 46.
6. W. E. B. Du Bois, *The Souls of Black Folk* (Chicago: A. C. McClurg & Co., 1903).
7. Since 2004, this pattern of representation has been changing, largely in response to major analytical studies and activist work by the Geena Davis Institute on Gender in Media.

8. Valerie Walkerdine, *Daddy's Girl: Young Girls and Popular Culture* (Cambridge, MA: Harvard University Press, 1997), 166.

9. Angela McRobbie, 'Settling Accounts with Subcultures', *Screen Series*, vol. 34 (1980), 38.

10. Gladys Knight, *Between Each Line of Pain and Glory: My Life Story* (New York: Hyperion, 1997).

11. Juan Williams, *Eyes on the Prize: America's Civil Rights Years 1954–65* (New York: Penguin, 1987).

12. Kyra Gaunt, *The Games Black Girls Play: Learning the Ropes from Double-Dutch to Hip Hop* (New York: New York University Press, 2006).

13. Ken Emerson, *Always Magic in the Air: The Bomp and the Brilliance of the Brill Building Era* (New York: Penguin Books, 2006).

14. Ronnie Spector, with Vince Waldron, *Be My Baby: How I Survived Mascara, Miniskirts and Madness, or My Life as a Fabulous Ronette* (New York: Harmony Books, 1990), 46.

15. Debbie Harry, *Face It: A Memoir* (New York: Dey Street Books, 2019).

16. Cited in Charlotte Grieg, *Will You Still Love Me Tomorrow? Girl Groups from the 50s On* (London: Virago, 1989), 134.

17. Anonymous, 'The Smiths' Historic First Recording – a 60s' Girl Group Cover – Has Surfaced Online', *Slicingupeyeballs.com*, www.slicingupeyeballs.com /2019/12/15/smiths-i-want-a-boy-for-my-birthday-full-song/ (accessed 15 December 2019). My thanks to Tom Appleyard for bringing this to my attention!

Further Reading

Gaunt, Kyra. *The Games Black Girls Play: Learning the Ropes from Double-Dutch to Hip Hop* (New York: New York University Press, 2006).

McRobbie, Angela. *Feminism and Youth Culture: From 'Jackie' to 'Just Seventeen'* (London: Macmillan, 1991).

Stras, Laurie (ed.). *She's So Fine: Reflections on Whiteness, Femininity, Adolescence and Class in 1960s Music* (Farnham: Ashgate, 2010).

Warwick, Jacqueline. *Girl Groups, Girl Culture: Popular Music and Identity in the 1960s* (New York: Routledge, 2007).

9 | Women and Rock

LEAH BRANSTETTER

What is a 'woman in rock'? The answer may seem simple: a woman who plays music that could be marketed as 'rock and roll', or maybe just 'rock'. But under closer examination, this definition becomes complicated. What constitutes 'rock music'? Why do we care when women do or don't participate? How do we know if a woman 'rocks', and are the qualities such a woman embodies consistent across time and place?

The phrase 'women in rock' and its variants ('women who rock', 'girls rock', etc.) are common. Books and articles with these titles proliferate, as well as magazine issues, compilation albums, playlists, museum exhibits, and television specials. Some of this is important and necessary feminist recovery work addressing women's inadequate representation in history and criticism. At the same time, numerous critics have argued that the construction creates a marked category (there's no parallel construction for 'men who rock') and causes us to consider women's participation differently. Some musicians feel that existing within this category is harmful, marginalising, or just exhausting. Many bristle at the designation or claim not to think of themselves according to their gender or as doing feminist work. Editor Barbara O'Dair wrote in her introduction to *Trouble Girls: The Rolling Stone Book of Women in Rock* in 1997: 'is it any wonder that "women in rock" hate to be characterised as such, and are often on the defensive? The responses to the subject from female artists today range from irritated to bemused.' The irritated and bemused women quoted in her essay included Kim Deal, Tina Weymouth, and Patti Smith.[1]

This tension persists. In 2014, for example, Neko Case made waves online when she engaged with *Playboy Magazine* on Twitter after the publication posted its review of her album *The Worse Things Get, the Harder I Fight, the Harder I Fight, the More I Love You*:

@PlayboyDotCom: Artist @NekoCase is breaking the mold of what women in the music industry should be: . . .

@NekoCase: @PlayboyDotCom Am I? IM NOT A FUCKING 'WOMAN IN MUSIC', IM A FUCKING MUSICIAN IN MUSIC![2]

Case followed this with an essay on her website about the label 'women musicians'. She did not want it to be quoted out of context, but the sentiments of both her tweets and her essay struck a nerve and received media coverage and a large number of social-media shares. Some people – particularly men – thought *Playboy*'s tweet should be taken as a compliment.[3] But Case's complaint resonated with many women. It also resonates across eras and disciplines. Artist Georgia O'Keeffe, who frequently rejected the gendering of her work, reportedly stated that 'men put me down as the best woman painter . . . I think I'm one of the best painters'.[4]

How did we get to a point where a publication known for objectifying women could draw upon the 'woman-in-music' trope and consider it a feminist act? Something about 'rock' creates a particular impulse to take note when women participate. This isn't because women were ever absent; instead, it reflects how we think about both categories. This chapter, therefore, will focus on women *and* rock more than *in* rock. Women's contributions to this diverse art form have been immense over the course of decades, and I don't wish to create a biographical list of performers expected to stand in for thousands who contributed in myriad ways. Rather, I would like to consider how these categories have had their definitions negotiated and renegotiated in relation to one another throughout the twentieth century. Because rock and roll originated in the United States and American culture shaped the initial discourse on rock, I will focus primarily on examples from American rock here; however, the genre has long since become an international form, and many of the observations in this chapter can be extrapolated or further explored within other cultural contexts.

As a starting point, I will use the analytical strategies sketched out by Joanna Russ in *How to Suppress Women's Writing*. Russ's focus is literature, but she demonstrates how boundaries are moved to keep marginalised groups on the margins of an art form. She writes:

In a nominally egalitarian society the ideal situation (socially speaking) is one in which the members of the 'wrong' groups have the freedom to engage in literature (or equally significant activities) and yet do not do so, thus proving that they can't. But, alas, give them the least real freedom and they will do it. The trick thus becomes to make the freedom as nominal a freedom as possible and then – since some of the so-and-so's will do it anyway – develop various strategies for ignoring, condemning, or belittling the artistic works that result.[5]

Much of Russ's theorising applies to music. A 2018 study by the Annenberg Foundation's Inclusion initiative found that in the most popular music on the *Billboard* charts between 2012 and 2017, women were under-represented as artists, songwriters, producers, and award winners.[6] The study urged examination of biases in history texts, and concluded that inclusion required changing the 'values and strategies of the industry'.[7] Russ's work can help us to understand what those values and strategies have been. Her theory invites us to identify ways the categories 'women' and 'rock' were developed in opposition to one another.

Early Rock and Roll and Anomalousness

Rock and roll became a phenomenon in the United States in the mid-1950s, a time when we frequently think of American women as housewives who stayed home with children. Images from contemporaneous media, such as sitcoms about idealised suburban family life, inform collective memories of the era. What lifestyle could be more opposite to rock and roll than a domestic one?

Rock histories therefore frequently state that there were few, if any, women in early rock and roll. One textbook from 2013 claims, for example:

Clearly the essential conservatism of the 1950s, politically and culturally, made it a particularly inauspicious time to be seen as a rebellious and empowered young woman. The rebellious, empowered young men of early rock 'n' roll proved controversial enough, and most teenagers of the period – male and female – were happy admiring these men from a safe distance, and without wishing the rock 'n' roll attitude to cross the gender divide. Given the tenor of the times, an empowered black female rock 'n' roll idol would have been even more unlikely – which is why African American women have played no part in this discussion.[8]

Texts like these tend to offer a small number of exceptions. Wanda Jackson – a country-turned-rockabilly performer often compared to Elvis Presley – is frequently cited in this context. The same textbook states: 'Jackson stands revealed on [her] records as a performer who could readily go toe-to-toe (or pelvis to pelvis!) with Elvis Presley or with any of the other major male rock 'n' rollers of this period.'[9] Otherwise, we're told that early rock and roll was the domain of wild men; women were anomalies.

Anomalousness, according to Russ, acknowledges that women participate in an art form, but insists that 'she doesn't fit in'. It's a way of ensuring 'permanent marginality'.[10] Related is Russ's concept of isolation, which acknowledges that some women did participate, but claims that they were few.[11] If we're told that a woman performing rock and roll was an anomaly, then what incentive is there to seek more like her? Russ cautions that this thinking leads to complacency; we start to see small numbers of women as sufficient representation.[12] Wanda Jackson deserves her place in rock history, but when she is represented as an exception, others can be hidden.

Feminist scholars have revised some common narratives about domesticity in the post-Second-World-War era to better show that there was no singular experience shared by all women, a tactic which may help in reframing early rock and roll. Stephanie Coontz's work demonstrates that real life in the United States was both poorer and more racially diverse than mid-century television showed.[13] What feminist writer Betty Friedan described as the 'problem with no name' – the alienation and repression experienced by women told not to desire anything beyond domestic life – was centred on white middle- and upper-class women. As bell hooks writes in her assessment of Friedan: 'Specific problems and dilemmas of leisure-class white housewives were real concerns that merited consideration and change, but they were not the pressing political concerns of masses of women.'[14] Many American women, hooks reminds us, have had little choice but to work.[15] Women's employment in the United States did drop with the end of the Second World War, but by the mid-1950s, rose to levels higher than those seen during the war. The social acceptability of working women increased too, although they received lower pay and faced limits as to the types of work made available to them.[16]

'Rock and roller' was not a typical job. Anyone making a living at it was already striving for something unusual. Though the genre was controversial, it is difficult to find evidence of consensus as to who could acceptably perform it. While some critics found rock and roll too vulgar for women, there are counterexamples of male rockers facing critique for being too feminine. One columnist claimed in 1956: 'We live in the "sexbomb" age. A "sexbomb", in the entertainment world, is a performer who gets by on animal allure rather than on artistic merit. . . . . Until now, women have dominated the "sexbomb" field. Elvis Presley is the first to show it can also be a male industry.'[17] The performing conventions of rock and roll, therefore, weren't always seen as too controversial for women: they could also be seen as unremarkable *because* they were performed by a woman. Maureen Mahon writes, for example, about how black women, including Big Mama Thornton – who created sounds and gestural vocabularies central to rock – are frequently silenced while Presley is held up for the 'sexy masculinity [that] comes into being in part as he draws on Thornton's confrontational black femininity'.[18] Thornton, who recorded 'Hound Dog' before Presley, once said: 'I've been singing way before Elvis Presley was born, and he jumps up and becomes a millionaire before me ... off of something that I made popular. They gave him the right .... [N]ow, why do they do that? He makes a million and all this jive because his face is different from mine.'[19]

Both supporters and detractors expected rock and roll to be a fad. Few counted on long careers in the genre, and the idea that a young woman might be an entertainer until she married was not necessarily radical, particularly if she was working class. Record labels even sought 'female Elvises'. RCA promoted rockabilly Janis Martin under that epithet right alongside her labelmate, Elvis Presley. Another woman with the stage name 'Alis Lesley, the Female Presley' toured internationally with Eddie Cochran and Little Richard and played barefoot while shaking her hips.

Nearly everywhere men performed rock and roll, women did too; even if, as is the case today, they were not always present in equal numbers or had career arcs that differed from men's. Driven to capitalise on whatever could be labelled 'rock and roll' and sold to teens, the industry in the mid-1950s defined the term in a fairly catholic way, not yet uniformly rendered masculine. Examine the *Billboard* charts as rock and roll broke in 1955, and not far below Bill Haley's 'Rock around the Clock' and Chuck Berry's 'Maybelline', you'll see a record by Lillian Briggs – the self-proclaimed 'Queen of Rock and Roll' – of Louis Jordan's 'I Want You to Be My Baby'. One of the biggest hits of 1956 was Kay Starr's recording of 'Rock and Roll Waltz', which seemed to poke fun at rock and roll, but started as an inside joke for listeners of Alan Freed's famed rock and roll radio shows. Live performances and sock hops were also common venues for women. Freed's productions on air and in theatres always included women, which was not uncommon for package shows featuring multiple acts. Performers who made appearances on his shows included women from R&B, country, and pop backgrounds. Fans might hear LaVern Baker, Jo-Ann Campbell, Valerie Carr, the Chantels, Jean Chapel, Linda Laurie, Gloria Mann, Ruth McFadden, the Rhythmettes, Jodie Sands; even Freed's third wife, Inga Boling.[20] Ads for venues ranging from state fairs to urban clubs further show that women were working as musicians in rock and roll in many contexts.

The restrictions that women faced in the 1950s should not be discounted, barriers that were broken must be recognised, and the careers that might have blossomed under different circumstances deserve to be mourned. But we must take care to apply these narratives with precision so as to not create blinkers preventing us from seeing the women who did it anyway.

The 1960s and the Double Standard of Content

The first wave of rock and roll is often said to have ended around 1960. The standard story is that men from the early craze left the scene: Elvis Presley was drafted; Chuck Berry served prison time; Jerry Lee Lewis was enmeshed in scandal; Little Richard left music for religion; and a plane crash took the lives of Buddy Holly, Ritchie Valens, and J. P. Richardson (known as 'The Big Bopper'). Meanwhile, payola investigations and the standardising of radio formats took a toll on distribution. The first generation of fans headed into adult life, and the younger cohort coming up behind them had its own taste, which many critics characterise as tamer.

Still, many women produced music rooted in the teen-oriented customs of rock and roll in the early sixties. Connie Francis and Brenda Lee led a youthful group of singers, releasing impressive streaks of hit records. Mary Wells was cutting her first sides for Motown by 1960, as that label was poised for success. Wanda Jackson finally cracked the *Billboard* Top 40 with 'Let's Have a Party' (1960). The first nationally popular 'girl groups', including the Chantels and the Bobbettes, had emerged by the late 1950s and established a burgeoning trend. (See Chapter 8, 'Leaders of the Pack: Girl Groups of the 1960s' for an in-depth consideration of the American girl groups of the 1960s.)

So, was it men's departures or women's participation that signalled rock and roll's 'death', or at least its taming, to many critics? One critic claimed, for example, that it was not 'until rock'n'roll lost its spark of spontaneity and became a tributary of the musical mainstream, with its waters paddled by clean-cut kids, was it acceptable for white girls to dip a toe in'.[21] Another noted that 'female artists were also successful during this period. They were usually not categorised as teen idols, but their music followed the same pallid formulas . . . As is the case of the teen idols, girl groups were simply song stylists.'[22]

This discourse shows how anomalousness and isolation were less effective strategies for separating women from rock in the 1960s. The teen stars at the outset of the decade were just a few of the musicians who are still household names today, rendering the manoeuvre more difficult. The Supremes alone had twelve No. 1 US singles between 1964 and 1969, and they were only one act from a slate of Motown talent. Girl groups from other labels, including the Ronettes, the Shirelles, and the Crystals, had enduring hits, too. Solo singers also sold millions of records each; Aretha Franklin and Lesley Gore, for example, or Petula Clark and Dusty Springfield as part of the British

Invasion. In the countercultural movement, Janis Joplin and Grace Slick were both prominent in psychedelic rock, whereas on the folk side, artists like Joan Baez, Buffy Sainte-Marie, Nina Simone, Joni Mitchell, Janis Ian, and Odetta made an impact with socially conscious lyrics and ushered in a new age of singer-songwriters. (See Chapter 10, '"(You Make Me Feel Like) A Natural Woman": Women in Songwriting', for a consideration of women songwriters, including a discussion of Mitchell.)

Not only was 'rock and roll' undergoing redefinition, but the way we conceptualised the category of 'women' in the 1960s was also shifting. If the dominant narrative of the 1950s was one of repression, in the 1960s, we look towards the growing force of second-wave feminism in tandem with the civil rights movement and the 'free love' of the countercultural sexual revolution. The story is generally no longer one in which women are not participating, but their increased visibility allows narratives employing what Russ terms 'the double standard of content'. The double standard relegates women's art to a separate realm, proclaiming their work less universal than that produced by men. The lower social value placed on women's experiences leads to their art being devalued. Russ explains that even when the art isn't ignored, the double standard can hurt 'all women artists, both those whose art is specifically recognised as "feminine" (it is depreciated) and those whose art is not (it is misinterpreted)'.[23]

It's easy to find examples of music by women that was made throughout the 1960s being devalued, perhaps because of its meaning to women. Susan Douglas's 1994 essay 'Why the Shirelles Mattered' noted that the group's music voiced the concerns of girls but that:

Girl group music has been denied its rightful place in history by a host of male music critics who've either ignored it or trashed it. Typical is this pronouncement, by one of the contributors to *The Rolling Stone History of Rock & Roll*: 'The female group of the early 1960s served to drive the concept of art completely away from rock 'n' roll . . . I feel this genre represents the low point in the history of rock 'n' roll.'[24]

Critical appraisal of the girl groups seems to have shifted in a positive direction since Douglas's essay. Yet the centrality of the women's rights movement to the story of social change in the 1960s to this day has a narrative pull that can paradoxically bring about the double standard of content. The emergence of second-wave feminism can be a useful inter-pretive lens for music of the time, and there is an important body of scholarship showing how music helped young women voice political concerns, as both performers and listeners.[25]

Used uncritically, however, this lens becomes another way of claiming that music speaking to women must have had a limited audience and that the larger story of rock therefore needn't be too bothered by it. One male critic went so far as to blame feminism and the sexual revolution – in a book titled *Go, Girl, Go! The Women's Revolution in Music* – for women's lack of chart success in the 1960s, asking:

If men were exerting such domination over women, why would female record buyers – still the majority – purchase records that reflected that attitude? Why would they buy records such as Leslie [sic] Gore's 'You Don't Own Me' one minute, then turn around and buy Dion's 'Runaround Sue' or Elvis Presley's 'You're the Devil in Disguise'? The answer seems to be that when they wanted meaningful lyrics, they turned to female artists, but when they wanted to dance, when they wanted to tap into that inner male rage that skewed their hormonal balance, they flocked to the male artists who were not ashamed to give it to them.[26]

The sexual revolution and women's movement did not impact only women, just as the songs of Lesley Gore or the Shirelles were not heard by only girls. The double standard of content suggests that rock performances by women amount to the sum of their success or failure to achieve presumed feminist aims. And while discussions of the 1960s are particularly susceptible to this suppression tactic, it often crops up when the audience for a woman's music is believed to be feminine.

The Rock Era and False Categorisation

The term 'rock and roll' has never had a singular definition. By the 1970s, it was sometimes just 'rock', and the number of subgenres included under its umbrella increased. Broad depictions of rock from the 1970s into the 1980s will generally include varied sub-classifications including progressive rock, arena rock, glam, funk, punk, post-punk, new wave, hip-hop, and heavy metal. The umbrella had greater coverage, but the danger of a slippery definition of 'rock' for marginalised performers is that it can continually be redefined to exclude them.

Russ calls this move 'false categorisation', which can manifest as 'denying [creators] entry to the "right" category, by assigning them to the "wrong" category', or even rearranging or renaming phenomena in order to change their significance.[27] 'The assignment of genre can also function as false categorising', writes Russ, 'especially when work appears to fall between established genres and can thereby be assigned to either (and then called an imperfect example of it) or chided for belonging to neither'.[28] The establishment of rock criticism as a discipline over the course of the 1960s encouraged defining and categorising. As Norma Coates argues in her work on the masculinisation of rock, criticism sought to establish rock as serious and 'authentic'. Authenticity was a vague concept that was 'best defined by what it was not: not mass culture, not prefabricated, and not necessarily "popular"'. Coates notes that it was defined on the level of 'I know it when I hear it'.[29] Defining in the negative and on a subjective level makes exclusion easier.

The 'wrong' category for women can be pop, for instance, but it can also vaguely be 'not rock'. Even women who were stars during what we think of as the 'classic rock era' – generally the late 1960s through the 1980s – were frequently excluded from the category for reasons not applied equally to men. Sometimes this was an accusation of a lack of substance via claims that the woman's visual appeal supplanted musical talent. Sometimes it was criticism that she appealed to commercial interests. Sometimes it was because she didn't play an instrument or write her own songs; having her success attributed to a man is also recategorisation. Examples are, again, easy to find:

Pat Benatar may not be 'the rock and roll woman of the '80s', as her record company would have us believe. And after co-authoring only two songs on her debut album, one is still not sure where her mentor, producer Mike Chapman ends, and Pat Benatar picks up. (1980)[30]

If any of rock's male marauders (say Triumph, or Rush) opened up an LP with a stop 'n' start thumper about spotting a 17-year-old number by the record machine and taking said number home for some action, and if the thumper had a chorus like 'I love rock 'n' roll/So put another dime in the juke box, baby' . . . you can bet that the crapometer would be reading about 88% by the time the guitar solo came galloping around the bend. Joan Jett gets away with a lot of such hand-me-down foolishness. Part of her escape hatch is likeability (oh, all right, lustability, but who ever said that dark bangs and well-applied mascara had nothing to do with rock 'n' roll?). (1982)[31]

While these performers and their peers also received favourable reviews embracing them as rockers, comments like those above are frequent enough to destabilise how women were perceived with respect to rock.

False categorisation was hardly a new tactic in music. Jes Skolnik writes in her critique of the 'women-in-rock' trope that:

white rock music, too, has been given critical primacy, with black artists shunted off to subcategories and 'urban radio' (the modern version of 'race music'), and Latinx artists relegated to Spanish-speaking radio only, even artists who record primarily in English. The historical shared and tangled root of rock, R&B, folk, and country somehow divides fairly neatly for most critics, leading to the current overuse of tropes like 'genre-defying' to describe music that plumbs this root fully.[32]

These segregation practices had existed about as long as recorded music. The criticisms lobbed at Pat Benatar or Joan Jett for not 'rocking' correctly might not be given the chance to arise when an artist had already been relegated to another genre. Could Donna Summer be 'disco' as well as 'rock'? Can Chaka Khan's style be thought of as 'rock' in addition to R&B or funk? While many of us find it easy to answer these questions with an unqualified 'yes', significant enough doubt in rock's dominant discourse requires us to make these arguments constantly. And, as Russ noted, falling between genres can itself constitute suppression by recategorisation.

In the early 2000s, the term 'rockism' emerged to describe these gate-keeping practices.[33] Rockism can be difficult to defeat, because, as Kelefa Sanneh reasoned, 'the language of righteous struggle is the language of rock-ism itself.[34] The theme of rebellion and struggle against power is a consistent thread connecting rock culture to its varying subgenres. Empowerment and rebelliousness, however, can be difficult to delineate within an intersectional feminist framework because the patriarchal forces shaping rock – and the risks of reproducing them – do not act upon all people in the same way.[35] Patricia Hill Collins writes that 'empowerment for African-American women will never occur in a context characterised by oppression and social injustice. A group can gain power in such situations by dominating others, but this is not the type of empowerment I found within black women's thinking.'[36] Instead, Collins found empowerment that occurs in tandem with larger, networked efforts to address social injustice. As philosopher Monique Deveaux argues, feminist modes of empowerment can be hard to perceive. 'Feminists need to look at the inner processes that condition women's sense of freedom or choice in addition to external manifestations of power and dominance ... Women's "freedom" does not simply refer to objective possi-bilities for manoeuvring or resisting within a power dynamic but concerns whether a woman feels empowered in her specific context.'[37]

Judging whether a woman feels empowered by her circumstances is more complex than noticing if she has tattoos, wears leather, or plays electric guitar. Yet while we do not always know how performers navigated their options or asserted personal rebellions, we can complicate the idea that pleasing audiences of straight white men is evidence of rebellion. Dismantling such notions could trigger more significant disruptions. As

Russ writes of women in literature: 'In order to have her "belong" ..., the tradition to which she belongs must also be admitted. Other writers must be admitted along with their tradition, written and unwritten. Speech must be admitted. Canons of excellence and conceptions of excellence must change, perhaps beyond recognition.'[38] Would the concept of 'rock' survive such a dismantling?

Revivals and Lack of Models

In 1991, Barney Hoskyns declared that 'rock and roll is being hijacked by angry girls with electric guitars'. He continued:

Tired of playing airbrushed pop dollies for salivating male voyeurs, women on both sides of the Atlantic have seized the traditional rock weapon of phallic oppression and made it their own.

More importantly, they have exploded the Ideal Feminine of pop by singing of sweat and blood, lust and menstruation, fear and self-loathing. Inger Lorre of LA's infamous Nymphs quotes Rimbaud to the effect that when woman has thrown off her servitude she will 'discover strange, unfathomable, repellent, delicious things' – which is precisely what acts as diverse as Hole, Belly, L7, Daisy Chainsaw, PJ Harvey, The Breeders, and Babes in Toyland are busy doing on their new releases.[39]

Critics wrote so much about women's presence in rock around this time that Ann Powers once quipped, 'I've often joked that I wrote at least one article about the "year of women in rock" every single year in the 90s.'[40] An impulse to explore this apparent trend on a deeper level led to a new wave of cultural criticism and books on 'women in rock'. Many of the musicians profiled in this literature seemed to harken back to earlier subgenres in which women were particularly visible. The 1990s and early 2000s saw new girl groups, amongst them TLC, Destiny's Child, and the Spice Girls. Meanwhile, singer-songwriters including Tori Amos, Tracy Chapman, Sheryl Crow, Alanis Morissette, and Liz Phair echoed the movement of the 1960s and 1970s.

These revivals also demarcate a cycle of remembering and forgetting. Russ refers to this as 'lack of models'. She argues that it isn't contradictory to claim that women's traditions exist while also noting that contemporary women lack models. 'One difference is in the age of the women involved', she notes. 'Female support groups exist, but they must be created anew by each generation, so that what was missing during one's formative years may (with luck and drive) be built or discovered later on at considerable cost in time, energy, and self-confidence.'[41] Thus, 'women in rock' are reinvented every decade or two.

Looking back, for example, it seems that 1974 was also declared a 'year of women in rock'. One 1975 newspaper article bemoaned the proliferation of writing on the topic: '[T]he stories keep appearing. What they do is merge different styles of music and performers to substantiate a "new phenomenon", when in fact different types of female singers and groups of female singers have been with us right along.'[42] The columnist also mentions a new book documenting the phenomenon, *Rock 'n' Roll Woman*, by Katherine Orloff.[43] Orloff concluded that 'rock and roll' and 'women' were contradicting terms: 'If rock demonstrates that very masculine power, a woman is at odds with the definition immediately. While she can play the notes and sing the tunes, all the elements that have influenced her upbringing and attitudes tell her she is in the wrong place.'[44]

And around we go. The terms 'rock' and 'women' still resist rectification, so the trope of 'women in rock' continues. But Russ urges us to keep working on the problem. The worst thing we can do, she notes, is turn our backs.[45] Recovery is important, but we should also not mistake enlarging the existing canon for systemic change. We have to monitor the cultural work that the label 'women in rock' does, remaining cognisant of the history of suppression it contains. We must rethink how we define women *and* rock to break old cycles, prevent harm to musicians, and address inequality in the industry.

Notes

1. Barbara O'Dair (ed.), *Trouble Girls: The Rolling Stone Book of Women in Rock* (New York: Random House, 1997), xxiii.
2. *PlayboyDotCom*, Twitter post (21 May 2014, 5:25 p.m.), available at https://twitter.com/PlayboyPlus/status/469227393274900480?s=20 (accessed 11 December 2020); Neko Case, Twitter post (21 May 2014, 5:45 p.m.), available at https://twitter.com/NekoCase/status/469232638616543232?s=20 (accessed 11 December 2020).
3. Virginia Pelley, 'Internet Goes After Neko Case After She Rejects Playboy Magazine's "Compliments"', *Daily Banter* (24 May 2014, updated 17 February 2016), available at https://thedailybanter.com/2014/05/neko-case-cunt-ingratitude-toward-playboy-magazine/ (accessed 12 May 2018).
4. Quoted in Jennifer Lyn King, 'Georgia O'Keeffe and the Gender Debate: Can a Woman Be Great, or Only a Great Woman?', *Salon* (17 July 2016), available at www.salon.com/2016/07/16/georgia_okeeffe_and_the_gender_debate_can_a_woman_be_great_or_only_a_great_woman/ (accessed 12 November 2019).

5. Joanna Russ, *How to Suppress Women's Writing* (Austin, TX: University of Texas Press, 1983), 4–5.

6. Dr Stacy L. Smith et al., *Inclusion in the Recording Studio? Gender and Race/ Ethnicity of Artists, Songwriters & Producers across 600 Popular Songs from 2012–2017*, Annenberg Inclusion Initiative (January 2018).

7. Smith, *Inclusion*, 27.

8. Joseph G. Schloss, Larry Starr, and Christopher Alan Waterman, *Rock: Music, Culture, and Business* (New York: Oxford University Press, 2012), 73.

9. Schloss, Starr, and Waterman, *Rock*, 71.

10. Russ, *Suppress*, 85–6.

11. Russ, *Suppress*, 62.

12. Russ, *Suppress*, 85.

13. Stephanie Coontz, *A Strange Stirring: The Feminine Mystique and American Women at the Dawn of the 1960s* (New York: Basic Books, 2011), 60.

14. bell hooks, *Feminism Is for Everybody: Passionate Politics* (New York and London: Routledge, 2014), 2.

15. hooks, *Feminism*, 2–3; Coontz, *A Strange Stirring*, 60.

16. Coontz, *A Strange Stirring*, 59–62.

17. Hal Boyle, 'Elvis Not So Bad, Boyle Decides', *Associated Press* (5 August 1956), n.p.

18. Maureen Mahon, 'Listening for Willie Mae "Big Mama" Thornton's Voice: The Sound of Race and Gender Transgressions in Rock and Roll', *Women and Music: A Journal of Gender and Culture*, vol. 15 (November 2011), 10.

19. Quoted in Mahon, 'Listening for Willie Mae', 9.

20. Alan Freed's archives are available online at alanfreed.com. See https://web .archive.org/web/20180414030856/ http://www.alanfreed.com/ (accessed 14 April 2018).

21. John Pidgeon, 'Venus: The Role of Women in Fifties Music', *The History of Rock* (1981), available at www.rocksbackpages.com/article.html? ArticleID=12456 (accessed 21 September 2011).

22. Paul Friedlander with Peter Miller, *Rock & Roll: A Social History*, 2nd ed. (Boulder, CO: Westview Press, 2007), 70.

23. Russ, *Suppress*, 44.

24. Susan J. Douglas, *Where the Girls Are: Growing Up Female With the Mass Media* (London: Penguin Books, 1995), 85–6.

25. See Jacqueline Warwick, *Girl Groups, Girl Culture: Popular Music and Identity in the 1960s* (New York: Routledge, 2007); and Diane Pecknold, 'The Politics of Voice in Tween Girls' Music Criticism', *Jeunesse: Young People, Texts, Cultures*, vol. 9, no. 2 (2017), 70.

26. James L. Dickerson, *Go Girl Go! The Women's Revolution in Music* (New York: Schirmer Trade Books, 2005), 40.

27. Russ, *Suppress*, 49.

28. Russ, *Suppress*, 53.

29. Norma J. Coates, 'It's a Man's, Man's World: Television and the Masculinization of Rock Discourse and Culture' (PhD thesis, University of Wisconsin, Madison, WI, 2002), 27.

30. Dino Tortu, 'Pat Benatar and Band', *The Herald-News*, Passaic, NJ (11 January 1980), n.p.

31. Mitchel Cohen, 'Joan Jett: I Love Rock 'N' Roll', *Creem* (March 1982), n.p.

32. Jes Skolnik, 'The Hideous Persistence of the "Women in Rock" Issue', *Medium* (30 April 2018), https://medium.com/@modernistwitch/the-hideous-persistence-of-the-women-in-the-rock-issue-15e206fe5a7c (accessed 24 November 2019).

33. Miles Parks Grier, 'Said the Hooker to the Thief: "Some Way Out" of Rockism', *Journal of Popular Music Studies*, vol. 25, no. 1 (2013), 31.

34. Kelefa Sanneh, 'The Rap Against Rockism', *The New York Times* (31 October 2004), available at www.nytimes.com/2004/10/31/arts/music/the-rap-against-rockism.html (accessed 12 July 2020).

35. The term 'intersectional' was first defined by Kimberlé Williams Crenshaw. See Devon W. Carbado, Kimberlé Williams Crenshaw, Vickie M. Mays, and Barbara Tomlinson, 'Intersectionality: Mapping the Movements of a Theory', *Du Bois Review: Social Science Research on Race*, vol. 10, no. 2 (2013), 303–12.

36. Patricia Hill Collins, *Black Feminist Thought: Knowledge, Consciousness, and the Politics of Empowerment*, 2nd ed. (New York: Routledge, 2009), x.

37. Monique Deveaux, 'Feminism and Empowerment: A Critical Reading of Foucault', *Feminist Studies*, vol. 20, no. 2 (Summer 1994), 234.

38. Russ, *Suppress*, 85.

39. Barney Hoskyns, 'Angry Young Women', *Vogue* (1991).

40. Lucy O'Brien, *She-Bop: The Definitive History of Women in Popular Music*, revised 3rd ed. (London: Jawbone, 2012), 355.

41. Russ, *Suppress*, 86.

42. Tom Zito, 'Women's Role in Rock Stirs Debate', *The Philadelphia Inquirer* (3 January 1975), 28.

43. Katherine Orloff, *Rock 'n' Roll Woman* (Los Angeles: Nash Publishing, 1974).

44. Zito, 'Women's Role', 28.

45. Russ, *Suppress*, 109.

Further Reading

Mahon, Maureen. *Black Diamond Queens: African American Women and Rock and Roll* (Durham, NC: Duke University Press, 2020).

McDonnell, Evelyn (ed.). *Women Who Rock: Bessie to Beyoncé, Girl Groups to Riot Grrrl* (New York, NY: Black Dog & Leventhal, 2018).

10 | '(You Make Me Feel Like) A Natural Woman': Women in Songwriting

KATHERINE WILLIAMS

For over a hundred years, the history of popular music has been male-dominated, populated by the men who sing the songs, write the songs, produce the songs, and run the record companies and distribution strategies. The male experience in popular music can therefore be assumed to be well documented. The terrain would look very different without Billie Holiday's 'Fine and Mellow' (1939), Nina Simone's 'Mississippi Goddam' (1964), Carole King's '(You Make Me Feel Like) A Natural Woman' (1967), Joni Mitchell's *Blue* (1971), Kate Bush's 'Wuthering Heights' (1978), or Adele's *19* (or *21*, or *25*, released 2008, 2011, and 2015 respectively). Since Mitchell and King, these examples all come from one tradition: the confessional singer-songwriter that emerged from the 1960s New York folk club scene. As David Shumway has commented, the term singer-songwriter came into use in the early 1970s. Proponents of the idiom, according to him, '[are] not anyone who sings his or her own songs, but a performer whose self-presentation and musical form fit a certain model . . . [Joni Mitchell, Carole King, and others] created a new niche in the popular music market. These singer-songwriters were not apolitical, but they took a confessional stance in their songs, revealing their interior selves and their private struggles.'[1]

Lucy O'Brien explains that throughout popular music history, female songwriters have sought to 'make sense of their world, to clear an inviolable space that is theirs rather than the possession of a man'.[2] The female perspective could be understood from this standpoint: these songs were an authentic representation of the singer-songwriter's experiences, and they were able to connect with their audience through both their music and through sharing a close physical space with the singer-songwriters in the bars and coffee shops in which this tradition began. The four case studies I explore in this chapter – Carole King, Joni Mitchell, Kate Bush, and Adele – are singer-songwriters. I differentiate here between performing singer-songwriters and behind-the-scenes songwriters such as librettist Dorothy Fields (1904–74) or songwriter Diane Warren (b.1956). I explore their early lives and musical experiences, their emergence on the scene as singer-songwriters, and what – if anything – makes their female perspective stand out from the male norm in popular music.

Carole King

Carole King was born Carol Joan Klein on 9 February 1942 in Brooklyn, and added the 'e' to her first name to stand out from two high school peers with the same name. Following in a long line of Jewish entertainers who sought success under a non-ethnic name, she chose 'King' to replace 'Klein'.[3] King learnt to play the piano as a child, and was encouraged in this by her parents. She attended James Madison High School in Brooklyn. While a high school student, she volunteered to contribute to the annual James Madison High School Sing, and writes in her autobiography that she found writing and arranging songs very satisfying. She explains that although she performed some of her songs herself, she gained the most pleasure from teaching other students to sing what she had written, eventually forming a doo-wop group from her Advanced Mathematics class (the 'Co-Sines'). Although her main goal at this point was to complete the arrangements and hear them performed, she realised that if she sang one of the four vocal lines herself, she needed to bring in fewer performers.[4] The focus of her recollections suggests that she did not write songs as a vehicle for herself as performer, but that she performed them as a way to get the music heard.

At this time, King's main musical influences were the popular records that Alan Freed played on his radio shows.[5] As King recalled: 'The music that had informed the songwriters on the records Alan played was a lot more gritty and diverse than the simple pop ditties, show tunes, and classical music to which I had been listening for most of my life. But I was determined to learn, and the timing in popular music and political history was favourable.'[6]

King recalls how her arranging technique over the years stems from her high school experiences:

In those days I wrote exclusively on piano ... I've always loved wrapping layers around a melody. When arranging for voices with a band, usually I begin with a foundation consisting of melody, lyrics, and the chords and rhythm coming from my piano. Then I bring in the rhythm section: a drumbeat on a kit with three drums, several cymbals, and a pair of sticks, mallets or brushes; a bass line that's pretty close to what my left hand plays on the piano; a rhythm guitar that complements my piano; and sometimes a lead guitar to add accents and fills to the mix of piano, rhythm guitar, bass and drums. Then I add vocal harmonies. And if I'm lucky enough to have the use of an orchestra, I add a final layer of orchestral instruments.[7]

She was aware that the weakness in her songwriting lay in her lyric writing, commenting:

Though I wasn't good at writing lyrics myself, I knew how important they could be in a pop song ... Lyrics aimed at my generation didn't need to be good, but they needed to be relevant to the burning issues of a teenager's life. As far as I knew, the biggest concern of girls in the fifties was 'Does he like me?'[8]

After graduating high school in June 1958, she set about obtaining a record contract. While supportive of her endeavours, King's parents encouraged her to attend the nearby Queens College and study for a teaching qualification as a fallback.

King met Gerry Goffin at Queens College, and they began to collaborate on songs, with King writing the music and Goffin the lyrics. By August 1959 they were married and King was pregnant with their first daughter Louise, who was followed later by Sherry. Since leaving high school, King had visited the Brill Building on Broadway regularly to try and sell her songs, and now did so with Goffin. One day in 1960 she bumped into singer-songwriter Neil Sedaka, who suggested she meet with Don Kirshner and Al Nevin, with whose publishing company he had recently signed. She set up a meeting and played them some songs in their office. They suggested she return with Goffin the next day, and the pair were immediately signed with Aldon music, and given an office at 1650 Broadway, which along with 1619 Broadway, was known as the 'Brill Building'. The songwriters hired by Brill Building producers were younger than traditional popular music songwriters, and therefore closer in age to their intended audience. An important development from the pop music that had come before was the inclusion of women. As Mary E. Rohlfing comments: 'It was at this time that women made their entry into rock'n'roll ... as composers, players, and producers.'[9]

Crucially, these songwriters could write about and therefore validate important life experiences for their listeners. In his 2002 categorisation of forms of authenticity in rock, Allan Moore suggests that authenticity is not created from certain musical features, but rather from the interpretation that can be brought by listeners. Goffin and King's songs offered 'second-person authenticity' to many fans: '[This] occurs when a performance succeeds in conveying the impression to a listener that that listener's experience of life is being validated, that the music is "telling it like it is" for them.'[10] Their first major hit was 'Will You Still Love Me Tomorrow?', recorded by the Shirelles and released on 21 November 1960. The song stayed at No. 1 in the Billboard 100 for ten weeks. As King had predicted, 'Does he like me?' was the issue that spoke most keenly to the popular music audience, which was largely comprised of teenage girls. The song documented the insecurities and anxieties faced by a young woman after a one-night stand, with lines such as:

Tonight you're mine, completely . . .
But will you love me tomorrow?
Is this a lasting treasure
Or just a moment's pleasure . . .
So tell me now and I won't ask again
Will you still love me tomorrow?

However, as King has commented:

A lot of people think I wrote the lyrics for 'Will You Still Love Me Tomorrow?' because they express so keenly the emotions of a teenage girl worried that her boyfriend won't love her anymore once she gives him her most precious one-time-only prize. Those lyrics were written by Gerry, whose understanding of human nature transcended gender. My contribution to 'Will You Still Love Me Tomorrow?' included writing the melody, playing piano in the studio, and arranging the string parts.[11]

(See also Chapter 8, 'Leaders of the Pack: Girl Groups of the 1960s'.) After this hit, both King and Goffin were able to give up their day jobs to focus on their writing. During the 1960s, the pair wrote a number of classic songs for a variety of artists. Throughout her career thus far, King had been indifferent to performing her own songs. Her voice, and her piano skills, provided a method through which to hear her music.

King and Goffin divorced in 1968. She moved to Laurel Canyon in Los Angeles with her two daughters, and continued songwriting, as well as reactivating her performing career by forming The City. Her position as a behind-the-scenes songwriter was to change still further in 1971, when she released her second studio album.[12] *Tapestry* (Ode Records, produced by Lou Adler) was a collection of songs written or co-written by King, and performed by King at the piano (Box 10.1).

Box 10.1 *Tapestry*, track listing and songwriter credits

Side 1
1. I Feel the Earth Move
2. So Far Away
3. It's Too Late (lyrics by Toni Stern)
4. Home Again
5. Beautiful
6. Way Over Yonder

Side 2
7. You've Got a Friend
8. Where You Lead (lyrics by Carole King and Toni Stern)
9. Will You Still Love Me Tomorrow? (lyrics by Gerry Goffin)
10. Smackwater Jack
11. Tapestry
12. (You Make Me Feel Like) A Natural Woman (Goffin, King, Jerry Wexler)

Tapestry was to become one of the best-selling albums ever, with over 25 million copies sold worldwide. It was also well received critically, with esteemed rock critics claiming that her unadorned and untrained voice would provide a touchstone for female singer-songwriters, and that *Tapestry* surpassed previous milestones of personal intimacy and musical accomplishment.[13] In 1972, it received four Grammys: Album of the Year, Best Pop Vocal Performance (Female), Record of the Year, (for 'It's Too Late'), and Song of the Year (for 'You've Got a Friend').

King cut her teeth working as the musical half of the songwriting team Goffin and King, essentially working behind the scenes providing songs for famous performing artists. Despite a lack of confidence in her own lyric-writing ability, she had given a good deal of thought to the subjects that would appeal to a popular music audience comprised predominantly of young adults in her demographic. However, it was when she recorded an album of her own performances of a collection of such songs that she reached significant success. She was able to connect with her audience in two ways: through creating relevant material and content, and through her accessibility as a performer.

Joni Mitchell

'Will You Still Love Me Tomorrow?' was No. 1 while Joni Mitchell (born Roberta Joan Anderson, in Fort Macleod Alberta, 7 November 1943) was establishing herself as a performer on the folk circuit in Saskatoon, Saskatchewan and Toronto, Ontario. The folk scene in each city tended to accord veteran folk performers the exclusive right to perform their signature songs, which were most often not written by the performer. Mitchell resolved to write her own songs, which often reflected personal concerns of love, sorrow, and joy, as well as wider political and environmental anxieties.

In 1964, Mitchell was touring the folk circuit in Ontario. She was pregnant by an ex-boyfriend, and unable to raise the child. She gave her daughter, Kelly Dale Anderson, up for adoption. She later attributed the inspiration for her early songwriting endeavours to this experience, claiming it forced her to write songs that put her personal emotions and experiences on show. In late 1965, she left Canada for the first time with American folk singer Chuck Mitchell. They moved to Detroit in the United states, and married in June 1965. This marriage and musical partnership ended in early 1967. Joni kept his surname and moved to New York City, playing venues up and down the East Coast. She performed frequently in coffeehouses and folk clubs, and by now her repertoire often included her own material. By this time she was beginning to become well known for her unique songwriting and her innovative guitar style, informed in part by disabilities caused by a childhood bout of polio.

In addition to the success of other artists' versions of her songs, Mitchell continued to rise in prominence for her own performances and interpretations of her own work, becoming, to many, the archetypal 1960s confessional singer-songwriter. Renowned singer-songwriter David Crosby heard her performing in a club in Coconut Grove, Florida, and introduced her to friends in his musical circle back in Los Angeles. As a result of this, Elliot Roberts became her manager. Roberts introduced her to producer David Geffen, and she was eventually signed to Reprise in 1968.

Mitchell's best known album is her fourth studio album. *Blue* was released just four months after *Tapestry*, in June 1971. The period 1970–71 was a fruitful one for Mitchell and King, both of whom recorded their albums at the same time in Sunset Sound in Hollywood. The two singer-songwriters were part of the same musical community, and as well as sharing recording space, shared musical collaborators. While recording her album, Mitchell was in the throes of a love affair with singer-songwriter James Taylor, who played guitar on the tracks 'All I Want' and 'A Case of You'. *Blue* documents several romantic relationships she had during its creation. People were keen to speculate on Mitchell's liaisons and often let gossip preclude discussion of her music, as the following comment by Jack Hamilton shows: '"A Case of You" is (maybe) about Leonard Cohen; "My Old Man" is (likely) about Graham Nash; "Carey" is (almost certainly) about an unfamous expat bartender that Mitchell met while vacationing in Crete.'[14] 'The Last Time I Saw Richard' is about leaving Chuck Mitchell. King had met James Taylor in 1970, and the pair established a long-standing musical relationship. Taylor was recording his own album *Mud Slide Slim and the Blue Horizon* at Sunset Sound concurrently to King's *Tapestry*, and both albums featured versions of 'You've Got a Friend'. King played piano on *Mud Slide Slim*, while Mitchell sang backing vocals. Taylor played guitar on *Tapestry*, and both Taylor and Mitchell appeared as backing vocalists.

Box 10.2 *Blue*, track listing. All songs written and performed by Joni Mitchell

Side 1
1. All I Want
2. My Old Man
3. Little Green
4. Carey
5. Blue

Side 2
6. California
7. This Flight Tonight
8. River
9. A Case of You
10. The Last Time I Saw Richard

Joni Mitchell wrote the songs for *Blue* during a self-imposed sabbatical in Europe. The songs, which develop and refine the idiom of the confessional and relatable singer-songwriter, traverse a range of life experiences and the associated emotions. As her biographer Mark Bego has commented:

She had dug deep inside herself and created a masterpiece. Joni admits '*Blue* was the first of my confessional albums, and it was an attempt to say, "You want to worship me? Well, okay, I'm just like you. I'm a lonely person." Because that's all we have in common.'[15]

The opening song, 'All I Want' is the most uptempo and upbeat song on the album. It is addressed to the man she loves, and she sings of the many ways she plans to express her devotion:

All I really, really want our love to do
Is to bring out the best in me and in you
I wanna talk to you, I wanna shampoo you . . .

I wanna knit you a sweater,
Wanna write you a love letter

She also addresses the depression when she and her lover hurt each other:

Do you see how you hurt me baby
So I hurt you too
Then we both get so blue

In the third song on the album, 'Little Green', Mitchell addresses the child she gave up for adoption. She nicknames the child Kelly Green, and sings of the devastation she felt at giving her up and all the events she will miss in the child's life:

Choose her a name she'll answer to
Call her green and the winters cannot fade her
Call her green for the children who have made her little, green ...
There'll be crocuses to bring to school tomorrow ...
There'll be icicles and birthday clothes and sometimes
There'll be sorrow

This is a song from the 1967 era, and the only accompaniment is Mitchell herself on guitar. This serves to make the song more intimate and personal, and projects the feelings behind the song to her audience. The audience seeks and believes that the music they are hearing communicates authenticity of experience: a confessional singer-songwriter is someone who writes lyrics about their own experiences, and sings and accompanies themselves in performance. The unadorned vocal and accompaniment styles of both King and Mitchell help portray the idea of an unmediated, authentic persona, and their music may be seen as a direct line of communication to an audience that is always searching to validate their own experiences. In addition to the second-person authenticity (validation of experience) of King and Goffin, King's solo work and Mitchell's confessional style exhibit 'first-person authenticity', or 'authenticity as expression'. As Moore explains, here an unadorned vocal and instrumental style can help reduce any perceived mediation of content. The audience feels closer to the performer because they believe they are sharing autobiographical experiences, which they themselves may have experienced too.[16]

Mitchell accompanies herself on piano for the title song, 'Blue'. This song is purportedly about her relationship with James Taylor, and she sings of his melancholy, and his tendency to bury his feelings with a variety of methods:

You can make it through these waves
Acid, booze, and ass
Needles, guns, and grass
Lots of laughs

Mitchell continued her live touring and studio recording practices throughout the 1970s and 1980s. Her style evolved throughout her career, as shown by jazz and pop influences on later albums including *Court and Spark* (1974) and *Mingus* (1979). In 1994, she won a Grammy for the album *Turbulent Indigo*. *Taming the Tiger* (1998) was her last album of new original songs for some time: in 2000 she released an album of reinterpretations of jazz standards, *Both Sides Now*, followed two years later by *Travelogue*, an album of reworkings of her own material. In 2006, she released *Shine*, a much-anticipated album of new songs. Her influence on musicians around her has continued to be evidenced through her entire career: in September 2007, the prominent jazz musician Herbie Hancock released an album of jazz covers of Mitchell's songs entitled *River: The Joni Letters*. Throughout her career, Mitchell asserted her creative authority by producing all her albums herself. In recent years she has suffered from a variety of health issues, and at the time of writing (August 2019) does not perform any more but occasionally appears in public to speak on environmental issues.

Kate Bush

The English singer-songwriter Kate Bush was born Catherine Bush on 30 July 1958. She began songwriting aged eleven, and after sharing many of her self-recorded songs with family friend Ricky Hopper, who passed them on to Dave Gilmour (guitarist from Pink Floyd), was signed by EMI at sixteen. O'Brien has commented that Bush's 1978 No. 1 debut single, 'Wuthering Heights', 'an offering to the lost love of Cathy and Heathcliff, was a brittle, shivering pop song with a folk base incorporating strings, piano and mournful echo. Nothing like it had been heard before: especially the voice – a high-pitched wander through octaves that pierced through the banality of daytime radio.'[17] 'Wuthering Heights' debuted at No. 1 in the UK singles chart, where it remained for four weeks. Bush was the first female UK singer-songwriter to achieve a No. 1 with a self-penned song. 'Wuthering Heights' was released just a month before her debut album *The Kick Inside*, which also topped the album charts in the UK. The album was named after the eponymous song, which took an old English folk tale about an incestuous pregnancy and consequent suicide as its inspiration.

Box 10.3 *The Kick Inside,* **track listing. All songs written by Kate Bush**

Side 1
1. Moving
2. The Saxophone Song
3. Strange Phenomena
4. Kite
5. The Man with the Child in His Eyes
6. Wuthering Heights

Side 2
7. James and the Cold Gun
8. Feel It
9. Oh to Be in Love
10. L'Amour Looks Something Like You
11. Them Heavy People
12. Room for the Life
13. The Kick Inside

Kate Bush's musical style incorporates a number of musical influences including pop, classical music, glam rock, folk and ethnic styles, and studio effects. Her primary instrument, piano, is the feature upon which most of her accompaniments are built. It is worth noting here that female singer-songwriters have historically been more readily accepted when their primary instrument is typically understood to be feminine. Lucy Green's suggested 'performance of femininity' is not disrupted by the piano-playing of King and Bush, nor by Mitchell's acoustic guitar.[18]

Bush's soprano voice is unusual in the singer-songwriter idiom, and the listener's attention is immediately grabbed by its high frequency and clear timbre. Her music has been described as 'surreal', in part for her frequent references to literature and the cinema, and for her rapid switches between emotional states.[19] Unlike King, who appealed largely to universal emotions, and Mitchell, who validated thousands of listeners' personal experiences, Bush embodied characters she had

created in her songs, making them believable through her vocal por-
trayal. After Simon Frith and Philip Auslander, Moore defines this
type of character construction in popular song as 'song character', or
'song personality'.[20]

In 1979, Bush embarked on a six-week tour of her rapidly
produced second album *Lionheart*. She had recently begun to study
dance, and the shows utilised complex choreography, lighting, several
costume changes, and Bush performed onstage alongside a magician.
After this tour, dubbed The Tour of Life, Bush refused to do live tours
of her work, choosing to save her creativity for the studio and music
videos. She produced a *Live on Stage* EP from her tour, and co-produced
her 1980 album *Never for Ever*. Like Mitchell before her, she asserted
authorial authority by self-producing all ensuing albums. All her studio
albums charted, as did many of her singles.

This hiatus in live performance lasted until her 2014 Before the Dawn
residency at the Hammersmith Apollo. The Beatles had famously set
a precedent for artists that chose to perform and create in the studio, by
refusing to perform live after August 1966. As they had demonstrated
before her, it was possible to produce much more intricate soundscapes
in the recording studio than those it would be possible to perform live. Her
albums utilised synthesisers, drum machines, huge orchestras, and double
tracking and layering of her own voice. Once again, the pattern for existing
in the popular music world had been established and reinforced by male
'genius' figures. Bush continued to write and record studio albums through
the 1980s and early 1990s before taking a career break to focus on marriage
and motherhood until *Aerial*, which was released in November 2005.

Bush represented the evolution of female singer-songwriters: no longer
bound to confessional songs based on personal experiences and understandings of the world, and no longer restricted to unadorned simplicity of
vocal style, she was able to extend her expressivity and musical style with
a range of techniques and references.

Adele

Adele Laurie Blue Adkins was born on 5 May 1988, in Tottenham, North
London. Adele (the name which she later used as her stage name) graduated from the BRIT School of Performing Arts in Croydon (South
London) in 2006. A friend posted a demo song she had written for a class
project on Myspace, which led to a phone call from Richard Russell, owner

of the independent record label XL Recordings. She was signed by the label in September 2006. Adele is a contemporary pop singer, and credits her musical influences to such towering figures as 'Etta [James] to get a bit of soul, Ella [Fitzgerald] for my chromatic scales and Roberta Flack for control'.[21] Her first two albums, *19* (2008), and *21* (2011), were famously break-up albums, attributed to different failed relationships. They are titled after her age during the main writing and recording period of the albums. Her first album included her first song, 'Hometown Glory', written aged sixteen, about West Norwood in South London, where she spent a good deal of her youth.[22] The album *19* also included 'First Love', 'Daydreamer', and 'Tired', providing a focal point for audiences who wanted to associate with a public figure who wasn't afraid to advertise her romantic failures. The lyrics to 'Tired', for example, show a despondent acceptance of her partner's lack of interest:

I'm tired of trying
Your teasing ain't enough
Fed up of biding your time
When I don't get nothing back

Adele's audiences, like Mitchell's and King's before her, seek the second-person authenticity defined by Moore as 'authenticity of experience'. The album was hugely successful, gaining platinum status eight times in the United Kingdom, and three times in the United States. Adele commenced the first of three world tours to promote the album, playing enormous and prominent venues such as Wembley Stadium and the American TV show *Saturday Night Live*, setting her far away from the intimate venues in which King and Mitchell performed in their early careers.

Box 10.4 *19*, track listing and songwriter credits

1. Daydreamer (Adele Adkins)
2. Best for Last (Adkins)
3. Chasing Pavements (Adkins/Eg White)
4. Cold Shoulder (Adkins/Sacha Skarbek)
5. Crazy for You (Adkins)
6. Melt My Heart to Stone (Adkins/White)
7. First Love (Adkins)

8. Right as Rain (Adkins/Leon Michels/Jeff Silverman/Nick Movshon/
   Clay Holley)
9. Make You Feel My Love (Bob Dylan)
10. My Same (Adkins)
11. Tired (Adkins/White)
12. Hometown Glory (Adkins)

As Box 10.4 shows, Adele herself was the primary songwriter for *19*, which helped provide her audience with a sense of intimacy and the authenticity of shared experience. Sarah Suhadolnik argued in 2016 that, although Adele tried to retain some ownership as songwriter of her material with her second album, audiences were by now focused on the power of her voice and her vocal delivery. 'Recurring themes on fan commentary', Suhadolnik writes, 'consistently point to the sounds of sincere, heartfelt angst as a primary draw.'[23] Many of the songs on 2011's *21* were collaboratively written (see Box 10.5), as Adele's public figure shifted from one that commanded second-person authenticity through the experiences expressed, to one who begins to embody third-person authenticity, or 'authenticity of execution'. As Moore explains: '"third person authenticity" ... arises ... when a performer succeeds in conveying the impression of accurately representing the ideas of another, embedded within a tradition of performance'.[24] Adele's command of the bluesy, soulful style, along with the association with the African American singers she lists as inspiration, situates her within a distant tradition that connotes pain and hardship.

Adele's breakthrough successful album was *21*, which won her six Grammys, two BRIT awards, and three American Music Awards, achieving platinum status seventeen times in the United Kingdom, and certified diamond status in the United States. Having established a reputation and public profile as an authentic singer-songwriter who spoke to shared experiences through perceived autobiographical content and her singing voice, sole authorship of the musical and lyrical material became less crucial.

Box 10.5 *21*, track listing and songwriter credits

1. Rolling in the Deep (Adele Adkins/Paul Epworth)
2. Rumour Has It (Adkins/Ryan Tedder)
3. Turning Tables (Adkins/Tedder)

> **Box 10.5 (cont.)**
>
> 4. Don't You Remember (Adkins/Dan Wilson)
> 5. Set Fire to the Rain (Adkins/Fraser T. Smith)
> 6. He Won't Go (Adkins/Epworth)
> 7. Take It All (Adkins/Francis White)
> 8. I'll Be Waiting (Adkins/Epworth)
> 9. One and Only (Adkins/Wilson/Greg Wells)
> 10. Lovesong (Robert Smith/Laurence Tolhurst/Simon Gallup/Boris Williams/Pearl Thompson/Roger O'Donnell)
> 11. Someone Like You (Adkins/Wilson)

Adele is also an interesting case study for the idea of the constructed persona. As Moore has suggested: '[when listening to popular song] it is usually more helpful to recognise that we are listening to a persona, projected by a singer, in other words to an artificial construction that may, or may not, be identical with the person(ality) of the singer'.[25] This disjunct is underscored further by the personality that comes across in interviews. Suhadolnik comments:

Adele has … drawn clear distinctions between her instrument and her self, constructing a performer identity that is generally obscured by her music. Ask her, as *Vogue* did in 2012, about what it is like to be a girl who 'sings her own blues', and she will likely respond that she is the total opposite of her records. In the extensive interview, Adele characterised herself as 'chatty, bubbly and kind of carefree really'.[26]

The difference between Adele's artistic and performed persona and her off-stage personality is underlined by her acceptance speech at the BRIT awards in 2012:

Nothing makes me prouder than coming home with six Grammys, and coming to the BRITs and winning Album of the Year. I'm so, so, proud to be British, and to be flying our flag, and I'm so proud to be in the room with all of you –

[HOST JAMES CORDEN MOUNTS THE STAGE]: I'm so, so sorry, and I can't believe I'm about to do this –
ADELE: You're going to cut me off?
CORDEN: I'm so sorry!
ADELE: Can I just say then, goodbye, and I'll see you next time round, yeah?
    [Flips the middle finger]

Adele took a short career break after the worldwide success and fame *21* brought. She released *25* on 27 November 2015, commenting:

My last record was a break-up record, and if I had to label this one, I would call it a make-up record. Making up for lost time. Making up for everything I ever did and never did. *25* is about getting to know who I've become without realizing. And I'm sorry it took so long but, you know, life happened.[27]

The 'life happen[ing]' that she alluded to included settling down into a long-term relationship with Simon Konecki, and giving birth to her first son Angelo in October 2012. Her relationship with Konecki was confirmed to have ended in April 2019.[28]

Box 10.6 *25*, track listing and songwriter credits

1. Hello (Adele Adkins/Greg Kurstin)
2. Send My Love (To Your New Lover) (Adkins/Max Martin/ Shellback)
3. I Miss You (Adkins/Paul Epworth)
4. When We Were Young (Adkins/Tobias Jesso Jr.)
5. Remedy (Adkins/Ryan Tedder)
6. Water Under the Bridge (Adkins/Kurstin)
7. River Lea (Adkins/Brian Burton)
8. Love in the Dark (Adkins/Samuel Dixon)
9. Million Years Ago (Adkins/Kurstin)
10. All I Ask (Adkins/Bruno Mars/Philip Lawrence/Christopher Brody Brown)
11. Sweetest Devotion (Adkins/Epworth)

As on *21*, all these songs are collaborations. Adele made her name as an authentic down-to-earth performer, with a powerful, soul-inspired voice. It seems that a direct line of communication expressing her own experiences is of lesser concern to her audiences than it was earlier in her career. The album *25* is credited with rekindling British record sales: it was the best-selling album worldwide for 2015, and debuted as No. 1 in 25 countries. The album won many accolades: including the BRIT award for British Album of the Year in 2016, and Grammys the following year for Album of the Year and Best Pop Vocal Album. The opening single 'Hello' won Grammys for Record of the Year, Song of the Year, and Best Pop Solo Performance the following year.

Conclusion

Carole King, Joni Mitchell, Kate Bush, Adele; my focus on performing songwriters in this chapter has provided an explanation for why female singer-songwriters evoke strong feelings of authenticity and relatability from their audiences. By writing about their own experiences, and then performing these songs themselves in fairly unmediated formats and venues, King, Mitchell, and Adele represent a seemingly direct line of communication, from emotional narrator to emotional receiver. These examples, along with other female singer-songwriters, provide a visible focal point for audiences. Bush is an outlier to this trajectory, and has been included in this chapter to showcase the commercial success that can be achieved by a female singer-songwriter who is unapologetic about using extensive artistic reference points and studio techniques.

Notes

1. David R. Shumway, 'The Emergence of the Singer-Songwriter', in Katherine Williams and Justin A. Williams (eds.), *The Cambridge Companion to the Singer-Songwriter* (Cambridge: Cambridge University Press, 2016), 11.
2. Lucy O'Brien, *She Bop: The Definitive History of Women in Rock, Pop and Soul* (London: Penguin Books, 1995), 176.
3. Sheila Weller, *Girls Like Us: Carole King, Joni Mitchell, Carly Simon, and the Journey of a Generation* (New York: Washington Square Press, 2009), 5.
4. Ibid., 60.
5. Most histories of popular music include an extensive section on Freed's career and significance. See, for example, Phil Hardy, *The Faber Companion to 20th-Century Popular Music* (London: Faber and Faber, 1990), 358–9.
6. Ibid., 44.
7. Ibid., 60–1.
8. Ibid., 73.
9. Mary E. Rohlfing, 'Don't Say Nothin' Bad About My Baby: A Re-Evaluation of Women's Roles in the Brill Building Era of Early Rock and Roll', *Critical Studies in Mass* Communication, vol. 13, no. 2 (1996), 94.
10. Allan Moore, 'Authenticity as Authentication', *Popular Music*, vol. 21, no. 2 (May 2002), 220.
    Allan Moore, *Song Means: Analysing and Interpreting Recorded Popular Song* (Aldershot: Ashgate Publishing, 2012), 179.

11. Carole King, *A Natural Woman* (London: Virago Press, 2012), 95.

12. King had released her first album as both songwriter and performer, *Writer*, in 1970. *Writer* was also produced by Lou Adler and released by Ode Records.

13. Robert Christgau, 'Consumer Guide '70s: K', *Christgau's Record Guide: Rock Albums of the Seventies*, available at www.robertchristgau.com/get_chap.php?k=K&bk=70 (accessed 28 February 2019).

14. Jack Hamilton, 'Why Joni Mitchell's 'Blue' Is the Greatest Relationship Album Ever', *The Atlantic*, 14 February 2013, available at: www.theatlantic.com/entertainment/archive/2013/02/why-joni-mitchells-blue-is-the-greatest-relationship-album-ever/273147/ (accessed 14 April 2020).

15. Mark Bego, *Joni Mitchell* (New York: Taylor Trade Publishing, 2005) 95–6.

16. Moore, 'Authenticity', 213.

17. O'Brien, *She Bop*, 188.

18. Lucy Green, *Music, Gender, Education* (Cambridge: Cambridge University Press, 1997).

19. Sue Hudson, 'The Unique Poetry of Kate Bush', *Hi-Fi and Record Review*, December 1985, available at: http://gaffa.org/reaching/i85_hifi.html (accessed 31 August 2019).

20. Moore, *Song Means*, 180. See also Simon Frith, *Performing Rites: On the Value of Popular Music* (Cambridge, MA: Harvard University Press, 1996), 196–9; and Philip Auslander, 'Musical Persona: the Physical Performance of Popular Music', in Derek B. Scott (ed.) *The Ashgate Research Companion to Popular Musicology* (Farnham: Ashgate, 2009), 305.

21. Kara Manning, 'Lady Adele', *Jazziz*, vol. 25, no. 6 (2008), 46.

22. Sophie Heawood, 'Adele-ation Starts Here', *The Times*, 28 December 2007.

23. Sarah Suhadolnik, 'Outside Voices and the Construction of Adele's Singer-Songwriter Persona', in Katherine Williams and Justin A. Williams (eds.), *The Cambridge Companion to the Singer-Songwriter* (Cambridge: Cambridge University Press, 2016), 179.

24. Moore, 'Authenticity', 218.

25. Moore, *Song Means*, 179.

26. Ibid., 181.

27. Anonymous, 'Adele Confirms New Album Is Called 25', *BBC News*, 21 October 2015, available at: www.bbc.co.uk/news/uk-northern-ireland-34594035 (accessed 23 August 2019).

28. Jeff Nelson and Robyn Merrett, 'Adele and Husband Simon Konecki Split After More Than 7 Years Together', *People* (19 April 2019), available at: https://people.com/music/adele-simon-konecki-split/ (accessed 23 August 2019).

Further Reading

Covach, John and Andy Flory. *What's That Sound? An Introduction to Popular Music and Its History*, 3rd ed. (New York and London: W. W. Norton and Company, 2012).

O'Brien, Lucy. *She-Bop: The Definitive History of Women in Pop, Rock & Soul* (London: Penguin Books, 1995).

Williams, Katherine and Justin A. Williams. *The Cambridge Companion to the Singer-Songwriter* (Cambridge: Cambridge University Press, 2016).

11 | The British Folk Revival: Mythology and the 'Non-Figuring' and 'Figuring' Woman

MICHAEL BROCKEN

During the mid-1990s (1994–1997) I successfully completed my doctoral research concerning the British folk revival, its histories, and its various manifestations up until that time. A year or so after my graduation in 1998, the thesis was uploaded in its entirety to Rod Stradling's *Musical Traditions* electronic magazine-cum-website (www.mustrad.org.uk). Following this, in 2002 Ashgate enquired about publishing the research in book form. As a consequence, in 2003 under the title of *The British Folk Revival 1944–2002*, about two-thirds of the work was edited and published by Ashgate; it has remained more or less in print ever since.[1]

It is now, however, in need of a thorough update-cum-rewrite and I suggest this because (i) it appears somewhat historically prescient and also because (ii) in 2014 I effectively 'returned' to the folk revival when BBC Radio Merseyside asked me to present the *Folkscene* radio programme alternating each week with the legendary folk music broadcaster Stan Ambrose.[2] Sadly, Stan passed away in 2016, so I am now the sole 'voice' of the show. Re-immersing myself as I did, I could see that the folk scene had thrown off at least some of its weighty ideologically constructed demons, and by doing so had rearticulated itself into a far more exciting, proactive, and entertaining environment than the one I had previously studied – especially regarding the contemporary 'figuring' of women (versus historical 'non-figuring')[3] – although there is much still to be done.

Gender and My Mid-1990s Thesis

For that earlier doctoral research, I had not considered writing much about gender issues. I felt that my research findings were controversial enough as they stood: drawing attention to the many problems encountered by myself regarding the trajectory of folk music ideology, business, and dissemination at that time. Also, not being female, I did not feel entirely qualified to engage with the alarming stereotyping of women I had come across. However, in the seventh chapter of the thesis gender was discussed a little. As one example, I cited an interview with my former guitar tutor, local folk singer Bob Buckle. Bob informed me of a gig that he and his singing partner Pete Douglas ('the Leesiders') had played at Ewan MacColl's folk club (I think it was the Scots Hoose in Moore Street, London) in the 1960s. After the evening's proceedings had 'officially' drawn to a close, he asked MacColl a question: 'what about women?' Bob recalled the response:

From what I can remember it was just when women's rights started to get a little press. Ewan said that women had to stand in line behind the rest of 'us' [i.e. the implication being that the 'us' was men]. The class war came first; then we could deal with women's issues. But I was never really convinced that he had any interest in gender issues. He had laid out his political stall years before, and stuck to it.[4]

I can still recall feelings of revulsion upon hearing this. Although I had never been a follower or fan of MacColl (I didn't care for his Marxist and later Maoist politics or his Critics Group purisms), I certainly respected much of both his and Bert Lloyd's research. However, the more I learnt about this folk 'axis', the more I mistrusted their formalist a priori critical/historical determinisms, which appeared to hold scant respect for any kind of radical emancipation for women (or anyone else, for that matter). MacColl's reported misogynist comments certainly resonated across my research, for these masculine tropes disguised as 'policy' reeked of the folk revival that I had come to know.

Looking back now, I suppose it all reflected the misogynist nature of British society at that time: one seldom feels that the popular music scene to which one is drawn is a representation of broader society, but (one way or another) it usually is. I much later learnt that the legendary folk singer Shirley Collins had also found both MacColl's and Lloyd's attitudes towards her as a female artist contemptible. According to Colin Irwin:

Shirley never really conformed to the perceived wisdom of the folk revival, as voiced by Ewan MacColl, Bert Lloyd and others of an ilk who sought to shape folk song . . . to further their political agendas . . . She doesn't have much good to say about the MacColl school of revivalism – or Bert Lloyd come to that . . . she never did forgive Lloyd for his patronising (Shirley used the word 'snidey') original sleeve note description of her on [the LP] *Sweet Primeroses* as 'a sweet singer from Sussex'. 'I didn't like either of them [stated Shirley]. They were Svengalis in their way who wanted to shape people and shape the way things were . . . I wanted to go it alone and do what I thought was right and do what I wanted to do.'[5]

Such blithe dismissals of women in the British post-Second-World-War folk revival (a kind of 'here, but not here' ghostly shadow) should also be placed into the historical-political matrix of mid-twentieth-century British Marxism. As Nancy Fraser and Linda Nicholson have commented:

When in the 1960s, women in the new left began to extend prior talk about 'women's rights' into the more encompassing discussion of 'women's liberation', they encountered the fear and hostility of their male comrades and the use of Marxist political theory as a support for these reactions. Many men of the new left argued that the gender issues were of secondary importance because subsumable under more basic modes of oppression, namely class and race.[6]

Both Bob Buckle's comments concerning MacColl and the above quote from Fraser and Nicholson made it into my PhD thesis, but were not present in the published Ashgate text. I cannot recall whether the decision to omit these important statements was mine, or my editor's, but I know that I later regretted it, for it was quite evident that the one key element of the British folk revival's musical-historical discourse was its overtly masculine narrative. Indeed, it was only via such a limited, myopic focus that the folk scene's self-directed hagiography could even exist: stitching together 'acceptable' folk fragments in a male-oriented *post hoc ergo propter hoc* fallacy. This artificial masculine linear narrative ('because of this came this') connected only those 'facts' deemed appropriate.

I found all folk clubs to be particularly problematic in this respect, with most members projecting into folk performances particular kinds of masculine-interpreted social and musical fantasies that gratified their folk 'historical' inclinations. Ruth Finnegan (whose work I still admire) acknowledged that 'folkies' in Milton Keynes in the late-1980s 'associated their music, and hence themselves, with "the folk" – ordinary people – in the past and present',[7] but I felt that she had neither recognised or articulated that this 'ordinary people' visage-cum-fantasy was effectively a masculine-centric hypothesis (the authentic working-class male) communicated within a male-dominated environment (the folk club, the pub). To me, it all appeared, not only part of the male sphere of socialisation, but also authority.

Towards the end of my research I came to feel that I had not even scratched the surface of the 'non-figuring' folk woman, and felt that as long as folk music performances in British folk clubs continued to be devised from masculinised politico-heritage tropes, they would continue to marginalise in song and dance not only female roles, but also other partially hidden folk music narratives (e.g. those concerning race, sexuality, mental illness, etc.). To me, the folk club was a recidivist environment: a patriarchal, self-indulgent (albeit somewhat contested) place of worship, out of step with broader societal developments. Back in 1989, Finnegan had also suggested that women felt relatively comfortable in the folk clubs she attended in Milton Keynes, but from my own research I found this not to be the case (I still hold ethnographic research on the topic). By 1993 Georgina Boyes was already declaring:

For all its apparent innovation and variety, the Revival was **hidebound** [my emphasis] by historical theory. Determinedly reproducing a policy of authenticity ... the Folk Revival had succeeded ... but unless its fundamental concepts of the Folk and folk culture were rejected, the movement had no possibility for development.[8]

Folk clubs were undoubtedly in a demographic predicament of vast proportions: for example in an article concerning the young folk club organiser Jane Threlfall, *Folk Roots* editor Ian A. Anderson suggested that:

For the future a new generation of organisers is required; clubs in the '60s were run in the main by people barely out of their teens, and there's no reason why this can't happen in the '90s. For though Jane Threlfall wasn't deterred by the people round her being twenty-odd years her senior, many young people, even those that enjoy the music, are put off.[9]

Actually, as projected in my thesis, a marked decline of folk clubs did come about. These days the 'traditional' club is merely one facet of a healthier, disparate, and voluminous folk music environment.[10] There exists a folk scene that encapsulates all different kinds of venues, events, and musical performances from great festivals and concert halls, to arts centres, and tiny house gigs. The folk scene still has a long way to travel in advocating a plurality of ethics, beliefs, and epistemologies, but at least it has now largely rejected the concept of humanity as a unitary male-informed 'given'. What follows are, I hope, examples of this: firstly, excerpts from two discussions between myself and two 'figuring' women currently involved in the 2019 British folk music scene: one, a female folk music performer, the other a female folk music business woman. Secondly, I also include in my summary a small vignette concerning one of my former music students, 'Mary'.

Folk Music Performance: Emily Portman

Emily Portman is an integral part of the British folk scene's current 'new wave'; she is a highly regarded singer, writer, and concertina player, and has recently won several awards.[11] For example, she was the 2013 holder of the

BBC Radio Two Folk Award for 'Best Original Song', and in the 2016 Folk Awards she was nominated for 'Best Singer'. In addition, Emily is a member of the Furrow Collective. This group also features Lucy Farrell, Rachel Newton, and Alasdair Roberts. They were awarded the prestigious 'Best Band' in the 2017 BBC Folk Awards. Emily lives in Liverpool, and she briefly presented BBC Radio Merseyside's *Folkscene* prior to myself. She has written articles for *fROOTS* magazine, and has given lectures on ballad studies at Cecil Sharp House and at The International Ballad Conference. She also teaches on the traditional music degree at Newcastle University. I would admit that I'm a fan of her work and have played several Emily Portman and Furrow Collective tracks on *Folkscene*.

As a new Furrow Collective tour approached (including an important gig lined up on 23 April 2019 at the Liverpool Philharmonic Music Room), Emily came into BBC Radio Merseyside to co-present *Folkscene*. Rather than interview guests per se, I have a policy of asking guests to co-present the programme. So, in addition to promoting their event and/or new release they might simply comment as and when they feel is appropriate. This awards the programme a more relaxed 'organic' feel which at the same time befits the aesthetics of the twenty-first-century folk scene. I also later visited Emily at her home, on 30 May 2019, to continue our conversation a little.

Following a lively discussion of both Emily's solo career and the Furrow Collective tour and latest album, I asked her, what it was like as a woman on the folk scene in 2019. Emily responded:

I only have my own experiences to go on; the other weekend I was down at King's Place in London, part of a 'Women in Music' panel discussion, and there was a conversation going on about women and folk music . . . Rachel Newton was leading the discussion, my agent Sarah Coxon, *Songlines* editor Jo Frost, and Sarah Jones of the EFDSS (English Folk Dance and Song Society) were on the panel. Conversations like these are important: raising issues like the casual objectification of women on stage, and gender imbalance on festival line-ups. I hope that young female performers today won't face any of the things that myself and other female performers have faced – those over-familiar older male fans (or promoters, or hosts) who insist on hugs, comperes who comment on your appearance rather than your music, or the patronising sound engineers who assume you know nothing. These small instances can add up to create inequalities, but with a little awareness they can be prevented.[12]

I responded by stating that during my mid-'90s research, I came across a great deal of tokenism, with folk authenticity residing for many in the masculine, not the feminine. Emily replied:

Yes; organisations such as FairPlé (in Ireland)[13] and the BIT Collective (in Scotland)[14] discuss the lack of visibility for female instrumentalists. ... Female folk singers, often surrounded by male accompanists, are considered the norm. But less is expected of female instrumentalists. It's a common story for audiences and promoters alike to *still* be surprised when female instrumentalists can actually play as well as their male counterparts! There are some brilliant instrumentalists out there, for example Kathryn Tickell, Rachel Newton [to name but two] who incidentally are the only women to have ever won instrumentalist of the year at the Folk Awards. Why is that and why are less women choosing to forge musical careers, particularly as instrumentalists? Perhaps they think it's not viable or they're losing confidence at some level.

Partly it's to do with visibility and challenging stereotypes. PRS Research has shown there are a lot of girls learning instruments but they're not going on to be performers. I remember when I went to university playing guitar, I looked at all the brilliant male guitarists and felt there was no point in continuing to play. I considered my experience an isolated one, but it came up on the panel discussion that most of us had lost confidence and given up playing at some point.

We can start countering this early on, with parents and teachers taking care not to lead their child into an instrument because they are a girl or a boy. A lot of instruments are unconsciously gendered – not just the guitar – we need more female pipers, for sure! I do think there's a growing awareness in education: Lucy Green's work, for example, and traditional music can offer so many different ways of learning.

Emily also remarked:

Maybe it's a bit naïve to think that [on the folk scene] we're exempt from these gender biases. The folk scene is known for being inclusive – so some women have felt very vulnerable when starting a conversation about gender inequalities, nobody wants to cause offence, especially to all those wonderful people who put their heart and soul into encouraging young folkies – we don't mean you! It's hard to criticise or speak out without coming under fire for being 'man-hating' or just whinging about nothing. But what seems to be emerging is a growing sense of awareness that can hopefully move us towards making the folk scene as enabling towards women as men.

Also, from personal experience, wider issues about being a self-employed parent and musician need addressing. Being freelance is precarious and not always conducive to earning money and freelance women can end up looking after the children and forgoing their careers. It can be difficult to justify childcare costs and even more difficult to go away on tour. You don't want to turn down the gig: aside from loving performing there's the money needed to live, band dynamics, and of course the perceived pressure of keeping up your visibility.

For me, seeing performers like Eliza Carthy and Nancy Kerr have families and continue to perform was inspiring and it's becoming, quite rightly, far more usual. Not to say it hasn't been a challenge. I toured with both my kids when they were babies and found some venues to be wonderful and others to be hugely challenging, sometimes with no back-stage area or any space to breastfeed or store milk. Ultimately it makes all the difference if venues are able to accommodate musician parents – it means we can continue to do our jobs, in a profession that isn't geared towards family life. It's also a great step forward to see folk festivals taking the need for gender equality on board and questioning whether they always need that all-male band to end the evening. Hopefully this won't just turn out to be tokenism and will create a sea-change in the way that things are programmed, in the gendering of musical instruments, in the way that people think it's alright to comment on what a woman is wearing rather than what instrument she's playing . . . We're heading in the right direction and hopefully soon these panel discussions won't be deemed necessary!

(On the practicalities of trying to combine a freelance career with parent-hood, see also Chapter 16, 'Women in the Music Industries: The Art of Juggling'.)

Emily also brought up the issue of singing what might be described as 'badly chosen' traditional song material. We discussed this at some length, agreeing that the rape, infanticide, and murder narratives contained in some ballads and traditional songs require at the very least discussion, re-contextualisation or perhaps 'answering' in a new song (as Emily has done in her song 'Borrowed and Blue'). After all, popular music is kinetic and perhaps, just like Marx's 'modern man', should **not** be preserved as if 'in aspic'. (For another account of a woman's experiences in the contemporary British folk scene, see 'In Her Own Words: Practitioner Contribution 2', by Virginia Kettle.)

Folk Music Business: Rose Price

Rose Price is a folk and acoustic music promoter 'born, bred, and buttered within the city walls of Chester'.[15] For the past five years Rose has promoted under the name of SoundBox at such venues in the city as 'Upstairs at the Lock Keeper', St Mary's Creative Space, and St Mary's Handbridge Centre. Rose was previously an editor for two editions of the *Chester Standard* series of local newspapers. The 'SoundBox' moniker emerged from her weekly 'what's on' column of the same name. Kate Rusby and Jacqui McShee's Pentangle were two early promotions, together with a stint for Chester Fringe, devising, and curating pop-up music events, and also booking O'Hooley & Tidow for what was their debut performance in Chester. Rose had been involved in folk and acoustic music for a long time:

I started comparatively young by the standards of the day and was fifteen at the time. Chester was a very 'folkie' place when I was younger, and it was a distinctly male-dominated environment. I'd been asked to join an established folk duo, prominent in the folk scene then and had never been into a folk club before . . . There were scarcely any local female groups or solo performers. This was undoubtedly due to the generally accepted perception of a 'woman's place' . . . etc. The guys called the shots and I felt that I had to follow. I suppose I respected their experience, too – that was the way it was. Now times have caught up with all that – ostensibly![16]

Rose also informed me that:

Opportunities to study folk at music colleges have resulted in increased numbers of females emerging in performance and recording contexts. Yet women are still not necessarily well represented at folk festivals. Ironically, attempts to integrate and be accorded the same respect in the business of music making and promotion, has often highlighted a resistance from males that's out of step with contemporary assumptions about 'equality' for women. Attitudes can still be bullying, however passively (or not), sometimes.

I asked her whether she felt it actually 'mattered' being a 'female folk music promoter' (i.e. whether a discussion about gender and folk promotion was even relevant), to which, she replied:

It does matter, but I suppose there's always an element of subjectivity. If you mean do I feel that being a female promoter makes a negative difference, I think possibly it can do. Not so much in working 'remotely' with male booking agents, but perhaps locally. Worse, I think, is when a woman feels 'grateful' for being treated with any semblance of respect by male colleagues! I've developed as a person and a promoter over the last twenty years – but yes, I'm wary – and some of that wariness is justified. I'm now more aware of the potential for obstructive male attitudes to frustrate and hamper the endeavours of women in the folk music industry; from committee room to concert stage. In the North-West [of England] there are definitely certain factions and still a lot of ground to be made-up . . . [For example] local festivals can still demonstrate an appalling gender imbalance in their programming.

Regarding the current folk music industry, Rose found that 'if you don't go through an agent and deal directly with the artists, it can be far easier'. I replied that as a radio presenter I dealt on a regular basis with many female publicity people, to which Rose replied that one might interpret this as women 'being handed the worst job'. She knew 'from personal experience' that press release work was a 'very time consuming, and often thankless, job'. She suggested, too, that such work might even be 'passed on to women, referencing the secretarial/admin role, traditionally associated with females'. However, she also stated 'these days, from an agency perspective, it's not overly male dominated, especially in the larger agencies where they need to cover a wide artist roster'.

I enquired whether, as a female promoter in Chester, she ever felt exposed:

Yes sometimes, if I'm honest. At times it's a bit like fighting an establishment; this can be territorial too – so yes, I do. Also, I feel 'tested' sometimes [i.e. as if others are 'testing' her]. At meetings with council officials and councillors, and non-governmental committees, they can be inappropriately competitive. Whereas we all seem to get on OK on the surface, perhaps with a nod to political correctness, occasionally I feel that the male 'pulls rank' (whether or not he holds any rank!). A female making the same stand would be viewed as … troublesome and an irritant!

The discussion moved on to folk music festival organisation: we both noted that the 2019 Wirral Folk Festival had returned following a year's absence in 2018 brought about by the illness of one of the organising committee. Previously, Rose and I had discussed taking over the festival's management for a year, rather than see its removal from the UK festival calendar; but nothing came of it. Upon its restoration, the festival continued to be organised by a committee. I asked Rose whether she might have put herself into a position of joining a committee to help organise and/or promote a folk festival (i.e. rather than sole-promote, as she currently did). She replied that she felt there might be 'too many battles that would be unwanted distractions' and felt that at present:

Hanging on to the reins at SoundBox is preferable, even though there are still some administrative hurdles. All things considered, the SoundBox venture allows certain freedoms to permit use of personal judgement, integrity, and gut instinct regarding programming, how SoundBox presents to its audiences, how I deal with our venue owners/managers, agents, artistes, etc. Whilst it's not a doddle by any means, it's distinctly preferable to being on a committee with those who may not share the same core values. The 'faffing' around that goes on in many committee meetings can also become an [unwanted] entity in itself.

Rose also suggested that:

A festival committee around here might be very entrenched! Also, as a woman, I might end up conceding an argument that I should really win. So, I would rather promote on my own, with the support sometimes from two or three people I already know and trust; if anything goes wrong, then it's my responsibility. I would rather not retreat into currently male-dominated environments, such as festival-based committees or pub-based folk clubs.

Rose had booked an interesting line-up of artists to play at both 'Upstairs at The Lock Keeper' and at St Mary's Creative Space between September and December 2019: mixed-gendered band Road Not Taken, the Chris Cleverley Trio (including Kim Lowings and Kathy Pilkinton), Chris Foster, Hannah Sanders & Ben Savage, Mishra, and Belinda O'Hooley & Heidi Tidow.

Overall, one might argue that this is an extremely well-balanced programme as far as gender is concerned; out of the fifteen 'featured' artists presented, eight are women and seven are men. These figures might also represent a growth in gender equality across the twenty-first-century British folk scene. For example, since my return to BBC Radio Merseyside in 2014, over 65 per cent of the 2,000-plus tracks I have presented on *Folkscene* have been performed by women: as soloists, in single-gender or mixed-gender duos, trios, and bands. In fact, as Rose has mentioned to me on several occasions, she tends to book those she admires, or those who have previously 'gone down well' at the venues she uses; for example, such popular artists might include (say) O'Hooley and Tidow, as much as (say) Jim Moray; at the very least, 'promising' news for the budding female folk artist.

Summary

I recall supervising a female folk-rock performer at Liverpool Hope University shortly before resuming my radio career in 2014. 'Mary' was approaching completion of her third-year dissertation, the topic of which was the logistics of self-promotion and performing in a mixed-gendered 'folk-style' band. She fronted a mixed female/male unit consisting of two guitarists, a bassist, a fiddle and part-time melodeon player, and a percussionist. They were raw, but had a good sound. They were looking forward to a busy summer, having received several festival bookings between June and September: 'almost enough to make a living' she quipped. 'Mary' informed me that a discussion had taken place the previous day between herself and a Liverpool-based promoter: the band had been booked as a support, but were informed by the promoter that some 'disappointment' had been expressed because they were not an all-girl band. Apparently, the promoter suggested that a former female member of the group, who had recently left, might be encouraged to return 'so that they would appear more of a girl band to the local brewery "guys" sponsoring the gig'. More females on stage apparently 'avoided the likelihood of complaints': tokenism, of course.

'Mary' asked whether I thought they should continue with the booking. I suggested that they might consider withdrawing, because, not only was it typecasting women, but also took no account of the guys in the band. It also struck me that such issues were not simply tokenistic, but also redolent of 'non-figuring' female choices and status. However, a little later that day, I came to change my mind: after all, those anti-female philosophical mono-discourses we persuaded ourselves to follow had been replaced by a tapestry of micro-threads of convergences and contingencies together with micro-circumstances demanding contingent responses.[17] Therefore, I determined to speak to 'Mary' again. I would tell her that there was little to be gained from reducing such complexities to one overall meta-philosophical stance: take the money, play the gig, have a good time, move on.

I saw 'Mary' again on campus the following morning and before I could even get a word in edgeways, she said 'we've decided to keep the gig and are taking the advice to add back "Emma" [the musician who had previously left]. The money's good, we are only on for forty minutes, so: "so what?"' As it turned-out, the promoter in question was female and pressure from the (surprise, surprise) all-male brewery marketing staff was falling on her, rather than the band per se. Although this female promoter appeared to possess power, that power was considered disruptive by the brewery team. 'Mary' suggested that the promoter lacked 'real' authority because she was a woman. So, she and her band had realised they were not victim-performers, per se, and attempted to debate a more multi-layered resolu-tion to this convergent sphere of music performance and music business activity. This created a different starting point for 'Mary' to reflect on her role as a female folk/rock bandleader, as she fashioned a more contingent time-based inflection to the issue: it was more conditional than universal. By doing so, she might have even helped the promoter to maintain her hard-won music business-related status. Evidently, circumstances were not ideal, but neither were they as binary as first appeared. Yes, perhaps the promoter had attempted to 'swerve' the issue by placing it into the hands of 'Mary' and the band. Yet 'Mary' had geared her response specifically towards the micro-context: convergence and contingency supervened mono-philosophical thought.

Any configuration of language-games is contingent: even those mono-historical 'tablets of stone' previously placed before us older 'folkies' by MacColl and Lloyd. Further, all popular music futures are determined by tolerances, borderlines, and frames of reference; for all music scenes create borders and 'frames'. Scenes tolerate as they define via contingent and con-textual fields of representation. However, borders surrounding 'tradition(s)' can exist to encapsulate or purify. As important as they might be in the name of tradition, symbols created by and through the historically rooted folk orthodoxy should no longer frame a so-called 'consensus': one in which the woman 'figures' only via male rhetorical tropes.

Perhaps the most useful way of understanding the many strands of the twenty-first-century British folk scene is via how it has come to recognise and respond to contextual, transient, and discursive musical and social spaces, interventions, and interactions. Within such discursive spaces we are able to allow representations from the past to stand, but can then critique them via the edges and limits of our sonic inspirations and delineations. Whether we like it or not, historical misogyny was once as integral to the social framework of the British folk scene as it was to the social framework of British society. We should not deny this historical fact, but instead express our subjective freedom by and through our actions and creative responses; such subjectivity will serve us well as a reminder not to withdraw into the British folk revival's previous patterns of behaviour, especially regarding the 'non-figuring' woman.

In all the examples discussed above, contingent, contextual, and provisional 'figurings' appear to be far more stable representations of female realities than the masculine-informed folk mythologies in which women were conceived as the 'non-figuring other'. If the British folk scene of the twenty-first-century can be truly described as vitally important popular music praxis, one in which social and cultural mores and issues such as feminism and gender equality are openly debated alongside a priori tropes of tradition, then in spite of the afore-discussed historically apprised recidivism, the awareness that abounds across the scene in terms of egalitarianism and fairness should help foster a variety of exciting and relevant discourses in which young women (and men) might pro-actively engage and 'figure'.

Notes

1. Michael Brocken, *The British Folk Revival 1944–2002* (Aldershot: Ashgate, 2003).
2. I had also previously presented a BBC radio show between 1998 and 2007: *Brock 'n' Roll*.
3. The expression 'figure' is drawn from the work of Meaghan Morris; see Meaghan Morris, *The Pirate's Fiancée: Feminism, Reading, Postmodernism* (London and New York: Verso, 1988), 1–23.
4. Bob Buckle to Mike Brocken (interview), December 1995.

5. Colin Irwin, sleeve notes to the Shirley Collins reissue CD, *The Sweet Primeroses*, Topic Treasure Series, Topic TTSCD003 (2018).

6. Nancy Fraser and Linda Nicholson, 'Social Criticism Without Philosophy: An Encounter Between Feminism and Postmodernism', in Thomas Docherty (ed.), *Postmodernism: A Reader* (London: Harvester Wheatsheaf, 1993), 422.

7. Ruth Finnegan, *The Hidden Musicians: Music-Making in an English Town* (Cambridge: Cambridge University Press, 1989), 67.

8. Georgina Boyes, *The Imagined Village: Culture, Ideology and the English Folk Revival* (Manchester: Manchester University Press, 1993), 240–1.

9. Ian A. Anderson, *Folk Roots*, 136 (October 1994), p. 31.

10. 'Traditional' in the sense of existing within the matrix/history of the post-Second-World-War British folk revival.

11. See Portman's website at: www.emilyportman.co.uk/ (accessed 11 December 2020).

12. Emily Portman to Michael Brocken (interview), 30 May 2019.

13. FairPlé, formed in 2018, helps to address the gender imbalance in Irish traditional and folk music; see: www.fairple.com/(accessed 11 December 2020).

14. The BIT Collective identifies, explores, and helps to deal with gender inequality in Scottish folk and traditional music scenes; https://en-gb.facebook.com /thebitcollective/(accessed 11 December 2020).

15. See Price's website at: https://roseprice.jimdofree.com/ (accessed 11 December 2020).

16. Rose Price to Michael Brocken (interview), 13 May 2019 at Telford's Warehouse, Chester.

17. For example, see Jean-François Lyotard, 'Some of the Things at Stake in Women's Struggles', translated by D. J. Clarke, W. Woodhull, and J. Mowitt, *Sub-Stance*, 20 (1978), 9–17.

Further Reading

Brocken, Michael. *The British Folk Revival 1944–2002* (Aldershot: Ashgate, 2003).

Finnegan, Ruth. *The Hidden Musicians: Music-Making in an English Town* (Cambridge: Cambridge University Press, 1989).

12 | How MTV Idols Got Us in Formation: Solo Women and Their Brands Make Space for Truth Telling, Trauma, and Survival in Popular Music from 1981 to the Present

KRISTIN J. LIEB

MTV and what we now recognise as star 'brands' saved the music industry, or at least postponed its demise, by turning music into an accessory to visuals. Al Teller, who ran Columbia and CBS Records from 1981 to 1988, noted that 'the biggest win' for a music company in the MTV era was to 'develop superstar careers'.[1] For solo women stars hoping to reach new markets, or launch new careers, MTV represented a marriage made in heaven: MTV needed content, the new pop playbook had yet to be written, and this seemingly rebellious outlet promised liberation – or at least mass exposure – for them in the midst of the ongoing battle for gender equality. MTV's first big solo stars, Cyndi Lauper and Madonna, who were both young and white, bent the short-form music video to their will, greasing the gears for Tina Turner and other charismatic, videogenic stars eager to transcend tired notions of gender and transform ideas of what an aspirational woman could be, do, or look like.

But as the industry moved away from artist development (the practice of investing in artists, albums, and tours over years to build sustainable careers) and towards shorter-term video and brand development, appearance quickly assumed dominance. The visual medium made visual demands, especially of women, who had 'always felt the pressure to look decorative or pleasing', but were now expected to please a 'mass gaze', a meta-level, coordinated male gaze, which increased this pressure 'tenfold'.[2] Art had taken a hard turn into commerce, and videogenic women now promised the best returns for labels, which functioned as artists' banks and advertising agencies. Given that MTV itself was 'one nearly continuous advertisement', which merely featured 'different *kinds* of ads' throughout the day and night, the challenge became finding content that would resonate.[3]

Videogenic stars who met the appearance criteria dominated those ad positions and had the option of engaging taboo subjects to spark audience excitement. Cyndi Lauper released 'She Bop', an ode to female masturbation and pleasure in 1983, and at the first annual MTV Video Awards Show the following year, Madonna shocked audiences when she 'writhed around in a giant wedding dress, pantomimed masturbating and sang, "It feels so good inside"'.[4]

Eighties stars asserted the power of the single, the sound bite, and the ad. Madonna excelled in all three, using them to make once-and-still-dreaded female power erotic and sexy. Many of today's power moves trace back to Madonna, the artist who, perhaps more than any other, authored the pop star playbook for modern times. Madonna's brand prioritised linear or successive reinvention around a core theme (sexual adventure),[5] and created 'a whole new set of feminine subject positions' for other stars to inhabit and explore.[6] She also challenged popular culture to reconsider where its boundaries belonged.[7]

This chapter considers the influence and lasting effects of MTV and superstar branding on current mainstream women solo artists – now known as person brands or corporeal brands[8] – particularly with regard to how they build and maintain personal narratives, fight back against abuse and exploitation, and recover from crisis. These ideas will be explored using case studies, artist examples, and four recurring themes: The human sacrifice of being a pop star;[9] the sharing of narratives about abuse and exploitation; the recasting of the hot mess as a survivor;[10] and the exploration of taboo subjects and identities. In telling these stories, a clear link will emerge between past and present stars and how they have navigated these themes across several decades.

Tina Turner: The Power of the Branded Self, the Survivor Narrative, and the Redemptive Comeback

In some ways, MTV was really nothing new.[11] Sound had already met image – to powerful effect – on television decades before, in live appearances on shows like *The Ed Sullivan Show* and *American Bandstand*, on music-centred television programmes like *The Monkees* and *The Partridge Family,* and on variety shows such as *Soul Train, Solid Gold,* and *Saturday Night Live.* But in this new environment, a different kind of storytelling emerged, with solo women leading the charge. Some stars sought to build in protection as they told their stories, creating branded selves to absorb the anticipated body blows associated with female daring. Cyndi Lauper turned herself, with the help of her handlers, into a cartoon in the video for 'She Bop', presumably so she could say she was just having a laugh, though she was clearly arguing in favour of female pleasure. Janet Jackson used cheeky humour and choreographed spectacles to encourage audiences to amplify the punchline ('Ms. Jackson if you nasty') while her songs explored heteronormative power dynamics and women's need for autonomy and control. These strategies of loading subversive messages of resistance into gender-normative packaging worked – and stuck.[12] Both Lauper and Jackson experienced spikes in recognition in 2016 when 'Girls Just Want To Have Fun' came back as 'Girls Just Want To Have Fun(damental) Rights' signs at the Women's March, and Jackson's 'Nasty' went viral in meme form after Donald Trump dismissed presidential nominee Hillary Clinton as 'such a nasty woman'. The lesson learned and passed onto future stars was this: Conform to gender expectations and you can resist, as long as you seem playful, and you maintain an image of youth, femininity, and desirability. (Think of Dolly Parton's '9 to 5' – and her overall brand presentation throughout her career – as an example of this theory in action.)

The branded self was also a new mechanism for sharing and selling gendered and sexualised violence and exploitation, as numerous scholars, such as Susan Bordo, have suggested through their examinations of Madonna's videos.[13] But traditional forms of power-based domination, such as domestic abuse and sexual violence, had plagued stars' careers long before MTV. The new music channel gave bold stars a worldwide platform to engage with these issues creatively, with the potential for unprecedented reach and impact.[14] Tina Turner provides a compelling example of an artist whose backstory, image, and resulting brand catapulted her to unprecedented success on MTV. Turner had literally sacrificed everything she had, including her physical safety, to pursue her dream. After enduring years of abuse at the hands of her husband and manager, Ike Turner, Tina broke free and became a star.[15] Her solo debut, *Private Dancer* (1984), served as a fiery, defiant declaration of independence, earning her multiple hit singles and videos, three Grammys, and international recognition and acclaim. (Turner quickly capitalised on these opportunities, venturing into the wider entertainment business with *Mad Max Beyond Thunderdome*.)

As an industry veteran in the midst of a major comeback, Turner used personal narratives to propel her performances, and to resonate with audiences hungry for justice via sing-along empowerment anthems. In her wonderfully campy 'Private Dancer' video, Turner draws parallels between sex work and pop stardom, roasting the ethics, integrity, and short-term, transactional focus of music-industry players. 'I'm your private dancer, dancer for money', she sings; 'Do what you want me to do'. Then, acknowledging music's new subservience to spectatorship, she concedes:

'And any old music will do'. It is worth noting that the lyrics to 'Private Dancer' were penned by Mark Knopfler, lead singer of Dire Straits, whose song 'Money For Nothing', was an MTV smash despite its open hostility towards MTV and its effects on the industry.[16] Predictably, internalising the channel's formula catapulted Knopfler and his band to wider mainstream success and greater critical acclaim than ever before. Knopfler sold 'Private Dancer' to a more reliable (woman) narrator, but in 'Money For Nothing' he cast himself as the prostituted protagonist, sickened by the 'little faggot(s)'[17] who sell out with ease to make their 'money for nothing'.[18] This telling epithet suggests that acquiescing to exploitation is for women, men who play the game are feminine or gay, and sexism and homophobia pervade the industry.

'Better Be Good To Me' finds Turner, the industry's first middle-aged sex symbol, in a black leather bodysuit, staring down the camera. She is grounded in her new expectations – she 'has no use' for what her love interest 'loosely call(s) the truth' and that she doesn't 'have the time for (his) overloaded lies'. Towards the end of the video, she literally grabs a white man ('The Man?') in a comic turn, and demands: 'Why can't you be good to me?' In 'What's Love Got To Do With It', Turner struts through the city – presumably to show off her famous legs – and collects interested glances from those she passes. But *she's* not interested, dismissing love as 'a second-hand emotion', and 'a sweet old-fashioned notion' and opting to prioritise her 'own protection' instead, at least for the moment. The title of this song also became the title to Turner's biopic, released in 1993.

Sinéad O'Connor: The Cycle of Abuse, Rebellion, Sacrifice, and Recovery

While MTV and brand building empowered artists such as Turner, giving them new levels of exposure and creative agency via branding, it disempowered or erased others; especially those who refused to even pretend to play by the new rules. The precipitous rise and savage takedown of Sinéad O'Connor perhaps best captures the perils of being a solo woman pop star in the 'ring of spectatorship' in which stars are 'plumped for the slaughter, then primed for the comeback'.[19] Through O'Connor's story we see the four aforementioned themes in action, and find that 'one of the biggest challenges for a woman in pop is to express herself from the core'.[20]

From the beginning of her career, O'Connor was clear she 'didn't want to be a fucking pop star', but did want to be 'a protest singer'.[21] Ensign

Records founder Nigel Grainge signed O'Connor precisely because she was a serious artist who didn't play by the rules, but then dared to suggest an image change. O'Connor rebelled:

Nigel and Chris ... suggested to me that I grow my hair really long and start wearing mini-skirts and thigh boots and get all sexed up, and that really wasn't me. Not that I've any objection to that, but I didn't wanna sell myself on my physicality ... I went and got it [her head] shaved.[22]

This had immediate implications for her brand when she hit the market with *The Lion and the Cobra* (1987), which was recorded while she was pregnant. Framed as an 'androgynous pixie' who was a 'striking contrast to the sexual potency of the reigning pop diva, Madonna',[23] O'Connor successfully differentiated herself from the beginning. Her look endured for more complicated and personal reasons. 'In the pagan tradition, they say the goddess has four faces. In one the goddess is shaven headed', she said. 'When the goddess is being her true self, she has no sexuality the way that men perceive earthly sexuality. But her sexuality comes from her soul.' Her photographer combined these notions, observing that hearing O'Connor's voice was 'like being French kissed by the angels'.[24]

When O'Connor's album was released in the UK, its cover depicted shaven-headed Sinéad, crossing her wrists across her chest as if protecting herself from a punch, and with her mouth wide open, suggesting a scream, or a cobra about to strike. Her eyes look in the direction of her presumed attacker. When it was released in the United States and Canada, the cover was edited, presumably to make her more gender-normative, and thus palatable to less forgiving markets. O'Connor's mouth is closed, her eyes are cast down at the ground, and her expression suggests defeat. Her arms still form an 'X' across her chest, but now O'Connor looks passive, as if she has resigned herself to being hit without fighting back. She also appears to have a black eye. One explanation for the difference could be that female passivity was expected to sell better than female rage.

In writing about Blondie, rock critic Lester Bangs described the dynamics between powerful woman stars and their male admirers in a way that might shed light on the strategy behind the more acquiescent positioning on the US cover.[25]

I think if most guys in America could somehow get their fave-rave poster girl in bed and have total license to do whatever they wanted with this legendary body for one afternoon, at least seventy-five percent of the guys in the country would beat her up.[26]

Writer Cheryl Cline responded to Bangs' observation, noting the fact '[that] a powerful woman brings out a desire in men to conquer her – if not to actually beat her into submission, then to bring her under his sway in some other way – is hardly a novel idea'.[27] Cline also suggested that the increasing popularity and acceptance of eroticised male domination was emboldening men to be more direct about such desires. 'Ten or twelve years before, Janis Joplin brought out similar reactions in male writers', she wrote. But they expressed fantasies about 'being the guy who comforted a "sad", "hurt" Janis after she'd been brutalised by some other cad – or by the hard life of a rebel girl'.[28]

O'Connor's second album, *I Do Not Want What I Haven't Got,* was released in 1990. O'Connor appeared in a video for its breakout hit, a cover of Prince's 'Nothing Compares 2 U', two days after ending her romantic relationship with Fachtna O'Ceallaigh, who was also her manager. In the video, striking for its simplicity and vulnerability on the heels of '80s excess, O'Connor's face appears in close-up, set against a black background. There is nothing between O'Connor and the audience – no pretence, no eighties effects, no big hair – and she has such a harrowing story to tell that she actually begins crying. (O'Connor maintains that her tears were real and shed for her mother, who died in 1986, when O'Connor was nineteen). Writing for the *New Yorker*, Amanda Petrusich captured the rare, revealing, meta-narrative of the video: '"This is all of my humanity", her face seems to say. "Don't you dare look away"'.[29]

O'Connor's next single, 'The Emperor's New Clothes' (1990), maintained this intense connection, exploring the trials of fame and criticism, post-partum depression, gaslighting, abuse and exploitation, male impunity and female 'hysteria', mental health, reality versus perception, and the consequences of truth telling: 'They laugh cause they know they're untouchable, not because what I said was wrong'. And audiences loved it, until they didn't.

O'Connor began to rebel strenuously against her rising fame, and by 1991, her brand was morphing from powerful protest singer to compassionate-but-exasperating contrarian. After rejecting four Grammy nominations – and one Grammy win – O'Connor did battle with a New Jersey concert venue to prevent the American National Anthem from being played before her performance. This angered Frank Sinatra, who called her a 'stupid broad' and said he'd like to 'kick her ass'.[30]

Then, in 1992, O'Connor released her third album, *Am I Not Your Girl,* which featured covers of jazz standards, not the pop hits fans had come to expect. The album was considered commercial suicide by fans and critics alike; and some paying close attention even wondered if its release was designed to stall O'Connor's career, and put her in self-imposed exile. Her behaviour on *Saturday Night Live* (*SNL*) on 3 October 1992 solidified growing perceptions of O'Connor as difficult, cantankerous, and disrespectful. She sang Bob Marley's 'War' – an odd choice given that it was not on the album she was there to promote – adapting the lyrics to focus on child abuse. As she sang the word 'evil', she held up a photo of Pope John Paul II, ripped it apart, and shouted 'fight the real enemy'.[31]

Without sufficient context for her rage and actions – O'Connor was a child abuse survivor who was deeply committed to God but enraged at the leadership of the Roman Catholic Church for covering up priests' crimes against children – the backlash was immediate and violent. During Joe Pesci's opening monologue on *SNL* the following week, he held up the same photo, explaining he had taped it back together, and then destroyed a photo of O'Connor, saying that if he had been hosting the previous week, he would have given her 'such a smack'.[32] Music industry mogul Jonathan King, told *Billboard* that O'Connor needed a spanking.[33] (King was later convicted of multiple counts of sexual assault on teenaged boys and sentenced to seven years in prison.)[34]

Thirteen days after O'Connor's fateful appearance on *SNL*, she performed at Bob Dylan's thirtieth anniversary concert at Madison Square Garden. When she took the stage, she heard 'a thundering mixture of cheers and jeers' that sounded, to her, like good and evil warring.[35] Although the sound made her 'want to puke', O'Connor doubled down, screaming 'War' to be heard above the crowd. Then she glared defiantly at the audience, walked off stage, and hugged legendary songwriter Kris Kristofferson, who had been asked to remove her from the stage, but had declined in solidarity. After this incident, O'Connor announced she was quitting her music career at twenty-five. A VH1 documentary explained the paradox: 'Sinéad may have had the "profile of a pop star", but she also had "the low self-esteem of a child abuse victim"'.[36] O'Connor sank into a 'life-threatening depression' for seven years following the event, and tried to kill herself eight times in one year.[37] Reflecting back on her actions, O'Connor acknowledges she could have contextualised her anger more effectively for audiences, but remains convinced she did the right thing.

O'Connor returned to music two years later, releasing *Universal Mother* in 1994, *Gospel Oak* in 1997, and *Faith and Courage* in 2010. She credits God with giving her the voice that enabled her comeback and recovery. 'That voice is what lifted me out of hell', she said. 'Like if I had not sung, god only knows, I'd be Kurt Cobain now'.[38] Retrospectively, she's proud she spoke her truth on *SNL*. 'If that's all I ever did on Planet Earth, I would be happy', O'Connor said in 2013. 'I am really proud that I got to be that person.'[39] O'Connor converted to Islam in 2018, and took the name Shuhada Sadaqat in 2019. Shuhada is an Arabic name meaning 'witnesses' or 'martyrs'.

Alanis Morissette: The Connections Between Emotional Pain, Pop Stardom, and Mental Health

O'Connor's work opened up space for emerging pop and indie artists who wanted to use their platforms to share disappointment, express rage, and hold men accountable. PJ Harvey's *Dry* (1992) and *Rid of Me* (1992) and Liz Phair's *Exile in Guyville* (1993) made women's anger palpable in indie rock circles – and in critical reviews in mainstream outlets – amplifying the ideas espoused via the more DIY riot grrrl movement.[40] With Alanis Morissette's *Jagged Little Pill* (1995), such themes exploded into the mainstream, became popular, and got audiences talking.[41] But mainstream success came with unexpected consequences.[42] In an interview with Oprah Winfrey, Morissette revealed she pursued fame to cure her emotional pain, believing: 'I will be less lonely, and I will be understood, and I will be loved. And that love will go in and heal any of the broken parts.'[43] Instead, fame exacerbated underlying issues, led to PTSD,[44] and 'one dimensionalised' her brand, first typecasting her as angry woman. She recalled:

I have not always been direct with my anger in my relationships, which is part of why I'd write about it in my songs because I had such fear around expressing anger as a woman. I thought I would be retaliated against or physically hit or vilified. Anger has been a really big deal for women: how can we express it without feeling that, as the physically weaker sex, we won't get killed. The alpha-woman was burned at the stake and had her head chopped off in days of old.[45]

Morissette described feeling particularly vulnerable and violated when excited fans would try to cut bits of her hair or skin off as souvenirs.[46] Scholar Kathryn Lofton places such moments in context, explaining: 'Transforming flesh into commodity has a long history, a history that includes far less voluntary formats of commodification than those experienced by Britney Spears . . . But to make something that is human something that is marketable . . . is, undeniably, a procedure of atomisation, valuation, and dehumanisation.'[47] By building human brands to be short-term, highly lucrative, and then disposable, the industry facilitates this dehumanisation, and ensures stars who are women can only be so powerful for so long. Once woman superstar brands are shunned or shut down, so too are their platforms, until a subsequent generation of stars notice the same cultural issues decades later and get in formation to try to fix them. But if each successive group of stars reinvents the wheel, it spins furiously but makes little progress.

As O'Connor and Morissette work to heal their personal selves from past pain and trauma,[48] their brands are also being rehabilitated by peers and audiences eager to celebrate the fearless contributions they made in less empathetic times.[49] In *Variety*, singer Kay Hanley admitted feeling jealous and threatened by Morissette's fearlessness. 'Her singing was guttural, primal, unconventional, terrifying, real . . . her lyricised revenge, fist-pumping catharsis', Hanley wrote. 'I didn't understand how to write the way Alanis was writing and I found her authenticity deeply upsetting.'[50]

Fiona Apple: The Necessity of Setting Self-Protective Career Boundaries

Aspiring stars who watched O'Connor be sacrificed, and Morissette be bashed despite – or because of – her popularity, could read the tea leaves. Some opted out of the branded pop star game to preserve their sanity and longevity. One artist who intuited the value of self-preservation from O'Connor is Fiona Apple, who wrote her solo debut, *Tidal* (1996), when she was seventeen, and released it when she was eighteen. Her natural trajectory was quick and clear; pop stardom. (She scored three hit singles, earned instant acclaim and popularity, and her album went platinum.) She also won the Grammy for Best Female Rock Vocal Performance for 'Criminal' in 1996 and the MTV Video Music Award for Best New Artist in a Video for 'Sleep to Dream' in 1997. But when critics accused her of glorifying child pornography in her 'Criminal' video, and of looking too young and emaciated, she fired back, revealing painful personal reasons for wanting to stay slim.[51]

Apple quickly encoded the industry's terms and rejected them; just saying no to top-level fame. She made herself difficult to market, releasing a sophomore effort with a ninety-word title and behaving aggressively at awards shows, calling the world and the industry 'bullshit'.[52] Her actions created a career ceiling; her music would never again be as popular or mainstream as it was on *Tidal*. She could retreat to the music-first world of the indie star, but perhaps this choice paid other dividends with respect to mental health and career longevity, so her choice should be more appropriately understood as a victory, not a defeat.

Apple's third album, the knowingly titled *Extraordinary Machine* (2005), found her embracing her choices and her humanity: 'I am likely to miss the main event', she sings on 'Better Version of Me', 'if I stop to cry or complain again'. Buoyed by her choice and exhausted by the 'folderol' and 'hauling over coals', she continues: 'So I will keep a deliberate pace', she sings, 'let the damned breeze dry my face'. After O'Connor posted a video of herself crying in the midst of a psychiatric episode (on Facebook on 5 August 2017), Apple responded with two videos. In the first, Apple calls O'Connor her 'hero' and offers her support, and in the second, she screams and thrashes along to a live performance of 'Mandinka', erupting into applause at the end.[53]

Gaining Awareness, Giving Credit Where It's Due, and Building Upon Past Sacrifices

Janet Jackson dominated the pop charts alongside Madonna throughout the mid-to-late 1980s, and was still so resonant in 2004, she was tapped to perform at the Super Bowl halftime show with Justin Timberlake. During the performance, Timberlake ripped Jackson's top, revealing a strategically covered nipple, for 9/16 of a second, to 143 million television viewers.[54] This 'wardrobe malfunction', also known as 'Nipplegate', resulted in Jackson being banned from the Grammys that year, while Timberlake was permitted to attend and perform.[55] Jackson's songs and videos were also banned by Clear Channel Communications, which controlled MTV, CBS, and many radio stations, compromising *Damita Jo* (2004), which became Jackson's worst-selling album since 1984. As *Billboard* summarised: 'Jackson was made a public example of; the new millennium's modern witch put on trial.' In 2017, Timberlake was invited to perform at the Super Bowl again, and did.[56] Black feminist critic Janell Hobson, amongst others, identified the intersecting racism and sexism that sacrificed Jackson, a black woman, but absolved Timberlake, a white man.[57] Such stories, once marginalised, have become mainstream.

Stefani Germanotta had humbler beginnings than Jackson, Apple, and O'Connor, but, after being dropped by Def Jam after only three months on its roster, Germanotta went all in, creating one of the best-known pop brands of all-time: Lady Gaga.[58] Drawing on Madonna's visuals and choreographed spectacles ('Born This Way'), Turner's narratives of sexual abuse and exploitation ('Bad Romance'), and O'Connor's taboo-violating silence-breaking about sexual abuse ('Til It Happens to You'), Gaga adapted Madonna's pop star playbook and extended its vision. Madonna fought powerfully for gay rights, and Gaga effectively 'queered the mainstream'.[59] This made it safer for numerous high-profile pop stars, such as Miley Cyrus, Halsey, Kesha, Janelle Monáe, and Hayley Kiyoko, to come out and provide better multidimensional representation for their industry peers and queer audiences.[60]

Beyoncé followed a similar trajectory, leveraging Jackson's choreographed-spectacle-as-protest idea, Tina Turner's survivor narratives, and Madonna's boss-bitch business acumen, to effectively become an industry unto herself. With these moves, Beyoncé pushed back against male dominance and white supremacy, and gained cultural power rather than losing it.[61] Beyoncé's approach has been dynamic and immersive reinvention, around her over-arching brand theme of complicated, resistant, and self-affirming black womanhood. (Beyoncé's approach also put Madonna's call for continuous brand reinvention on an accelerated timeline). While clearly liberating for some fans, this branding strategy was also optimised for demanding followers who had been trained by social media, streaming services, and Amazon.com to expect instant gratification.

Conclusion: Surviving, Speaking Out, Finding Support, and Sticking Around . . .

The human sacrifices of being a post-MTV pop star are abundant and clear: there's no privacy, fans expect full-time access to stars' lives, and if fans don't like something a star does, she might be destroyed as quickly as she was embraced. For those daring to share personal or professional narratives about abuse and exploitation, or exhibiting real, human signs of struggle in their private lives, the likelihood of fierce rejection, humiliation, and back-lash increases exponentially. But Turner, O'Connor, and Morissette had the courage not only to share their experiences, but also to keep talking about them, despite the vitriol they inspired. They are pop stars who bottomed out and survived, showing others that such a trajectory was possible.

The stars featured in this chapter articulated women's desires, ambi-tions, identities, and sources of anger and rage in highly compelling ways and then made their resulting need for respect, autonomy, and justice seem not only fair, but obvious. These stars sacrificed their own comfort and well-being to build a safer platform for those coming up behind them to explore similar themes of exploitation and abuse, cultural taboos, and underexplored dimensions of identity. The careers of Miley Cyrus, Lady Gaga, Beyoncé, Kesha, Demi Lovato, and Billie Eilish would be unimaginable without them. Pop stars tacitly agree to serve as our representational proxies through their songs and performances. If we appreciate their efforts, we should reciprocate with love, support, respect, and a determination to change the sexist culture that continually demands their sacrifice. 'People say I'm controversial', Madonna told a crowd of industry insiders at the Billboard Women in Music Event in 2016. 'But I think the most controversial thing I have ever done is to stick around.'[62]

Notes

1. Marc Eliot, 'Rockonomics', in Lucy O'Brien, *She Bop, The Definitive History of Women in Rock, Pop, and Soul*, 3rd ed. (London: Continuum, 2012), 176.
2. Lucy O'Brien, *She Bop: The Definitive History of Women in Popular Music*, 3rd ed. (London: Continuum, 2012), 168.
3. E. Ann Kaplan, *Rocking Around the Clock: Music Television, Postmodernism and Consumer Culture* (New York: Routledge, 1987), 143.
4. Matt Mullen, 'Madonna's Now-Famous "Like a Virgin" Performance Was Thanks to a Wardrobe Malfunction', *Biography* (11 June 2019), available at www.biography.com/news/madonna-like-a-virgin-vmas-1984 (accessed 17 July 2020).
5. Kristin J. Lieb, *Gender, Branding, and the Modern Music Industry: The Social Construction of Female Popular Music Stars* (New York: Routledge, 2013); Kristin J. Lieb, *Gender, Branding, and the Modern Music Industry: The Social Construction of Female Popular Music Stars*, 2nd ed. (New York: Routledge, 2018).
6. Susan McClary, *Feminine Endings: Music, Gender and Sexuality* (Minneapolis: University of Minnesota Press, 2002), 148–166.
7. Key works about Madonna include: E. Ann Kaplan, *Rocking Around the Clock*; bell hooks, 'Madonna: Plantation Mistress or Soul Sister?' in *Black Looks: Race and Representation* (New York: Routledge, 2014), 157–64; Susan McClary, *Feminine Endings*, 148-166; Susan Bordo, *Unbearable Weight: Feminism, Western Culture, and the Body* (Berkeley: University of California Press, 1993), 272–4; O'Brien, *She Bop*, 2012 edition; Bidisha, 'Madonna Is Superhuman. She Has to Be to Survive the Ugly Abuse', *The Guardian* (26 February 2015),

available at www.theguardian.com/commentisfree/2015/feb/26/madonna-superhuman-abuse-brit-awards-fall (accessed 17 July 2020); Caitlin Moscatello, 'Madonna Tells Howard Stern Her Rape Was "Too Humiliating" to Report', *Glamour* (12 March 2015), available at www.glamour.com/story/madonna-stern-rape (accessed 17 July 2020).

8. Lieb, *Gender, Branding,* 32–49; Susan Fournier, 'Contemplating the Futures of Branding', in Susan Fournier, Michael J. Breazeale, and Jill Avery (eds.), *Strong Brands, Strong Relationships* (New York: Routledge, 2015), 398–99; Lieb, *Gender, Branding,* 18–19 and 42–26.

9. Kathryn Lofton, 'Religion and the American Celebrity', *Social Compass*, vol. 58, no. 3 (2011), 346–52.

10. Lieb, *Gender, Branding,* 155–65.

11. Jordan McClain and Amanda McClain, 'Online Music Television: New Media, Same Celebrity', *Journal of Entertainment and Media Studies*, vol. 2, no. 2 (2016).

12. James Dickerson 's *Women on Top: The Quiet Revolution That's Rocking the American Music Industry* (New York: Billboard Books, 1998), 29.

13. Bordo, *Unbearable Weight*, 272–4.

14. MTV certainly did not mark the beginning of such discussions – and many women in previous decades deserve credit for addressing these topics before the stars of MTV did. But MTV had greater reach than anything before it, which is why this is the focus of this chapter.

15. Bill Higgins, 'Hollywood Flashback: Tina Turner's Abuse by Husband Ike Made Headlines 40 Years Ago', *Hollywood Reporter* (3 March 2016), available at www.hollywoodreporter.com/news/hollywood-flashback-tina-turners-abuse-871542 (accessed 17 July 2020).

16. Knopfler co-wrote the song with Sting.

17. See 'Money for Nothing by Dire Straits', *Songfacts* (2019) available at www.songfacts.com/facts/dire-straits/money-for-nothing (accessed 17 July 2020) and Claire Shaffer, 'How The Dire Straits' "Money for Nothing" Video Helped CGI Go Mainstream', *Garage* (11 March 2019), available at https://garage.vice.com/en_us/article/9kpmzp/dire-straits-money-for-nothing-video (accessed 17 July 2020).

18. Craig Marks and Rob Tannenbaum, *I Want My MTV: The Uncensored Story of the Music Video Revolution* (New York: Plume, 2014), 238.

19. Lofton, 'Religion', 351.

20. O'Brien, *She Bop*, 179.

21. George Moll, '*Sinéad O'Connor Behind the Music*', VH1 (2000), available at https://youtu.be/uJMHp4n8Stc (accessed 17 July 2020).

22. Moll, 'Sinéad O'Connor'.

23. Moll, 'Sinéad O'Connor'.

24. Moll, 'Sinéad O'Connor'.

25. Lester Bangs cited in Cheryl Cline, 'Little Songs of Misogyny', *Bitch*, vol.16 (1987), in Evelyn McDonnell. and Ann Powers (eds.), Rock She Wrote: Women Write About Rock, Pop, and Rap (Medford, NJ: Plexus, 1995), 369–375.

26. Lester Bangs cited in Cheryl Cline, 'Little Songs', 372.

27. Cheryl Cline, 'Little Songs of Misogyny', 369–75.

28. Cheryl Cline, 'Little Songs of Misogyny'.

29. Amanda Petrusich, 'The Feminist Trailblazing of Sinéad O'Connor', *The New Yorker* (26 May 2016), available at www.newyorker.com/culture/culture-desk/the-feminist-trailblazing-of-sinead-oconnor (accessed 17 July 2020).

30. Mark Trecka, 'Remembering Why Sinéad O'Connor Tore Up the Pope's Picture on National TV', *PRI* (3 October 2014), available at www.pri.org /stories/2014-10-03/remembering-why-sinead-oconnor-tore-popes-picture-national-tv (accessed 17 July 2020).

31. Trecka, 'Remembering Why'.

32. Trecka, 'Remembering Why'.

33. Trecka, 'Remembering Why'.

34. Trecka, 'Remembering Why'.

35. Moll, 'Sinéad O'Connor'.

36. Moll, 'Sinéad O'Connor'.

37. Dr. Phil, 'Sinéad O'Connor Describes Event She Says Made Her Suicidal: "I Lost My Mind"', *YouTube* (12 September 2017), available at https://youtu.be /gmnhY3Jih-U (accessed 17 July 2020); Antoinette Bueno, 'Sinéad O'Connor Talks Alleged Physical and Sexual Abuse by Her Mother in Heartbreaking Interview with Dr. Phil', *ET* (7 September 2017), available at www .etonline.com/sinead-oconnor-talks-alleged-physical-and-sexual-abuse-her-mother-heartbreaking-interview-dr-phil (accessed 17 July 2020).

38. Moll, 'Sinéad O'Connor'.

39. *Wall Street Journal*, 'Sinéad O'Connor on Miley Cyrus, Infamous SNL Appearance', *YouTube* (12 November 2013), available at https://youtu.be /kuyrVLtoOBs (accessed 17 July 2020).

40. Sara Marcus, *Girls to the Front: The True Story of the Riot Grrrl Revolution* (New York: Harper Perennial, 2010), 42–54; Catherine Strong, *Grunge: Music and Memory* (Farnham: Ashgate, 2011), 128; Andi Zeisler, *We Were Feminists Once: From Riot Grrrl to Cover Girl, the Buying & Selling of a Political Movement* (New York: PublicAffairs, 2016), 169–92.

41. David Wild, 'Q&A: Alanis Morissette', *Rolling Stone* (11 April 2002), 48.

42. Andrew Billen, 'Am I Happy? I Work on It Every Day', *The Times* (29 April 2003), available at www.thetimes.co.uk/article/am-i-happy-i-work-on-it-every-day-7khw22krksw (accessed 17 July 2020); Oprah Winfrey, 'Alanis Morissette: Is Happiness Temporary? (Maybe That's Okay)', *Oprah's SuperSoul Conversations* (23 August 2017) available at https://youtu.be /iO_V5ZtBxMc (accessed 17 July 2020); Andrea Shea, 'On Addiction, Healing, Compassion: A Conversation With Alanis Morissette', *The ARTery*

(30 May 2018), available at www.wbur.org/artery/2018/05/30/alanis-morissette-jagged-little-pill (accessed 17 July 2020); Nicole Cliffe, 'Alanis Morissette on Pregnancy at 45, Childbirth, Postpartum Depression, and #MeToo', *Self* (26 June 2019), available at www.self.com/story/alanis-morissette (accessed 17 July 2020).

43. Winfrey, 'Alanis Morissette: Is Happiness Temporary?'

44. Alanis Morissette, 'I Still Have PTSD From the Jagged Little Pill Era. It Was a Profound Violation', *The Guardian* (16 August 2012), available at www .theguardian.com/music/2012/aug/16/alanis-morissette-profound-violation (accessed 17 July 2020).

45. Morissette, 'I Still Have PTSD'.

46. Winfrey, 'Alanis Morissette'.

47. Lofton, 'Religion', 348.

48. Winfrey, 'Alanis Morissette'; Michael Agresta, 'The Redemption of Sinéad O'Connor', *The Atlantic* (2 October 2012), available at www.theatlantic.com /entertainment/archive/2012/10/the-redemption-of-sinead-oconnor/263020/ (accessed 17 July 2020).

49. As this chapter went to press, Morissette's musical, *Jagged Little Pill*, was set to open on Broadway, and O'Connor had just announced plans for a tour of the United States.

50. Kay Hanley, 'In Defense of Alanis Morissette's Jagged Little Pill', *Variety* (29 March 2019), available at https://variety.com/2019/music/news/alanis-morissettes-jagged-little-pill-defense-letters-to-cleo-kay-hanley-1203175891/ (accessed 17 July 2020).

51. Chris Heath, 'Fiona: The Caged Bird Sings', *Rolling Stone* (22 January 1998), available at www.rollingstone.com/music/music-news/fiona-the-caged-bird-sings-244221/ (accessed 17 July 2020).

52. 'Fiona Apple's Bad, Bad Girl Moments', *Rolling Stone* (24 April 2012), available at www.rollingstone.com/music/music-lists/fiona-apples-bad-bad-girl-moments-22292/ (accessed 17 July 2020).

53. Fiona Apple Rocks, 'A Message to Sinéad O'Connor From Fiona Apple', *YouTube* (10 August 2017), available at https://youtu.be/4ah51vQfRL8 (accessed 17 July 2020); Fiona Apple Rocks, 'Fiona Apple – "Sinéad O'Connor Is My Hero"', *YouTube* (11 August 2017), available at https://youtu.be/f91v2a-1kjQ (accessed 17 July 2020).

54. Shira Karsen, 'What Happened After Janet Jackson's 2004 Super Bowl "Nipplegate" Incident', *Billboard* (23 October 2017), available at www .billboard.com/articles/news/super-bowl/8007041/janet-jackson-justin-timberlake-2004-super-bowl-what-happened (accessed 17 July 2020).

55. Shira Karsen, 'What Happened After'.

56. Shira Karsen, 'What Happened After'.

57. Janell Hobson, *Venus in the Dark: Blackness and Beauty in Popular Culture* (New York: Routledge, 2005).

58. Paul Lester, *Looking For Fame: The Life of a Pop Princess* (London: Omnibus Press, 2010), 39–51.

59. Bryan O'Flynn, '10 Years of Lady Gaga: How She Queered Mainstream Pop Forever', *The Guardian* (10 April 2018), available at www.theguardian.com /music/2018/apr/10/10-years-of-lady-gaga-how-she-queered-mainstream- pop-forever (accessed 17 July 2020).

60. Kristin J. Lieb, '2018 Is the Year of the Queer Woman Pop Star', *BuzzFeed News* (20 September 2018), available at www.buzzfeednews.com/article/kristinlieb/ queer-women-in-pop-katy-perry-hayley-kiyoko-janelle-monae (accessed 17 July 2020).

61. Wesley Morris, 'Beyoncé Unearths Pain and Lets It Flow in "Lemonade"', *The New York Times* (24 April 2016), available at www.nytimes.com/2016/04/25/ arts/music/beyonce-unearths-pain-and-lets-it-flow-in-lemonade.html (accessed 17 July 2020).

62. Wesley Morris, '60 Times Madonna Changed Our Culture', *The New York Times* (8 August 2018), available at www.nytimes.com/interactive/2018/08/16/ arts/music/madonna-birthday-impact.html (accessed 17 July 2020).

Further Reading

Coates, Norma. 'Moms Don't Rock: The Popular Demonisation of Courtney Love', in M. Ladd-Taylor & L. Umansky (eds.), *Bad Mothers: The Politics of Blame in Twentieth-Century America* (New York: New York University Press, 1998).

Gaar, Gillian G. *She's a Rebel: The History of Women in Rock & Roll*, 2nd ed. (New York: Seal Press, 2002).

Lieb, Kristin J. *Gender, Branding, and the Modern Music Industry: The Social Construction of Female Popular Music Stars*, 2nd ed. (New York: Routledge, 2018).

O'Brien, Lucy. *She Bop: The Definitive History of Women in Popular Music*, 3rd ed. (London: Continuum, 2012).

In Her Own Words: Practitioner Contribution 2

VIRGINIA KETTLE

I look back in wonder sometimes at the speed of change. Aged twenty, I was busking in Trafalgar Square during the 'Free Nelson Mandela' non-stop protests of the late 1980s. Eight years later, I was busking in Johannesburg when the same Nelson Mandela had been elected President of South Africa after nearly three decades in prison! As musicians we get the chance to write our share of the soundtrack to an ever-shifting, terrifying, awe-inspiring world.

Most women in popular music are not world-famous. Still they sing, play, write, create, teach, and inspire others. They compose advertising jingles, run open-mic nights, perform in care homes, work as music therapists for people living with dementia or anxiety, sing on cruise ships, write for theatre productions and television dramas, play in tribute bands. Some even write the 'hold' music we listen to when we're in a queue and our call will be answered as soon as possible! Some women are just starting out on their musical journey. They are embarking on an apprenticeship that may last years, on what we used to call 'The Toilet Tour'; pubs all over the country (UK) and in Europe, with sticky floors and all too often a crowd who can't contain their indifference. Late nights, little money, spirit-crushing venues.

Many, like me, have at one time or another, done many of these different jobs. To keep afloat and hone your craft you learn to be flexible, adaptable, and willing to wear many musical hats. A huge number of women in music, myself included, have also maintained a day job, to pay the rent and the bills when the wonderful wishing well of music dries up for a while, as so often it can. I've been a musician for thirty-five years, I'm known and respected in the genres within which I work. When I started out, I dreamed of being world-famous. Along the way, I realised it was the creative process that really drove me. I found an attainable vision for a future as a woman in music and began to aspire to more achievable goals:

1. Stop trying to be famous and get real.
2. Don't put pen to paper unless you've got something to say. Write songs that touch people, music that's relevant to their lives.

3. Accept that many of the jobs you'll get offered are not going to be remotely glamorous. (I once wrote and sang heritage songs from inside a mine at the National Coal Mining Museum in Huddersfield; £60 for two days' work!)
4. Learn your rights and develop the confidence to stand up for yourself as a woman, knowing that your value as a musician is equal to that of a man.
5. Believe in yourself and what you are trying to achieve, even when literally no one else does.
6. Get out from your own backside! Lose the ego, find some humility and humour.
7. Practise!
8. Practise!
9. Practise!

My dad smoked a pipe. My earliest musical memories are infused with the smell of tobacco. The whole family in the small living room of our Manchester semi; early 1970s, *Top of the Pops* on the telly. Melodies I remember, but what really struck me, even then, were lyrics. The fascination of songs with a narrative. Some of them frightening to a small child, like 'Billy Don't Be a Hero' (performed by Paper Lace, written by Mitch Mitchell and Peter Callander, 1974); 'Maxwell's Silver Hammer' (Lennon and McCartney, 1969); and 'Seasons in the Sun' (sung by Terry Jacks; originally 'Le Moribond' by Jacques Brel and rewritten by Rod McKuen, 1974). I loved them and learned every word, enjoying that delicious childhood combination of fear and intrigue. Those were the days of the record player. As the youngest of four, you had to play whatever records your three older siblings had bought, knowing you'd be dead if you put a single scratch on them.

When I was about five years old my primary school music teacher, Miss Smith, sent me home with a letter to my Mum and Dad. She'd been teaching the class a song and I, unable to reach the high notes, had instinctively sung a lower harmony throughout. She'd suggested that, if we had the money, I receive some private singing tuition. We couldn't afford it, but we did have a piano, and my musical mum taught us lots of songs and encouraged us to sing.

As I grew, I began to absorb the political and social times I was living in through the music that was being created, particularly by young people. The early '80s in the UK brought exciting fusions between white punks and black ska and reggae artists. These were the sounds of fused communities, blending their cultures to create new genres, voices reacting to racism, unemployment, and riots. These were the Margaret Thatcher years of the poll tax and miners' strikes. Different styles of song were soaring up the pop charts; hits from sharp-edged two-tone to flamboyant New Romantic escapism and New Wave imports from America were all pumping through our young veins.

Women's voices were changing too. Alongside the usual musical catwalk of pop princesses came a fresh brand of female musicians. These girls were young and brave; their outspoken individuality was exciting and infectious. They weren't ashamed to be something other than just pretty. Women like Siouxsie Sioux, Annie Lennox, Chrissie Hynde, and Toyah Wilcox were giving young teenagers like me a sense that women could play a more relevant part in popular music, coming from their own place and time, with no one pulling their strings.

Aged sixteen, I went to college in Chester to do A levels in English and Drama. I began busking with a friend who played guitar. He had been a choirboy and the sweet combination of our voices was a hit with the tourists who flocked to the beautiful, historic city. Vocal projection was learned on the job by a crude process of elimination: finding the balance between singing too quietly and being ignored by the passers-by, to shouting the words and watching people cringe!

I discovered folk clubs during this time. I made friends with a talented guitarist, Stewart Lupton. He kindly lent me an old guitar and patiently taught me a few chords. Chester's folk scene was really buzzing in the early 1980s. Clubs like The Raven were born in the late 1970s and are still going strong to this day. Hanging around with young songwriters and being introduced to the music of John Martyn, Richard Thompson, Joni Mitchell, Paul Simon, Bob Dylan, and Tom Waits; these truly were my most musically formative years and it comes as no surprise to me that I ended up making songwriting my vocation.

Folk wasn't my only musical influence, however. The 1980s produced some outstanding hip-hop and funk artists and I was out clubbing as much as possible, dressed in old men's long johns bought at jumble sales, combined with monkey boots and a battered Victorian dinner jacket borrowed from the college drama department. Mine was the generation who ritually taped the top 40 onto cassette every Sunday. I would write down the lyrics to my favourites, so I could be word-perfect ready for the dance floor the following weekend. The highlights of the early 1980s culminated in a pilgrimage to Manchester's mighty Hacienda Club to see Grandmaster Flash and the Furious Five, and my first Glastonbury in 1984, with Ian Dury, Joan Baez, and Dr John amongst the headliners.

The following year, I began writing my own songs. At first, I found myself limited to the few guitar chords I'd learned. Gradually I got better, adding minor keys and more complex melodies. A friend had a four-track recorder and helped me to make my first demo. Not long after that I was in London, living in a squat on Charing Cross Road, next to Denmark Street (aka 'Tin Pan Alley'). I bought my first acoustic guitar there, from Andy's Guitar Shop. It cost £80.

I busked every day in the Underground at Tottenham Court Road, earning enough to get by. My songwriting was flourishing; within a year I had twenty decent songs to my name. I made another demo cassette and began trying to put a band together. The problem with London's music scene was that it was so transitory; musicians were moving on all the time. In those days you often had to 'pay to play' at venues. If you were unknown, you had little chance of pulling a crowd. It was particularly difficult to get gigs playing original music. Cover bands seemed to be the only ones making money.

I spent the next twenty years touring in bands and as a solo artist, in the UK, France, and Spain, and several years on the 'Madchester' music scene of the early '90s. I toured the British folk club circuit. For those of you unfamiliar with the UK folk scene, many of the clubs are small and friendly, run by passionate enthusiasts who often provide trays of sandwiches for the crowd. People from all walks of life get up and play a couple of songs. Regardless of their level of talent, they are enthusiastically received, and the ethos of the clubs is that everyone is welcome. In those days, the fee for the guest artist was usually £50 and you were given a one-hour slot straight after the raffle!

In 2010, my husband, John Kettle – formally of Wigan band, The Tansads – invited me to join a new folk-rock band he was forming with his brothers, Bob on mandolin and Andrew on vocals, I was to share songwriting duties and sing alongside my brother-in-law. From the very beginning, we all knew there was something special about coming together at this time in our lives. Each of us arrived as individuals, but what we created, and continue to create, is shared. Our values and responses to politics, diversity, conflict, injustice. Our age, our humour, and our musical skills have all blended together to create Merry Hell. Now in our eighth year. We are currently working on our sixth album. We've won several awards and have reached a level where we are playing theatres and festivals across the UK and in Europe.

Someone asked me recently if I ever suffered from stage fright. I realised I very rarely do these days. As I've got older, it's become less about me and more about the audience. I feel so genuinely privileged that people take the time out of their busy lives, buy tickets, drive through traffic, turn up at our concerts hoping to leave behind their troubles for a while. As a band, we always aim to switch off from what's going on in our own lives and deliver what people have come for: uplifting, thought-provoking entertainment.

From a woman's perspective, I've found the modern folk scene to be particularly non-sexist and non-ageist. Perhaps because its audiences seem to value good songwriting and playing above image. Many musicians, especially women, can feel that they lose their value as they get older and/or if they don't fit the narrow bandwidth of young, sexy, skinny. The folk industry is much kinder and more mellow. Older female artists are highly respected. Like fine wine, they are said to develop more richness and depth as they mature into their vintage years!

I've witnessed the music industry undergo profound changes in the last couple of decades. The way music is shared via the internet has brought financial and copyright challenges for the artist, but at the same time, a significant power shift away from the traditional record company control into the hands of musicians themselves. I'm now in my early fifties and at present have absolutely no plans to slow down. I'll shortly be venturing into the world of television, writing music for a drama about the Pendle Witches.

PART III

Women and Music Technology

13 | Case Studies of Women in Electronic Music: The Early Pioneers

LOUIS NIEBUR

While composers and engineers had experimented with electronic instruments and music since the beginning of the twentieth century, work really began in earnest in the 1950s with the availability of magnetic tape. *Musique concrète* ('concrete music', or music that involved the manipulation of preexisting sound into a new form) had been developed in the 1940s by engineer Pierre Schaeffer at the Radiodiffusion-Télévision Française (RTF), France's national public broadcasting system, through the alteration of sonic materials on shellac phonograph discs. But magnetic tape, besides being much cheaper than shellac discs, was a vastly more flexible medium, allowing for cutting, rearranging, looping, slowing down or speeding up, playing in reverse, and layering sonic material much more easily. This music wasn't inherently 'electronic' (*musique concrète* merely implied the use of any recorded sound as its material), but from the beginning composers applied electronic treatments to their sounds such as filters and ring modulators. For example, husband-and-wife team Louis and Bebe Barron combined tape manipulation with sound-generating electronic circuits to compose the first fully electronic film score, *Forbidden Planet* (1956). Around the same time, cutting-edge computers began to be used to generate compositions. In the early years of electronic and computer music composition, however, the cost of the equipment (tape recorders, echo machines, sound generators, electronic filters, mainframe computers) made working as an independent composer prohibitively expensive. Almost all experimentation and composition happened from within government-funded institutions such as radio and television networks and universities. Without institutional backing, it was practically impossible to gain a foothold in electronic music.

Nevertheless, women were involved from the very beginning. Daphne Oram, one of the earliest pioneers of tape music, was a co-founder of the British Broadcasting Corporation's (BBC) electronic music studio, the Radiophonic Workshop, in the United Kingdom. The influential Delia Derbyshire also began her career at the BBC's Radiophonic Workshop. Often, women were able to triumph over institutional bias by moving laterally from other positions; both Oram and Derbyshire (like their colleague Maddalena Fagandini) began by doing other things at the BBC before making the transition into composing. Pauline Oliveros had the support of the University of California to fund her work, enabling her co-founding of the San Francisco Tape Music Center in the early 1960s. With the emergence of less expensive sound synthesisers around the same time, Wendy Carlos benefited from an ad hoc sponsorship from the Moog synthesiser company for the acquisition of their equipment. Suzanne Ciani also struggled for institutional support, but by working at the San Francisco Tape Music Center had access to Don Buchla's new synthesiser system. These five pioneering women were certainly not alone in the early years of electronic music, but can serve as case studies for some of the ways in which women were able to position themselves in a field that was (and still is, to some extent) not friendly to the inclusion of women. These case studies are a small sample of the many women who had an important part to play in the development and incorporation of electronic sound into mainstream musical culture.

Daphne Oram (1925–2003)

Initially, the BBC hired Daphne Oram as a 'music balancer' during the Second World War because of her background in classical music, a job that required her to control the various input and output levels from microphones during broadcast. At the same time, she trained as a recording engineer and by the early 1950s had been promoted to the role of studio manager, responsible for recording and playing back music and sound effects during broadcasts.

Already by 1956 she was working towards the creation of an electronic music studio at the BBC and had been privately experimenting on her own with the limited resources available to her, including tape recorders and primitive noise-generating equipment. Her engineering training and interest in electronics allowed her to make adjustments to this equipment to suit her own needs, as well as to supplement these with hardware of her own construction, such as sound-altering filters. In 1958 she contributed tape effects to several radio broadcasts as well as to the first television programme to contain electronic sounds in Britain, *Amphitryon 38*. When the decision was made to open a dedicated electronic music studio at the BBC, she was the first person considered to run it. Her classical training and experience gave the Workshop a much-needed dash of musical credibility. Staffing for the opening of the Radiophonic Workshop also included another woman, Jeannie MacDowell, as a junior engineer. Initially, Oram operated as the Workshop's only full-time composer, which newspapers announced at the time of the studio's opening as: 'A team of enthusiasts, led by musician and technician Daphne Oram', who would 'yet dazzle their continental counterparts by their independent discoveries and ambitions'.[1]

From the start, Oram struggled with the lack of autonomy that she faced at the Workshop, particularly the requirement that the studio provide what she considered insignificant sound effects (what the BBC called 'Special Sound') rather than more substantial music. Consequently, Oram left within six months of the studio's opening, and spent the rest of her career building and refining her own private music studio in her home. In particular, she focused on a project she called 'Oramics', a process of creating electronic music from fluctuating light patterns. Oram's specially crafted instruments consisted of photoelectric cells that read an image drawn with black ink onto plastic sheets, converting that image into sound. Eventually Oram adapted this technology to personal computers, developing software to exploit the possibilities of Oramics. Oram's position on the process of composition and her ideas about music in general can be read in her fascinating autobiography, *An Individual Note*, written as she worked through the implications of her Oramics system.[2]

Throughout the 1960s and '70s, Oram divided her compositional output between occasional 'concert' pieces such as 'Four Aspects' (1968) and music for art installations and exhibits such as *Pulse Persephone* (1965), incidental music for theatre, like the soundtrack for Fred Hoyle's and John Elliot's play *Rockets in Ursa Major* (1962), and more commercial work. In the commercial field she achieved a great deal of success, contributing music and sound effects to advertisements for Lego, Schweppes, Nestea, and others; mainstream films such as *The Innocents* (1961) and *Dr. No* (1962); and commercial films like *Power Tools* (1965) for Atlas Copco, *Rotolock* (1967) for Rayant Films, and *Costain Mine* (1977). She also composed music for two fascinating projects, *Electronic Sound Patterns* and *Listen, Move and Dance* (both 1962), a collaboration with educator Vera Grey, intended for teachers to use as an instructional aid, with Oram's electronic swoops, dips, and whooshes imaginatively mirrored by the movement of children.

While until relatively recently Oram's contributions to the history of electronic music have been neglected, after her death in 2003 a resurgence of interest led to several commercial releases of her music.[3] Her Oramics machine is on permanent display at the Science Museum in London, and Goldsmiths, University of London has been digitising the hundreds of reel-to-reel tapes she left to them.[4] Future research will hopefully give a fuller account of the profound influence that Oram had on the field of electronic music.

Delia Derbyshire (1937–2001)

While the BBC had historically hired women in primarily clerical roles in the 1950s and 1960s, as Oram's colleague Fagandini acknowledged, there had also been a tradition of employing them as engineers during the Second World War. These same women, however, faced 'quite a cutback after the war when the surviving gentlemen came back and wanted their jobs'.[5] Certainly these prejudices were still very much in place in the early 1960s when Delia Derbyshire arrived at the Workshop. She had studied mathematics and music at the University of Cambridge, recalling that: 'There were only a few women at the University at that time and so we were treated terribly. But I had the solace of my music'.[6] After an unsuccessful application to Decca Records, where she was told that 'they didn't employ women in the recording studio', she toured for a time with the Pembroke University Players' production of *Julius Caesar*, providing off-stage electronic sound effects, before being hired at the BBC as a studio manager.[7] After discovering the Radiophonic Workshop, she requested a three-month attachment, and once employed there, she quickly earned a reputation as one of the studio's most talented and original composers; one who combined her love of music and mathematics to create revelatory new sounds.

    Derbyshire was still new to the Workshop when she was assigned what would become her most famous contribution to electronic music: realising the signature tune for the new television series *Doctor Who* (1963). One of her standard methods involved analysing complex concrete sounds using an oscilloscope, then reconstructing the sounds using banks of Jason valve oscillators. For *Doctor Who*, composer Ron Grainer is said to have 'scribbled a melody and bass line on a piece of paper',[8] leaving it to Derbyshire and engineer Dick Mills to 'realise' his score completely using electronic sound. Producer Verity Lambert, one of the first women at the BBC to fill that role, wanted the signature tune to 'use music, whether electronic or otherwise that had a melody rather than just *musique concrète*'.[9] Derbyshire took Grainer's melody and slowly pieced together the tune: 'I was dead into using as much electronic sound as possible. The boss was on record as saying that it was impossible to make a beautiful

sound electronically and it was my pleasure to prove him wrong'.[10] The
result, however, was worth the effort. She recalled later, 'In those days
people were so cynical about electronic music and so *Doctor Who* was my
private delight. It proved them all wrong ... [Ron Grainer] said "I can't
believe you've been able to do this! I want you to have half my royalties".
Unfortunately, that wasn't allowed'.[11] While she may not have received the
financial compensation she deserved, her arrangement helped bring electronic music to a larger, mainstream audience. With the subsequent success of *Doctor Who*, everyone had heard electronic music.

After *Doctor Who*, probably the most important project Derbyshire
worked on at the Radiophonic Workshop was the four *Inventions for
Radio* (1964–65), collaborations with playwright Barry Bermange. 'The
Dreams', 'Amor Dei', 'The Afterlife', and 'The Evenings of Certain Lives'
each used a similar collage technique to explore single themes. For the
premiere *Invention*, 'The Dreams', like the others on different topics,
Bermange interviewed a diverse group of ordinary people on their thoughts
related to dreaming, recorded their comments, and edited and shaped the
responses into a cohesive whole. The resulting product resembled
a scripted work. Specially composed radiophonic music by Derbyshire
then provided the background to these spoken-word collages, often occu-
pying quite a substantial role in them, with purely musical interludes
separating individual sections and topics, and, more importantly, creating
an electronic musical glue that held together and unified the often disparate
voices.

In 'Amor Dei', ('The Love of God'), Derbyshire was responsible, as she
had been for 'The Dreams', for constructing the radiophonic accompaniment to Bermange's collage of voices, who were this time discussing the
role God has in ordinary people's lives. It was agreed that all radiophonic
sound would be derived from the sound of the human voice. Perhaps due
to her study of mathematics at Cambridge, Derbyshire loved using complex formulae to construct elaborate structures for even the simplest of
signature tunes. This may have been an attempt for her and her works to be
taken more seriously. At the top of the first page of notes for this work is
outlined the 'Dies Irae' melody, but she quickly settled on a library recording of the more expansive Advent antiphon 'Rorate coeli desuper et nubes
pluant justum' ('Drop down dew, ye heavens, from above, and let the
clouds rain the just').[12] In her notes for the construction of this piece, she
writes on the first day: 'Take "rorate", make detailed analysis, serial, statistic
and linguistic, rebuild a fragmented variation, serially organised fragments
of voice. Find best tech for cutting fragments: normal cut, switched,

scanned, long cut, spaced fade up, etc. Very very fast at first in short groups, then in breathtakingly long complex dramatic sections'.[13] From these basic ideas, throughout the last weeks of May 1964, she began working with the prerecorded chant, first rerecording it, isolating each individual pitch, and rearranging them into a new musical utterance.

By the early 1970s, Derbyshire, like Oram before her, had grown tired of the limited opportunities for making her own music at the BBC, and she left in 1972. By that time she had developed a reputation as a skilled, witty, and effective composer of electronic music in her own right, having worked on projects outside the BBC, including scoring Yoko Ono's short film *Wrapping* in 1967; written a song, 'Moogies Bloogies', with the West End singer Anthony Newley in 1966; composed the electronic score for Peter Hall's film *Work Is a Four-Letter Word* (1968); and, with David Vorhaus and fellow Radiophonic Workshop composer Brian Hodgson, had formed the band White Noise and released an album, *An Electric Storm*, in 1968 on Island Records. As 'Kaleidophon', Vorhaus, Hodgson, and Derbyshire moonlighted an album of television stock music and scored incidental music for several other stage plays in the late 1960s. Upon her leaving the BBC, she worked with Hodgson as 'Electrophon Ltd.', composing the music library for the 1970s British children's science fiction television series *The Tomorrow People* for Thames Television. But by the mid-1970s, she had almost entirely retired from music.[14] According to Hodgson, Derbyshire's primary frustration had always been with inflexible equipment, and the consequent inability to see a vision through:

She always felt the limitations of the technology. It was so difficult, you were wrestling with it the whole time, and the deadline would be creeping up and there was no time if you had an idea and it wasn't working. There would come a point where you couldn't go back and try a new idea because the deadline was going to be there. It just took so long to do anything.[15]

In the 1990s, Derbyshire's non-*Who* work was rediscovered by a new generation of popular electronic musicians, and she began collaborating with younger composers. Sadly, her untimely death in 2001 ended any new projects she had been working on, but since her death her reputation has grown exponentially. Numerous recordings of her works, as well as documentaries and a radio play based on her life, have all helped restore her legacy to its rightful place in the history of electronic music. In 2013, Delia Derbyshire Day was established as a registered charity to 'advance the art of British electronic music via the archive and works of Delia Derbyshire'.[16] Finally, in 2017 Derbyshire was honoured by a commemorative blue plaque placed on her home in Coventry from the British Plaque Trust which reads 'BBC Radiophonic Workshop pioneer who influenced the course of electronic music lived and worked here'.

Wendy Carlos (1939–)

Women composers of electronic music have consistently faced institutionalised obstacles to success, particularly a feeling by studios that audiences wouldn't be receptive to music known to have been produced by women. At the BBC both Oram's and Derbyshire's work was almost always credited to the generic 'Radiophonic Workshop' rather than by their names. And things were no different in the United States. According to *Switched-On Bach*'s record jacket (1968), the album-length Columbia Masterworks collection of some of Johann Sebastian Bach's most popular works interpreted on the new Moog synthesiser was produced by the anonymous, corporate-sounding 'Trans-Electronic Music Productions, Inc', or 'TEMPI'. In actual fact, this project was a collaboration between electronic music pioneer Wendy Carlos and jazz-singer-turned-producer Rachel Elkind, with contributions made from musicologist and musician Benjamin Folkman. Wendy Carlos – who was identified as 'Walter Carlos' on subsequent albums until the mid-1970s, when her identity as a transgender woman was acknowledged with the credit 'Wendy Carlos' on album covers – had started her studies at the Columbia-Princeton Electronic Music Studio in 1962, working with the famous composer Vladimir Ussechevsky. However, Carlos found herself frustrated by the constraints under which composers were then held, with the contemporary academic trend for techniques like serialism and other dissonant styles.

Carlos and Folkman were both graduate students at Columbia and together worked on a simple electronic arrangement of Bach's 'Invention in F', amongst other experiments. When Elkind heard this, it seemed like the perfect way for the composer Carlos to show the public that electronic music could be accessible, and hopefully pave the way for original compositions in a less dissonant style. The problem, however, was that before Robert Moog's synthesiser innovations, there was no practical way, economically or artistically, to get the kinds of nuanced performances required of Bach's works. Carlos had been looking for a way to demonstrate the power and potential musicality of the electronic music equipment coming out of Robert Moog's studio.

Carlos had met Moog at the annual meeting of the Audio Engineering Society in 1964, and they immediately became friends, with Carlos frequently testing Moog's latest products. Meanwhile, Carlos was building a small studio of her own. She assembled an Ampex 8-track tape recorder out of spare and used parts, and gradually acquired other pieces of equipment. Unlike today's more compact digital keyboards, the so-called 'modular' analogue synthesisers of this time were custom-built and often had very large combinations of components. Carlos's small studio apartment eventually housed an assemblage of oscillators, filters, a white noise source, an artificial echo generator, and an envelope generator for constructing more complex sounds, as well as a chord generator, which chained a series of oscillators together to form harmonies, created by Moog for Carlos to realise Bach's continuo parts. The final innovation was a touch-sensitive keyboard that enabled greater sensitivity in performance.

All was not perfect, however. Tuning was the notorious bugbear of early synthesisers; the slightest change in temperature could affect a sound's pitch. In the notes to her *Switched-On* boxset, Carlos remembers the agonising process behind achieving a perfectly tuned synthesiser melody:

Each recorded take on our first albums had to be tediously checked for pitch immediately before and after. You'd practice the line you were about to play, then do a precision tuning, quickly hit record and perform the note or notes, hit stop and recheck the tuning. If it was still near correct pitch, you assumed the take was too.[17]

Carlos and Elkind organised the first album, originally titled *The Electronic Bach*, in such a way that each track highlighted a different strength of the new synthesiser. Bach's music was the perfect candidate, in their eyes, for this project, since, as Carlos explains on her website, 'It was contrapuntal ... it used clean, Baroque lines, not demanding great "expressivo" (a weakness in the Moog at the time), and it was neutral as to orchestration (Bach freely used many variations on what instruments played what)'.[18]

Carlos, Elkind, and Folkman weren't prepared for the massive success of the album upon its release, and had no immediate plans for a sequel. Folkman went on to a career as a successful musicologist and composer. Carlos and Elkind, for their part, took the opportunity of making a follow-up to perfect their techniques, and for their second album, they took and expanded the repertoire to include contemporaries of Bach's, as well as a version of his Fourth Brandenburg Concerto. This too, achieved both notoriety and success, with the Canadian pianist Glenn Gould declaring that 'Carlos's realisation of the Fourth Brandenburg Concerto is, to put it bluntly, the finest performance of any of the Brandenburgs – live, canned, or intuited – I've ever heard'.[19]

Over four albums from 1968 to 1979 (*Switched-On Bach, The Well-Tempered Synthesizer, Switched-On Bach II,* and *Switched-On Brandenburgs*), Carlos and Elkind successfully produced electronic interpretations of the works of Bach and other Baroque composers, using each album to refine their equipment and techniques, though the joyous spirit of experimentalism is strong throughout all of the recordings. They all display a level of virtuosity unheard of in electronic popular music up to that point, and the relative paucity of Carlos and Elkind's output can be traced to their methodical approach of assembling each track.

Elkind left music as a producer in the early 1980s and now lives in France. In her later work, Carlos continued to expand the boundaries of electronic music, perhaps most memorably in the film scores to Stanley Kubrick's *A Clockwork Orange* (1971) and Disney's *Tron* (1982). She, more than anyone else, was responsible for acclimating audiences to the sound of the synthesiser, to showing music lovers that there was more to electronic music than science fiction and scary movies, and that electronic music could both convey a sense of the modern and the beautiful.

Pauline Oliveros (1932–2016)

As a representative of the academic side of music, Pauline Oliveros is unique amongst these case studies. While electronic music formed only a small part of Oliveros's total compositional output, what she did write has had an outsized influence on later composers, through both her technical procedures and in her philosophy of music as expressed through her works and writings. Oliveros developed an interest in electronic music in the 1960s through her composition teacher Robert Erickson at the San Francisco Conservatory of Music (although influence undoubtedly flowed in both directions) and was a member of the San Francisco Tape Music Center from its founding in 1962. There, alongside fellow composers Ramon Sender, Terry Riley, and Loren Rush, Oliveros explored electronic and electroacoustic music in relation to improvisational techniques. In 1967, both she and Erickson accepted positions at the University of California, San Diego, where she went on to teach composition for twenty years, directing the university's Center for Music Experiment for four of those years. One of Oliveros's most important contributions to music in the second half of the twentieth century was her emphasis on focused listening, particularly to the musical background of modern life. Drones, especially, are a persistent theme of both her own works and her writing. In 1970, she recalled how the ubiquity of drones began infiltrating her own works:

Drones of all kinds (such as motors, fluorescent lighting, freeway noise), are ever present. The mantra of the electronic age is *hum* rather than Om ... I began to seek out drones of all kinds and to listen to them consciously, allowing myself to hear the myriad shifting, changing partials of a constant tone, broad and narrow band noise. My subsequent music, both electronic and instrumental, reflected this interest. Whole pieces became single tonal centers or noise bands with characteristic timbral shaping. I was quite satisfied with this work emotionally and intellectually, although I had apparently abandoned Western harmonic practice.[20]

In electronic works such as *Bye Bye Butterfly* (1965) and *I and II of IV* (1966) slowly shifting electronic notes foreground static and repetitive bass figures. But by gradually adding up and removing musical elements, these works generate a sense of forward motion and momentum in a familiar way that makes them accessible rather than alienating for audiences. Indeed, investment and involvement on the part of audiences (and in fact, the removal of the boundaries between 'audience' and 'musician') was of vital importance to her.

The prejudice she faced as a woman composer was a persistent theme in her writings, and in an essay for the *New York Times* entitled, 'And Don't Call Them Lady Composers' (1970), she mused that,

Women have been taught to despise activity outside of the domestic realm as unfeminine, just as men have been taught to despise domestic duties ... Many critics and professors cannot refer to women who are also composers without using cute or condescending language. She is a 'lady composer'. Rightly, this expression is anathema to many self-respecting women composers. It effectively separates women's efforts from the mainstream.[21]

Despite her initial frustration at the perceived separation between male and female composers in academic circles, she later came to embrace that difference, and throughout the 1970s and '80s, with her ♀ ensemble, Oliveros brought her ideas of 'sonic awareness' to large audiences through workshops and lectures. Towards the end of her life, Oliveros returned to electronic sound as part of her 'deep listening' project, an extension of her lifelong interest in ambient music.

Suzanne Ciani (1946–)

Walking in the footsteps of Oliveros, Suzanne Ciani also began her electronic music career in the San Francisco area. But it was a career that moved in a very different direction; whereas Oliveros chose an academic path, Ciani has spent the majority of her career in the commercial and media realm. Ciani's interest in electronic music began in earnest while studying for a master's in music composition at the University of California, Berkeley, where she was able to merge her classical music education from her undergraduate years at Wesleyan with her passion for cutting-edge technology. Mills College owned a new Buchla synthesiser, and Ciani's discovery of this instrument cemented her commitment to electronic sound. Whereas the Moog, primarily through the work of Carlos, encouraged music that followed a standard tuning system and emulated the sounds of traditional instruments, the layout of the Buchla promoted a more inherently abstract style. She recalls:

I think that awareness of the future for me being a composer as a woman [*sic*], and when I met Don [Buchla] and I entered this room of walls of toys and all those things, just crystallised right there that this was my path. I could be independent. I could do it. I didn't need anybody else, I didn't depend on the political system, I didn't have to please anybody. All I had to do was make enough money to get one of those things.[22]

This she did by working at the San Francisco Tape Music Center, where she built instruments for Buchla and continued her own composing: 'From the moment that I was able to actually get my hands on one, that was my sole possession. I had a Buchla, I didn't have anything else. That went on for ten years. It was my constant companion. It was on all the time. I never shut it off. It was like a living being in my space'.[23]

As was made clear in Ciani's release of *Buchla Concerts 1975* (2016), her work with the Buchla, while tonal and diatonic, has more in common with the drone music of Riley or Oliveros than the pop sensibility of Carlos's Moog work. Ironic, then, that Ciani had her first big successes writing electronic commercial jingles for companies such as Coca-Cola and Energizer, with distinctive sound designs and accessible timbres appealing to a wide audience. Film scores have also formed a significant component of her output. Indeed, her work on *The Incredible Shrinking Woman* (1982) made her the first woman to score a major Hollywood film, and with its alternation between the sound of gratingly cheerful advertising jingles, abstract electronic textures, and comforting tonal synth pads, the score can be seen as a demonstration of her primary stylistic technique.

That same year, Ciani released her first solo album, *Seven Waves*, a recording of electronic synthesiser music which started a long and successful career in the New Age genre (an umbrella marketing term to describe largely instrumental music perceived as relaxing, meditative, or inspirational). Over the course of twenty-three solo albums, Ciani's music frequently employed the acoustic piano in combination with banks of synthesisers for a commercial, accessible sound that made her one of the most important contemporary New Age musicians in America. In recent years, Ciani has returned to the Buchla, presenting a quadrophonic Buchla concert in San Francisco in 2016 with a limited-edition vinyl release, releasing old recordings she had made in the 1970s and never released, and composing new works for the instrument.

Conclusion

While these case studies, by necessity of space, have been limited to English-speaking countries, there have of course been women from all over the world who have made huge contributions to electronic music's early years. Else Marie Pade (1924–2016) was Denmark's first electronic musician, and like Oram, experimented from within her state-run radio station, where she worked from 1952. Influenced by her studies with *musique concrète* inventor Schaeffer at France's RTF in the late 1950s, she presented a series of radio lectures on *musique concrète,* and composed Denmark's first electronic score for a television programme. She is remarkable, like the British composer Elisabeth Lutyens (who is discussed in Chapter 2, 'Women in Composition 2: The Cold War in Music'), for her adoption of serial techniques in composition, and participated in the summer programme at Darmstadt in the 1960s and 1970s. Likewise, French composer Éliane Radigue (1932–) began her career studying with Schaeffer in the late 1950s, but since the mid-1970s, the course of her career has been influenced more by her adherence to Tibetan Buddhism. In particular, her music, as realised primarily through the ARP synthesiser, explores the meditative aspect of subtly evolving drones. In works like the *Adnos* trilogy (1974, 1980, 1982), she clearly articulated her ethos, which she explained in an interview: 'For me, maintaining the sound did not interest me as such; it was primarily a means to bring out the overtones, harmonics and subharmonics. This is what made it possible to develop this inner richness of sound'.[24] The work of Kaija Saariaho (1952–) of Finland – discussed further in Chapter 4, 'Still Exceptional? Women in Composition Approaching the Twenty-First Century' – initially explored the combination of acoustic and electronic sounds within the context of serialism, but after attending the Darmstadt summer course in 1980 and later worked IRCAM, her style evolved into a more textural and abstract language.[25] For example, *Jardin Secret I* for tape (1984–85) superficially resembles Karlheinz Stockhausen's mathematically rigorous *Gesang der Jünglinge* (1955–56) but upon closer examination reveals itself to be far more interested in contrasting timbres and an exploration of shifting textures.

Women have had a permanent and lasting influence on the development of electronic music. Some of the most essential contributors to its history have been women, and the individuals discussed in this chapter have made it possible for subsequent generations of composers and innovators of any gender to continue the pioneering work begun in the 1950s and 1960s. The fact that their accomplishments have only been acknowledged relatively recently does nothing to diminish their importance, and in the future, as the full scale of their contributions are better understood, their reputations can only grow in prominence.

Notes

1. Madeau Stewart, 'Is It Really Music?', *The Tablet* (26 April 1958), n.p.
2. Daphne Oram, *An Individual Note of Music, Sound and Electronics* (Wakefield: Anomie Academic, 2016).
3. *Oramics* (Paradigm Discs, 2007). *The Oram Tapes, Volume One* (Young Americans, 2011). *Electronic Sound Patterns/Electronic Movements* (Trunk Records, 2013). *Pop Tryouts* (Mondo Hebden, 2015).
4. See Daphne Oram Collection, www.gold.ac.uk/ems/oram/ (accessed 11 December 2020).
5. Louis Niebur, *Special Sound: The Creation and Legacy of the BBC Radiophonic Workshop* (New York: Oxford University Press, 2010), 73.
6. Austin Atkinson-Broadbelt, 'Soundhouse: Delia Derbyshire', *Doctor Who Magazine*, no. 199 (12 May 1993), 14.
7. Interview available at www.delia-derbyshire.org/interview_surface.php (accessed 11 December 2020).
8. Atkinson-Broadbelt, 'Soundhouse: Delia Derbyshire', 14.
9. John Tulloch and Manuel Alvarado, *Doctor Who: The Unfolding Text* (New York: St. Martin's Press, 1983), 19.
10. Ibid., 14.
11. Marcus Hearn, 'The Dawn of Knowledge', *Doctor Who Magazine*, no. 207 (22 December 1993), 15.
12. The original recording is labeled in the script for the work as 'Plain Song Antiphon, unaccompanied. Back, band 1, Lib. No. LP 27101'.

13. Delia Derbyshire, undated notes. Delia Derbyshire Archive, Centre for Screen Studies, University of Manchester.

14. Although, as David Butler has recently shown, she did contribute to a few projects in the later 1970s and early 1980s, including collaborations with the film-makers Elsa Stansfield and Madelon Hooykaas, and Polish artist Elisabeth Kozmian. David Butler, 'Whatever Happened to Delia Derbyshire?: Delia Derbyshire, Visual Art, and the Myth of Her Post-BBC Activity', *British Art Studies*, vol. 12 (May 2019). Available at: https://dx.doi.org/10.17658/issn.2058 -5462/issue-12/dbutler (accessed 13 December 2019).

15. Interview with Brian Hodgson, quoted in Niebur, *Special Sound*, 142.

16. Delia Derbyshire Day, 'About', https://deliaderbyshireday.com/about/ (accessed 17 May 2020).

17. Wendy Carlos, *Switched-On Boxed Set*, East Side Digital – ESD 81422 (1999), 72–3.

18. See Wendy Carlos's website, www.wendycarlos.com/+sob.html (accessed 11 December 2020).

19. *Wendy Carlos Switched-On Boxed Set Book One: New Notes*, 15.

20. Pauline Oliveros, 'On Sonic Meditation', reprinted in *Software for People: Collected Writings 1963–1980* (Baltimore, MD: Smith Publications, 1984), 147.

21. Pauline Oliveros, 'And Don't Call Them Lady Composers', *The New York Times* (13 September 1970); reprinted in *Software for People*, 47–8.

22. Aaron Gonsher, 'Instrumental Instruments: Buchla', *Red Bull Music Academy* (14 October 2016); taken from original interview, Frosty, 'Encounters: Suzanne Ciani and Morton Subotnick', *Red Bull Music Academy* (24 June 2016).

23. Ibid.

24. Julien Bécourt, 'Eliane Radigue: The Mysterious Power of the Infinitesimal', https://daily.redbullmusicacademy.com/specials/2015-eliane-radigue-feature/ (accessed 11 December 2020).

25. Kimmo Korhonen, *Finnish Composers since the 1960s* (Helsinki: Finnish Music Information Centre, 1995), 74–9.

Further Reading

Niebur, Louis. *Special Sound: The Creation and Legacy of the BBC Radiophonic Workshop* (New York: Oxford University Press, 2010).

Oliveros, Pauline. *Software for People: Collected Writings 1963–1980* (Baltimore, MD: Smith Publications, 1984).

Sewell, Amanda. *Wendy Carlos: A Biography* (New York: Oxford University Press, 2020).

14 | The Star-Eaters: A 2019 Survey of Female and Gender-Non-Conforming Individuals Using Electronics for Music

MARGARET SCHEDEL AND FLANNERY CUNNINGHAM

The invention of magnetic tape during the Second World War afforded greater flexibility, durability, and reproducibility of recorded sound outside factory processes and brought about a wave of new work that took advantage of tape's potential. It was the development of digital sound in the late 1960s, however, that caused a true explosion in the number of artists working with sound. The development of progressively cheaper and more powerful personal computers has both opened up sonic transformations that are impossible through purely analogue means and have made such techniques accessible to a much broader range of sound-makers. The increasing availability of high-quality consumer or 'pro-sumer' recording equipment, the development of gestural interfaces for controlling digitally produced sound, and the possibility of sharing one's work widely on the internet have all fundamentally changed who produces artistic work with sound and how they do so. As one might expect, these changes have been particularly transformative for women and gender-non-conforming musicians. Where once male composers and technicians could limit access to expensive studio spaces to 'experts', today an entire professional production studio can be contained in a laptop. Our title is borrowed from electronic pioneer Joanna M. Beyer's song for soprano and clarinet, *Ballad of the Star-Eater* (1934), and refers to the star power usually reserved for white, cisgender men. Though there are still barriers to access, today's composers, sound artists, performers, and sound-makers who use electronics represent a far more diverse array of working methods, aesthetics, and backgrounds (in terms of gender, race, geography, income, and much more) than ever before.

In this chapter we cover some of the diversity of this late-twentieth-century and contemporary work through artists' own words. We developed a survey of fifteen questions (see Appendix for these) which we sent to twenty-four composers, sound artists, instrument builders, and programmers.[1] Our respondents range from emerging experimental artists to pillars of academic electroacoustic music; they also represent a cross-section of genre influences, working processes, technical means, and aesthetic aims. Despite their varied backgrounds and the sometimes vastly different sounding effects of their final audio output, a number of important commonalities emerged in our respondents' descriptions of their work and processes. Taken together, along with our own perspectives as women working with electronics, these commonalities begin to describe a state of the art for electronic sound at the beginning of the twenty-first century. In general, our respondents do not work in popular music, although synthesisers and digital audio workstations have come to dominate production of the vernacular sound of the late twentieth and early twenty-first centuries.

Perhaps the most important trait our surveyed artists share is their unabashed love of the sonic medium. This holds true regardless of the avenue that brought an artist to working with electronics. Some of our respondents followed a relatively well-trodden path through playing an instrument, beginning to compose, and studying a traditional curriculum of Western art music, while others studied audio engineering, visual art, or other fields. Our survey, while non-comprehensive, confirmed our intuition that younger artists come from a wider range of educational backgrounds. Nearly all respondents seem to have been drawn to electronics for the expansive range of ways they allow one to manipulate sound. Mara Helmuth, for instance, often writes for instruments in combination with interactive electronics and 'love[s] to work off the performer's unique sounds and set up environments for them to improvise or perform with', while Niloufar Nourbakhsh 'enjoy[s] using electronically produced sounds that would not otherwise be possible with an instrument'. Many employ a range of methods and position the resultant sound, rather than particular technical processes, as the driving force of their work. Seongah Shin feels particularly strongly about the priority of sound over means: 'I consider myself a composer who is dealing with all sorts of sonic events on this earth . . . The method of making music and sonic events does not really mean anything to me.' Karen Power concurs: 'I use whatever is necessary for the needs of an individual piece. For me, it's all about the sound.'

Identities

Many of these artists also seemed reluctant to subscribe to a single label for themselves. Though some were content to call themselves by familiar names like 'composer' or 'sound artist', many either listed a number of such terms, preferred to talk about the range of ways that they work rather than artistic identities, or even resisted particular terms on principle. Pamela Z calls herself 'an extremely "hyphenated" artist', noting that while she is 'best known for [her] solo performances of works for voice and electronics with gesture-controlled sound and video', she 'work[s] as a composer/performer – sound artist – installation artist – voice artist – composer for dance, film, and video – experimental theatre artist – etc.' Cecilia Lopez goes further, disliking even a multi-category identity: 'I don't usually observe the distinction between music and sound art and I am, in fact, specially interested in producing works that inhabit the intersections of these disciplines or concepts.' Lauren Sarah Hayes feels somewhat similarly: 'I move through such a mixture of domains and making sound and music that it seems funny to try to draw such distinctions in my practice. People can call it what they like, although I don't really see much difference in what I do when I improvise noisy electronics versus sitting down to play some Schubert on the piano.' She goes on to say that she describes herself as an improviser and sound artist, mainly to avoid using the term composer, which she doesn't really identify with anymore. Others also resist the term composer in particular. Sadah Espii Proctor writes that she calls herself a sound artist because she struggles with the title 'composer', as she associates it with 'traditional classical or jazz composition and do[es] not see a space for [her]'. Russell Butler argues for a broader, more general conception of their practice, while acknowledging the necessity of describing their work in ways legible to audiences: 'I choose to use the broader title of artist, as this better represents my potential in exploring the creative process . . . "sound artist" or "musician" function more as convenient terms that I use to say that I use sound to express myself and to connect'. Jess Rowland describes her work in similarly general terms, eloquently tying that decision to her way of being in the world:

I never know quite what to call myself – that goes for my art and my identity more generally. I usually just say 'artist', which covers most things (composing, sound arting, inventing, building, etc.). I have always staked out ground that falls between the cracks, no matter where those cracks form. Maybe this comes from being a contrarian, or also because this is where I feel comfortable in a world where I never felt like I quite fit.

Finally, some have even coined new terms that they feel best convey the breadth of their practices; Elizabeth A. Baker, for instance, calls herself a 'New Renaissance Artist' encompassing her many artistic practices.

Approaches and Practices

In general, our respondents work in and across four main areas of electronics: fixed media, live electronics, instrument or environment building, and installation works. Much like the artists themselves, the boundaries between these four areas are not always neat, and multiple identities can overlap within a given work. For example, many pieces contain both prerecorded fixed media and live, interactive elements. Helmuth has written pieces with electronics that are entirely fixed and others that are 'completely interactive', but she often mixes these methods to facilitate the technical needs of the work. Her *Irresistible Flux* (2014) for tárogató and electronics uses this 'best of both worlds' approach, triggering sound files when it would be too difficult to accomplish particular processing live. Other artists also use prerecorded audio as an element to be triggered or manipulated by a live performer. Power often writes music using self-made field recordings of environmental sound combined with instruments. In Nourbakhsh's *METRO* (2018) for dancer and electronics, the dancer moves around a self-assembled Arduino-based sensor system that controls playback of electronic material consisting mainly of recordings of female-only train carriages in Nourbakhsh's native Iran. Using sensors in this way allows for a gesturally rich exploration of the particular social and sonic space of these train carriages, using the dancer's body to sketch the train's confines both physically and sonically. Though all the piece's sound is prerecorded, its performance is dynamic and demanding. Finally, while there can be a striking difference in the demands of performing with fixed-media track and live electronics, in practice these two experiences can sometimes be closer than one might think for an audience. As Nourbakhsh observes, 'depending on the piece, fixed media can actually work in a way that looks [as] if it's interactive'. She writes: 'There is a certain flexibility in timing that comes along with live electronics that I highly enjoy. At the same time, the advantage of fixed media is the predictability of it. So, I try to use both elements in my pieces.'

Even when the actions of performance are digital, the sounds sparked by those actions can draw on acoustic sources. *Unmute* (2018), a laptop ensemble piece by Flannery Cunningham (one of the authors of this chapter), uses such a technique, with 'quasi-vocal' samples of voices resonating piano strings controlled through facial motions via a webcam, hand tracking with a motion sensor, and keyboard input. In this way, *Unmute* aims to open up the experience of communal singing to those who cannot (or do not want to) use a physical voice through a kind of 'voiceless choir'. Rebecca Fiebrink also loves the richness of acoustic sounds and the skills of acoustic players, noting that '[h]aving this expertise at hand takes some pressure off the technology to be capable of the range of expression, structure, improvisational flexibility, etc. that an expert acoustic musician can bring to the table'.

Fiebrink presents an interesting case in terms of identity; she is a musician, performer, and composer, but professionally she considers herself primarily a programmer and 'interaction designer'. She views herself foremost as 'someone who makes tools for others, informed by a variety of other people's practices and experiences'. Her own artistic practices do aid her work, by 'giving [her] some intuition about what is likely to be useful to others', but her goal is to make software that is interesting and broadly useful for other artists. Her Wekinator software has become a standard for musicians who wish to leverage the power of machine learning in their practice, through providing an open-source platform in which an artist can feed a system examples of their desired behaviour through simply matching input and output data. Though working with machine learning presents new challenges of its own, such an adaptive 'black box' allows for the creation of systems that would not only be almost impossibly complex to code, but that are also robust to the variability of human gesture. Margaret Schedel (one of the authors of this chapter) used Wekinator to create *After | Apple Box* (2018), which was inspired by her mentor Pauline Oliveros' piece *Apple Box* (1965). In *After | Apple Box*, performers 'fill' ammunition crates with the sounds of loved ones who have passed away through recordings of those loved ones and their memories of them. Using Wekinator the performers then 'train' their boxes so that tapping in different positions triggers and affects the prerecorded sounds, allowing simple wooden boxes to become expressive instruments.

While Wekinator provides an environment that facilitates the creation of a wide range of pieces, other artists build hardware, software, or combined set-ups that they conceptualise as more akin to musical instruments; systems that are distinctive (and thus not limitless in potential), but which offer sufficient variety and richness to sustain multiple works. Such a tradition of instrument-building stems back to work such as Laurie Spiegel's mid-1980s 'Music Mouse' intelligent instrument. Spiegel writes that:

It is extremely gratifying to have created an instrument that has enabled many more of the people who love music but lack previous musical training to be able to play music of their own, and to help expert music-makers to break free from entrenched musical habits and find new ways to love the process of making music again as though it is fresh and still new.

Today, such set-ups are sometimes called NIMEs (New Interfaces for Musical Expression), though some artists prefer simply to call them instruments. Artists build these systems for a range of reasons, but often seem to create them to fill a sonic, gestural, or experiential vacuum in existing acoustic or electronic instruments. Akiko Hatakeyama, for instance, feels that 'there are no other instruments or interfaces that allow [her] to realise the world that [she] want[s] to create with [her] music [...]'. For Hatakeyama, 'creating and playing custom-made instruments enables [her] to reflect certain bodily gestures that come from deep inside [her], cultural associations, personal experiences, and memories in [her] performances'. Contemporary research and development of NIMEs often focuses on expanding the sonic possibilities of acoustic instruments or restoring the tactile, vibrational feedback of acoustic instruments to digital or hybrid digital/analogue systems. Hayes, for instance, played classical piano from the age of four. She writes: 'When much later I started to perform with computers, the disconnect between sound and touch left me unfulfilled as a musician.' This missing linkage between touch and sonic result led Hayes to develop a hybrid piano, with digitally augmented sound as well as vibration-based haptic feedback.

Besides the hybrid piano, Hayes performs using a variety of combined analogue/digital electronic systems. She describes these as 'assemblages of various components, including analogue synthesisers, hardware drum machines, various MIDI and game controllers, foot pedals, and bespoke software built using Max/MSP'. This kind of hybrid practice, especially the adaptation of existing game/MIDI controllers or building new controllers to create a personal set-up, was pioneered by artists such as Pamela Z and has become a fairly widespread approach. Z performs primarily with her voice, electronics, and video using custom gestural controllers (built with her collaborator, Don Swearingen) with Max/MSP and Isadora software to create 'dense, complex sonic layers' through processing her voice in real-time. Z has worked with this system over a long period and has a single Max patch that serves as her main console for performance. While new works sometimes require her to add new effects to her patch, this continuity has helped Z develop a deep compositional and performative virtuosity on her instrument, which she considers to be the entire system of her voice and electronics set-up. Indeed, the possibility of developing physical skills akin to those required to perform on wholly acoustic instruments is a core attraction of an instrument-building approach. Z observes: 'I think of music as a very physical thing. I think that part of its power is that it gets into our bodies [. . .] I find it very moving and engaging to watch musicians playing music that requires great physical skill and concentration [. . .]'. Hatakeyama shares this view on the importance of physicality, and is particularly interested in physicality as a way of knowing; she writes that 'the presence of a human body, particularly my body presence is extremely important in my art . . . Many times, my body navigates for me the ways to move in my performances.'

Besides her large-scale solo voice/electronics works, another area of Z's practice is installation works. Other respondents, especially Rowland and Proctor, shared this dual pursuit of performance and installation works, which are meant to be experienced on a timescale that the viewer's/listener controls rather than one determined by the composer or performer. Often these installations involve sounds that are the result of the viewer's/listener's interactions with the piece. Rowland, for instance, uses a digital design process to create plans for conductive material, and the conductive material is then cut and 'printed' onto flat materials like paper with analogue circuitry. As she explains, 'at that point, the final product is a physical object which can be explored and interacted with without using any digital technology at all', giving her audiences a concrete, material way to engage with Rowland's work. Proctor often takes a less material approach to interaction, but it is nonetheless important to her, as in her works for virtual reality in which an avatar's movement in an artificial landscape determines the sonic progression of her pre-composed material. Whether interaction is physical or not, a visual element is often an important aspect of a viewer's/listener's interaction with installation-based work. Indeed, installation-based sound art can even be deeply concerned with sound without *sounding* at all. Maria Chavez's sound art spans a wide range of experiential approaches that range from carefully placed speakers that listeners must stand between to hear fragmented sections of text to paintings of microscopic images of vinyl records and turntable needles; the latter works make no sound, but Chavez still considers them sound art pieces. She explains: 'Sound art doesn't just have to be about emitted sound . . . I'm interested in sound in all of its physicalities, whether it's how you visualise it in your mind, how it presents itself through speakers in a space, or how you can present sound beyond sonic emission.' Besides sounding or non-sounding installations, though, Proctor, Rowland, and Chavez all also create works meant to be experienced within the more controlled timescale of a performance, further demonstrating the ways in which many of the artists we surveyed work across multiple electronic practices.

Alongside this widespread fluidity, some artists also have deep-seated aesthetic or philosophical commitments to particular practices. Schedel is deeply interested in interactivity, rarely creating fixed media. While she does not completely eschew using recorded audio material, she is interested in a more extensive kind of in-the-moment interactivity than, say, triggering short sections of audio. Indeed, it may be most useful to conceptualise both 'liveness' and interactivity on a kind of spectrum, from wholly pre-arranged fixed media played back on speakers, through practices such as in-performance triggering of fundamentally fixed audio material, to something like Schedel's 'ferocious interactivity', in which extracted data about musical parameters and/or performer decisions often deeply affect the form or sound of a work.

Hardware and Software

Our respondents use a wide range of technologies to create sound. For artists with long careers, the gear they use has often undergone significant changes over time. Joan LaBarbara, for instance, began performing solo with her voice and electronics around 1974 and primarily used commercially available hardware audio units such as the Roland Space Echo, Electro-Harmonix Frequency Analyzer, and others to modify the signal from her vocal mic. During the period from the 1970s to 1990 she moved to multitrack analogue recording, and around 1990 she began to work more with digital audio workstations (DAWs). Today, DAWs such as ProTools (which is LaBarbara's software of choice) provide powerful, flexible environments for artists to record acoustic instruments; create sound with software instruments built from sample libraries; modify tracks with audio effects and plug-ins; and arrange their sounds with the help of visual interfaces. In general, DAWs have allowed more detailed editing to be done much more quickly than would have been possible before the advent of digital sound. Z reflects on the effect on her compositional choices: 'I make a lot more minute sound edits with digital editing software than I would have had the patience to make when I needed to use a razor blade and splicing tape for each one.' Today, artists creating fixed media may need no more than one or two microphones, an audio interface, a laptop or desktop running a DAW, and studio monitors or monitoring headphones to create their music.

For artists who work with interactive elements instead of or alongside fixed media, other software becomes important. Max and its open-source cousin PureData (Pd) – visual programming environments built for working with audio – are the most commonly used software programmes for controlling interactive elements amongst our respondents. Both environments allow users to extract data from audio inputs, process sound in various ways, and output it to a flexible number of channels through an interface consisting of boxed 'objects' interacting in a 'patch'. This is in contrast to platforms like ChucK, SuperCollider, C#, and C++, which are more traditional line-based coding languages used for audio applications that are also used by our respondents.

Some artists also draw on software that was not specifically developed for audio or music. Helmuth and Proctor both employ the game engine Unity in their installation work, and game engines have become widespread and powerful tools in the burgeoning field of virtual reality (VR). A fair number of our surveyed artists also work with video in addition to audio, drawing in a visual component to their work. This can be fixed video that is created with recording and video-editing software, algorithmic visuals reactive to audio parameters, or other means controlled by the composer/sound artist, but often such projects represent a collaboration with other artists. Both Proctor and Spiegel, for instance, have worked significantly in creating sound for theatre. When doing so, Spiegel tries 'to support the emotional content of the central-focus medium', while other artists negotiate the role of sound in multimedia productions differently. Across the board, though, our surveyed artists (including those who do not work with video or other 'scored' visual elements) displayed a deep cognisance of the importance of an audience's visual experience to their understanding of the work. Some even draw in other senses besides vision and hearing, as in Hayes' use of embedded transducers in risers to create a tactile response for audiences. Nearly all of our respondents understand an audience's reading of their work as one in which sound cannot easily be teased out from other modes of reception. Jennifer Walshe puts it succinctly: 'I don't agree that people can listen in a pure way which ignores all non-sonic information. If we could do that they wouldn't need blind auditions for orchestras.'

Whether for audio with video or audio alone, software-based set-ups are more common today largely because they allow new sonic control, flexibility, and possibilities for interactivity or algorithmic control. Fiebrink reflects on the effects of this access: 'I wouldn't be in this field if electronic music still required such specialised equipment. I got into programming and electronic music because they were activities that were possible on my home PC in the mid-1990s.' Software set-ups also often reduce the costs of creative innovation; adding an audio effect to a Max patch does not require buying something new, as adding an effects pedal would. Transitioning from an analogue to a digital composition and/or performance set-up is not unambiguously positive, however. Analogue gear has a physicality like that of acoustic instruments, which we have already seen artists such as Hayes try to emulate in NIME design. Even digital recreations of analogue equipment lack their materiality. Spiegel, for instance, notes that '[t]he response curves of emulated control devices are ... often not well designed', and she thinks that 'the quality and design of digital simulation of analogue control ... makes [it] less musical when in actual use'. Though Z ultimately prefers her current digital set-up, she 'found that [she] both gained and lost in the process of moving from hardware processors to software. It became possible to be completely accurate with delay time, for example. But I lost the ability to do some pieces that were built around some of the strange quirks of my hardware delays.'

Indeed, besides physicality, it is the very fallibility or imperfection of some kinds of hardware that attracts certain artists. Lopez, for instance writes that 'in terms of technology, there is something about precariousness that [she's] interested in'. Furthermore, she connects this attraction to broader social attention:

There is something about hi-fi technology related to sound, that it's supposed to be neutral and it's not. For me it talks about many things that come up that are related to class, social structures, power structures. And I guess for me it's interesting to break that down, or investigate other ways in which technology works that it's more marginal, or the noise of an apparatus.

That investigation has included creating unstable acoustic feedback systems in works like Lopez's sculpture/instrument *RED* (2015). Other artists working with non-digital materials share this interest in using their process or in interrogating social structures or barriers. Though Chavez's work as an abstract turntablist seems more motivated by an aesthetics of exploration than of precarity, she also uses breakdown (in the form of damaged or broken records) as a driver of sound and structure. While digital sound has opened up access and possibilities for many creators, there is a significant subset of artists who continue to use analogue hardware exclusively, repurpose that hardware in new contexts, or combine it with digital techniques. Some even resist an analogue/ digital divide. Butler finds it 'a tiresome debate that [they] really wish would go to bed' and 'feel[s] that any artist in this age must interact with a hybrid of either technology to their own taste and ease', pointing out that they use a (digital) computer to record (analogue) modular synthesisers. Others draw on both technologies, but do feel them to be separate strands of their practice: Cat Hope 'think[s] digital and analogue creation and reproduction both sound so different, so [she] use[s] them very much as different instruments'. Hope exclusively uses analogue effects pedals in her solo electric bass performance, a practice drawn from experimental rock, but works with digital production in other streams of her music making. Overall, it is an age of hybridity for many artists in terms of the gear and techniques that they use.

Along these lines, our respondents tend not to have an ideological attachment to particular kinds of software or hardware. Many express interest in using new technologies in the future, especially DIY circuitry, and some note the constant process of learning that working with electronics today entails. Nourbakhsh, for instance, calls herself a 'generalist' and says that she tries 'to challenge [herself] to learn something new with every piece'. Most of our surveyed artists choose technologies that they feel will best allow them to create the sound or performative experience that interests them in a particular piece. Some of our respondents also expressed frustration with or resistance to expectations of demonstrating membership of a scene through having the 'right' gear or displaying technical mastery of that gear. Such expectations can sometimes have uncomfortably gendered overtones based in historical assumptions about who belongs in particular spaces and has the intellectual chops to create 'complex' electronic music. Hope 'hate[s] shopping for gear' and writes: 'I often feel I have to prove my technical prowess (even when I don't have it) due to my gender.' Others actively resist such pressure. Hayes writes that she is 'not interested in working environments where the goal is to demonstrate some kind of technical mastery, make the most noise, or show off the most gear', explaining that she 'spent a long time in those scenes and . . . find[s] them quite boring' despite her interest in technical work. While many of our surveyed artists in fact cited warm support from mentors and colleagues – men as well as women and gender-non-conforming artists – in the communities they work in, others described a gradual process of overcoming worries that they came from insufficiently technical/musical backgrounds. Spiegel explains how she was discouraged from pursuing music:

Because I had not had a standard childhood music education, of ongoing music lessons on a classical European instrument, I was told very clearly there was no way I could become a musician. Later[,] after I had persisted anyway, I was told I might, if I was lucky and worked very hard, get far enough with music to be able to teach it. I was never encouraged. I was told it was impressive that I could write music at all because women generally couldn't do that.

In contrast, Proctor found huge support and encouragement through the laptop orchestra and the Digital Interactive Sound and Intermedia Studio at Virginia Tech, where she was 'inspired to not be embarrassed about [her] arts background and to embrace the advantage in building a story/experience, and [learned that] the math and science can be learned to support that rather than withdrawing because of it'.

Of course, there is a final piece to the gear puzzle, and one that is not always so directly in artists' control: speakers and microphones. High-quality speakers and microphones can be prohibitively expensive and bulky to own and transport, meaning that many artists depend on venues to provide them. Most of our respondents primarily use stereo sound, meaning two channels (left and right). A stereo set-up allows for one's work to be performed/diffused in a wide array of venues, and its low number of speakers also maximises the chances of high-quality equipment. (Some artists even take the simplicity of stereo a step further; Shin often works in what she calls 'big mono', aiming for a particularly robust sound with a single audio channel.) Even those who work in other set-ups often utilise stereo as a fallback option. Practicality married with a deep concern about sound quality/audience experience is a hallmark of nearly all the artists we surveyed, and it speaks to both the constraints our respondents are accustomed to and their creative responses to such constraints.

The main alternative to stereo seems to be a quadrophonic set-up ('quad'), which still involves a relatively low number of speakers but allows for basic spatialisation of sound because of its introduction of rear left and right speakers. Power writes the majority of her works in quad, and LaBarbara and Walshe each also have at least a few works designed specifically for the set-up. Those who work with larger numbers of speakers are more apt to work with *much* larger numbers, such as the hundreds of speakers Proctor used at The Cube at Virginia Tech or at the SARC (Sonic Arts Research Centre) at Queen's University, Belfast. In these cases, spatialisation of the sound becomes a primary feature of the work, and the resulting pieces are tied to a small number of possible venues.

Of course, it is not only the number or arrangement of speakers that matters, but also the type. All speakers 'colour' sound by boosting some frequencies and attenuating others, and they vary greatly in both self-noise and power. Many of our respondents preferred not to make particular requests that venues might not be able to accommodate. Walshe never requests particular models of speakers, and besides her custom-built speakers, Rowland is not usually particularly concerned with the speaker set-up. Others do feel strongly about particular speaker choices for particular works. Hope always makes specific requests, and she enjoys using a wide range of speakers, including instrument amplifiers, multiple large subwoofers, and 'tiny, quiet speakers'.

Finally, some artists even assemble or build their own custom speakers or microphones. Baker designs her own microphones and is thinking of selling her hydrophones (microphones made to work under water), while Rowland creates her own speakers. Elizabeth Hoffman (author of the section 'In Her Own Words: Practitioner Contribution 1' within the current volume) spent months hunting for an alternative to standard public address (PA) speakers for her permanent installation *Retu(r)nings* (2019) in New York University's Elmer Holmes Bobst Library. She eventually discovered a model of studio monitors with sufficient power to project in the library's atrium when mounted on the space's catwalks. Rowland builds her own speakers out of paper, with printed circuits, for many of her sound artworks. In these works, 'the material object – musical instruments/interface/ graphic score/speaker – is complicated into one charged piece of material', as in her installation using a malleable 100-foot speaker and audio work, *The Very Long Sound* (2016). In general, in an installation setting – where a speaker set-up might sound continuously for days, weeks, or even years – the upfront logistical costs of sourcing or making more (or less standard) speakers may seem more worthwhile.

Challenges

The challenges of dealing with speakers are in many ways illustrative of the challenges of working with electronics today more broadly. Though we have sketched a number of widespread approaches, aims, and types of equipment, there is no real consensus about so many of the techniques that go into creating music or sound with electronics. Just as artists come up with their own individual responses to lack of speaker standardisation and availability, individual creators have their own solutions to a whole range of other challenges: producing sounds that feel like they equal the richness and complexity of acoustic performance, finding ways to inject physicality into performing with computers, designing systems that facilitate rehearsal for performers who may not be experienced with electronics, figuring out how to quickly adjust levels and effects in (often very short) soundchecks, working with precarious or unreliable systems, and much more. Many artists might welcome some sort of standardisation of approaches to these problems: a kind of shared set of best practices that has not yet fully evolved. At the same time, however, the individual problem-solving that the state of the field has necessitated has led to a certain thoughtfulness about means and aims that might not otherwise exist. A lack of common practice has led to groundbreaking individual solutions and many conceptually rich approaches to working with electronics.

Above all, the artists we have surveyed are practical-minded, serious people. They work within the constraints they experience in terms of cost and availability of equipment, access to the knowledge required to create particular tools (such as DIY hardware), restrictions of venues, and more, to deliver personal, persuasive, and often innovative sonic experiences. Many think deeply about the experience of their audiences and find ways to invite them into the work, including by using and transforming familiar natural sounds (Helmuth, *Abandoned Lake in Maine* (1997), *LOONSPACE* (2000)); creating possibilities for physical interaction by viewers/listeners in installation settings (Rowland, paper speakers and piano-roll interfaces); drawing in the element of touch through embedded transducers (Hayes); using a deeply personal reflection of self in performances with significant elements of improvisation (described as 'me at the moment of performance like a diary') in order to invite audiences to meditate on their own experiences and emotions (Hatakeyama); or setting up 'feedback loops' with an audience through groove box performances that 'giv[e] them something to process, integrat[e] their responses, and push out that interpretation' (Butler). They also often hope to challenge listeners/viewers, provide novel experiences, or provoke creative reimagining, such as through confronting audiences with 'impossible transition[s] ... outside our constrained conception of what sound is or could be' (Rowland), or accepting their own sense of 'be[ing] a stranger in any kind of society' and the difficulty for understanding that that may pose for listeners (Shin). Taking a broader view, there is no question that this field (and the people populating it) looks different from what it did sixty, forty or even twenty years ago. It *is* more representative, and there have been positive shifts in the way, for example, mentorship structures have been conceived: away from single mentors and towards mentorship networks. Although institutional affiliations remain vital, advancement and access are no longer necessarily contingent on contact with a single, well-placed mentor. There is, in other words, an emerging lateral network of participants whose diverse backgrounds and approaches are transforming this area. Attending to this network and supporting it will help to continue to diversify and strengthen the future of the field.

Notes

1. The survey was carried out from May to July 2019.

Further Reading

Baker, Elizabeth A. *The Resonant Life: Attack. Decay. Sustain. Release. Resonate* (USA: 2018).

Fiebink, Rebecca. The Wekinator (n.d.). www.wekinator.org/ (accessed 11 December 2020).

Rowland, Jess. 'Flexible Audio Speakers for Composition and Art Practice.' *Leonardo Music Journal* (2013), 33–6.

In Her Own Words: Practitioner Contribution 3

MANUELLA BLACKBURN

This practitioner contribution documents a series of compositions created between 2013 and 2018, when my compositional process and research trajectory distinctly altered as a result of life changes. My work as an electroacoustic music composer has consistently explored sound recordings of objects, instruments, and environments captured from the real world. My interest in this field was cultivated during my undergraduate music degree at the University of Manchester, where I learned how to combine composition with computer technology.

My earlier fixed-media works (from 2006 to 2013) exhibited a preoccupation with foreign, unfamiliar, and exotic sound sources. Armed with a portable field recorder, I travelled the world to capture culture-specific sound materials; anything from street musicians and jukeboxes to languages and traditional instruments. I would bring these sonic treasures home like souvenirs,[1] unpack them, and give them pride of place within my fixed-media compositions. These globally sourced sounds can be heard in my works *Sonidos Bailables* (2006), *Cajón!* (2008), *Dance Machine* (2009), *Karita oto* (2009), *Javaari* (2012–13), and *New Shruti* (2013), in which the search for sound involved field trips to Argentina, Mexico, Portugal, Japan, and India respectively. A shift in focus to home-sourced sounds led to the creation of a series of works derived entirely from domestic sources: *Time Will Tell* (2013), *Ice Breaker* (2015), *Snap Happy* (2017), and *Landline* (2018). The shift was propagated by a significant life-changing milestone; the birth of my two children.

The Domestic and Creativity

Having two children in close succession resulted in more time spent around the home and less time travelling overseas for recording projects. This elongated period at home was unusual, and grounded me in a single location for long stretches of time both in the pre- and antenatal stages. Sounds found around the home, which had always been there, suddenly became points of inspiration for compositional work, since I noticed and appreciated them more for their consistency and association with my home space; I was also around them more than usual. I came to view these home-based sound sources as personal sounds, and they began to mean more to me, as they marked out a period of time that signified importance and change. This shift in sonic focus functioned as a reminder of the emotional connections and memories one can have with the personal possessions that one is surrounded by daily. The re-imagining of the domestic 'mundane' is a sentiment I share here with sound artist Felicity Ford, and her concept of the 'domestic soundscape'.[2] Ford's use of everyday sound as documented in her research has been used to highlight daily activities that take place within the home, such as home decorating, knitting, cooking, and other sounds from the kitchen. The home environment as an impetus for creating music is not by any means a novel or exclusively (female) gendered approach; take, for example, the kitchen environment which has inspired a wealth of electroacoustic music repertoire from male composers:

- Jonty Harrison's *Klang* (1982) uses two earthenware casseroles dishes as the sole sonic material.
- Paul Lansky's *Table's Clear* (1992) uses kitchen utensil sounds and recordings of a domestic scene in a kitchen.
- Matthew Herbert's *Around the House* (2002) uses samples of washing machines, toasters, and toothbrushes, processed into swinging grooves.
- Amon Tobin's *Kitchen Sink* (2007) constructs trip-hop music through looped samples of water splashing and pans clattering, inspired by *musique concrète* processes.
- Konstantinos Karathanasis's *Ode to Kitchen* (2015) showcases hundreds of sounds from kitchen objects clustered together.
- Matmos's *Ultimate Care II* (2016) derives every sound from the duo's washing machine. The thirty-eight-minute duration mimics a single wash cycle.

Exploring the work of installation artist Fran Cottell and her *House Projects* (2001) furthered my interest in this area. Cottell's own domestic home space was converted into a 'museum' venue accessible to visitors, initially established for the public to view 'the honesty and truthfulness of mess over domestic order'.[3] In one of these projects, visitors had access to Cottell's home through specially constructed walkways to observe the reality of domestic life (with young children) along with the objects that inhabited this space. Assessing the domestic through the perspective of anthropology, Mihaly Csikszentmihalyi and Eugene Rochbert-Halton's *The Meaning of Things* has also shaped my understanding of the relationship of the self to personal objects (like those objects that appear sonically in my music). This text suggests that: 'to understand what people are and what they might become, one must understand what goes on between people and things. What things are cherished, and why, should become part of our knowledge of human beings.'[4]

The home as a site for artistic creation and contemplation has clearly inspired many, but there is something curiously subversive about the mix of motherhood and the use of domestic objects as a means for creativity within the examples I have encountered. Having an opportunity to take ownership of a domestic symbol, one that has such stereotypical connotations or associations with the 'housewife' role in the traditional sense, feels like an empowering move, most likely for its unconventional application and transformation within an artistic context. The remarkable (and often unbelievable) time and spaces these examples emerge from is also worth a note here. Finding a window to 'make' and continue practice in light of children arriving on the scene is significant and provides the subject for a growing body of practice from voices discussing and representing this impossible juggling act (consider, for instance, the national initiative Mothers Who Make).[5] Academic study has also begun to follow suit, as articulated by the work and theories of dance practitioner Sarah Black. Black's research led to new terminology when she considered the combination of creative practice and mothering.[6] Her concepts of 'maternal ethics', 'mother as curator', and 'mother-artists' are particularly significant in this context.[7]

My collection of compositions, under the heading of 'Domestic Bliss', adds to this emerging body of work from women practitioners that document periods of transition, in which those artists are still eager to be creative. My contribution, from the perspective of a woman electro-acoustic music composer, discusses decisions to use home-sourced sounds in my music making, and explains the connection these sounds have to my changing circumstance. From the outside, and without reading this as evidence or verification, listeners of my compositions are unlikely to receive this level of context, significance, or meaning, but to myself, as composer, I look back on these works and catch the symbolism, memories, and connections embedded within the timbres and structures.

Domestic Bliss (2013–2018)

Time Will Tell *(2013)*

In 2013 I was given a commission from EMPAC (Experimental Media and Performing Arts Centre), Troy, New York. This residency in spring 2013 gave me access to the Goodman Studio,[8] a team of technicians, and carte blanche to create a new work for performance at EMPAC. On arrival my only preconception for a new composition was to continue my interest in short sounds (initiated in my earlier work, *Switched on*, 2011). Part of my sound-collection activity led me to a clock shop in a nearby town, Waterford. These clock sound recordings were added to my collection as part of my residency, a collection which also included the sounds of the EMPAC building, the surrounding environment, and a thunderstorm I experienced during my stay. On my return from my residency, I continued to work on the sound materials that I had gathered, but it was my extended malaise with hyperemesis gravidarum that solidified my focus upon clock sounds featured in *Time Will Tell*. Non-stop sickness and the knowledge that symptoms might ease off in the second trimester kept my mind on the passage of time, checking off dates on the calendar, and working on the mantra of 'taking one day at a time'. Hearing the sounds of the house during this seemingly endless 'housebound' time was a new experience, one that I had not previously had the 'luxury' of. The previously unnoticed clocks tick-tocking in the house that continued to mark out each day found their way into my commission. *Time Will Tell* was premiered in EMPAC in November 2013, when I was four months pregnant.

Ice Breaker *(2015)*

My first daughter was born in June 2014. The summer of this year was unusually hot for the UK, and I remember the sound of ice cubes becoming the 'soundtrack' to this time. Copious cold drinks, ice packs, cooling down, and wanting to live in the freezer to escape the heat initiated my fascination with the phenomenon of differential expansion. Placing ice into drinks resulted in the satisfying cracking sound of the ice expanding due to the sudden change of temperature. Five weeks postpartum I developed sepsis and, as a result, spent all of my maternity leave recovering. Recording ice crack and pop sounds was a welcome distraction conducted at nap times. *Ice Breaker* was premiered at the L'Espace du son festival at Théâtre Marni in Brussels, Belgium, in 2015, sixteen months post-partum.

Snap Happy *(2017)*

Part way through my second maternity leave in 2016, I discovered a box filled with old cameras, which had been tucked away in my loft for some time. After contemplating the camera function on my iPhone, which adopted the classic shutter sound to accompany picture taking, I realised these recently discovered older-style cameras had much more to offer in the sound domain, such as flashes, zooms, clicks, film-roll winds, disc-cartridge cranks, and function button switches. The use of my camera in this antenatal period struck me as a fundamental part of bonding with my second daughter, capturing the passage of time, gathering one-off moments, and documenting developmental milestones that would freeze these memories amidst my particularly acute sleep-deprived state. I chose camera sounds to represent this 'happy' time. *Snap Happy* was premiered in the Martin Harris Centre for Music and Drama at the University of Manchester, UK, in 2017.

Landline *(2018)*

The discovery of my landline phone behind my sofa, caked in dust, reinforced how little this household object had been used in recent times. This discovery took me back to my memories of the rotary phone my parents had in my childhood home. This shiny black patent object took pride of place in the hallway, complete with telephone table and phone book. It was the first object to greet you as you entered the home. Like the cameras I stumbled upon in my loft, the phone as a device has undergone great developments, rendering the older styles obsolete. My role as composer was to document these changes sonically, fix these endangered 'historic' sounds within a musical form, and also to celebrate the newer sounds emitted by modern phone cameras. In my composition, I explored dial tones, touch tones, rings and ringtones, the engaged tone, and rotary dials from older phones. I received permission to use a rotary dial phone sound from the Conserve the Sound Online Museum,[9] which approximated the sounds of the phone in my memory, as my parents no longer had possession of the phone I recalled from my childhood. This work became concerned with recreating a domestic space from a childhood memory; a time hop to an earlier time, forced from the reflections I had been having of being a child, which tends to happen after one has had children. *Landline* was premiered at Edith Cowan University in Perth, Australia, in 2018.

Notes

1. Manuella Blackburn, 'Importing the Sonic Souvenir: Issues of Cross-Cultural Composition', Electroacoustic Music Studies Network Conference proceedings (New York, 201); available at www.ems-network.org/IMG/pdf_EMS11_Blackburn .pdf. (accessed 10 December 2020).
2. Felicity Ford, 'The Domestic Soundscape and Beyond . . . Presenting Everyday Sounds to Audiences', PhD thesis (Oxford Brooks University, 2010).
3. Fran Cottell, www.francottell.com/ (accessed 5 June 2019).
4. Mihaly Csikszentmihalyi and Eugene Rochbert-Halton, *The Meaning of Things: Domestic Symbols and the Self* (Cambridge: Cambridge University Press, 1981), 1.
5. Mothers Who Make website: www.improbable.co.uk/motherswhomake/ (accessed 11 December 2020).
6. Sarah Black, 'Mother as Curator: Performance, Family and Ethics' (PhD thesis, Middlesex University, 2018).
7. Ibid.
8. The Goodman studio at EMPAC can be viewed here: https://empac.rpi.edu /about/building/venues/studio-1-goodman (accessed 5 December 2020).
9. Rotary phone sound sourced from Conserve the Sound project, available at www.conservethesound.de/en/ (telephone name: Fernsprechtischapparat, Manufacturer: Deutsche Bundespost) (accessed 4 October 2017).

PART IV

Women's Wider Work in Music

Women and Music Education in Schools:
Pedagogues, Curricula, and Role Models

ROBERT LEGG

To Watch, to Nurse, and to Rear: Women in General Education

Compared with other salaried occupations, the teaching profession has a recent history of being relatively open to women. By the second half of the nineteenth century, women represented a majority of those employed as teachers in both the United Kingdom and the United States, whereas on either side of the Atlantic the individual careers of physicians such as Elizabeth Blackwell and Elizabeth Garrett Anderson were isolated examples in an overwhelmingly male-dominated medical profession. In the same period, Clara Brett Martin and Ethel Benjamin became the first female barristers to succeed in contesting women's professional exclusion from the British Empire's legal structures. The prohibition of the employment of women in the British armed forces continued until 1949, and women continued to be excluded from the ranks of the Anglican clergy until 1992, the latter exclusion maintained to this day in the context of the Roman Catholic Church. While the medical, legal, military, and religious professions represented closed avenues for most women of the early twentieth century, teaching in its various guises was a popular and well-travelled career path for women, and had been so since long before 1900.

The issues explored in this chapter have significance across many areas of education, but it is women's experience and representation in formal, compulsory music education in the classroom that provide the principal focus here. The comparative openness of schools to the employment of women from the early years of general education resulted rather less from a radical commitment to equality on the part of agitators than from the view that for a woman, to teach was to extend her essential nurturing role, and was therefore a 'natural' and good thing. The impediments to female membership of the other professions did not apply. Unlike the surgeon, the teacher does not draw blood or delve into open bodies; unlike the lawyer, her domain is not that of adversarial argumentation and logic; unlike the soldier, she does not kill; unlike the clergyman, she holds no responsibility for sacramental leadership; rather, her domain is the raising of the young.

As early as 1829 the American advocate of female education Catharine Beecher made explicit this elision between the practices of teaching and child-rearing, and emphasised women's lack of preparation for both these vital roles:

It is to mothers and to teachers that the world is to look for the character which is to be enstamped on each succeeding generation, for it is to them that the great business of education is almost exclusively committed. And will it not appear by examination that neither mothers nor teachers have ever been properly educated for their profession? What is the profession of a Woman? Is it not to form immortal minds, and to watch, to nurse, and to rear the bodily system, so fearfully and wonderfully made, and upon the order and regulation of which, the health and well-being of mind so greatly depends?[1]

Beecher's view is echoed and amplified in countless texts from the period. The perceived suitability of the female sex for careers in teaching predominates as a societal belief today, even as the corresponding, paternalistic view that teaching is a uniquely suitable job for middle-class women has been eroded. Notwithstanding the twentieth century's near consensus over the appropriateness of female employment in teaching, it perhaps goes without saying that women's involvement as professionals in the provision of formal education has also been subject to many of the societal restrictions and frustrations that have arisen across a wide range of occupations. These have included, amongst other barriers, limits on the employment of married women, who were discouraged or excluded by regulation in many jurisdictions before 1945; a variety of discriminatory employment practices; and exclusion from roles of responsibility; not to mention difficulties arising from domestic and family responsibilities.

Justified contemporaneously as safeguards of family and community life, it is now hard to view these restrictions as anything other than self-interested checks on women's financial and intellectual independence, devised by and for the benefit of a moneyed male elite. In the UK, the Forster Act of 1870, the Balfour Act of 1902, and the Butler Act of 1944 each brought compulsory free education to significant numbers of new students; while in the United States, legislation was enacted mandating elementary education on a state-by-state basis. As new tranches of children were ushered into the scope of universal free education, more women were brought into the workforce to teach them. Statistical analysis of female participation in the education sector in the first half of the twentieth century shows demographic factors relating to students as important determinants of women teachers' acceptability. Where the students were young, or from low socio-economic backgrounds, the employment of a female teacher was more likely. Thus, universities and fee-paying schools were staffed mainly by men, whereas women teachers predominated in elementary schools, inviting us again to identify expedience as the primary motivation for this setting aside of society's reluctance to emancipate women through employment.

Late nineteenth- and early-twentieth-century society, as it began to educate its masses, had no choice but to deploy its women as educators. Then, as now, women were greatly under-represented in leadership roles. Post-1945, the implementation of universal general education in the developed world, first to the age of fourteen, then sixteen, and in many countries eventually to eighteen and beyond, has required a larger workforce, in which women are increasingly represented, although not always on an equal basis with men. Recent research into the gender pay gap amongst rank-and-file teachers in the UK showed that male teachers' wages were greater by between 2 (for primary school practitioners) and 4 per cent (in secondary education), while amongst school and college leaders men were on average 17 per cent better paid.[2] These differentials represent both historical improvement and, clearly, unfinished business. In recent decades, qualitative studies into the experiences of women working in education, both as teachers and leaders, have shown the variety of barriers they must overcome to achieve positions of influence as well as the stereotyping they face when exercising power in the workplace.[3] Despite the narrative of female suitedness for teaching, despite the profession's ostensibly family-friendly working hours and holidays, and despite the evident success of twentieth-century women in building careers in teaching, it is also true that the scholastic environment has presented – and still presents – many female teachers with significant challenges.

Body and Mind: Women Working in Music Education

The opportunities and challenges that apply to women teachers in general are, by and large, shared by those who choose to work in the field of music education. Although the proportion of music teachers who are women has differed very little from the proportion of women working in the sector as a whole, and although the historical imposition of barriers and limits to employment as a music educator have been similar to those experienced by other teachers, certain features are specific to our subject. In order to understand the structures that distinguish the experiences of women teaching music in schools from those of their colleagues in other subjects, it is worth considering the musical realm from a theoretical perspective as well as from the perspective of individual practitioners.

Many persuasive theoretical accounts of gender issues in music and education employ a body/mind dualism,[4] in which various musical activities and roles are apportioned, facilitated, celebrated, or proscribed according to their being understood either as an aspect of (bodily) display or (cerebral) control, with the former delineated as consistent with femininity, the latter with masculinity. Hence social approbation for women singers – whose display of the body as the physical origin of the voice is consistent with normative ideas of femininity – but opprobrium for female composers and conductors – whose minds are conspicuously deployed in the creative management and direction of others (perhaps especially including men), thereby disrupting feminine norms. A succinct summary of the specific ways in which this theory plays out in relation to music composition is offered by Victoria Armstrong, drawing upon the scholarship of Marcia J. Citron and Lucy Green:

> [Citron] asserts that 'the mental, or the mind, has been considered fundamental to creativity' reinforcing the mind-body dualism that acts as a means of excluding women, creating an ideological separation between the 'intellectual purity' of the masculine mind and the messy, uncontrollable female body. Whereas the female singer affirms her femininity through the perceived alliance of her sound with her 'natural' body, the female composer, devoid of the need to control or employ external forms of technology, challenges traditional notions of femininity (Green 1997). In order to create music, the composer must have technical knowledge of instruments and harmony ... 'Composition requires knowledge and control of technology and technique', leading Green to suggest that composition becomes a 'metaphorical display of the mind'; the notion of the mind is delineated as masculine. As a result, this metaphorical display of the mind when applied to a female composer 'conflicts with her natural submission of the body' (88). Composition becomes both materially and ideologically associated with masculinity.[5]

The material and ideological positioning of a key component of musical practice as antithetical to femininity has had implications for women teachers and female students, of course, but also for the curriculum itself. In the first half of the twentieth century, problematic delineated associations of composition with masculinity meant that while many women studied musical performance to a high standard – an accomplishment for the most part in harmony with a socially approved performance of femininity – the opportunities for women to study composition, notable exceptions notwithstanding, were far fewer. When coupled with the preponderance of women working in the profession during this early period, this in turn led to the omission of composition from the school music curriculum.

Problematic ideology (and often inadequate resources) meant that prescribed curricula pre-1970 in the United Kingdom were for the most part limited to – as in many cases even identified as – class singing. The other main focus of the school curriculum was listening and music appreciation, drawing on and simultaneously reinforcing a small canon of music by male composers who worked in the 'common-practice' tradition of European art music.[6] The view expounded by George Upton in 1886 was that while 'at first glance it would seem that musical composition is a province in which women should excel', closer examination, evidently, showed women to be 'receptive rather than creative' in their engagement with music, having 'failed to create important and enduring works'.[7]

While women's compositional output was thus unjustly excluded from the pedagogical canon, women were influential in the development, testing, and publication of pedagogical principles and practices. Sondra Wieland Howe's recent work has shown how, in the United States, women took the lead in the writing of textbooks and instructional works, with series of texts for schools appearing under the authorship of Eleanor Smith, M. Teresa Armitage, Mabelle Glenn, and Lilla Bell Pitts, while pedagogues such as Angela Diller, Elizabeth Quaile, and Leila Fletcher published popular piano methods.[8] In Great Britain, meanwhile, the confidence – certainty, even – with which a woman author might address music-pedagogical matters was amply demonstrated in the highly influential and frequently quoted philosophy of Annie Curwen, an Anglo-Irish writer of books for music teachers:

1. Teach the easy before the difficult.
2. Teach the *thing* before the *sign*.
3. Teach one fact at a time, and the commonest fact first.
4. Leave out all exceptions and anomalies until the general rule is understood.
5. In training the mind, teach the concrete before the abstract.
6. In developing physical skill, teach the elemental before the compound, and do one thing at a time.

7. Proceed from the known to the unknown.
8. Let each lesson, as far as possible, rise out of that which goes before, and lead up to that which follows.
9. Call in the understanding to help the skill at every step.
10. Let the first impression be a correct one; leave no room for misunderstanding.
11. Never tell a pupil anything that you can help him to discover for himself.
12. Let the pupil, as soon as possible, derive some pleasure from his knowledge. Interest can only be kept up by a sense of growth in independent power.[9]

Pedagogy was thus understood as a domain in which female authority could be asserted and accepted. Curwen's role in providing a pedagogical interpretation or realisation of theories and practices developed by a man better established in the public sphere – in this case her father-in-law, John Curwen, the pioneer of tonic sol-fa – was not an unusual one. Two of the leading 'methods' popularised in the middle part of the twentieth century, Orff-Schulwerk and Dalcroze Eurhythmics, although ostensibly founded by men, were furnished with pedagogies by female music educators. In the former case, the substantial input of Dorothee Günther, Gunild Keetman, and (especially in the anglophone world) Margaret Murray belies the movement's eponymous title. Working at the progressive Günther-Schule in Munich, Keetman's work 'putting [Orff's] ideas into practice'[10] resulted in the lead authorship of all five volumes of *Musik für Kinder* (*Music for Children*), published in German between 1949 and 1954, and in Margaret Murray's English editions in the later 1950s. The influence of these volumes on music-pedagogical practice in the coming decades was great. Meanwhile, the practical development of Dalcroze Eurhythmics on the foundations of Émile Jaques-Dalcroze's groundbreaking concept was also largely in the hands of women such as Suzanne Ferrière and Marguerite Heaton, who founded the first training centre in the United States; Marie Eckhard, the founder of the Dalcroze Society of Great Britain and Northern Ireland; and Heather Gell, who initiated the lively Dalcroze scene in Australia. The trend for music-pedagogical innovation and refinement to be discharged by women has continued, with significant contributions from writers like Ruth Harris and Elizabeth Hawksley, for example, providing practical elucidations of the ideas normally ascribed to John Paynter, in their highly regarded and much-used text of 1989.[11]

By the 1950s, individual women teachers were making significant progress, too, in securing positions in higher education institutions. Helen Just, the cellist in the English String Quartet, was in the early generation of women to be appointed to permanent professorial roles at London's Royal College of Music (RCM), following in the footsteps of pioneers such as Marguerite Long, who became professor of piano at the Paris Conservatoire in 1920, and the composer Nadia Boulanger, who worked at the American School at Fontainebleau throughout the 1920s. In common with many other pioneers, Just relied on charisma and the force of her personality to gain acceptance in this male-dominated environment, in which she encountered resistance on a regular basis. In the following account of a postgraduate chamber music coaching session, a male violist provides insight into her dialogic teaching style while also demonstrating, probably inadvertently, the readiness of a young male student to challenge the authority of a female professor:

All went much as expected to begin with – we played a movement (or perhaps just an exposition) and then received good advice on tempo or balance, phrasing or tone quality. 'Walk about, walk about!' was a favourite phrase used to engender forward movement when Helen felt we were hanging about to no good purpose. Then occasionally out would come some statement so musically challenging as to be provocative. I found myself opening my mouth and saying, 'I don't know that I agree with that, Miss Just' – which produced tangible silence and looks of frozen horror from my three colleagues. 'Why not?' came the reasonable retort – and I would have to think hard to marshal cogent musical arguments to support a different view of the passage in question. Quite often Helen and I would achieve quite a sustained argument – frequently resolved by trying out both approaches in turn.[12]

Helen Just occupied her position at the Royal College deservedly, as one of the most musically gifted, technically able, and frequently broadcast performing cellists of her generation, yet it is illustrative of her experience – and that of other women performers of her era – that published accounts of her success were quick to assert the patronage of her husband, the cellist Ivor James, an RCM professor of an earlier generation.[13]

Mind the Gap: Role Models and Curricula

In the second half of the twentieth century, a clear gap emerged between the distance travelled by individual women and the general stagnation of the music education world where issues of gender politics were concerned. Female educators were central to the flourishing of organisations like the Music Educators National Conference (MENC) in the United States, and the National Association of Music Educators (NAME) in the United Kingdom, as well as to the establishment of the International Society for Music Education (ISME) itself. New opportunities afforded by broadcast media and music publishing were seized by women like the flautist and concert animateur Atarah Ben-Tovim, whose relentless advocacy of high-quality universal music education led her to be viewed first as 'just another crazy woman with a bee in her bonnet',[14] and eventually as an imaginative pedagogue with a talent for inspiring children's interest in all kinds of musical material. Ben-Tovim's work for the BBC resulted in a number of television and radio series, including *Atarah's Music Box* and *Atarah's Band*, which aired in the late 1970s and early 1980s.

In the United States, similar influence was gained by the conductor and teacher Doreen Rao, whose work encompasses professional performance and pedagogical leadership. Rao's contribution to choral pedagogy, primarily through the editing of an extensive and popular series of graded repertoire for children and adults, and by regular mediatised appearances, has been significant. Other women have achieved prominence as a result of their ability to match artistry and pedagogical innovation. Lin Marsh's success as a prodigious composer of outstanding music for children has been unsurpassed since her emergence in the 1990s as a leading British music pedagogue. Practitioners like Mary King, whose work includes television programmes like *Operatunity* (2003) and *Musicality* (2004) for the UK broadcaster Channel 4, have made a similarly powerful and long-lasting impact through their writings and music educational leadership.

The success of these individuals in pursuing careers at the highest level has clearly benefited the wider music education community, but in other ways music educational practice has been unhelpfully constrained by narrow attitudes towards women. As Roberta Lamb, Lori-Ann Dolloff, and Sondra Wieland Howe rightly suggest in their review of gender themes as they relate to this discipline, 'Music education did not demonstrate concern with issues addressed in second wave educational feminism: uncovering sexism in historical perspectives of music education; justifying equal opportunities and affirmative educational programmes; and creating non-sexist curricula in music.'[15] This inaction in relation to feminism's second wave – that is, in relation to the idea that discrimination in education was structural, and that women's personal, cultural, and political inequalities were necessarily bound together – is perhaps particularly surprising, given that colleagues in other subject disciplines were grappling with how to rebalance – to detoxify, even – curricula that had focused disproportionately on the white European male experience. Thus, while history educators were engaging in a factional struggle for control of their curriculum,[16] and while sexism and racism were being acknowledged and challenged in English literature,[17] music educationalists were failing to address a number of their own historiographical myths. These included the absence of women in the historical narrative of musical development, and a musical version of the historian Thomas Carlyle's theory that decisive, courageous, and influential individuals, rather than communities, technologies, or circumstantial factors, are primarily responsible for the advancement of culture.[18] A tendency to neglect these important issues, casting the musical past and present as apolitical and uncontested, has been all too common. Educationalists have done too little to respond to Jane Bowers and Judith Tick's factual observation that 'The absence of women in the standard music histories is not due to their absence in the musical past.'[19] In the United Kingdom, for example, the first generation 'GCE Advanced-level' examination that functioned as a gateway between secondary and higher education between 1951 and 1986 prescribed the detailed study of a few hundred composers – all of them white, all of them European, none of them women[20] – seemingly without a word of criticism at this bias being set down in print.

At the establishment of the UK's first national curriculum, similarly problematic canon-formation was demonstrated in the preeminent textbooks, and, again, went unchallenged: listening examples were offered from myriad historical periods, genres, and cultures for use with students between the ages of eleven and fourteen; yet the only role models for females as composers were a handful of singer-songwriters.[21] Syllabuses for public examinations have been similarly problematic. In 2016, a campaign led by the seventeen-year-old Jessy McCabe resulted in one of the main providers of post-sixteen music qualifications in the United Kingdom, Pearson Edexcel, abandoning its plan to revalidate its Advanced-level Music specification with an updated list of exclusively male composers. The publisher's response to pressure exercised through an online petition was to issue a revised list of set works, following consultation, which now includes pieces by Clara Schumann, Rachel Portman, Kate Bush, Anoushka Shankar, and Kaija Saariaho.

Despite such successes, and perhaps as a result of the failure to recontextualise the historiography of previous generations as, at best, partial, music educators of both sexes have unwittingly reproduced sexist ideas within our curricula. These range from ideas about which instruments 'suit' girls and boys respectively – a tedious playing out in the classroom of the wider 'pink is for girls, blue is for boys' trope, which has resulted in the gender imbalance observed in some instrumental areas going unchallenged[22] – to arguably yet more unsettling ideas about the nature and distribution of human creativity. Green's research, later replicated in British Columbia by Betty Hanley,[23] showed how inequality in music education was not a simple 'one-dimensional assertion of power by men over women' but rather a complex web of 'tolerance and repression, collusion and resistance, that systematically furthers the ... divisions from which musical patriarchy springs'.[24] Green reveals an alarming discourse on the nature of girls' and boys' aptitude for musical composition amongst music educators themselves. Synthesising evidence from open-ended questionnaires and interviews, she showed how teachers of the 1990s ascribed boys' success to 'imagination, exploratory inclinations, inventiveness, creativity, improvisatory ability and natural talent' while achievement by girls was 'characterised as conservative, traditional and reliant on notation'.[25] While we can only speculate about the significant power of this discourse to discourage girls from engaging in musical creativity, early evidence has already suggested that music teachers' sexist beliefs of this kind lead to the unfair assessment of musical works that are dependent on the assessors' perception of the composer as female or male.[26] Meanwhile, as Armstrong has demonstrated, composition at secondary school level has become increasingly driven by and mediated through digital technologies and the virtual, rather than by social relationships and the physical. As discussed in more detail below, this 'technicisation' of musical creativity, she suggests, risks the further exclusion of girls from what can be characterised, simplistically but influentially, as a uniquely male-friendly domain.[27]

Women and Pedagogical Debates in the Twenty-First Century

With notable exceptions – the discussions around Pearson Edexcel's curricular decisions being a good example – gender has hardly been at the forefront of recent curricular debates, at least as far as classroom music education at primary and secondary level is concerned. It would be misleading, however, to cast music pedagogy and curricula per se as uncontested territories, and it is worth exploring the ways in which the debates that are currently being waged advance or impinge upon ideas of progress as far as women working and studying in music education are concerned. Addressing an international conference of music educators in 2009, Magne Espeland set out three ways in which music pedagogy was then perceived to be subject to significant and dichotomous differences of opinion:

I will denote the dichotomies I am referring to as having to do with: (1) technology/ digital proponents versus non-technology/analogue proponents; (2) a formal/ formalist position versus an informal/informalist position, and, finally; (3) educator/teacher views versus artist/musician views.[28]

It is worth dwelling on these issues, since they represent the foci of the discursive energies of the music education community. In the first case, as suggested above, the debate is evidently one that can readily be construed as highly gendered. The further integration of technology into music educational practices, as Espeland asserts, can facilitate the realisation of individual potential by releasing the expression of musical ideas from the confines of the individual's instrumental or vocal ability. It also enables practices in the classroom to mirror practices observed in parts of the music industry. On the other hand, an increased focus on technology risks the development of 'machine qualities as opposed to human qualities in music education', the loss of 'practical, aesthetic, and expressive activities involving body and mind', and even 'social delimitation, unhealthy individualisation and body de-focused practices'.[29] Espeland cites Wayne Bowman's persuasive account of all human cognition as characterised by 'the inseparability of mind and body ... [and] the indispensability of corporeal experience to all human knowledge'.[30] From this vantage, he highlights the potential for delineated meanings around gender – particularly in relation to the body/mind dualism – to intersect in harmful ways with practices that prioritise learning approaches in which individuals work with machines, instead of those in which learning is collective and embodied. In her more elaborated critique of music technological learning in the music classroom, Armstrong shares these fears, adding that 'male teachers and male pupils dominate social interactions that focus around technological talk [and that] the prevalence of an "*ad hoc*" way of learning about technology largely favours boys' ways of engaging with technology'.[31]

A sociological reading of these music education technologies, therefore, must consider the possibility that unthinking enthusiasm for the practice of addressing musical composition uniquely in a digitally mediated context risks a fresh approach to the practice of limiting female creativity in schools. Clearly, neither Espeland nor Armstrong takes an unenthusiastic position overall in respect of computers; the central question for each of them is *how* rather than *whether* we should employ technology in music educational contexts, enabling the numbers of women now finding creative and fulfilling roles in this field to be increased further. A key point for the latter writer seems to be that the question of technology should first be understood as a gendered one and that its gendered effects in relation to students and teachers be weighed appropriately as new policies and practices are devised; secondly, as Armstrong sets out below, a crude stereotyping of computers as inherently male business should be firmly resisted:

as Grint and Gill (1995) note, we must not take for granted the idea that technology and masculinity go together. Women's supposed 'alienation' from technology is a product of the historical and cultural construction of technology as masculine. Understanding these gendered processes . . . powerfully demonstrates that it is not technology itself that is the 'problem' for women but the cultural context in which it is used.[32]

(For a detailed consideration of women and music technology, see Part III.)

The second of Espeland's contemporary dichotomies, between formal and informal approaches to learning, rests on the degree to which practices observed amongst learners in non-institutional settings – amongst those who learn in a 'garage band', by studying online videos, or orally in the setting of traditional music cultures – should be imported into institutional contexts. Informal pedagogies in music can be understood variously, but many writers have relied on the key principles laid out by Green, drawing upon her research into the learning practices of popular musicians. Informal learning in music, according to Green, is:

1. Learning music that pupils choose, like, and identify with.
2. Learning by listening and copying recordings.
3. Learning with friends.
4. Personal, often haphazard without structured guidance.
5. Integration of listening, performing, improvising, and composing.[33]

The Musical Futures pedagogical approach,[34] inspired by these five principles and motivated by the perceived stagnation and rejection of traditional ways of teaching music in the classroom, has been enthusiastically received in some quarters and fiercely opposed in others. Many schools in the United Kingdom adopted its brand of self-directed, independent learning, reporting that students who approached musical tasks in this way, while working in friendship groups, showed greater engagement with the subject than those working in a conventional, teacher-directed way. Its introduction has been challenged by critics as signalling a break with the

Deweyan concept of 'democratic' public education, in that by allowing students to learn with friends – effectively to choose the students with whom they will interact musically, consistent with Green's third principle – priority is given 'to egoism and personal priorities as more important in learning situations than altruism and democratic and social values'.[35]

By relaxing teacher control on the sequencing of activities and the selection of repertoire, students are free to interact with activities and repertoire of their own. This raises two important possibilities where gender is concerned. The first is that individuals can elect to pursue roles within informal working groups that are consistent with their own gender identities and self-concept; playing, singing, composing, or improvising in ways that they choose themselves. Thus, while they might very well still be subject to limitations imposed by society and their own imaginations in their choice-making, they are unlikely to choose roles for which society has adjudged them unsuited. The second is that by allowing students to copy the music of musicians that they themselves select, the number of women musicians and composers brought into the classroom is likely increased; the power of music education professionals to curate 'role models' in the ways that have historically resulted in the near elimination of female musicianship from the scholastic canon, meanwhile, is diminished. What can be said about these discussions is that to date very little empirical evidence relating to gender has been wielded either in support of informal learning approaches or in defence of more traditional methods. While we can speculate about the impact of this debate in relation to women teachers and female students, more research is required before conclusions can fruitfully be drawn.

The third contemporary dichotomy, that between the 'educator/teacher' and the 'artist/musician' is perhaps the one that has evolved most significantly in the decade since Espeland's address, in the sense that it has been brought into the political realm and has been amplified and extended as part of turf wars fought between factions in the political class, perhaps especially in the UK, where the governments in office since 2010 have unambiguously sought to redefine music education as merely the learning of musical instruments and singing. The potential conflict between the privileging of artistry and the privileging of pedagogy is itself one that can be easily revealed as having little substance; revealed, that is, 'as a dichotomy of the past, and not as a real dichotomy with strong opposing ... views'.[36] What has become increasingly challenged in some political quarters, however, is the very notion of a thoroughgoing and comprehensive music education delivered by professional educators and made available as part of a universal compulsory education; which is to say that, in respect of this third dichotomy, the stakes have been raised considerably. While the gendering of this debate might not be immediately apparent, familiarity with feminist accounts of schooling and learning invite us to read its subtexts critically.

On one side of the current debate are advocates of broad musical learning as articulated, for example, in early versions of England's national curriculum and in the roughly contemporaneous US national standards devised by the National Association for Music Education (NAfME) in 1994. In brief, they argue for a universal music education that is creative as well as re-creative, that addresses many styles and genres, and that privileges the sharing of musical experiences of value as the key site of musical learning. On the other side, focus is increasingly directed towards instrumental and vocal expertise, towards individual and re-creative practices rather than social and creative ones, and towards an ever narrower group of acknowledged great works: 'the best in the musical canon',[37] to echo the words of the current national curriculum in England. Further, those on this side of the debate conceive of the notion of a universal entitlement rather differently, focusing on the idea of sifting and selecting from the student population in order to find those most suited to intensive musical learning, rather than providing a curriculum for all.

If we are attuned to the gendered subtexts in all the above we might legitimately raise four concerns. First, by emphasising and narrowing the existing canon of works and (male) composers – that is, leaning in the opposite direction to that which grass-roots pressure has obliged Pearson Edexcel to travel – we deny female students helpful role models and risk limiting female creativity in ways that have already been presented in this chapter. While progress in this respect has clearly been made in tertiary and post-compulsory secondary education, for the vast majority of students for whom music is compulsory, change has been regressive. Second, by focusing governmental funding mainly on instrumental and vocal expertise rather than broader forms of musical learning we move our discipline towards the problematic realm of gendered instrument choice.[38] Third, by focusing on individual rather than social learning we privilege behaviours and modes of learning that are often societally approved amongst males but discouraged amongst females, increasing rather than diminishing male advantage. Fourth, by increasing selection within our education systems we risk introducing or reintroducing tools that have been found historically to advance male learners and teachers.

Coda

In 2002, Lamb, Dolloff, and Howe called for significant change in the way scholars of music education think about the nature and boundaries of their work. Drawing on the persuasive analysis of Ellen Koskoff, they made reference once again to the idea that our disciplinary domain is attitudinally and philosophically conservative:

If feminism, feminist research, and gender research are to have the kind of impact on music education that they have had on education and on music, then music education scholars will need to challenge disciplinarity in music education. Such a challenge involves looking at these issues with imagination … [asking] 'First, to what degree does a society's gender ideology and resulting gender-related behaviours affect its musical thought and practice? And second, how does music function in society to reflect or affect inter-gender relations?'[39]

These questions still provide an excellent starting point for gender-based discussions. Examining ways in which music education cultures prescribe gender as much as they describe it will be fundamental to a mature debate about meaningful improvements.

Notes

1. Catharine E. Beecher, *Suggestions Respecting Improvements in Education, Presented to the Trustees of the Hartford Female Seminary, and Published at Their Request* (Hartford, CT: Packer & Butler, 1829), 7–8.
2. Office for National Statistics, *Gender Pay Gap in the UK: 2018* (London: Office for National Statistics, 2018).
3. See Sharon D. Kruse and Sandra Spickard Prettyman, 'Women, Leadership, and Power: Revisiting the Wicked Witch of the West', *Gender and Education*, vol. 20, no. 5 (1994), 451–64.
4. See, for example, Suzanne G. Cusick, 'Feminist Theory, Music Theory, and the Mind/Body Problem', *Perspectives of New Music*, vol. 32, no. 1 (1994), 8–27. The first systematic account of the body/mind dualism in music education is offered in Lucy Green, *Music, Gender, Education* (Cambridge: Cambridge University Press, 1997).
5. Victoria Armstrong, 'Hard Bargaining on the Hard Drive: Gender Bias in the Music Technology Classroom', *Gender and Education*, vol. 20, no. 4 (2008), 375–86.
6. See Robert Legg, 'Bach, Beethoven, Bourdieu: Cultural Capital and the Scholastic Canon in England's A-level Examinations', *The Curriculum Journal*, vol. 23, no. 2 (2012), 157–72. See also Adam Whittaker, 'Investigating the Canon in A-level

Music: Musical Prescription in A-level Music Syllabuses (for First Examination in 2018)', *British Journal of Music Education*, vol. 37, no. 1 (2018), 17–27.

7. George Unwin, *Women in Music* (Chicago: McClurg, 1886), 18–19.

8. Sondra Wieland Howe, *Women Music Educators in the United States: A History* (Lanham, MD: Scarecrow Press, 2014).

9. Annie Jessy Curwen ('Mrs. Curwen'), *The Teacher's Guide to Mrs. Curwen's Pianoforte Method. (The Child Pianist.) Being a Practical Course of the Elements of Music* (London: J. Curwen & Sons, 1886), viii.

10. Gunild Keetman, 'Erinnerungen an die Günther-Schule' in Barbara Haselbach (ed.), *Studientexte zu Theorie und Praxis des Orff-Schulwerks: Basistexte aus den Jahren 1932–2010* (Mainz: Schott Music, 2011), 45–65.

11. Ruth Harris and Elizabeth Hawksley, *Composing in the Classroom* (Cambridge: Cambridge University Press, 1989).

12. Christopher Wellington, 'Quartet Coaching with Helen Just (1903–1989)', *RCM Magazine* (Autumn Term, 1990), 62–3.

13. See, for example, Margaret Campbell, *The Great Cellists* (London: Gollancz, 1988).

14. Atarah Ben-Tovim, *Children and Music* (London: A. & C. Black, 1979), 138.

15. Roberta Lamb, Lori-Anne Dolloff, and Sondra Wieland Howe, 'Feminism, Feminist Research, and Gender Research in Music Education', in Richard Colwell and Carol Richardson (eds.), *The New Handbook of Research on Music Teaching and Learning* (Oxford: Oxford University Press, 2002), 655.

16. See Keith Crawford, 'A History of the Right: The Battle for Control of National Curriculum History 1989–1994', *British Journal of Educational Studies*, vol. 43, no. 4 (1995), 433–56.

17. See, for example, Judith Stinton, *Racism & Sexism in Children's Books* (London: Writers and Readers Publishing Cooperative, 1979).

18. Thomas Carlyle, *On Heroes, Hero-Worship, and the Heroic in History* (London: Fraser, 1841).

19. Jane Bowers and Judith Tick, *Women Making Music: The Western Art Tradition, 1150–1950* (Urbana and Chicago: University of Illinois Press, 1987), 3.

20. Legg, 'Bach, Beethoven, Bourdieu', 161–4.

21. Chris Hiscock and Marian Metcalfe, *Music Matters* (Oxford: Heinemann Educational, 1992); Chris Hiscock and Marian Metcalfe, *New Music Matters* (Oxford: Heinemann Educational, published in three volumes 1998–2000).

22. Susan Hallam, Lynne Rogers, and Andrea Creech, 'Gender Differences in Musical Instrument Choice' *International Journal of Music Education*, vol. 26, no. 1 (2008), 7–19.

23. Betty Hanley, 'Gender in Secondary Music Education in British Columbia', *British Journal of Music Education*, vol. 15, no. 1 (1998), 51–69.

24. Green, *Music, Gender, Education*, 15.

25. Green, *Music, Gender, Education*, 196.

26. Robert Legg, 'One Equal Music: An Exploration of Gender Perceptions and the Fair Assessment by Beginning Music Teachers of Musical Compositions', *Music Education Research*, vol. 12, no. 2 (2010), 141–9; Robert Legg and David Jeffery, 'Suleika and Hatem Revisited: Uncovering the Material Advantages of Identifying as a Male Composer', *Music Education Research*, vol. 20, no. 1 (2018), 1–10.

27. Victoria Armstrong, *Technology and the Gendering of Music Education* (Abingdon: Routledge, 2011).

28. Magne Espeland, 'Dichotomies in Music Education: Real or Unreal?', *Music Education Research*, vol. 12, no. 2 (2009), 129–39.

29. Espeland, 'Dichotomies', 130.

30. Espeland, 'Dichotomies', 130.

31. Armstrong, 'Hard Bargaining', 384.

32. Armstrong, 'Hard Bargaining', 384.

33. Lucy Green, *Music, Informal Learning and the School: A New Classroom Pedagogy* (Aldershot: Ashgate, 2008).

34. Abigail D'Amore, *Musical Futures: An Approach to Teaching and Learning* (London: Paul Hamlyn, 2009).

35. Espeland, 'Dichotomies', 135.

36. Espeland, 'Dichotomies', 137.

37. Department for Education, *National Curriculum for Music* (London: National Archives, 2013).

38. Hallam, Rogers, and Creech, 'Gender Differences'.

39. Lamb, Dolloff, and Howe, 'Feminism in Music Education', 667.

Further Reading

Green, Lucy. *Music, Gender, Education* (Cambridge: Cambridge University Press, 1997).

Howe, Sondra Wieland. *Women Music Educators in the United States: A History* (Lanham, MD: Scarecrow Press, 2014).

Lamb, Roberta, Lori-Anne Dolloff, and Sondra Wieland Howe, 'Feminism, Feminist Research, and Gender Research in Music Education', in Richard Colwell and Carol Richardson (eds.), *The New Handbook of Research on Music Teaching and Learning* (Oxford: Oxford University Press, 2002), 648–74.

16 | Women in the Music Industries: The Art of Juggling

CLARE K. DUFFIN

The ability to multitask successfully is often jokingly linked to women. Joking aside, as a mother of two young children, a drummer, a driver, an artist manager, a lecturer, and a community music practitioner – I am, perhaps, a fitting example of such multitasking, or multi-working, in a sense. My own experience of working in the music business has seemingly burgeoned as a result of my ability to juggle a series of short-term creative and overlapping roles over the years. However, this has taken time to master and make successful – over ten years in fact – with a great deal of self-reflection along the way. It could be perceived as a painstaking journey. As a result, in part, I decided to focus my PhD research on, predominantly, female independent music artists (FIMAs) who live, work, or were born in Scotland. For a long time, while working within various music roles over the years, it struck me that women were still – in many areas across live performance, the recording studio, and songwriting – subject to the working conditions set by males; and that some of these conditions make it comparatively more difficult for women to succeed in the same ways as their male counterparts. Frith and McRobbie aptly observe aspects of this pertinent to the rock genre: 'In rock, women have little control of their music, their images, their performances; to succeed they have to fit into male grooves'.[1] Further, 'the problems of women in rock reach much further than those of surviving the business; oppressive images of women are built into the very foundations of the pop/rock edifice'.[2] While we are almost thirty years on from when this was published, it is nevertheless important to recognise that those who are, or identify as being, 'women' in the music industries, have been outnumbered and given fewer opportunities compared to males. Some women have simply been 'lost', in the sense that histories of women in music have seldom been told from a female perspective, as put forth in the seminal text by Reddington regarding punk musicians of 1976 to 1984.[3] In metal music production, females remain unequal in representational terms, as depicted in the Berkers and Schaaps longitudinal study,[4] which shows only a minor and slow annual increase in women's participation in the said genre has occurred, from about 2 per cent in the 1980s to a maximum of 4 per cent in the 2010s.[5] My question here is whether the music industries have progressed 'enough' in terms of gender equality.

Indeed, the music industries have long been male dominated and there is evidence – as will be discussed in more detail later in this chapter – that such male dominance remains the case in 2019. Roles in production, engineering, and performance have historically been formed around males, with roles in PR and administration assigned more to females. What this means is that notions of these roles, created in the infancy of the recording industry in the late 1880s to the early 1900s, have become so tightly tied to that of the male that it has made it arguably more difficult to reimagine what such roles would have developed into, in the purest sense, had females been first to hold them.

Males and females are, of course, built differently. While I have no intention to provide a biology or psychology lesson here – I am certainly no expert – it is important to take cognisance of the very basic notion that the moulding of any professional role, in the creative industries or otherwise, is intrinsically linked to the whole person within that role. More specifically, what is fundamental to the *functioning* of that whole person is their biology. One very obvious distinction that can be made between males and females is that females can bear children. Males, of course, cannot. The repercussions of such a distinction in a working-world context are that women naturally have to take time out of work for – and to recover from – childbirth.[6] However, for independent workers in the music industries, including the self-employed, agency workers, and for some on zero-hour contracts, we see an arguably more difficult terrain for females by comparison to industries built more firmly and predominantly on salary-based roles, where short-term contracts and freelance work are far less pervasive. Thus, while the structure of the music industries – and creative industries more broadly – continues to function on the basis of so-called 'precarious labour',[7] it will subsequently continue to obstruct certain freedoms for its women workers. The result of this is a necessary 'juggling' of music work and the cultivation of entrepreneurial skills to manage them.

Contextualising the Case Studies: Gender Inequality, the Portfolio Career, and Precarious Labour

While not focused on independent artists, nor Scottish ones as pertains to my PhD research, a report entitled *Inclusion in the Recording Studio?* highlights some of the disparity across three main creative roles in the

United States,[8] analysing the inclusion of women in 700 popular songs between 2012 and 2018. These roles were: artists, songwriters, and producers, for which the percentage of females were reported as being 17.1 per cent, 12.3 per cent, and 2.1 percent, respectively. A similarly low percentage of female participation was reported by UK publishing organisation PRS for Music in 2018, showing that only 17 per cent of their writer members were female.[9] Why such a gender gap? While the answer is far from being clean-cut and simple, there are foundational aspects upon which the music industries have been built that may provide a starting point to any explanation. Firstly, there has been a fairly rapid change in the nature of what once was 'the record business' through, in part, the impact of technology; and secondly, there is the changing nature of the operational side of working within 'the business', more aptly known in academic terms as 'the music industries'. The operational side I will discuss in this chapter pertains to the types of music work that can be, but is not limited to, the constitution of a music worker's portfolio, and the work ethic of independent workers; one, I argue, that brings about *essential entrepreneurialism*. 'Essential', through the necessary behaviours required to monetise the music work as a means to sustain a career; while *entrepreneurialism* is understood to mean the very spirit embodied in the work connected to entrepreneurship, whereby one is alert to opportunities that will render an economic outcome: thus, 'entrepreneurial alertness must include the entrepreneur's perception of the way in which creative and imaginative action may vitally shape the kind of transactions that will be entered into'.[10] Thus, as will be presented in the case studies, there is the possibility that there may be a challenge in terms of striking a balance between the artistic decisions being made and the transportation of the art (in these cases, 'the songs') to a place of 'higher productivity and greater yield'.[11] Say discusses this shift in relation to 'economic resources'.[12] As such, one question that may be raised here is whether the women in the case studies consider their art to be economic resources, art for art's sake, or perhaps something entirely new.

Further, Lewis links the entrepreneurial to the concept of identity construction,[13] where, in Lewis's study, women self-consciously adopt a 'feminised' entrepreneurial identity: 'within the institutional context of entrepreneurship, women's identity is understood as something that is actively constructed and worked upon as opposed to something that is understood as an elemental essence'.[14] Indeed, it is not my intention to discuss the concepts of *identity* and *authenticity* in detail here, as the related literature is fairly plentiful elsewhere. However, there is value in drawing some attention to the relationship both serve to the motivational factors connected to working entrepreneurially. As will be demonstrated in the case studies analysed, I highlight the challenges women in the modern music industries face in the navigation and active construction of their identities as part of professional and practice-based role-creation. (For a study of the gendered dimensions facing female freelance musicians in the contemporary classical-music industry, see the Afterword, 'Challenges and Opportunities: Ways Forward for Women Working in Music'.)

Gender Equality Campaigns in Music

It can be said that positive progress has been made to help undo some of the role-framing and male-dominated operational grounding of the music industries. One such campaign is 'Keychange' – which was originally rolled out by Vanessa Reed during her time in a leadership role at the PRS Foundation – which 'invests in emerging talent whilst encouraging music festivals, orchestras, conservatoires, broadcasters, concert halls, agents, record labels and all music organisations to sign up to a 50:50 gender balance pledge by 2022'.[15] The Women in Music (WIM) organisation, launched in 1985, similarly encourages gender equality in the music industries through raising awareness, opportunities, diversity, heritage, opportunities, and cultural aspects of women in the musical arts through education, support, empowerment, and recognition.[16] Broadly, such campaigning exists as an attempt to even the playing field, serving to improve the working lives of women in music.

However, given Keychange 50:50 aims to achieve gender balance by 2022, it remains to be seen whether such initiatives are fully effective. On the one hand, the very existence of such initiatives could be seen to be a step in the right direction to achieve the gender balance so desired. Coupled with the fact that over 300 organisations have signed up to the campaign, this further underlines that such initiatives are indeed being impactful from the viewpoint of general progress. On the other hand, however, it may be that the practical implementation is more cumbersome if promoters become overly reliant on their existing contacts or networks, which have seemingly come to accept a belief that there are simply not enough female performers out there. As a means to combat this barrier, Vick Bain – the former CEO of the British Academy of Songwriters, Composers and Authors (BASCA) – has produced an extensive database of female artists on her blog, 'Counting the Music Industry', to highlight that there are indeed female artists of a suitable standard available to be booked.[17] Nonetheless, the working environment and opportunities as such for women in music remains somewhat precarious.

Precarious Labour

A very basic example of precarious labour for women in music – one that applies to many people working on a self-employed basis not least in the music industries – is the lack of support for maternity leave. Fundamentally, it is a precarious type of employment to be self-employed within the creative industries. Banks refers to such precariousness as 'injustices',[18] whereby creative and cultural work may be overlooked by comparison to other traditional forms of work outside of said categories. However, internal and external factors linked to kinds of 'practice', he argues, may help recognise the standing of the work more broadly.[19] When discussing work in the creative and cultural industries, of which the music industries are a part, the notion of 'practice' is thus important to consider. The internal and external factors to which Banks refers are arguably key to understanding at least some of the reasons why there may be disparity between notions of 'real' work,[20] which is economically motivated, and work that renders an outcome of non-economic value. Indeed, music work can and does produce results in the economic sense. We need only look at the finances of major record labels such as Universal Music or Warner Music to see evidence of this. However, in Banks's chapter focused on the work of musicians,[21] he states that those who choose to work as professional musicians often do *not* do so for the money.[22] Thus, the precarious work being underlined here is not that pertinent to the roles within the music industries that are relatively secure, those jobs that are to some extent office-based, and that are tied mainly to major record labels; but rather the roles and the practices of those operating at the margins of the major or larger independent record labels, often on an independent, self-employed, or partially self-employed basis. (For simplification, I will refer to this group of workers as independent workers for the remainder of the chapter.) As such, building on the work of Stahl, Sholette, Morgan, Wood, and Nelligan, Eikhof and Warhurst,[23] and the aforementioned Banks,[24] this chapter explores and problematises the work of FIMAs as a vehicle for explaining some of the issues linked to topics such as: work ethic and the portfolio career; gender inequality; and perspectives on 'success' as mapped to women operating as independent workers in the music industries more broadly. Granted, there are nuances across these areas which apply to non-artists; for example, those working purely in administration. However, the ideas set forth here are designed to help address recurring themes and issues pertinent to independent workers, particularly women, in the music industries. To do so, I present two case studies of real independent artists currently working in the music industries as a means to unpack the said themes and convey live issues pertinent to their work ethic, portfolio careers, and ideas about their own sense of success, while also considering aspects of gender inequality.

The Changing Nature of the Music Industries: Mobilising the 'Portfolio Career'

The modern music 'business' is complex. We now talk about the 'music industries' as this term better reflects its multifaceted nature, which extends beyond the 'record industry',[25] technologically and economically speaking. One such complexity is the underlying layers of 'people work': the fragmented roles people undertake, such as that of promoter, artist manager, self-managed artist, community music practitioner, label manager, or studio owner, that ultimately fuel these industries. As such, the case studies in this chapter take a closer look at the work of women in the music industries, primarily that of so-called independent music artists. Its perspective is drawn from a UK standpoint and more specifically, addresses the work of FIMAs in Scotland. The women in each of the case studies are Glasgow-based and share something in common: the ability to make their careers in the music business (and beyond) 'work': to make these careers meaningful and significant to them, amidst the challenge of juggling a portfolio of artistic endeavours that make up a rich tapestry of artistic being against the backdrop of our modern and somewhat intricate economy. My fieldwork in this area has thus far suggested to me that the unusual patterns of creative and precarious labour tied to the role of FIMAs in Scotland are indeed a key challenge in terms of making such careers 'work' – and indeed, of making them sustainable. Perhaps this is often because there are various levels at which such artists work in terms of the components that make up their whole 'portfolio'. There is no 'one size fits all', necessarily. The multifarious nature of portfolio work can be chaotic. It can also offer flexibility. Organising oneself across various roles requires diligence and a great deal of autonomy. My own work in this field, perhaps more aptly defined as that of a 'music practitioner', has certainly taught me this. What has been important in operating autonomously in this portfolio capacity has been steering and maintaining a moral course, arguably core to any and all related decision-making. Often, this means mulling over of the value of the type of work involved in a project before engaging in it.

Collinson Scott and Scott discuss the portfolio career in practice,[26] raising valuable points in relation to the generation of two types of esteem in creative practice: *creative esteem*, where there is value attached to the creative work and professional practice; and *self-esteem*, where there is enjoyment of music making.[27] Both, they argue, are particularly important to artists operating broadly on an independent level.[28] As such, the case studies presented in this chapter will seek to unpack some of the issues tied to self-management in terms of decision-making in this sense, and consider key issues at the forefront of creative practice for each.

The first of the two case studies in this chapter addresses the idea that motherhood may hinder opportunities in the progression of a career in the music industries, particularly for independent singer-songwriters. The second case study also looks at an independent music artist, but one with a career spanning over thirty years, comprising a history of major record label engagement. In both cases, the notion of independent work – often linked with precarious labour – is discussed: this is a core element when considering the contemporary work of women's freelance roles in the music industries.

Navigating the Case Studies

Each case study provides background information on the independent music artist in question, followed by an analysis of their current operation within the music industries. Broadly, the key areas for consideration pertain to: (i) 'work ethic' – where 'essential entrepreneurialism' is given some attention; (ii) components of their 'portfolio career' – where self-management is considered in connection with some (though not an exhaustive list of) ideas linked with identity, gender inequality, and, again, entrepreneurialism. Finally, I conclude with (iii) perspectives on the notion of 'success' in the context of independent working and music making – in this section, I provide the briefest of commentary on what this means to artists and their conflicts with commercial operations.

Case Study 1 – Emma Gillespie: Mothering and Music Making

Background

The first case study considers the career and work ethic of singer-songwriter Emma Gillespie, previously known under the pseudonym, 'Emma's Imagination'. Originally from Dumfries, Emma embarked upon the early parts of her performing career frequenting the pub circuit in Glasgow, further honing her craft through busking. A few years later, Emma decided to audition for a new music talent show to be shown live on Sky TV, called *Must Be the Music*. Unlike other music reality TV shows such as *Pop Idol* or *X Factor* where the winner would already be committed to a predetermined recording contract, the grand prize for the winner of this particular show was to be £100,000 cash. The judges on the show were Sharleen Spiteri, Dizzee Rascal, and Jamie Cullum. To cut a long story short, Emma went on to win first prize in this show. This was in 2010. Due to the weekly live broadcasting of the show, Emma saw her online audience dramatically increase via her Facebook page. At a time when audiences were becoming increasingly fragmented due to the increase in online channels in general, the TV exposure alone was enough to help significantly grow her fan base.

With £100,000 in the bank, a song in the UK top ten, and a captive audience primed through her TV appearances, Emma then had a string of record deal offers made to her. At the time she had no management in place. As such, she had to make what is ultimately a business decision, without having any business advice: the kind of advice that an artist manager would traditionally provide. She eventually signed with Future Records, a label owned by Gary Barlow and a subsidiary of Universal Music.

Analysis

Independent artists without management in place arguably have a dilemma: the inevitable conflict between art and commerce. While this is not a new discussion, it makes sense to take stock of it given that, as I will argue, independent artists with a desire to be 'successful' must adopt one or more aspects of entrepreneurship – and the inevitable consequence of this is a practice–purpose dissonance. For Emma, this would pertain to subsequent and essential behaviours related to her work as a songwriter and performer. For example, proactively sharing her new songs on online platforms such as Bandcamp, SoundCloud, Music Glue, or Facebook, required Emma to consider which were the best techniques to use in order to attract the attention of existing and new audiences. There are two key facts here: (i) Emma would like people to listen to and buy her music; (ii) Emma understands that if in order to optimise online sales opportunities, the evidence within her online engagement analytics suggests there would be value in employing business-like skills in order to maximise music views, streams, listens, and sales. Thus, there is an apparent manner of acting entrepreneurially. What may prove problematic for Emma, however, is the notion of another 'self' that governs her creativity in the crafting of her songs. This self writes 'freely' without any concern about the songs' economic success. As such, any reluctance connected to profit seeking unlocks a dissonance between the freedom of her writing process and the economic value attached to the practice of songwriting. The qualitative research of Haynes and Marshall underlines this idea, stating that 'while the musicians in our study are routinely involved in activities that could be construed as entrepreneurial, generally they were reluctant to label themselves as entrepreneurs'.[29]

Indeed, Emma self-labels as an artist rather than as an entrepreneur. It is part of her identity. In recent years, Emma became a mother and, as an independent worker in the contemporary music industries, had to negotiate creative space (physically and mentally) with mothering. The practicalities of breastfeeding in the context of independent music making, for instance, should not be underestimated. The image in Figure 16.1 depicts Emma cradling her toddler while attempting to capture a vocal take in the microphone. Here, Emma, as prime carer for her child on this particular day, had to make a decision about taking an opportunity – the kind that can come and go quickly in the music industries due to the competitive nature of its fringe[30] – to juggle a typical act of mothering (holding and comforting a child) with a typical act of recording a vocal take. (On the practicalities of working as a freelance musician and parenting, see also Chapter 11, 'The British Folk Revival: Mythology and the "Non-Figuring" and "Figuring" Woman'.) Governing Emma's music practice are the two principles of *creative esteem* and *self-esteem*, whereby value is being sought for the music-making practice and where Emma engages in the practice for the enjoyment of it; and also *essential entrepreneurialism*, where Emma is utilising her voice as an economic resource with which to render an output of economic value, beyond art for art's sake.

The sustaining of Emma's music career is, in her view, what makes it a 'success'. However, the reality is that to do this in the current music

Figure 16.1 Singer-songwriter Emma Gillespie and her son, Oscar. Photo credit: Thomas Brumby

industries on an independent level requires sufficient income to be generated. Given that musicians in the UK earned an average income of £23,059 in 2018,[31] and statistics reported by WIM highlight that '50% of freelance women earn less than £10,000 annually in the UK',[32] there is concern that women – and arguably mothers even more so, given that no maternity pay exists in this freelance context – may be experiencing more barriers than non-female musicians in terms of mobilising their creative resources into an area of greater yield. In other words: mothering could be perceived as a prohibitive measure in the progression of a FIMA's music career. While campaigns for positive discrimination are increasing awareness of gender inequality, given the current structure of the music industries, it will likely be difficult in the short term to effect a scenario whereby mothers are afforded a version of maternity leave more closely matching the conditions set by other more favourable industries, such as in the 'teacher, training and education sector' in the UK. Indeed, short-term contracts exist here, too.

An HM Revenue and Customs report outlining personal income statistics for the period 2016–17 stated that 'there were more male than female taxpayers in every age range and males had higher median income throughout', further suggesting that self-employed women in the UK may well be in a more precarious position,[33] due, in part, to the meagre or non-existent pay received during maternity 'leave'.

Case Study 2 – Carol Laula: A Career Spanning Over Thirty Years

Background

The second case study looks at the work of singer-songwriter Carol Laula. Carol's career spans over thirty years, having signed a development deal

Figure 16.2 Singer-songwriter Carol Laula featured on the front cover of her eighth studio album, *The Bones of It*, released in 2016 by Vertical Records. Photo credit: Julie Vance. Sleeve design: John Eaden

with Chrysalis Records in 1989 followed shortly by a record deal with Iona Gold[34] in 1991 and subsequent reviews in Billboard magazine. Carol took some time out to complete a university degree after her contract with these record labels had drawn to a close, then revived her music career with a series of self-releases and smaller label releases, as well as organising a range of live dates, all the while being heavily involved in community music projects. Carol's community music projects, alone, vary widely. For example, her weekly operations as a practitioner in this context see her function as a songwriting tutor to young carers and to female prisoners (some of whom are more broadly under some form of surveillance), and as a training co-ordinator for BookBug, a programme run by the Scottish Book Trust; she has also previously held roles as a project co-ordinator for Scottish youth music initiative, Hear! Glasgow.

In Carol's more recent activity as a singer-songwriter, she works more independently. Gone are the marketing team; gone are the people that spent large parts of their day in a 'full-time work' capacity seeking out live dates and synchronisation opportunities on Carol's behalf. Now, Carol works with a part-time music manager to help tackle some of these administration-based tasks. Her most recent record (and eighth studio album), *The Bones of It*, was released in 2016 by a small Scottish folk label, Vertical Records. Carol largely funded the record, from its production through to manufacturing – and its marketing, too. Alongside her commercial musical output, Carol supplements her income through a separate role as a community music practitioner, working across Scotland with a range of (mainly) young people delivering songwriting workshops. These tend to be funded by Creative Scotland, local councils, and/or small charitable funds such as Cashback for Communities.

Analysis

For the last few years, Carol has operated in such a fashion as to make her career in music 'work'. Essentially, what this means is to strike a balance between the production of creative output (primarily songs) and generating sufficient income. Why such a mix of roles? Ultimately, Carol epitomises the typical work of the independent music artist, who is focused on sustaining their music careers through practice. Practice in many different forms.

For a songwriter keen to maintain creative control, 'self-funding' is a frequent source of expense – and in order for them to self-fund, there must be other work available, to provide funds where royalties from songwriting (from collection management organisations (CMOs) such as PRS for Music and/or PPL) are insufficient or fluctuate greatly. The inconsistent payment for creative work can be problematic for such artists insofar as the decision-making and self-management aspects go.

Looking for the next short-term contract for Carol often means having to make a decision about where and how to dedicate her time for the next few months. Sometimes, the inconsistent nature of such work means taking on 'last-minute' opportunities, whereby Carol may agree to cover the work of another freelancer, usually someone within her creative industries network. To a certain extent, Carol is able to decide when she wishes to engage in her community music work. However, her work as a singer-songwriter has often had to make way. This 'weighing up' of opportunities under the broader sense of music-making or music production is fundamental to the maintenance of a portfolio career. At times, the income from royalties is not sufficient to fund the next step in her creative practice in a timely enough fashion, whether this is production, session musician, or website-hosting costs, not to mention covering the mortgage/rent and food. Thus, Carol exercises her talent in the aforementioned community music or music co-ordinator roles.

The result is a new kind of independent artist. An artist, still; yes, but perhaps more accurately termed a 'music practitioner', to cover more thoroughly the ground within the music industries and creative and cultural industries on which she works. The kind of practitioner who makes a meaningful contribution in local communities but who can also continue engaging in 'music as practice' (i.e. covering their whole portfolio of work) and who is also afforded the necessary flexibility to engage in songwriting that matches her own artistic identity. It is the latter that is of the utmost importance to artists like Carol. This is a key part of her identity.

Conclusion

In my contextualising introduction I referred to several key areas at the heart of the issues facing contemporary women operating within the music industries. The case studies were subsequently used as a means to draw closer attention to the sea of women working in music who identify as independent music artists, not least to shine a spotlight on the complex nature of their operations as a whole, and perhaps more aptly, the work they engage in as 'music practitioners'. It is this term that more closely embodies the components that make up the portfolio career. It comprises an unusual compounding of various music-making activities that serve in the production of the enjoyment and value aspects pertinent to the practice itself. I have argued that as part of negotiating the portfolio career, the independent workers presented in the case studies enact essential entrepreneurialism as a means to sustain their music-making activities, but they often do so reluctantly. For women in music, the decision-making attached to their practice sometimes, if not often, must incorporate childbearing and/or childcare concerns, which may compromise opportunities to progress their music careers. Put simply, the physical and mental pressures attached to mothering appear not to be best catered for in the modern music industries for independent workers. Thus, this may be a significant contributing factor to the gender gap across the music industries more broadly.

For the women depicted in the case studies, their attempts to make a 'success' of a music career appears intrinsically linked to notions of sustainment. Furthermore, what drives the proficiency of career sustainment, at least at an independent level, appears, in both case studies, to be the aptitude for, or the art of, juggling a number of separate yet connected roles in music: this is the lifeblood of the portfolio career.

Notes

1. Simon Frith and Angela McRobbie, 'Rock and Sexuality', in Simon Frith (ed.), *Ashgate Contemporary Thinkers on Critical Musicology Series: Taking Popular Music Seriously. Selected Essays* (London: Routledge, 2007), 47.
2. Ibid., 47.
3. Helen Reddington *The Lost Women of Rock Music: Female Musicians of the Punk Era*, 2nd ed. (London: Equinox Publishing Ltd, 2012).
4. Pauwke Berkers and Julian Schaap, *Gender Inequality in Metal Music Production* (Brighton: Emerald Group Publishing, 2018).
5. Berkers and Schaap, *Gender Inequality in Metal Music Production*, 103–4.
6. The Maternity and Parental Leave etc. Regulations 1999, available at: www .legislation.gov.uk/uksi/1999/3312/contents/made (accessed 10 July 2019).
7. Joseph Choonara, *Insecurity, Precarious Work and Labour Markets: Challenging the Orthodoxy* (London: Palgrave Macmillan, 2019); George Morgan and Pariece Nelligan, *The Creativity Hoax: Precarious Work and the Gig Economy* (London: Anthem Press, 2018).
8. Stacy L. Smith, Marc Choueiti and Katherine Pieper, *Inclusion in the Recording Studio? Gender and Race/Ethnicity of Artists, Songwriters & Producers across 700 Popular Songs* (2019), available at http://assets.uscannenberg.org/docs/aii-inclusion-recording-studio-2019.pdf (accessed 10 July 2019).

9. PRS Foundation for Music, '200 Female Songwriters Assemble to #GETHEARD and Address Gender Disparity in Songwriting: Only 17% of Songwriters are Women', PRS for Music website (2018), available at: www .prsformusic.com/press/2018/female-songwriters-getheard-address-gender-disparity-in-songwriting (accessed 10 July 2019).

10. Israel M. Kirzner, 'Creativity and/or Alertness: A Reconsideration of the Schumpeterian Entrepreneur', *Review of Austrian Economics*, vol. 11 (1999), 10.

11. Jean-Baptiste Say, c. 1800; cited in Peter F. Drucker, *Innovation and Entrepreneurship* (London: William Heinemann Ltd, 1985), 19.

12. Ibid., 24.

13. Patricia Lewis, 'The Search for an Authentic Entrepreneurial Identity: Difference and Professionalism among Women Business Owners', *Gender, Work and Organization*, vol. 20 (2013), 252–66.

14. Lewis, 'The Search for an Authentic Entrepreneurial Identity', 377.

15. See 'About Us', Keychange website: https://keychange.eu/about-us/ (accessed 20 July 2019).

16. Women in Music, 'Mission Statement', available at www.womeninmusic.org /about-us.html (accessed 21 July 2019).

17. See Vick Bain's website at https://vbain.co.uk/ (accessed 19 April 2020).

18. Mark Banks, *Creative Justice: Cultural Industries, Work and Inequality* (London: Rowman & Littlefield International, 2017).

19. Banks, *Creative Justice*, 2.

20. Ibid., 2.

21. Ibid., 2.

22. Banks, *Creative Justice*, 44.

23. Matt Stahl, *Unfree Masters: Recording Artists and the Politics of Work* (Durham, NC: Duke University Press, 2012); Gregory Sholette, *Dark Matter: Art and Politics in the Age of Enterprise Culture* (London: Pluto Press, 2011); George Morgan, Julian Wood, and Pariece Nelligan, 'Beyond the Vocational Fragments: Creative Work, Precarious Labour and the Idea of "Flexploitation"', *The Economic and Labour Relations Review*, vol. 24, no. 3 (2013), 397–415; Doris Ruth Eikhof and Chris Warhurst, 'The Promised Land? Why Social Inequalities Are Systemic in the Creative Industries', *Employee Regulations*, vol. 35 (2013), 495–508.

24. Banks, *Creative Justice: Cultural Industries, Work and Inequality*.

25. John Williamson and Martin Cloonan, 'Rethinking the Music Industry', *Popular Music*, vol. 26 (2007), 305–22.

26. Jo Collinson Scott and David Scott, 'The Portfolio Career in Practice: Key Aspects of Building and Sustaining a Songwriting Career in the Digital Era', in Justin Williams and Katherine Williams (eds.), *The Singer-Songwriter's Handbook* (New York: Bloomsbury Academic, 2017),191–203.

27. Collinson Scott and Scott, 'The Portfolio Career in Practice', 195.

28. Ibid., 195.

29. Jo Haynes and Lee Marshall, 'Reluctant Entrepreneurs: Musicians and Entrepreneurs in the "New" Music Industry', *British Journal of Sociology*, vol. 69 (2017), 459.

30. François Moreau, 'The Disruptive Nature of Digitization: The Case of the Recorded Music Industry', *International Journal of Arts Management*, vol. 15 (2013), 19.

31. UK Music, *Music by Numbers, available at* www.ukmusic.org/assets/general/ Music_By_Numbers_2019_Report.pdf (accessed: 2 April 2020).

32. Women in Music, 'Mission Statement': www.womeninmusic.org/about-us.html (accessed 21 July 2019).

33. HM Revenue & Customs *Personal Income Statistics 2016–17*: https://assets .publishing.service.gov.uk/government/uploads/system/uploads/ attachment_data/file/783132/ National_Statistics_T3_1_to_T3_11_and_T3_16_tax_year_1617_-_FINAL .pdf (accessed 21 July 2019), 10.

34. Iona Gold officially launched in 1992, however the deal was signed in 1991.

Further Reading

Bayton, Mavis. *Frock Rock: Women Performing Popular Music* (Oxford: Oxford University Press, 1998).

Leonard, Marion. *Gender in the Music Industry: Rock, Discourse and Girl Power* (Farnham: Ashgate, 2007).

Whiteley, Sheila. *Women and Popular Music: Sexuality, Identity and Subjectivity* (London and New York: Routledge, 2000).

In Her Own Words: Practitioner Contribution 4

From Polymath to Portfolio Career – Reclaiming 'Renaissance Woman'

STEPH POWER

At some point in our journeys to becoming a professional – and often quite early on – we musicians typically narrow our focus to a particular discipline and hone our skills accordingly. Nonetheless, even within specialisms, many of us will go on to work across sectors and genres, continually adapting to different artistic and industry environments. Orchestral players, for instance, often teach and/or perform in chamber groups, while session musicians might improvise or adapt parts *in situ*, playing in pit bands by night. Classical composers arguably need to be as skilled at fundraising, networking, and writing programme notes as they are at writing music. This presents both opportunities and challenges, some of which apply particularly to women, as I've found in my own work across an unusually wide range of disciplines, from international performing and examining to composing and critical writing.[1]

When I graduated from the University of York in 1987, the term 'portfolio career' was a long way from being coined. My immediate need was to take stock after an academically high-flying but emotionally bruising few years, not helped by the homophobia I encountered coming out as gay. Moreover, I was one of only a few music students from a working-class background in the department at that time, as well as years from being equipped to face the serious abuse I had suffered in childhood. Finding support within a department which had, in those days, exclusively male and sometimes overtly sexist lecturers was not easy.

Immediately post-York, I gladly accepted invitations to join two new contemporary music ensembles as guitarist and percussionist: Jane's Minstrels, founded by the distinguished soprano Jane Manning (in residence in my final year) and Icebreaker, a post-minimalist band inspired by the Dutch scene. I expected a short sojourn away from academia before returning to study for a PhD on Berg's *Lulu*. But, with further performing and teaching commitments, it was over two decades before I eventually enrolled at King's College, London, only for spine surgeries to stop play.

However, as I convalesced, exciting new writing and composing opportunities came along and, ultimately, the sheer breadth of my interests led me to pursue these alongside what was already a host of different freelance musical directions. While each has had highs and lows, none have proved especially progressive or regressive from a gender perspective relative to others. Rather, the central challenge has been juggling the mix in a world in which people are routinely pigeonholed – even if that is, ironically, as 'polymath' – often to the particular detriment of women.

Those who decry sexism in any industry are often challenged to define exactly how and to what extent this has directly affected their careers. For me as for many women, there have of course been clear instances, and further homophobia. But the main point – and this is especially poignant for those of us who have suffered sexual violence in any context – is that these are symptoms of a wider structural problem that permeates our culture, underpinning everything from everyday micro-aggressive 'banter' – and the 'benevolent' and 'choice' sexism so vividly described by Soraya Chemaly, and so often practised by women themselves[2] – to extreme misogyny and existential threat.

In my final year at York, I'd been propelled by male students' ridicule of female composers – and by hearing the then London Sinfonietta artistic director Michael Vyner declare on national radio that 'women can't compose' – to mount a three-day festival of women composers, *Women of Note*. With help from the violinist Lucy Russell, and others, the event was a success. But not before many run-ins with objectors, and a summons by a lecturer to answer (anonymous and incorrect) claims that men would be excluded from participating. Despite then chairing the student new music group ANeMonE, I had quietly stopped presenting my own compositions in year one.[3]

Today, gender inequality continues to be rife in music as elsewhere, with conscious, and unconscious bias of all kinds underpinned by unequal pay, discriminatory working conditions, and more. And of course sexist attitudes linger irrespective of the positive strides made. For instance, in my own experience, interviewees are still sometimes surprised when a mere journalist shows high levels of musical expertise; the more so if that journalist is female. Likewise, female music examiners are not always afforded the same respect in the field as their male counterparts, while female writers and critics too often find themselves wincing when male colleagues write inappropriately about, say, a female performer's appearance.

The tired cliché that critics, teachers, musicologists, and so on only work in those arenas because they themselves can't create or perform music obviously falls down in my case, as it does in very many others'. Yet it persists, assuming as its creator ideal the usual pantheon of dead, white, male super-composers. The continued relative lack of women and black and minority-ethnic composers, conductors, professors, producers, and industry leaders – despite supposed social progress over the years – is a great cause for concern.

It is vital for our collective cultural health that women are enabled on equal terms with men to excel in all areas of music. At the same time, the lack of women in key places is an indication that the system itself needs complete reform. Multidisciplinary, portfolio working is now so widespread, for example, that, if it were held in greater social and economic esteem, women in particular would stand to benefit; not least those who interrupt careers to have children, or who choose to combine a career with parenting. Society might better equip young musicians to deal with the real world, rather than selling them spurious notions about 'talent' and being 'discovered' that very few will experience. Above all, it might facilitate a much-needed cultural shift away from unhelpful post-Romantic assumptions about the nature of creativity and genius that we see reflected in the worship of icons past and present from Beethoven to Beyoncé.

But social attitudes and economic practice would need to change radically for this to happen. While, on the surface, equality of opportunity appears to have improved since I graduated some thirty-four years ago, in reality the situation has barely changed for many women, with exceptions of course; Beyoncé has not come from nowhere. For others, it has actually worsened. The 2008 global economic crash and subsequent 'austerity' governmental policies have impacted women especially, with a devastating increase in poverty as the wealth of the richest few has spiralled.[4]

Recent surges in populist politics and religious fundamentalism are seeing hard-won moves towards gender equality threatened across the spectrum by social conservatives, with an extreme right emboldened by Trump in the USA, Brexit in the UK, and other movements around the globe. How far these developments have directly impacted women in music to date is hard to say. But the last decade hardly points to a blossoming of women's involvement, while savage cuts to arts funding and music education budgets do not bode well for a socially equitable future.

Alongside wider campaigns for social justice such as #MeToo and Black Lives Matter, much-needed quotas and new industry initiatives are seeking to redress gender imbalances: the PRS Foundation and partners' Keychange project (also discussed in Chapter 16) is an excellent international example, whereby music festivals and organisations have pledged to achieve 50:50 gender parity in new commissions by 2022. Such campaigns – where they are not actively resisted as threats to the status quo – are often dismissed as identity politics. But the reality is that, taken together, in the current sociopolitical climate they form an important part of what's become a fight not just for equal representation within the arts, but for the arts themselves, and, indeed, for democracy; an aspiration which is in any case impossible to realise without gender parity.

Meanwhile, women – intersecting with the working classes and ethnic minorities – continue to be very much second-class economic citizens in music as elsewhere. In 2019, women are still far more likely than men to combine careers with unpaid domestic and caring roles, and we are likely to be less well paid than our male counterparts, and to receive less money for equal work.[5] For women musicians, this can mean being forced rather than choosing to work in multiple arenas simultaneously. And that's musicians in full- or part-time employment, with the concomitant rights to paid holidays, maternity leave, sick leave, and pensions that those statuses confer.

For freelancers like myself, without employment rights or support beyond the rudimentary benefits afforded *in extremis* by an eroded welfare state, working across disciplines has increasingly become a matter of financial necessity. In such circumstances, 'portfolio career' becomes but a glitzy euphemism for unpredictable work patterns. There is irony but greater realism in another recently coined phrase: 'gig economy'. This references long-used musicians' slang to describe the recent proliferation of short-term, temporary, and zero-hours contracts; a situation familiar for better or worse to large numbers of musicians, female and male, since long before the term 'Renaissance Man' was coined.

Of course Renaissance Woman – however brilliantly multiskilled – was assumed to be muse or mistress rather than master, so to speak. We women should reclaim the epithet: as I suspect large numbers merit it, not just as experts – polymaths, even – working across numerous professional fields, but as experts in managing that work alongside domestic demands. Yet far too many freelancers are constantly exhorted to take on work – whether it be to write a piece of music or a review, or to deliver a pre-concert talk – for very little or no remuneration, nor even expenses.[6] While women in particular tend to be far too understanding when negotiating terms, it's also clear that we are just as liable as men to be the ones touting unpaid projects.

Nonetheless, the benefits of freelance working can outweigh the drawbacks for women like myself, who tolerate the disadvantages in order to claim the freedom to pursue different disciplines that self-employment brings. And there is the satisfaction of knowing that, merely by existing, an independent, creative woman posits an ideological challenge to an androcentric, patriarchal culture. Make no mistake, it is immensely fulfilling – even exhilarating – to work across different musical spheres utilising very different skills. And that in itself can, I hope, be a positive force for change at a time when long-embedded binary thinking is being questioned, along with the familiar, crude, and outdated stereotypes on which it depends. Such stereotypes around gender are amongst the most pernicious, and often underlie so-called musical and artistic 'traditions'.

Arts practitioners of all kinds need to be at the forefront of movements for reform, or risk the diminishment of the very arts they profess to love. Thanks to the work of enlightened music historians, performers, and promoters we are now coming to understand the immense loss not just women, but our entire culture has incurred over hundreds of years due to gender inequality and worse. Partial change has come for some, but far too slowly; the need to properly redress that inequality for present and future generations is now critical.

Notes

1. My use of the gender terms women/men etc. includes trans women and men, who experience additional obstacles to equality, as do those from black and minority communities, people with disabilities, and more. I am white and able-bodied, which automatically confers certain privileges.
2. Soraya Chemaly, *Rage Becomes Her: The Power of Women's Anger* (London: Simon & Schuster, 2018).
3. Shortly after graduating I succeeded in securing funding for the then-nascent organisation Women in Music, to create an office and administrator post.
4. Sean Coughlan and David Brown , 'Inequality Driving Deaths of Despair', BBC News (14 May 2019); available at www.bbc.co.uk/news/education-48229037 (accessed 11 December 2020).
5. Pamela Duncan, Niamh McIntyre , and Caroline Davies, 'Gender Pay Gap Figures Show Eight in 10 UK Firms Pay Men More Than Women', *The*

Guardian (4 April 2019); www.theguardian.com/world/2019/apr/04/gender-pay-gap-figures-show-eight-in-10-uk-firms-pay-men-more-than-women (accessed 5 December 2020).

6. As is typical in academic publishing, my contribution to this volume is unpaid in cash terms, though Cambridge University Press are unusual in providing £150 worth of their books (in addition to the more usual free copy of this book) to contributors. My hope is that ensuing debate will help effect much-needed reform in this arena.

Afterword: Challenges and Opportunities: Ways Forward for Women Working in Music

VICTORIA ARMSTRONG

Introduction

Mark Banks asserts that too little is known about the conditions under which the creative cultural worker produces their work, often because it is regarded as 'fun' and not work at all.[1] It is described as a 'vocation' because it is committed to values of a 'higher' nature whereby creativity is seen as a 'calling'.[2] David Hesmondhalgh and Sarah Baker argue that, 'some of the celebrations of creative labour are deeply complacent about the conditions of such work and the reality of the labour markets involved',[3] in which a highly skilled workforce is expected (and deemed willing) to endure the vagaries of a precarious, insecure, and often poorly paid working life to pursue their 'calling'. This lack of criticality serves to fetishise creativity,[4] while simultaneously invoking a neoliberal economic ideology that emphasises individualism, competition, and entrepreneurialism, whereby the individual is held responsible for their own successes and failures, and where hard work pays, and success is rewarded.[5] Problematically, neoliberal orthodoxies redirect our gaze *away* from the sociopolitical sphere and *towards* the self: it is the *self* that is deemed lacking and in need of change and improvement, so a lack of work or opportunities is read as 'self-inflicted'.[6] As Rosalind Gill rightly notes, 'sexism, racism and other patterns of structural discrimination remain unspoken because there is a reluctance to puncture neoliberal mythologies of individual achievement'.[7]

Too often, governments and policy makers are quick to laud the success of the creative industries and its contribution to the UK economy,[8] while ignoring the working conditions of those who contribute to its success. In 2012, income from musical theatre and classical ticket sales to overseas tourists visiting London was estimated to be £67 million, with British orchestras alone generating a total income of £150 million during that period, and yet, having surveyed 2,000 musicians across the UK, a report by the Musicians' Union (MU) found that

56 per cent had earned less than £20,000 that year and 60 per cent reported working for free in the previous twelve months.[9] This lack of critical engagement with cultural work results in a failure to acknowledge the structural inequalities in these industries, where their gender, ethnicity, or socio-economic background can profoundly shape cultural workers' experiences because they rely on a model of production which can exacerbate social inequalities in the workplace.[10]

Women account for 32 per cent of all music-industry-related jobs in the UK, but in comparison to men they earn less, experience greater barriers to progression, and exit the workforce sooner.[11] Women also experience both vertical segregation, such as being under-represented in positions of authority, and horizontal segregation, which, in the classical music profession,[12] results in a persistent under-representation of women in the fields of composition, conducting, and music technology.[13] In contrast, Dawn Bennett notes that women are over-represented in the teaching profession, which is viewed as both less prestigious and less desirable as a career.[14] Therefore, in a cultural economy that insists individuals take personal responsibility for their successes and failures with little or no regard for the material challenges and constraints in which they work, women warrant particular attention because gendered structures, attitudes, and cultures inevitably shape and inform their experiences of work in ways that are significantly different to those encountered by men.

'Good' and 'Bad' Work in the Cultural Industries

Despite the inequalities and discrimination they are likely to face together with the uncertainties of pursuing a professional career, female musicians assert there are significant rewards and challenges which enable them to forge meaningful, successful, and fulfilling musical lives and careers.[15] Herein lies the contradiction at the centre of recent critiques of cultural work, in that the very qualities which supposedly attract people to this type of work also form the basis for exploitation and self-exploitation in an already precarious and insecure labour market.

As noted earlier, within policy discourse, cultural work is invariably presented as a neoliberal 'ideal', whereby the (mainly) self-employed, freelance, 'protean' worker develops and thrives within a competitive marketplace. These self-improving 'entrepreneurs' are continually networking,[16] and

constantly generating new projects and ideas while taking personal responsibility for their success or failure.[17] This 'permanently transitional' work is
characterised by self-advancement and self-reliance,[18] and the desire to
embrace the supposed 'freedom' that labour mobility brings with this peripa-
tetic career. In this conceptualisation of cultural work, individuals seamlessly
move from job to job, developing 'DIY biographies',[19] their rewards derived
from finding outlets for self-expression and creativity. It is argued that cultural
work is attractive because of its potential for personal creativity, autonomy,
self-actualisation, self-expression, and personal growth. Taken together, these
characteristics offer a validation of creative work as a model of what
Hesmondhalgh and Baker describe as 'good work'.[20]

In contrast, recent critiques focus on the precarious, insecure nature
of cultural work, which is invariably determined and constrained by
factors beyond the individual's control. In fact, cultural work can result
in low self-esteem, overwork, boredom, risk, poor-quality work, and
frustrated self-realisation, which Hesmondhalgh and Baker suggest
characterises 'bad work'.[21] Recognising the precarious, insecure nature
of cultural work, which is invariably determined and constrained by
factors beyond the individual's control, challenges the romantic and
over-celebratory notions of creative work as a 'calling', or a 'self-
actuating pleasure'.[22]

In the remainder of this chapter, I will explore this model of 'good' and
'bad' work drawing on data from my recent UK-based ethnographic study
into the working lives of twenty-four professional, classically trained
female composers, conductors, and performers through an examination
of the subjective, lived experiences of their working lives. Their portfolio
careers involve juggling numerous roles and jobs under challenging conditions; dealing with the uncertainties of irregular work; having to engage
in considerable strenuous self-activity to market and promote themselves,
while ensuring they are always 'work ready'; and dedicating regular time to
practice and preparation. Their musical lives may appear to be characterised by high levels of autonomy, which supposedly makes creative work
desirable, but, as Hesmondhalgh has commented, 'All autonomy is limited,
in that individuals and groups are, to some extent at least, socially constituted by others beyond themselves. Total autonomy in any sphere of
a life is an impossible ideal, because there is no life without constraints and
determinants.'[23]

Consequently, while the women in my study did experience much of
their musical lives as rewarding, fulfilling, and as providing opportunities
for creative and personally satisfying work – what would be considered

'good work' – their narratives revealed that certain factors (the constraints and determinants outlined above) could significantly alter their perception and subjective experiences of work previously characterised as 'good work' and turn it into 'bad work'. (For a study of the gendered dimensions facing female freelance musicians in the contemporary popular-music industry, see Chapter 16, 'Women in the Music Industries: The Art of Juggling'.)

Overview of the Study

The study involved twenty-four freelance, classically trained, professional female musicians, aged between twenty-three and sixty-five, working in a wide range of genres and contexts both at national and international level, and was undertaken during the period 2012–2017. Many of the subjects described themselves as composer-performers and adhered to Bennett's notion of a musician as 'someone who practices within the profession of music in one or more specialist fields',[24] and were located in London, the South East, and South West of England, encompassing both city and rural locations. The aim of the study was to gain insights into their subjective experiences of work, and their 'day-to-day' experiences of building and sustaining a freelance career.

Given the itinerant nature of their professional commitments, it was not possible to take the 'traditional' ethnographic approach, where the researcher embeds herself in the lives of the participants. To address this I developed a digital ethnographic approach, which involved each participant generating her own weekly 'digital diary' over a five-week period, uploaded to a designated Dropbox account. This resulted in a rich and diverse array of 'found' data, including photographs, audio clips, marketing and promotional material, written diaries, screenshots of scores, and rehearsal and performance videos that they felt best represented their working lives; this method gave ownership of data generation to the women, and allowed them to decide what was important and relevant to them.[25] At the end of this five-week period, the data was used as a basis for a one-to-one interview lasting from around ninety minutes to two hours. Stephanie Taylor suggests that a career is largely about identity; asking 'who am I', and positioning oneself in relation to others in the field.[26] The notion of professional identity is very strongly presented in my participants' narrative and can inform whether work is experienced as 'good' or 'bad'. In the remainder of the chapter I will focus on four themes emerging from the data: professional identity relating to paid and unpaid work; the affective qualities of work; motherhood and caring responsibilities; and aesthetic labour.

Paid and Unpaid Work

While the 'gifting of free labour' is common amongst creative workers,[27] generally rationalised as investing in the future in the hope that it might lead to paid work, for the composers in my study the lack of payment for their work profoundly shaped their sense of self, in ways that resulted in them feeling ambivalent about their status and that led them to question whether they could even call themselves professionals:

Who needs my music anyway? Am I actually a professional composer? Based on my ability and education: oh yes. Based on my recent PRS statement: not really. (Lili, Composer, 40s)

I need to earn a living wage. I have to just do it [music] like an amateur. I feel like a professional, I think like a professional, but actually I'm just a bloody amateur diddling about in little bits of spare time. (Mia, Composer, 40s)

Despite the lack of payment for their compositions, these women's works are regularly performed nationally and internationally, often by well-known players, but as funding is difficult to obtain, ensembles and performers rarely bother to apply for commissioning fees; it is time-consuming and more often than not futile. Therefore, what should have been experienced as 'good work', takes on aspects of 'bad work' for the composers, because being paid for their creative work is strongly associated with self-perception: when judging themselves against the criteria of what constitutes a professional, they feel they do not match up.

This sense of professional identity can also be undermined even when work is paid, in that it may not be experienced as 'good work' if the composer feels she has compromised over artistic quality. Libby (Composer/performer, 20s) had been taken on by an agency who commissioned music for TV indents and jingles, work that she viewed positively for the following reason:

What I like about it is that it makes me feel like a professional composer. Getting paid for the compositions is a boost but it can be a bit soul destroying when they send it back saying make it more cheesy, add bells.

To secure more paid work in this field, Libby was required to react to the needs of the client, resulting in a significant lack of creative autonomy and relinquishing artistic control. Consequently, the financial security this work afforded was counteracted by elements that are characterised as 'bad work', such as frustrated self-actualisation and limited control over the artistic product.

Affective Labour

The allure of creative labour, even when poorly paid or even unpaid, is said to lie in its affective qualities, which results in the work being experienced as 'good': feelings of satisfaction, connectedness to others, a sense of well-being, and emotional involvement. Angela McRobbie suggests that these affective elements have become a normative requirement in cultural labour,[28] leading us to overlook less appealing and potentially exploitative aspects of such work. For my participants, the reality was more complicated and could not easily be categorised as simply 'good' or 'bad'. Mia (Composer, 40s) received a large grant to 'write music for people who know nothing about music whatsoever' supported by 'a couple of millionaires who own properties all over the world'. Despite being paid well she felt no emotional connection to the work she was producing, stating that, 'although I was earning money it wasn't really where my heart was'. At that point, Mia said that she had started to wonder: 'Why I was even doing it? Why was I writing this stuff?' Shortly after, she was commissioned by an all-female international ensemble, for which she was less well paid, but she expressed a great deal of pride in this work as she felt it was 'useful' and 'purposeful', turning what might be considered 'bad work' (because it was poorly paid) into 'good work'.

This affective element was also discernible in Charlotte's (Composer/performer, 40s) description of successfully running singing workshop weekends held at her home. Her digital diaries were dominated by preparations for one of her madrigal weekends. She noted that the amount she earned from the event was not commensurate with the amount of effort required to make it a success. Few of the attendees could read music, so she spent a whole week recording the separate vocal parts, which she then sent to them in advance. She observed:

With the weekend residential, the work appears to happen all in the weekend, but the preparation for some workshops starts weeks earlier. For one workshop earlier in the year I actually spent five whole days writing the music for it, so it looks as if you're earning £1,000 in a day or two but in reality it isn't that.

This highlights how paid work also has the potential for self-exploitation and therefore constitutes 'bad work'. Charlotte vehemently refuted this notion because she considered this 'personalised service' gave her singers 'a better experience' from which she took great pleasure, also offering 'that extra bit of attentiveness', which included providing home-made cakes and biscuits. When I pointed out that it sounded like very hard work, she replied, 'I wouldn't do it if I didn't enjoy it'. For Charlotte, the opportunity to engage in fulfilling music-making activities, underpinned by the affective qualities of relationship building and care, and the ability to run this from her home, outweighed the relatively poor financial return.

Motherhood and Family Life

As also discussed in Chapter 16, 'Women in the Music Industries: The Art of Juggling', freelancers operate outside of conventional employment models which protect workers' rights, as they have limited access to social welfare and associated benefits such as maternity leave. Perhaps not surprisingly, the creative industries are dominated by workers without children, as they are perceived as more willing to accept poor working conditions involving long and irregular hours (in my study, nearly two-thirds of the participants did not have children). This reinforces McRobbie's point that the 'traditional conditions of youthfulness are normatively expected',[29] where the cultural worker, irrespective of age, is expected to be independent of family, flexible, mobile, and able to work beyond the confines of the nine to five. As Gill argues, it is not motherhood that is the 'issue', but the fact that caring responsibilities largely remain in the hands of women, a situation which is rarely challenged.[30]

This certainly characterises the experiences of those participants with children, who combined childcare with working long and unsociable hours involving extensive travel. When coupled with the need to juggle childcare, the rhetoric of 'choice', agency, and autonomy, as positive characteristics of cultural labour, become problematic. Stephanie Taylor and Karen Littleton observe that 'many women would now claim to be freed from the constraints which society placed on former generations but these supposed freedoms can be questioned'.[31] This point is exemplified in Adele Teague and Gareth Dylan Smith's study of five London-based professional drummers, in which the authors argue that men also have to 'reposition' their careers to accommodate changes in family circumstances.[32] However, it was telling that one of the male participants, who regularly played at gigs but stated he no longer toured due to family commitments, acknowledged that it was his wife who undertook most of the childcare responsibilities and it was *she* who had taken a nine-year career break from her performing career to bring up their family.

Without exception, those with childcare responsibilities powerfully describe a range of factors which have profoundly impacted hard-won professional achievements and work that had previously been experienced as fulfilling and rewarding. Earlier in her career, Margaret (Conductor, 50s) was appointed as the first female music director of a major organisation, a much-coveted position, which coincided with the birth of her child. She recounts the challenges of juggling family and professional life, and how this impacted her ability to maintain the professional standards necessary for the post. She believed this was one of the main reasons she ended up relinquishing the role:

I remember running from the tube, to running to the house. I'm the MD of X and I'm running home because my husband otherwise is going to be really cross that I'm already late for the supper that he's cooked us. And I was thinking what am I doing actually? And eventually it got to the point where I felt so tense that I couldn't do the music properly anyway and that's what led me to resign.

In contrast to her accounts of trying to maintain an acceptable work–life balance and not having sufficient time to prepare, she recounts that her male predecessor would just 'block out' the time prior to rehearsals two weeks before the rehearsals started; 'nobody was allowed to call him or speak to him unless the house was burning down', but 'it was impossible for me to do that given what was happening at home'. He too had a family but, from Margaret's perspective, there appeared to be little expectation that he should be similarly encumbered with domestic responsibilities. He appeared to be able to prioritise his professional responsibilities without recrimination and, from Margaret's description, it was accepted that he should not be burdened with additional responsibilities while preparing for rehearsals. The difference between their two experiences is stark, as Margaret explained:

It was just impossible to do that given my domestic situation. It just meant that I was trying to learn the music at night, deal with my child in the morning. Looking back, it was a completely impossible equation.

While many women are likely to experience challenges juggling work and childcare due to the continued expectation that they, rather than their male partners, will take on the majority of caring responsibilities, for these self-employed freelance musicians, taking maternity leave is a luxury few can afford, not only due to financial concerns, but also because they are worried about being viewed as 'unavailable', which might result in work 'drying up'. Martha (Performer, 30s) completed her digital diaries during her maternity leave, but her fears about turning down work and not being asked again meant she was working regularly during this time, often driving long distances to rehearsals and performances, and getting home in the early hours of the morning. During the period she was uploading data, she had to take her baby to a concert as her babysitter had let her down, and her musician husband also had work commitments that he could not cancel. Her innate professionalism compelled her to honour her contract, but her fear of losing future work was an even greater incentive. This was prestigious, well-paid work, playing with other well-known and respected musicians, and a regular fixture in her concert diary, and Martha felt she could not 'send a dep' (i.e. find a deputy musician to replace her), in case the 'dep' was offered the work in the future. This left her with little choice but to take her six-month-old baby with her to the performance. About this three-hour journey and the subsequent rehearsal, she wrote in her digital diary:

Arrived early and need to pump my boobs before the day starts. Battery on pump then dies. Oh shit! It's been a real nightmare. Rehearsals are an hour and a half then a tea break when I rush to the loo to pump while others go to get coffee. I will be glad to finish feeding but this is not the way to do it. It will be painful today and I will have to hand express every few hours. Arrrgh!

This regular high-profile work, which she had always looked forward to and which fulfilled the definition of 'good work', was transformed by the stress and anxiety of having to manage childcare alongside fears of not being offered the gig again if she did not honour her contract.

Trudy (Performer, 60s), a specialist in twentieth-century and contemporary repertoire, had made several successful recordings during her career, touring frequently in the UK and abroad. During the first two years following the birth of her first child, she managed to continue playing and touring, but it was proving hard to sustain, artistically, emotionally, and financially. To eke out the time needed to learn this demanding and time-consuming new repertoire, she paid for a part-time nanny. This extra time was crucial for maintaining her international playing career, but it was not financially sustainable in the long term, as the cost of childcare exceeded the income generated from her concerts. Echoing Margaret's experiences above, without this additional time, she was unable to prepare or perform to the standard required to sustain an international career. After the birth of her second child, she took on sole responsibility for childcare, relying on the income from her husband's 'stable' job. Trudy stopped accepting concert invitations and set up a private teaching practice at home; she did not perform professionally for another sixteen years. Of that time, she says:

I would do the same again but I wouldn't wait so long to go back. I lost my confidence not a little bit, a lot. I think I realised that I had been less than fully myself during those years. I think there was probably an underlying depression. I think the truth is, if you are a musician and that's been a huge part of your life, to actually give up is injurious.

While her concert career had been demanding and not always well paid, she relished the musical and intellectual challenges of the repertoire; but due to her change in circumstances, her paid work became a source of anxiety and stress because she felt she was producing poor-quality work which was therefore no longer creatively fulfilling, both characteristics of 'bad work'.

Aesthetic Labour

The role of 'aesthetic labour' and the different ways it shapes and informs attitudes towards work was also apparent in the women's narratives in relation to self-promotion and marketing. Chris Warhurst, Dennis Nickson, Anne Witz, and Anne Marie Cullen describe aesthetic labour as placing particular importance on a person's physical appearance.[33] It relies on an individual's embodied capacities, which are deliberately geared towards appealing to the senses of 'the customer' and managing physical appearances potentially to enhance career prospects. In her recent work on early-career female classical musicians, Christina Scharff notes that selling and marketing oneself may evoke the spectre of prostitution for some musicians.[34] Although this particular concern was not raised by my participants, the ways in which they negotiated and rationalised the use of often hyper-feminine and sexualised images were very diverse, ranging from resistance to acceptance or even denial. For others, particularly the conductors in the study, this focus on their embodied capacities and perceived level of attractiveness was unwelcome and actively resisted.

Sexuality, as a dimension of aesthetic labour, was especially evident in the promotional images of the younger women in my cohort. Conventional images of femininity and heterosexuality would often involve shots of slim legs, short black dresses, or long dresses with thigh-high splits in marketing material. Only two of the participants had representation, so publicity shots were paid for by the musicians and they were in control of which images to use. The digital diaries included many of these images and there was some resistance to the idea that they might be using their bodies to sell their 'product'. This is exemplified in Martha's interview (Performer, 30s) in which she initiated a discussion about the marketing materials used by her all-female quartet (they did not have representation so were responsible for their own publicity materials), all aged between their late twenties and early thirties. Without prompting, Martha pointed to one of their publicity photos, in which they were wearing short, black dresses and high heels while holding their instruments, and asserted:

I don't feel I should feel embarrassed about dressing up nicely with three girls who happen to be my friends and we look nice together. We don't do short, black dresses, basically a classy short. We're not going for anything tarty.

While Martha acknowledges that the dresses in the publicity shot were 'short', it is interesting to note her use of language, and there was a sense that she felt she had to 'defend' their choice of clothing. She refers to what they wore as 'classy short' (looking stylish and sophisticated) as opposed to appearing 'tarty' (an informal term used to describe a woman dressed in a sexually provocative manner). Martha was at pains to downplay the potentially sexual interpretation of their clothing choices, but it was evident from her later comment that she was aware that the ensemble may project a certain look that makes full use of their 'embodied capacities' and that has a level of commercial usefulness. She noted that, 'it just so happens that none of us are particularly large in size [and as we're] doing a lot of evening and drinks parties and corporate events it seems more *natural* to wear a shorter dress'. This suggests that she assumes corporate clients will have certain expectations of how a young, all-female ensemble should dress, and her allusion to adhering to notions of conventional femininity (young and slim) appears to collude with this.

However, others were more overt about the benefits of explicitly engaging in aesthetic labour, asserting their image could help raise their profile:

People do say, you know you play really well and everything but don't forget you've got lots of assets including, you know, one's body. But some artists manage to still do well without, you know, doing that. Doing a Vanessa Mae? I can't say I wouldn't –

you never know. It depends on how big the cheque is. That's the truth. Sex sells. (Alisha, Composer/Performer, 30s)

As a woman without an agent, looking to self-release a CD, it is perhaps not surprising that Alisha rationalises the use of her body to market herself in monetary terms. (The sexualisation, image, and marketing of female classical performers is also discussed in Chapter 6, 'Soloists and Divas: Evolving Opportunities, Identity, and Reception'.)

The issue of aesthetic labour for the conductors in the study revealed a completely different problem: the need to downplay and minimise their femininity for fear that their looks, bodies, or clothing choices might contribute to not being taken seriously, potentially undermining their professionalism. This was reinforced by their experiences of being a 'female conductor', and the very fact of them being a woman in the role resulting in discontent or resentment by others with whom they worked. This ranged from passive-aggressive behaviours such as being 'stared at the whole time by the male lead cellist as if being conducted by a woman was the worst thing that had ever happened' to gendered challenges to their authority, 'if a man is insistent, he's strong, if a woman is insistent, she's a bitch' (Margaret, Conductor, 50s). The conductors in the study expressed the need to 'emanate authority' when in front of an orchestra and were conscious of their clothing choices, not wearing anything tight-fitting where 'things are going to move around and be a distraction' (Kay, Conductor, 40s).

In contrast with Martha's narrative above, a (perceived) lack of attractiveness was considered a professional asset for conductors. Layla (Conductor, 20s), a talented young conductor in demand in the UK and Europe noted:

I've met female conductors who are blond and very beautiful, and they do find it's difficult. They conduct and people say, 'You're wonderful to watch' and she's thinking 'What about my conducting?' I'm not a conventional beauty so I don't have that problem as much and I've never had that sort of response.

Layla deliberately downplayed her femininity and made careful choices about her clothes on the podium, insisting she was 'grateful' she was not conventionally attractive; she felt it gave her an advantage because she felt her professional abilities were taken more seriously by the players. How women respond to the demands of managing personal aesthetics appears to vary across age and stage of career, and the type of musical activity in which they are involved, shaping their professional experiences in important ways. (The image of female conductors – with particular reference to Ethel Leginska and Marin Alsop – is also discussed in Chapter 5, 'On the Podium: Women Conductors'.)

Conclusion

Regardless of the uncertainties of such work, there is significant pleasure to be gained despite the long hours, financial insecurity,[35] and other challenges outlined above. As my study suggests, it is possible for women to sustain a fulfilling and rewarding career in music.[36] It is important when undertaking critical work about the creative industries to take into account that there *are* opportunities for positive and rewarding experiences, which should not be simply dismissed 'as the product of ideology or disciplinary discourse'.[37] In particular, paying greater attention to the affective aspects of cultural work provides interesting and more nuanced insights into how this work is experienced. Acknowledging this 'affective messiness' neither celebrates nor denies the negative aspects of cultural work but, instead, recognises 'the far more common quotidian problems and strengths of negotiating creative employment'.[38] In attempting to interrogate both the challenges and opportunities women experience in their working lives it becomes evident that there are serious limitations when defining work as either 'good' or 'bad' because, as discussed above, the context in which work is undertaken is key to understanding how it is experienced.

However, while recognising there are positive aspects to work in the music industries for women, this should not detract from the fact that this work is experienced as highly gendered and can result in discrimination and exploitation. Much is made of personal autonomy in policy discourses, and having freedom to make choices about one's life is the marker of an autonomous individual and important in the notion of agency. But the *contexts* in which the women undertake their work demonstrate the gendered dimensions of cultural work, and emphasise the importance of engaging with, and trying to understand, the materiality of their musical lives in order to uncover how these contexts shape and inform women's working lives.

Notes

1. Mark Banks, *The Politics of Cultural Work* (Basingstoke and New York: Palgrave Macmillan, 2007).
2. Rosalind Gill, '"Life Is a Pitch": Managing the Self in New Media Work', in Mark Deuze (ed.), *Managing Media Work* (Thousand Oaks, CA, Sage: 2010), 249–62.
3. David Hesmondhalgh and Sarah Baker, *Creative Labour: Media Work in Three Cultural Industries* (London and New York: Routledge, 2011), 7.

4. Bridget Conor, Rosalind Gill, and Stephanie Taylor (eds.), *Gender and Creative Labour* (Chichester: John Wiley & Sons, 2015).

5. Jim McGuigan, 'Creative Labour, Cultural Work and Individualisation', *International Journal of Cultural Policy*, vol. 16 (2010), 323–35.

6. Christina Scharff, *Gender, Subjectivity, and Cultural Work: The Classical Music Profession* (London and New York: Routledge, 2018).

7. Rosalind Gill, 'Unspeakable Inequalities: Post Feminism, Entrepreneurial Subjectivity, and the Repudiation of Sexism among Cultural Workers', *Social Politics*, vol. 21 (2014), 511.

8. Doris Ruth Eikhof and Chris Warhurst, 'The Promised Land? Why Social Inequalities Are Systemic in the Creative Industries', *Employee Relations*, vol. 35 (2013), 495–508.

9. Musicians' Union, *The Working Musician Report* (2012), available at www .musiciansunion.org.uk/Files/Reports/Industry/The-Working-Musician-report (accessed 24 April 2020).

10. Eikhof and Warhurst, 'The Promised Land'.

11. Creative and Cultural Skills, *Sector Skills Assessment for the Creative and Cultural Industries: An Analysis of the Skills Needs of the Creative and Cultural Industries in the UK* (2010). Previously available at www.ccskills.org.uk/ (accessed 14 July 2020).

12. Scharff, *Gender, Subjectivity, and Cultural Work*, 43–4 and 56–7.

13. Victoria Armstrong, *Technology and the Gendering of Music Education* (London and Farnham: Ashgate, 2011).

14. Dawn Bennett, *Understanding the Classical Music Profession: The Past, the Present and the Future* (Aldershot: Ashgate, 2008).

15. Victoria Armstrong, 'Women's Musical Lives: Self-Managing a Freelance Career', *Women: A Cultural Review*, vol. 24 (2013), 298–314.

16. Susan Coulson, 'Collaborating in a Competitive World: Musicians' Working Lives and Understandings of Entrepreneurship', *Work, Employment and Society*, vol. 26 (2012), 246–61.

17. Scharff, *Gender, Subjectivity, and Cultural Work*.

18. Angela McRobbie, 'From Holloway to Hollywood: Happiness at Work in the New Cultural Economy?', in Paul du Gay and Michael Pryke (eds.), *Cultural Economy: Cultural Analysis and Commercial Life* (London: Sage, 2002), 97–114.

19. Rosalind Gill, 'Creative Biographies in New Media: Social Innovation in Web Work', in Andy C. Pratt and Paul Jeffcutt (eds.), *Creativity, Innovation and the Cultural Economy* (London and New York: Routledge, 2009), 161–78.

20. Hesmondhalgh and Baker, *Creative Labour*, 39.

21. Hesmondhalgh and Baker, *Creative Labour*, 39.

22. Mark Banks and David Hesmondhalgh, 'Looking for Work in Creative Industries Policy', *International Journal of Cultural Policy*, vol. 15 (2009), 417.

23. David Hesmondhalgh, 'Normativity and Social Justice in the Analysis of Creative Labour', *Journal for Cultural Research*, vol. 14 (2010), 235.

24. Bennett, *Understanding the Classical Music Profession*, 14.

25. Karen O'Reilly, *Ethnographic Methods*, 2nd ed. (London and New York: Routledge, 2012).

26. Stephanie Taylor, 'Negotiating Oppositions and Uncertainties: Gendered Conflicts in Creative Identity Work', *Feminism and Psychology*, vol. 21 (2011), 354–71.

27. Gillian Ursell, 'Television Production: Issues of Exploitation, Commodification and Subjectivity in UK Television Labour Markets', *Media, Culture and Society*, vol. 22 (2000), 805–25.

28. Angela McRobbie, *Be Creative* (Cambridge and Malden: Polity Press, 2016).

29. McRobbie, 'From Holloway to Hollywood', 110.

30. Leung Wing-Fai, Rosalind Gill, and Keith Randle, 'Getting In, Getting On, Getting Out? Women as Career Scramblers in the UK Film Industries', *The Sociological Review*, vol. 63 (2015), 50–65.

31. Stephanie Taylor and Karen Littleton, *Contemporary Identities of Creativity and Creative Work* (Aldershot: Ashgate, 2012), 37.

32. Adele Teague and Gareth Dylan Smith, 'Portfolio Careers and Work-Life Balance among Musicians: An Initial Study into Implications for Higher Music Education', *British Journal of Music Education*, vol. 32 (2015), 177–93.

33. Chris Warhurst, Dennis Nickson, Anne Witz, and Anne Marie Cullen, 'Aesthetic Labour in Interactive Service Work: Some Case Study Evidence from the "New" Glasgow', *The Service Industries Journal*, vol. 20 (2000), 1–18.

34. Christina Scharff, 'Blowing Your Own Trumpet: Exploring the Gendered Dynamics of Self-Promotion in the Classical Music Profession', in Conor, Gill, and Taylor (eds.), *Gender and Creative Labour*, 97–112.

35. McRobbie, 'From Holloway to Hollywood'.

36. Armstrong, 'Women's Musical Lives'.

37. Hesmondhalgh and Baker, *Creative Labour*, 220.

38. Susan Luckman, *Locating Cultural Work: The Politics and Poetics of Rural, Regional and Remote Creativity* (Basingstoke: Palgrave Macmillan, 2012), 10.

Further Reading

Haworth, Catherine and Lisa Colton. *Gender, Age and Musical Creativity* (Farnham: Ashgate, 2015).

Macarthur, Sally. *Towards a Twenty-First-Century Feminist Politics of Music* (London and New York: Routledge, 2016).

Scharff, Christina. *Gender, Subjectivity, and Cultural Work: The Classical Music Profession* (London and New York: Routledge, 2018).

Appendix: Survey Questions for Chapter 14, The Star-Eaters: A 2019 Survey of Female and Gender-Non-Conforming Individuals Using Electronics for Music

1. Sound art and music have something of an uneasy relationship as terms. For some, sound art is any artistic practice using sound in some way that does not happen in a linear performance but can be experienced in one's own time, such as an installation in a gallery setting. Music for such observers is defined by its performance in time, such as a string quartet performed in a concert or a song sung in a jazz club. For others, though, music and sound art also have stylistic meanings. The string quartet or the jazz standard might be music, but not the improvised performance on a circuit-bending set-up using harsh and noisy timbres. Or, conversely, noise and/or the experience of sounds outside a formal performance might constitute important ground to stake out as belonging to the (esteemed, long-standing) category of music. In short, sound art and music are defined differently by different people. Do you consider yourself a composer, sound artist, a programmer, an instrument builder, a combination of these, or none of them? Does your work happen in a performance, installation, or another setting? Does it happen linearly in time, or can audience members change its progression or go back and listen again?

2. Digital sound has facilitated a range of audio manipulation by both broadening the array of possible effects and making many effects cheaper and easier to accomplish than in an analogue studio. It has also opened up possibilities for interactivity through live computation in the moment of performance (or audience interaction in an installation setting). Yet some artists prefer the physicality of analogue devices and find digital emulations of physical controllers (buttons, faders, knobs) unsatisfying; others express a preference for the sound of analogue gear (such as the surging popularity of Eurorack) or the aesthetics of failure that can result from pushing such devices to their limits. How do you use digital or analogue devices and why? How have these decisions impacted your

process and the sounds you draw on? Have you repurposed older analogue equipment?

3. A piece with electronics can mean many things. It can mean a work for a live human player playing an acoustic instrument along with a fixed-media audio track; the same player with a system taking microphone instruments and applying live processing to that player's sound; someone performing on an 'all-gear' set-up of synthesisers, transducers, no-input mixer, or other analogue equipment; video game or other kinds of controllers that control a laptop-based set-up; and much more. Some of these practices include acoustic instruments that are familiar to audiences and some do not. Do you use acoustic instruments in your work with electronics? Why or why not? If you use an all-gear set-up, do you feel that that set-up constitutes an instrument or a new interface for musical expression (NIME)? If you build instruments/NIMEs, do other people play them?

4. Developed in the 1950s, Pierre Schaeffer's concept of reduced listening calls for an aural practice in which one attempts to ignore the source or extra-sonic associations of sounds and focus solely on their sounding character. Such a practice still has strong influence in some musical spheres, and many electroacoustic composers continue to use Schaeffer's term 'acousmatic' to describe their work. At the same time, contemporary electronics have facilitated more theatrical work through sounds that have real-world associations (such as field recordings), easy integration with theatre and dance (it is often more feasible to hire a single composer to score a play with electronics than hire that composer and a chamber ensemble to perform), gestural interfaces and cameras such as the Kinect (which allow dancers or other physical performers who are not necessarily musicians to control sound), and other techniques. Does your work entail theatrical, narrative, visual, or extra-sonic elements? Why or why not? If so, how do you create and manage such elements? How do you feel this changes your audience's experience?

5. In the early days of electronic music, studios such as Studio d'Essai and the Columbia-Princeton Electronic Music Center were large spaces filled with bulky, extremely expensive, highly specialised equipment. They were considered spaces for experts only and required in-depth, specific knowledge and insider access. Today the computing power of the Columbia-Princeton studio is dwarfed by that of a relatively inexpensive consumer laptop, with no institutional credentials required. At the same

time, the scope of knowledge required to produce 'new' or 'cutting-edge' music with electronics has hugely expanded. In some sense, a composer or sound artist working today may not need to be a specialist in the same sense as one working in the 1950s, '60s, or '70s, but might be aided more by knowing a bit about a number of subfields and practices in order to have a sense of what techniques exist that could be useful for a given project. How has the increasing availability and affordability of electronics equipment facilitated or changed your work? Do you consider yourself a specialist in a particular area of electronics, a generalist who is able to learn the necessary tools for each new piece, or something else?

6. A huge range of speaker configurations for playing electronic music are possible today, from a traditional stereo set-up to complex surround-sound speaker arrays, crowd-sourcing low-fi sources such as audience phones, to using transducers to resonate acoustic objects. What kind of speaker set-up do you use most often in your work? If you use stereo, is this decision driven primarily by practicality and portability or by aesthetics? If you use more complex set-ups, what do you feel you gain and/or lose by doing so? Does the speaker constitute a fundamental part of the performance for you, and do you build your own speakers, travel with your own speakers, seek out venues that have systems you like, or make specific requests about speakers?

7. One might conceptualise work with electronics as existing along a continuum of interactivity, with a wholly fixed-media piece that simply requires an operator to press play on the low end to an installation or piece where every parameter of sound is influenced by user input in some way on the high end. Where would you say your work falls along this spectrum? How and why do you use and engage with interactivity (or not) in your work?

8. There is a significant strand of work in the past fifty years that treats sound production as fundamentally embodied, whether through gestural interfaces, amplification of bodily sound, playing with our understanding of the categories human and machine through vocal processing, or other means. Do you consider the performance of your work by human bodies to be important, and if so, how do you think about embodiment in your work? If your work is not performed by humans or you don't consider the physical aspects of performance salient to the audience's experience, why not, and what actions constitute the performance of the work, and do you still consider it to be embodied?

9. Do you buy most of your equipment ready-made or DIY it in some way (e.g. Arduinos, instrument building, hacking commercial hardware, etc.)? If you DIY, how do you do so and what led you to it? If not, what are the barriers to entry or what satisfies you about commercially available equipment? Do you program your computer, or primarily use DAWs to create your work, and why? If both, how do you choose what procedure to use? Do you create programs for other musicians working with electronics to use? If so, please explain why and give examples.

10. Electronic and electroacoustic music today includes a large range of sound sources: non-recorded, synthesised sounds in the tradition of *Elektronische Musik* (electronic music); emulation of acoustic instruments through sampled software instruments; live processing of acoustic instruments; and recorded sound, including field recordings or samples from pre-existing work. Which of these categories and/or what other sound sources do you draw on in your own work? What drives those choices?

11. Venues for performing electronic music or displaying sound art include traditional concert halls as well as universities, theatres, art galleries, bars/clubs, warehouses, and underground venues of various sorts. Some work is also rarely if ever performed and mostly encountered through recordings or other means. Where do audiences experience your work? Why do you choose the venues you do, and what are the challenges of those venues? Do you wish you could perform/display your work in other kinds of venues?

12. New technologies such as virtual reality (VR) and augmented reality (AR) platforms and increasingly sophisticated and responsive video and audio conferencing for telematics have enabled a broadened range of performance and experiential environments. Performers who are geographically distant can play together, audiences can watch/listen from at home, and composers/sound artists can create truly immersive audiovisual environments. Do you use VR or AR at all in your work? What about telematics/remote performance? If not, why not? If so, how and why?

13. Contemporary technology can facilitate extremely fine-grained, intentional control of all sorts of parameters of sound. Conversely, it also allows for randomness, complex algorithms with unpredictable results,

and even generative systems approaching artificial intelligence (or machine learning) that can generate or respond to material in ways outside the immediate control of the composer or performer. Do you ever take any elements of your sonic practice outside your direct control in any of these ways, and if so, how? Why or why not?

14. If you would like, please tell us about a time you felt particularly supported or unsupported as an artist working with electronics. Who has been a mentor, inspiration, or hero to you and why? Or who has been an anti-mentor, example of what you don't want to be, or source of frustration and why?

15. What have we missed here? This could be historical trajectories we've left out or important aspects of your own experience we haven't provided space to meditate on.

Select Bibliography

Abel, Samuel. *Opera in the Flesh* (Boulder, CO: Westview Press, 1996).

Armstrong, Victoria. 'Hard Bargaining on the Hard Drive: Gender Bias in the Music Technology Classroom.' *Gender and Education*, vol. 20, no. 4 (2008), 375–86.

Armstrong, Victoria. *Technology and the Gendering of Music Education* (Farnham: Ashgate, 2011).

Armstrong, Victoria. 'Women's Musical Lives: Self-Managing a Freelance Career.' *Women: A Cultural Review*, 24 (2013), 298–314.

Auslander, Philip. 'Musical Persona: The Physical Performance of Popular Music', in Derek B. Scott (ed.), *The Ashgate Research Companion to Popular Musicology* (Farnham: Ashgate, 2009), 303–16.

Auslander, Philip. 'Musical Personae.' *The Drama Review*, vol. 50, no. 1 (2006), 100–19.

Bacewicz, Grażyna. *A Distinguishing Mark*, trans. Anna Clarke and Andrew Cienski (Orleans, Ontario: Krzys Chmiel, 2004).

Banks, Mark. *Creative Justice: Cultural Industries, Work and Inequality* (London: Rowman & Littlefield International, 2017).

Banks, Mark. *The Politics of Cultural Work* (Basingstoke and New York: Palgrave Macmillan, 2007).

Banks, Mark, and David Hesmondhalgh. 'Looking for Work in Creative Industries Policy.' *International Journal of Cultural Policy*, vol. 15 (2009), 415–30.

Bego, Mark. *Joni Mitchell* (New York: Taylor Trade Publishing, 2005).

Bennett, Dawn. *Understanding the Classical Music Profession: The Past, the Present and the Future* (Aldershot: Ashgate, 2008).

Berger, Arthur. 'Stravinsky and the Younger American Composers.' *The Score*, no. 12 (June 1955), 39–40.

Berger, John. *Ways of Seeing* (London: Penguin Books, 1972).

Berkers, Pauwke, and Julian Schaap. *Gender Inequality in Metal Music Production* (Brighton: Emerald Group Publishing, 2018).

Black, Sarah. 'Mother as Curator: Performance, Family and Ethics' (PhD thesis, Middlesex University, 2018).

Block, Adrienne Fried. *Amy Beach: Passionate Victorian. The Life and Work of an American Composer 1867–1944* (New York and Oxford: Oxford University Press, 1998).

Bordo, Susan. *Unbearable Weight: Feminism, Western Culture, and the Body* (Berkeley: University of California Press, 1993).

Boulez, Pierre. *Notes of an Apprenticeship*, collected by Paul Thevenin, trans. Herbert Weinstock (New York: Knopf, 1968).

Bowers, Jane, and Judith Tick (eds.). *Women Making Music: The Western Art Tradition, 1150–1950* (Urbana and Chicago: University of Illinois Press, 1987).

Boyes, Georgina. *The Imagined Village: Culture, Ideology and the English Folk Revival* (Manchester: Manchester University Press, 1993).

Bridger, Sue. 'The Cold War and the Cosmos: Valentina Tereshkova and the First Woman's Space Flight', in Melanie Ilič, Susan E. Reid, and Lynne Attwood (eds.), *Women in the Khrushchev Era* (New York: Palgrave Macmillan, 2004), 222–37.

Broadbent, Marguerite, and Terry Broadbent. *Leginska: Forgotten Genius of Music, the Story of a Great Musician* (Wilmslow: The North West Player Piano Association, 2002).

Brocken, Michael. *The British Folk Revival 1944–2002* (Aldershot: Ashgate, 2003).

Brooks, Jeanice. '*Noble et grande servant de la musique*: Telling the Story of Nadia Boulanger's Conducting Career.' *Journal of Musicology*, vol. 14, no. 1 (Winter 1996), 92–116.

Bunzel, Anja, and Natasha Loges. *Musical Salon Culture in the Long Nineteenth Century* (Woodbridge and Rochester, NY: The Boydell Press, 2019).

Butler, Judith. *Gender Trouble: Feminism and the Subversion of Identity* (New York and London: Routledge, 1990).

Byrne, Vincent James. 'The Life and Work of Dorothy Howell' (MA thesis, University of Birmingham, 2015).

Chatelain, Marcia. *South Side Girls: Growing Up in the Great Migration* (Durham, NC: Duke University Press, 2015).

Chemaly, Soraya. *Rage Becomes Her: The Power of Women's Anger* (London: Simon & Schuster, 2018).

Choonara, Joseph. *Insecurity, Precarious Work and Labour Markets: Challenging the Orthodoxy* (London: Palgrave Macmillan, 2019).

Citron, Marcia J. 'Cécile Chaminade', in Julie Anne Sadie and Rhian Samuel (eds.), *The New Grove Dictionary of Women Composers* (London: Macmillan, 1994), 112–15.

Citron, Marcia J. *Gender and the Musical Canon* (Urbana and Chicago: University of Illinois Press, 1993).

Cizmic, Maria. *Performing Pain: Music and Trauma in Eastern Europe* (New York: Oxford University Press, 2012).

Coates, Norma J. 'It's a Man's, Man's World: Television and the Masculinization of Rock Discourse and Culture' (PhD thesis, University of Wisconsin, Madison, WI, 2002).

Cohen, Aaron, I. *International Encyclopedia of Women Composers*, second revised and enlarged ed. (New York: Books & Music USA, 1987).

Collins, Patricia Hill. *Black Feminist Thought: Knowledge, Consciousness, and the Politics of Empowerment* (New York: Routledge, 1990).

Collinson Scott, Jo, and David Scott. 'The Portfolio Career in Practice: Key Aspects of Building and Sustaining a Songwriting Career in the Digital Era', in Justin Williams and Katherine Williams (eds.), *The Singer-Songwriter's Handbook* (New York: Bloomsbury Academic, 2017), 191–203.

Conor, Bridget, Rosalind Gill, and Stephanie Taylor (eds). *Gender and Creative Labour* (Chichester: John Wiley & Sons, 2015).

Coontz, Stephanie. *A Strange Stirring: The Feminine Mystique and American Women at the Dawn of the 1960s* (New York: Basic Books, 2011).

Coulson, Susan. 'Collaborating in a Competitive World: Musicians' Working Lives and Understandings of Entrepreneurship.' *Work, Employment and Society*, vol. 26 (2012), 246–61.

Csikszentmihalyi, Mihaly, and Eugene Rochbert-Halton. *The Meaning of Things: Domestic Symbols and the Self* (Cambridge: Cambridge University Press, 1981).

Cusick, Suzanne G. 'Feminist Theory, Music Theory, and the Mind/Body Problem.' *Perspectives of New Music*, vol. 32, no. 1 (1994), 8–27.

Cusick, Suzanne G. *Francesca Caccini at the Medici Court: Music and the Circulation of Power* (Chicago: University of Chicago Press, 2009).

Cusick, Suzanne, G. 'Gender and the Cultural Work of a Classical Music Performance.' *Repercussions*, vol. 3, no. 1 (Spring 1994), 77–110.

Dahl, Linda. *Stormy Weather: The Music and Lives of a Century of Jazz Women* (New York: Limelight Editions, 1984).

Davidson, Jane. 'The Solo Performer's Identity', in Raymond MacDonald, David J. Hargreaves, and Dorothy Miell (eds.), *Musical Identities* (Oxford: Oxford University Press, 2002), 97–115.

Davies, Rhian. *Never So Pure a Sight: Morfydd Owen (1891–1918): A Life in Pictures* (Llandysul: Gomer, 1994).

Dempf, Linda. 'The Woman's Symphony Orchestra of Chicago.' *Notes*, Second Series, vol. 62, no. 4 (June 2006), 857–903.

Deveaux, Monique. 'Feminism and Empowerment: A Critical Reading of Foucault.' *Feminist Studies*, vol. 20, no. 2 (Summer 1994), 223–47.

Dickerson, James L., *Go Girl Go! The Women's Revolution in Music* (New York: Schirmer Trade Books, 2005).

Dickerson, James L. *Women on Top: The Quiet Revolution That's Rocking the American Music Industry* (New York: Billboard Books, 1998).

Doctor, Jenny, '"Working for Her Own Salvation": Vaughan Williams as Teacher of Elizabeth Maconchy, Grace Williams and Ina Boyle', in Lewis Foreman (ed.), *Vaughan Williams in Perspective: Studies of an English Press* (Illminster: Albion Press for the Vaughan Williams Society, 1998), 181–201.

Douglas, Susan J. *Where the Girls Are: Growing Up Female With the Mass Media* (London: Penguin Books, 1995).

Drucker, Peter F. *Innovation and Entrepreneurship* (London: William Heinemann Ltd, 1985).

Du Bois, W. E. B., *The Souls of Black Folk* (Chicago: A. C. McClurg & Co., 1903).

Dunbar, Julie, C. *Women, Music, Culture* (New York and London: Routledge, 2010).

Edwards, J. Michele 'Women on the Podium', in José Bowen (ed.), *The Cambridge Companion to Conducting* (Cambridge and New York: Cambridge University Press, 2003), 220–36. ·

Ehrenreich, Barbara, Elizabeth Hess, and Gloria Jacobs. 'Beatlemania: Girls Just Want to Have Fun', in Lisa Lewis (ed.), *The Adoring Audience: Fan Culture and Popular Media* (New York: Routledge, 1992), 84–106.

Eikhof, Doris Ruth, and Chris Warhurst, 'The Promised Land? Why Social Inequalities Are Systemic in the Creative Industries.' *Employee Regulations,* vol. 35 (2013), 495–508.

Elsen, Arthur. *Woman's Work in Music* (Boston, MA: L. C. Page & Co., 1904).

Emerson, Ken, *Always Magic in the Air: The Bomp and the Brilliance of the Brill Building Era* (New York: Penguin Books, 2006).

Espeland, Magne, 'Dichotomies in Music Education: Real or Unreal?', *Music Education Research*, Vol. 12, No. 2 (2009), 129–139.

Filtzer, Donald, 'Women Workers in the Khrushchev Era', in Melanie Ilič, Susan E. Reid, and Lynne Attwood (eds.), *Women in the Khrushchev Era* (New York: Palgrave Macmillan, 2004), 29–51.

Finnegan, Ruth, *The Hidden Musicians: Music-Making in an English Town* (Cambridge: Cambridge University Press, 1989).

Friedlander, Paul, with Peter Miller, *Rock & Roll: A Social History*, 2nd ed. (Boulder, CO: Westview Press, 2007).

Frith, Simon, *Performing Rites: On The Value of Popular Music* (Cambridge, Massachusetts: Harvard University Press, 1996).

Frith, Simon and Angela McRobbie, 'Rock and Sexuality', in Simon Frith and Andrew Goodwin (eds.), *Ashgate Contemporary Thinkers on Critical Musicology Series: Taking Popular Music Seriously. Selected Essays* (London: Routledge, 2007).

Fuller, Sophie, *The Pandora Guide to Women Composers: Britain and the United States, 1629–Present* (London: Pandora, 1994).

Fuller, Sophie, 'Women Composers during the British Musical Renaissance, 1880–1918' (PhD thesis, King's College, University of London, 1998).

Fuller, Sophie, '"Devoted Attention": Looking for Lesbian Musicians in Fin-de-Siècle Britain', in Sophie Fuller and Lloyd Whitesell (eds.), *Queer Episodes in Music and Modern Identity* (Urbana and Chicago: University of Illinois Press, 2002), 79–103.

Fuller, Sophie, 'Elgar and the Salons: The Significance of a Private Musical World', in Byron Adams (ed.), *Edward Elgar and His World* (Princeton: Princeton University Press, 2007), 223–247.

Fuller, Sophie, '"Putting the BBC and T. Beecham to Shame": The Macnaghten-Lemare Concerts, 1931–7' *Journal of the Royal Musical Association*, vol. 138, no. 2 (2013), 377–414.

Fuller, Sophie, and Jenny Doctor (eds.), *Music, Life, and Changing Times: Selected Correspondence between British Composers Elizabeth Maconchy and Grace Williams, 1927–77*, Vol. 1 (Abingdon and New York: Routledge 2019).

Gateward, Frances, and Murray Pomerance, *Sugar and Spice and Everything Nice: Cinemas of Girlhood* (Detroit: Wayne State University Press, 2002).

Gaunt, Kyra, *The Games Black Girls Play: Learning the Ropes from Double-Dutch to Hip Hop* (New York: New York University Press, 2006).

Gill, Rosalind. 'Creative Biographies in New Media: Social Innovation in Web Work', in Andy C. Pratt and Paul Jeffcutt (eds.), *Creativity, Innovation and the Cultural Economy* (London and New York: Routledge, 2009), 161–78.

Gill, Rosalind, '"Life Is a Pitch": Managing the Self in New Media Work', in Mark Deuze (ed.), *Managing Media Work* (Thousand Oaks, CA, Sage: 2010), 249–62.

Gill, Rosalind, 'Unspeakable Inequalities: Post Feminism, Entrepreneurial Subjectivity, and the Repudiation of Sexism among Cultural Workers', *Social Politics*, vol. 21 (2014), 509–28.

Green, Lucy, *Music, Gender, Education* (Cambridge: Cambridge University Press, 1997).

Green, Lucy, *Music, Informal Learning and the School: A New Classroom Pedagogy* (Aldershot: Ashgate, 2008).

Greer, David, *A Numerous and Fashionable Audience: The Story of Elsie Swinton* (London: Thames Publishing, 1997).

Grieg, Charlotte, *Will You Still Love Me Tomorrow? Girl Groups from the 50s On* (London: Virago, 1989).

Hallam, Susan, Lynne Rogers, and Andrea Creech, 'Gender Differences in Musical Instrument Choice.' *International Journal of Music Education*, Vol. 26, No. 1 (2008), 7–19.

Hamer, Laura, 'On the Conductor's Podium: Jane Evrard and the Orchestre féminin de Paris', *The Musical Times*, vol. 152, no. 1916 (Autumn 2011), 81–100.

Hamer, Laura, *Female Composers, Conductors, Performers: Musiciennes of Interwar France, 1919–1939* (Abingdon and New York: Routledge, 2018).

Handy, D. Antoinette, *Black Women in American Bands and Orchestras*, Second Edition (Lanham, Maryland: Scarecrow Press, 1998).

Hanley, Betty, 'Gender in Secondary Music Education in British Columbia.' *British Journal of Music Education*, Vol. 15, No. 1 (1998), 51–69.

Hardy, Phil, *The Faber Companion to 20th-Century Popular Music* (London: Faber and Faber, 1990).

Harry, Debbie, *Face It: A Memoir* (New York: Dey Street Books, 2019).

Haste, Cate, *Passionate Spirit: The Life of Alma Mahler* (London: Bloomsbury, 2019).

Haynes, Jo and Lee Marshall, 'Reluctant Entrepreneurs: Musicians and Entrepreneurship in the 'New' Music Industry', *British Journal of Sociology*, Vol. 69 (2017), 459–482.

Hesmondhalgh, David, 'Normativity and Social Justice in the Analysis of Creative Labour', *Journal for Cultural Research*, vol. 14 (2010), 231–49.

Hesmondhalgh, David and Sarah Baker, *Creative Labour: Media Work in Three Cultural Industries* (London and New York: Routledge, 2011).

Hisama, Ellie, *Gendering Musical Modernism: The Music of Ruth Crawford, Marion Bauer and Miriam Gideon* (Cambridge: Cambridge University Press, 2001).

Hobson, Janell. *Venus in the Dark: Blackness and Beauty in Popular Culture* (New York: Routledge, 2005).

hooks, bell, *Black Looks: Race and Representation* (New York: Routledge, 2014).

Huffington, Arianna, *Maria Callas: The Woman Behind the Legend* (Blue Ridge Summit, PA: Cooper Square Press, 2002).

Ilič, Melanie, 'Women in the Khrushchev Era: An Overview', in Melanie Ilič, Susan E. Reid, and Lynne Attwood (eds.), *Women in the Khrushchev Era* (New York: Palgrave Macmillan, 2004), 5–28.

Kahan, Sylvia, *Music's Modern Muse: A Life of Winnaretta Singer, Princesse de Polignac* (Rochester, NY: Rochester University Press, 2003).

Kaplan, E. Ann, *Rocking Around the Clock: Music Television, Postmodernism and Consumer Culture* (New York: Routledge, 1987).

Kelly, Jennifer, *In Her Own Words: Conversations with Composers in the United States* (Urbana: University of Illinois Press, 2013).

Kenny, Aisling, and Susan Wollenberg (eds.), *Women and the Nineteenth-Century Lied* (Farnham: Ashgate, 2015).

Kernodle, Tammy, *Soul on Soul: The Life and Music of Mary Lou Williams* (Boston, MA: Northeastern University Press, 2004).

King, Carole, *A Natural Woman: A Memoir* (London: Virago, 2012).

Kirzner, Israel M., 'Creativity and/or Alertness: A Reconsideration of the Schumpeterian Entrepreneur', *Review of Austrian Economics*, vol. 11 (1999), 5–17.

Korhonen, Kimmo, *Finnish Composers since the 1960s* (Helsinki: Finnish Music Information Centre, 1995).

Knight, Gladys, *Between Each Line of Pain and Glory: My Life Story* (New York: Hyperion, 1997).

Kruse, Sharon D. and Sandra Spickard Prettyman, 'Women, Leadership, and Power: Revisiting the Wicked Witch of the West', *Gender and Education*, vol. 20, no. 5 (1994), 451–64.

Lamb, Roberta, Lori-Anne Dolloff, and Sondra Wieland Howe, 'Feminism, Feminist Research, and Gender Research in Music Education', in Richard Colwell and Carol Richardson (eds.), *The New Handbook of Research on Music Teaching and Learning* (Oxford: Oxford University Press, 2002), 648–74.

Le Beau, Louise Adolpha, *Lebenserinnerungen einer Komponistin* (Baden-Baden: Emil Sommermayer, 1910).

Legg, Robert, 'One Equal Music: An Exploration of Gender Perceptions and the Fair Assessment by Beginning Music Teachers of Musical Compositions', *Music Education Research*, vol. 12, no. 2 (2010), 141–9.

Legg, Robert, 'Bach, Beethoven, Bourdieu: Cultural Capital and the Scholastic Canon in England's A-level Examinations', *The Curriculum Journal*, vol. 23, no. 2 (2012), 157–72.

Legg, Robert, and David Jeffery, 'Suleika and Hatem Revisited: Uncovering the Material Advantages of Identifying as a Male Composer', *Music Education Research*, Vol. 20, No. 1 (2018), 1–10.

Leonard, Kendra Preston, *Louise Talma: A Life in Composition* (Aldershot: Ashgate, 2014).

Lester, Paul, *Looking For Fame: The Life of a Pop Princess* (London: Omnibus Press, 2010).

Lewis, Patricia, 'The Search for an Authentic Entrepreneurial Identity: Difference and Professionalism among Women Business Owners', *Gender, Work and Organization*, vol. 20 (2013), 252–66.

Lieb, Kristin J., *Gender, Branding, and the Modern Music Industry: The Social Construction of Female Popular Music Stars*, 2nd ed. (New York: Routledge, 2018).

Luckman, Susan, *Locating Cultural Work: The Politics and Poetics of Rural, Regional and Remote Creativity* (Basingstoke: Palgrave Macmillan, 2012).

Lukomsky, Vera, '"The Eucharist in My Fantasy": Interview with Sofia Gubaidulina', *Tempo*, vol. 206 (1998), 29–35.

Lukomsky, Vera, '"Hearing the Subconscious": Interview with Sofia Gubaidulina', *Tempo*, vol. 209 (1999), 27–31.

Lutyens, Elisabeth, *A Goldfish Bowl* (London: Cassell, 1972).

Macarthur, Sally, Dawn Bennett, Talisha Goh, and Sophie Hennekam, 'The Rise and Fall, and the Rise (Again) of Feminist Research in Music: "What Goes Around Comes Around"', *Musicology Australia*, vol. 39, no. 2 (2017), 73–95.

Mahon, Maureen, 'Listening for Willie Mae "Big Mama" Thornton's Voice: The Sound of Race and Gender Transgressions in Rock and Roll', *Women and Music: A Journal of Gender and Culture*, vol. 15 (November 2011), 1–17.

Marcus, Sara, *Girls to the Front: The True Story of the Riot Grrrl Revolution* (New York: Harper Perennial, 2010).

Mathias, Rhiannon, *Lutyens, Maconchy, Williams and Twentieth-Century British Music: A Blest Trio of Sirens* (Farnham: Ashgate, 2012).

McBurney, Gerald, 'Encountering Gubaydulina', *The Musical Times* 129 (1988), 120–3, 125.

McCabe, Mary Ann, *Mabel Daniels: An American Composer in Transition* (Abingdon and New York: Routledge, 2017).

McClary, Susan, *Feminine Endings: Music, Gender and Sexuality* (Minneapolis: University of Minnesota Press, 2002).

McClary, Susan, 'Terminal Prestige: The Case of Avant-Garde Music Composition', *Cultural Critique*, No. 12 Discursive Strategies and the Economy of Prestige (1989), 57–81.

McDonnell, Evelyn and Ann Powers (eds.), *Rock She Wrote: Women Write About Rock, Pop, and Rap* (Medford, NJ: Plexus, 1995).

McGuigan, Jim, 'Creative Labour, Cultural Work and Individualisation', *International Journal of Cultural Policy*, vol. 16 (2010), 323–35.

McRobbie, Angela, 'Settling Accounts with Subcultures.' *Screen Series*, vol. 34 (1980), 37–49.

McRobbie, Angela, 'From Holloway to Hollywood: Happiness at Work in the New Cultural Economy?', in Paul du Gay and Michael Pryke (eds.), *Cultural Economy: Cultural Analysis and Commercial Life* (London: Sage, 2002), 97–114.

McRobbie, Angela, *Be Creative* (Cambridge and Malden: Polity Press, 2016).

Miller, Mark, *High Hat, Trumpet and Rhythm: The Life and Music of Valaida Snow* (Ontario, CA: The Mercury Press, 2007).

Moisala, Pirkko, *Kaija Saariaho* (Urbana: University of Illinois Press, 2009).

Moore, Allan, 'Authenticity as Authentication', *Popular Music*, vol. 21, no. 2 (May 2002), 209–23.

Moore, Allan, *Song Means: Analysing and Interpreting Recorded Popular Song* (Aldershot: Ashgate Publishing, 2012).

Moreau, François, 'The Disruptive Nature of Digitization: The Case of the Recorded Music Industry', *International Journal of Arts Management*, vol. 15 (2013), 18–31.

Morgan, George and Pariece Nelligan, *The Creativity Hoax: Precarious Work and the Gig Economy* (London: Anthem Press, 2018).

Morgan, George, Julian Wood, and Pariece Nelligan, 'Beyond the Vocational Fragments: Creative Work, Precarious Labour and the Idea of "Flexploitation"', *The Economic and Labour Relations Review*, vol. 24, no. 3 (2013), 297–415.

Morris, Meaghan, *The Pirate's Fiancée: Feminism, Reading, Postmodernism* (London and New York: Verso, 1988).

Morris, Monique W., *Pushout: The Criminalization of Black Girls in Schools* (New York: The New Press, 2016).

Morrison, Simon, 'Galina Ustvolskaya: Outside, Inside, and Beyond Music History', *Journal of Musicology*, vol. 36 (2019), 96–129.

Mulvey, Laura, 'Visual Pleasure and Narrative Cinema', *Screen*, vol. 16, no. 3 (1975), 6–18.

Nalimova, Elena, 'Demystifying Galina Ustvolskaya: Critical Examination and Performance Interpretation' (PhD Thesis, University of London, Goldsmiths, 2012).

Neuls-Bates, Carol, 'Women's Orchestras in the United States, 1925–45', in Jane Bowers and Judith Tick (eds.), *Women Making Music: The Western*

Art Tradition, 1150–1950 (Urbana and Chicago: University of Illinois Press, 1987), 349–69.

Neuls-Bates, Carol, *Women in Music: An Anthology of Source Readings from the Middle Ages to the Present*, 2nd ed. (Boston, MA: Northeastern University Press, 1996).

Niebur, Louis. *Special Sound: The Creation and Legacy of the BBC Radiophonic Workshop* (New York: Oxford University Press, 2010).

Noeske, Nina, 'Gender Discourse and Musical Life in the GDR', in Elaine Kelly and Amy Wlodarski (eds.), *Art Outside the Lines: New Perspectives on GDR Art Culture* (Amsterdam and New York: Rodopi, 2011), 175–91.

O'Brien, Lucy, *She Bop: The Definitive History of Women in Rock, Pop and Soul* (London: Penguin Books, 1995).

O'Dair, Barbara (ed.), *Trouble Girls: The Rolling Stone Book of Women in Rock* (New York: Random House, 1997).

O'Reilly, Karen, *Ethnographic Methods*, 2nd ed. (London and New York: Routledge, 2012).

Oliveros, Pauline. *Software for People: Collected Writings, 1963–1980* (Baltimore, MD: Smith Publications, 1984).

Olsen, Judith E., 'Louise Adolpha Le Beau: Composer in Late Nineteenth-Century Germany' in Jane Bowers and Judith Tick (eds.), *Women Making Music: The Western Art Tradition, 1150–1950* (Urbana and Chicago: University of Illinois Press, 1987).

Oram, Daphne, *An Individual Note of Music, Sound and Electronics* (Wakefield: Anomie Academic, 2016).

Orloff, Katherine, *Rock 'n' Roll Woman* (Los Angeles: Nash Publishing, 1974).

Parks Grier, Miles. 'Said the Hooker to the Thief: "Some Way Out" of Rockism', *Journal of Popular Music Studies*, vol. 25, no. 1 (2013), 31–55.

Pecknold, Diane, 'The Politics of Voice in Tween Girls' Music Criticism', *Jeunesse: Young People, Texts, Cultures*, vol. 9, no. 2 (2017), 69–90.

Peyser, Joan, *The Music of My Time* (New York & London: Pro/Am Music Resources, 1995).

Philipp, Beate, *Komponisten der neuen Musik* (Kassel: Furore-Verlag, 1993).

Placksin, Sally, *American Women in Jazz: 1900 to the Present: Their Words, Lives, and Music* (New York: Seaview Books, 1982).

Polin, Claire, 'Conversations in Leningrad, 1988', *Tempo*, vol. 168 (1989), 15–29.

Potter, Caroline, *Nadia and Lili Boulanger* (Farnham: Ashgate, 2006).

Prima, Diane di, *Recollections of My Life as a Woman* (New York: Viking, 2001).

Rees, Heward, 'Views and Revisions: Grace William in Interview with Heward Rees', *Welsh Music*, Vol. 5, No. 4 (1976–1977), 7–18.

Reich, Nancy B., 'Women as Musicians: A Question of Class', in Ruth A. Solie (ed.), *Musicology and Difference: Gender and Sexuality in Music Scholarship* (Berkeley and Los Angeles: University of California Press, 1995), 125–48.

Reid, Susan E., 'All Stalin's Women: Gender and Power in Soviet Art of the 1930s', *Slavic Review*, vol. 57 (1998), 133–73.

Reddington, Helen, *The Lost Women of Rock Music: Female Musicians of the Punk Era*, Second Edition (London: Equinox Publishing Ltd, 2012).

Rink, John, 'Impersonating the Music in Performance', in Raymond MacDonald, David J. Hargreaves, and Dorothy Miell (eds.), *Handbook of Musical identities* (Oxford: Oxford University Press, 2017), 345–63.

Robb, Mary, 'The Music of Miriam Gideon during the McCarthy Era, Including a Complete Catalogue of Her Works' (PhD thesis, University of Edinburgh, 2012).

Rogers, Victoria, *The Music of Peggy Glanville-Hicks* (Farnham and Burlington, VT: Ashgate, 2009).

Rohlfing, Mary E., 'Don't Say Nothin' Bad About My Baby: A Re-Evaluation of Women's Roles in the Brill Building Era of Early Rock and Roll', *Critical Studies in Mass Communication*, vol. 13, no. 2 (1996), 93–114.

Rosenstiel, Léonie, *The Life and Work of Lili Boulanger* (Madison, NJ: Fairleigh Dickinson University Press, 1978).

Rowbotham, Sheila, *A Century of Women: The History of Women in Britain and the United States* (London: Viking, 1997).

Russ, Joanna, *How to Suppress Women's Writing* (Austin, TX: University of Texas Press, 1983).

Sadie, Julie Anne and Rhian Samuel (eds.), *The New Grove Dictionary of Women Musicians* (New York: Norton, 1994).

Scharff, Christina, 'Blowing Your Own Trumpet: Exploring the Gendered Dynamics of Self-Promotion in the Classical Music Profession', in Bridget Conor, Rosalind Gill, and Stephanie Taylor (eds.), *Gender and Creative Labour* (Chichester: John Wiley & Sons, 2015), 97–112.

Scharff, Christina, *Gender, Subjectivity, and Cultural Work: The Classical Music Profession* (London and New York: Routledge, 2018).

Schloss, Joseph G., Larry Starr, and Christopher Alan Waterman, *Rock: Music, Culture, and Business* (New York: Oxford University Press, 2012).

Schmelz, Peter, *Such Freedom, If Only Musical* (New York: Oxford University Press, 2009).

Schreffler, Anne. C., 'The Myth of Empirical Historiography: A Response to Joseph N. Straus', *Musical Quarterly*, Vol. 84, No. 1 (2000), 30–39.

Seashore, Carl E., 'Why No Great Women Composers?' *Music Educators Journal*, vol. 26, no. 5 (March 1940), 21–88.

Shaw, George Bernard, *Music in London 1890-94*, revised edition (London: Constable, 1932).

Sholette, Gregory, *Dark Matter: Art and Politics in the Age of Enterprise Culture* (London: Pluto Press, 2011).

Shumway, David R., 'The Emergence of the Singer-Songwriter', in Katherine Williams and Justin A. Williams (eds.), *The Cambridge Companion to the Singer-Songwriter* (Cambridge: Cambridge University Press, 2016), 11–20.

Smyth, Ethel, *Female Pipings in Eden* (London: Peter Davis, 1934).

Spector, Ronnie, with Vince Waldron, *Be My Baby: How I Survived Mascara, Miniskirts and Madness, or My Life as a Fabulous Ronette* (New York: Harmony Books, 1990).

Stahl, Matt, *Unfree Masters: Recording Artists and the Politics of Work* (Durham, NC: Duke University Press, 2012).

Stam, Robert and Roberta Pearson, 'Hitchcock's Rear Window: Reflexivity and the Critique of Voyeurism', in Marshall Deutelbaum and Leland Poague (eds.), *A Hitchcock Reader* (Oxford: Blackwell Publishing, 2009), 199–211.

Straus, Joseph N., 'The Myth of Serial "Tyranny" in the 1950s and 1960s', *Musical Quarterly*, Vol. 83, No. 3 (1999), 301–343.

Strong, Catherine, *Grunge: Music and Memory* (Farnham: Ashgate, 2011).

Stürzbecher, Ursula, *Komponisten in der DDR: 17 Gespräche* (Hildesheim: Gerstenberg Verlag, 1979).

Suhadolnik, Sarah, 'Outside Voices and the Construction of Adele's Singer-Songwriter Persona', in Katherine Williams and Justin A. Williams (eds.), *The Cambridge Companion to the Singer-Songwriter* (Cambridge: Cambridge University Press, 2016), 179–186.

Tarnowski, Susan M., 'Gender Bias and Musical Instrument Preference.' *Update: Applications of Research in Music Education*, vol. 12, no. 1 (1993), 14–21.

Taylor, Stephanie, 'Negotiating Oppositions and Uncertainties: Gendered Conflicts in Creative Identity Work', *Feminism and Psychology*, vol. 21 (2011), 354–71.

Taylor, Stephanie and Karen Littleton, *Contemporary Identities of Creativity and Creative Work* (Aldershot: Ashgate, 2012).

Teague, Adele and Gareth Dylan Smith, 'Portfolio Careers and Work-Life Balance among Musicians: An Initial Study into Implications for Higher Music Education', *British Journal of Music Education*, vol. 32 (2015), 177–93.

Thomas, Adrian, *Polish Music since Szymanowski* (Cambridge: Cambridge University Press, 2005).

Thomson, Virgil, 'Elisabeth Lutyens', *Grand Street*, Vol. 2, No. 4 (Summer 1983), 182–184.

Tick, Judith, 'Passed Away Is the Piano Girl: Changes in American Life, 1870–1900', in Jane M. Bowers and Judith Tick (eds.), *Women Making Music: The Western Art Tradition, 1150–1950* (Urbana and Chicago: University of Illinois Press, 1987), 325–48.

Tick, Judith, *Ruth Crawford Seeger: A Composer's Search for American Music* (Oxford and New York: Oxford University Press, 1997).

Tulloch, John and Manuel Alvarado, *Doctor Who: The Unfolding Text* (New York: St. Martin's Press, 1983).

Upton, George, *Woman in Music* (Boston, MA: J. R. Osgood, 1880).

Ursell, Gillian, 'Television Production: Issues of Exploitation, Commodification and Subjectivity in UK Television Labour Markets', *Media, Culture and Society*, vol. 22 (2000), 805–25.

Vicinus, Martha, *Independent Women: Work and Community for Single Women, 1850-1920* (London: Virago, 1985).

Walkerdine, Valerie, *Daddy's Girl: Young Girls and Popular Culture* (Cambridge, MA: Harvard University Press, 1997).

Walker-Hill, Helen, *From Spirituals to Symphonies: African-American Women Composers and Their Music* (Champaign, IL: University of Illinois Press, 2015).

Warhurst, Chris, Dennis Nickson, Anne Witz, and Anne Marie Cullen, 'Aesthetic Labour in Interactive Service Work: Some Case Study Evidence from the "New" Glasgow', *The Service Industries Journal*, vol. 20 (2000), 1–18.

Warwick, Jacqueline. *Girl Groups, Girl Culture: Popular Music and Identity in the 1960s* (New York: Routledge, 2007).

Weller, Sheila, *Girls Like Us: Carole King, Joni Mitchell, Carly Simon, and the Journey of a Generation* (New York: Washington Square Press, 2009).

White, Maude Valérie, *My Indian Summer* (London: Grayson & Grayson, 1932).

Whiteley, Sheila (ed.), *Sexing the Groove: Popular Music and Gender* (London and New York: Routledge, 1997).

Whiteley, Sheila, *Women and Popular Music: Sexuality, Identity and Subjectivity* (London and New York: Routledge, 2000).

Whittaker, Adam, 'Investigating the Canon in A-level Music: Musical Prescription in A-level Music Syllabuses (for First Examination in 2018)', *British Journal of Music Education*, vol. 37, no. 1 (2018), 17–27.

Wieland Howe, Sondra, *Women Music Educators in the United States: A History* (Lanham, MD: Scarecrow Press, 2014).

Williams, Grace, 'How Welsh Is Welsh Music?', *Welsh Music*, 4 (Summer 1973), 7–12.

Williams, Grace, 'Composer's Portrait', *Welsh Music*, Vol. 8, No. 5 (1987), 6–16.

Williams, Juan, *Eyes on the Prize: America's Civil Rights Years 1954-65* (New York: Penguin, 1987).

Williams, Justin and Katherine Williams K (eds.), *The Singer-Songwriter's Handbook* (New York: Bloomsbury Academic, 2017).

Williamson, John and Martin Cloonan, 'Rethinking the Music Industry', *Popular Music*, vol. 26 (2007), 305–22.

Wing-Fai, Leung, Rosalind Gill, and Keith Randle, 'Getting In, Getting On, Getting Out? Women as Career Scramblers in the UK Film Industries', *The Sociological Review*, vol. 63 (2015), 50–65.

Wood Elizabeth, 'Lesbian Fugue: Ethel Smyth's Contrapuntal Arts' in Ruth A. Solie (ed.), *Musicology and Difference: Gender and Sexuality in Music Scholarship* (Berkeley: University of California Press, 1993).

Zeisler, Andi, *We Were Feminists Once: From Riot Grrl to Cover Girl, the Buying & Selling of a Political Movement* (New York: PublicAffairs, 2016).

Index

Made in the USA
Las Vegas, NV
13 March 2022

45576695R00197